# LESSON PLANS & TEACHER'S MANUAL
# BEGINNING
# BUILDING THINKING SKILLS®

### SERIES TITLES
BUILDING THINKING SKILLS®—BEGINNING FIGURAL
BUILDING THINKING SKILLS®—BOOK 1
BUILDING THINKING SKILLS®—BOOK 2
BUILDING THINKING SKILLS®—BOOK 3 FIGURAL
BUILDING THINKING SKILLS®—BOOK 3 VERBAL

## SANDRA PARKS, HOWARD BLACK, AND MARIA DE ARMAS

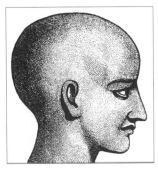

© 2000
## CRITICAL THINKING BOOKS & SOFTWARE
www.criticalthinking.com
P.O. Box 448 • Pacific Grove • CA 93950-0448
Phone 800-458-4849 • FAX 831-393-3277
ISBN 0-89455-763-7
Printed in the United States of America
Reproduction rights granted for single-classroom use only.

# Acknowledgements

We wish to thank the following people for their contributions to this book.

Ada Egusquiza, Educational Specialist in the Division of Advanced Academic Programs, Dade County Public Schools, Miami, FL: facilitated the field testing of activities and made suggestions for using the program with limited-English proficient students

Thelma Bear, Director of Special Programs, Weld County Public Schools, Greeley, CO: facilitated field testing of figural activities

Jan Bartram: made suggestions for teaching the program to kindergarten students

Raquel Kubala: reviewed the manuscript

Stephanie Pastore: supplied sample student responses

# Table of Contents

## INTRODUCTION

Program Design .................................................................................................. vii
Instructional Methods .......................................................................................... ix
Rationale and Description of Thinking Skills ...................................................... xii
Evaluating Building Thinking Skills Instruction ................................................. xiv
Instructional Recommendations ......................................................................... xvi
Vocabulary and Synonyms ................................................................................ xvii
Guide to Using the Lesson Plans ...................................................................... xix
Teaching Suggestions for Figural Lessons ........................................................ xxi
Teaching Suggestions for Verbal Lessons ........................................................ xxv

## LESSON PLANS

### CHAPTER ONE—DESCRIBING SHAPES

Matching Blocks to Shapes .................................................................................. 1
Finding Shapes—Select ....................................................................................... 3
Describing Shapes—Select A ............................................................................... 5
Finding Shapes—A ............................................................................................... 7
Finding Shapes—B ............................................................................................... 8
Describing Shapes—Select B ............................................................................. 10
Finding Shapes—C ............................................................................................. 12
Identifying Shapes by Color ............................................................................... 14
Following Directions—Select First to Last ......................................................... 16
Following Directions—Select First to Third ....................................................... 18
Following Directions—Select Left or Right ........................................................ 20
Following Directions—Select Top to Bottom ..................................................... 22
Following Directions—Select Above or Below ................................................... 24
Following Directions—Supply Above or Below .................................................. 26
Following Directions—Supply Right or Left ....................................................... 27
Naming Shapes—Select and Write–A ............................................................... 29
Describing Shapes—Select and Write–B ........................................................... 30
Describing Shapes—Explain (A) ........................................................................ 32
Describing Shapes—Explain (B) ........................................................................ 34

### CHAPTER TWO—FIGURAL SIMILARITIES AND DIFFERENCES

Matching Shapes—A ......................................................................................... 37
Matching Shapes—B ......................................................................................... 39
Matching Shapes—C ......................................................................................... 41
Matching Shapes by Shape and Color .............................................................. 44
Matching Shapes—D ......................................................................................... 45
Which Shape Does Not Match the Block? ......................................................... 47

Which Shape Does Not Match? ........................................................ 49
Copying a Figure ......................................................................... 52
Making a Figure .......................................................................... 53
Matching Figures with Cubes ........................................................ 54
Combining Attribute Blocks .......................................................... 56
Combining Interlocking Cubes ...................................................... 58
Covering Shapes with Equal Parts—Blocks .................................... 60
Covering Shapes with Equal Parts—Cubes ..................................... 63
Combining Shapes Made with Cubes ............................................. 64
Combining Shapes ...................................................................... 66
Comparing Shapes ...................................................................... 67

# CHAPTER THREE—FIGURAL SEQUENCES
Copying a Sequence of Cubes ....................................................... 71
Which Cube Comes Next?/Which Cube Is Missing? .......................... 72
What Group Comes Next? ............................................................ 75
Copying a Sequence of Blocks ...................................................... 77
Which Block Comes Next? ............................................................ 78
Describing Sequences of Cubes .................................................... 80
Describing Sequences of Shapes ................................................... 81

# CHAPTER FOUR—FIGURAL CLASSIFICATIONS
Comparing One Characteristic ...................................................... 85
Changing One Characteristic—Color, Size, or Shape ........................ 87
Comparing Two Characteristics ..................................................... 89
Changing Two Characteristics ....................................................... 91
Grouping Blocks by Shape, Color, or Size ....................................... 93
Describing a Group—What Belongs? .............................................. 95
Which Block Does Not Belong? ..................................................... 97
Describing a Group—Adding a Shape ............................................. 99
Complete the Group—What Belongs? ........................................... 100
Sorting Blocks by Color or Shape ................................................ 102
Find the One That Doesn't Belong ............................................... 104
Sorting Cube Figures ................................................................ 106
Forming Groups ....................................................................... 107
Forming Overlapping Groups ...................................................... 109
Overlapping Classes—Matrix A ................................................... 112
Overlapping Classes—Matrix B ................................................... 115
Overlapping Classes—Matrix C ................................................... 117
Describing Characteristics .......................................................... 119

# CHAPTER FIVE—DESCRIBING PEOPLE AND THINGS
Describing Family Members—Select .............................................. 121
Describing Family Members—Explain ............................................ 125
Describing Jobs—Select ............................................................. 128
Describing Jobs—Explain ........................................................... 132

Describing Foods—Select ........................................................................ 136
Describing Foods—Explain ...................................................................... 140
Describing Vehicles—Select .................................................................... 144
Describing Vehicles—Explain .................................................................. 147
Describing Animals—Select ..................................................................... 151
Describing Animals—Explain ................................................................... 154
Describing Buildings—Select ................................................................... 158
Describing Buildings—Explain ................................................................. 161

## CHAPTER SIX—DESCRIBING SIMILARITIES AND DIFFERENCES

Similar Family Members—Select ............................................................. 165
Similar Family Members—Explain ........................................................... 168
Similar Jobs—Select ............................................................................... 171
Similar Jobs—Explain ............................................................................. 174
Similar Foods—Select ............................................................................. 177
Similar Foods—Explain ........................................................................... 181
Similar Vehicles—Select ......................................................................... 184
Similar Vehicles—Explain ....................................................................... 188
Similar Animals—Select .......................................................................... 191
Similar Animals—Explain ........................................................................ 196
Similar Buildings—Select ........................................................................ 199
Similar Buildings—Explain ...................................................................... 203
Similarities and Differences—Jobs .......................................................... 206
Similarities and Differences—Foods ........................................................ 210
Similarities and Differences—Vehicles .................................................... 215
Similarities and Differences—Animals ..................................................... 219
Similarities and Differences—Buildings ................................................... 224

## CHAPTER SEVEN—VERBAL SEQUENCES

Ranking Family Members ......................................................................... 229
Ranking Jobs .......................................................................................... 232
Ranking Foods ........................................................................................ 234
Ranking Vehicles .................................................................................... 237
Ranking Animals ..................................................................................... 240
Ranking Buildings ................................................................................... 243

## CHAPTER EIGHT—VERBAL CLASSIFICATIONS

How Are These Family Members Alike? .................................................... 247
How Are These Jobs Alike? ..................................................................... 250
How Are These Foods Alike? Explain ....................................................... 254
How Are These Vehicles Alike? Explain ................................................... 257
How Are These Animals Alike? ................................................................ 261
How Are These Buildings Alike? .............................................................. 265
Explain the Exception—Family Members ................................................. 269
Explain the Exception—Jobs ................................................................... 272
Explain the Exception—Foods ................................................................. 276

Explain the Exception—Vehicles ....................................................................................... 279
Explain the Exception—Animals ....................................................................................... 283
Explain the Exception—Buildings ..................................................................................... 287
Sorting into Classes—Jobs ............................................................................................... 290
Sorting into Classes—Foods ............................................................................................ 293
Sorting into Classes—Vehicles ........................................................................................ 296
Sorting into Classes—Animals ......................................................................................... 299
Sorting into Classes—Buildings ....................................................................................... 302

## CHAPTER NINE—DESCRIBING ANALOGIES

Analogies Regarding Food—Select .................................................................................. 307
Analogies Regarding Community—Select ........................................................................ 311
Analogies Regarding Food—Explain ................................................................................ 315
Analogies Regarding Community—Explain ...................................................................... 319

## TRANSPARENCY MASTERS ................................................................ 325
## APPENDIX .......................................................................................... 351
## BIBLIOGRAPHY .................................................................................. 359

# INTRODUCTION

## PROGRAM DESIGN

### Rationale

*Beginning Building Thinking Skills* provides developmentally appropriate lessons for primary students. This introduction to the *Building Thinking Skills* series is the first of five carefully sequenced books that feature the same analysis skills. *The Building Thinking Skills* series includes five books on four levels:

- *Beginning Building Thinking Skills* for grades K-2 ability,
- Book 1 for grades 2-4 ability,
- Book 2 for grades 4-7 ability,
- Book 3 Figural and Book 3 Verbal for grade 7-adult ability.

*Beginning Building Thinking Skills* is a series of lessons that employ mathematics manipulatives and language integration techniques to teach analysis skills to students in kindergarten, first and second grade. This program is designed to:

- improve young children's observation and description skills;
- stimulate vocabulary development;
- clarify thinking processes integral to content learning (making observations, identifying similarities and differences, sequencing, classifying, and recognizing analogy)
- improve students' conceptualization of mathematics, social studies and science concepts taught in the primary grades.

To help students clarify their thinking processes, *Beginning Building Thinking Skills* features peer and class discussion of richly detailed pictures or mathematics manipulatives. Discussion helps teachers identify the knowledge base that young children have already developed or need to develop in order to understand social studies and science principles commonly taught in primary grades. *Beginning Building Thinking Skills* fosters students' abilities to systematically describe geometric shapes, family members, occupations, animals, food, vehicles, or buildings.

### Thinking Skills

- **Figural Skills**: describing shapes, figural similarities and differences, figural sequences, figural classifications
- **Verbal Skills**: describing things, verbal similarities and differences, verbal sequences, verbal classifications, verbal analogies

The five cognitive skills developed in this series (describing, finding similarities and differences, sequencing, classifying, and forming analogies) were selected because of their prevalence and relevance in academic disciplines. These analysis skills are required in all content areas, including the arts. Since improved school performance is an important goal of thinking skills instruction, many variations of each of these thinking skills are demonstrated in *Beginning Building Thinking Skills* exercises.

Analysis skills are sequenced in the order in which a child develops intellectually. A child first learns to observe and describe objects, to recognize the characteristics of an object and then to distinguish similarities and differences between the objects. Describing, comparing, and contrasting skills are integral to a learner's ability to put things in order, to group items by class, and to think analogically. Each analysis skill is presented first in the concrete figural form and then in the abstract verbal reasoning form.

### Teaching Options

Teachers may select from three alternatives for organizing *Beginning Building Thinking*

© 2000 CRITICAL THINKING BOOKS & SOFTWARE • WWW.CRITICALTHINKING.COM • 800-458-4849

*Skills* lessons:
1. teaching skills in the order in which they are presented in the student book, i.e., completing the figural exercises first and then teaching the verbal exercises;
2. alternating between figural and verbal forms of each skill;
3. scheduling the thinking skills exercises as they occur in content objectives.

Using any of these alternatives, the exercises dealing with *description* and *similarities and differences* in figural and verbal forms should be offered before more complex ones. The following flow chart illustrates the first two teaching options.

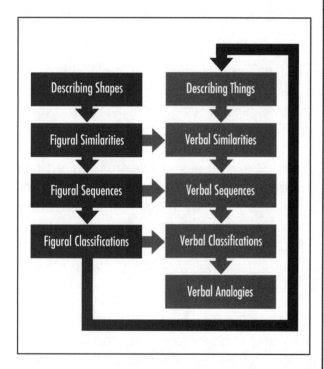

In both of the first two options, *Beginning Building Thinking Skills* is used as a structured program. Because students practice skillful thinking in many forms, they recognize their growing competence in carrying out the thinking tasks required in school. Program effectiveness evaluation of the *Building Thinking Skills* series over the last decade has shown that the careful sequencing of the complexity of the exercises and the repeated practice in consecutive lessons results in greater cognitive development growth gains than correlating the exercises with similar content lessons over the academic year.

The third teaching option involves linking thinking skills instruction to content objectives. By identifying thinking skills in the curriculum, one can offer a structured thinking skills program tailored for teaching content objectives to district needs rather than offering a "packaged program." This articulated program allows supervisors to identify and evaluate instruction, and is generally preferred by teachers because thinking skills instruction makes content learning more effective.

Because improved school performance is an important goal of thinking skills instruction, both teachers and students should identify thinking skills in the content curriculum. Skillful thinking enhances concept building, improves student confidence, and facilitates new content learning. Those benefits are best realized by identifying these five thinking skills (describing, finding similarities and differences, sequencing, classifying, and forming analogies) whenever teachers and students encounter similar examples or applications.

The Curriculum Applications section of each lesson plan identifies common content objectives and assists teachers in scheduling thinking skills lessons to correlate with appropriate curriculum material. For effective transfer, the thinking skills activity should be implemented in conjunction with, and just prior to, a content lesson which features the thinking process.

To transfer thinking skills instruction into content lessons, students must experience sufficient explanation, explicit practice, and metacognition of the thinking skill demonstrated in the lesson. By using *Beginning Building Thinking Skills* activities in conjunction with similar content lessons, teachers confirm students' confidence and competence in their skillful use of a variety of thinking processes.

The decision whether to use thinking skills instruction as a lesson supplement or as a sequential series depends on several factors:
1. how thinking skills instruction can be

effectively scheduled within the school program

2. how thinking skills instruction can be most easily managed and evaluated

3. whether teachers are more receptive to using a structured program with a carefully developed sequence of lessons or to correlating thinking skills lessons to existing instructional objectives

4. the extent to which student achievement on objective tests and classroom performance is expected to improve

For special education instruction, compensatory education classes, or bilingual programs, teaching thinking skills sequentially produces better results on tests of cognitive ability, vocabulary, and achievement than correlating *Beginning Building Thinking Skills* activities to content objectives.

### Item Design

In both the figural and verbal strands, exercises are sequenced in the order that the developing child learns: *cognition, evaluation,* and *convergent* production. The simplest form of each thinking task is recognizing the correct answer among several choices. These cognition exercises are labelled *select*.

Next in difficulty is the ability to explain or rank items. This evaluation step helps the learner clarify relationships between objects or concepts. Evaluation exercises contain the term *rank* or *explain*.

When the learner must supply a single correct answer from his own background and memory, the task becomes more difficult. This convergent production step is designated by the heading *supply*. Teachers may find it helpful to explain concepts in any discipline by remembering the simple "select, explain, then supply" process. The increasing difficulty of cognition, evaluation, and convergent production processes follows J. P. Guilford's *Structure of Intellect* model.

### Vocabulary Level

*Beginning Building Thinking Skills* employs manipulatives and pictures to allow learners with limited reading ability to develop more complex thinking skills. *Beginning Building Thinking Skills* uses vocabulary from the first thousand words that a child learns to read. Vocabulary designation is based on the *New Horizon Ladder Dictionary of the English Language* by John and Janet Shaw (New American Library, Inc., 1970). Because the vocabulary level is compounded by the thinking process, the resulting exercises may be more difficult than the vocabulary level alone suggests.

## INSTRUCTIONAL METHODS

Piagetian learning theory indicates that the learner proceeds from the concrete manipulative form of a task to the semiconcrete paper-and-pencil form of the task and, finally, to the abstract verbal form. The *Building Thinking Skills* program is based on that progression. Students should practice each cognitive task in concrete form. Attribute blocks and interlocking cubes are commonly available. Vocabulary exercises involve discussing richly detailed pictures and commonly available picture books.

The student book provides the paper-and-pencil form of the thinking task. Paper-and-pencil tasks alone do not offer the same cognitive benefit as experiencing the thinking in all three forms—manipulative, paper-and-pencil, and discussion.

The third step in this process—abstract, verbal expression of the thinking task—involves class discussion of the exercises. Discussion reinforces and confirms the thinking processes which the learner used to carry out the task. The discussion process clarifies the information the learner considered in formulating an answer and differentiates that thinking process from similar ones.

Discussion demonstrates differences in learning styles, allowing students to recognize and understand other ways of arriving at an answer and to value other people's processes for solving problems. For gifted students, discussion provides insight regarding how other equally bright learners can produce correct answers by different analyses.

Discussion reinforces the learner's memory of the thinking process, promoting transfer to similar tasks in content applications. Carrying out a thinking task in a nonthreatening learning situation enhances the learner's confidence in his or her ability to solve similar problems in a different context.

## Figural and Verbal Development

Class discussion also provides verbal stimulation for figural learners and is particularly helpful to students whose language skills are underdeveloped. Implementation of *Beginning Building Thinking Skills* with limited English, learning disabled, or hearing impaired students has indicated that developing students' thinking through figural tasks can be an effective strategy for language acquisition.

Figural observation skills are integral to scientific observation. Underdeveloped figural skills may explain why students who can make good grades on textbook tests sometimes perform less satisfactorily in science tasks that require observation.

## Discussion Principles

Discussion allows learners to clarify subtle aspects of their mental processing of the exercises. This clarification distinguishes a thinking task from subject content and provides alternative and creative ways of thinking through a problem. Through discussion, the learner ties a thinking skill to other school-related or common experiences and anticipates situations when using that thinking skill will be helpful.

For effective explanation and transfer of the thinking skill, the lesson proceeds from previous experience to new experience. When introducing a skill, the teacher should identify a school-related or nonacademic experience in which the learner has used that kind of thinking, cueing the learner that he or she already has some experience and competence doing that thinking task.

After explanation and guided practice of the thinking skill, the learner should identify other contexts in which he or she has used this skill. This association with past personal experience increases the learner's confidence in his or her thinking and encourages transfer of the skill.

The Thinking About Thinking section of each lesson reminds students of the thinking process practiced in the lesson and prompts students to express their thinking clearly. Research on thinking process instruction indicates that unless students can express the thinking that they practice in such instruction, subsequent transfer and demonstrated competence in improved thinking are greatly reduced. Metacognition is fostered by peer discussion, by class discussion as outlined in the lesson plan, by creating posters to describe the thinking process, or by student journaling.

## Supplemental Activities in Verbal Exercises

**Language integration activities**—Language acquisition research suggests several strategies to help young children develop and express new or partially-conceived concepts. Supplemental language acquisition activities in *Beginning Building Thinking Skills* lesson plans include drawing activities, using portfolio assessment, creating big books, story telling, telling riddles, and writing exercises.

- **Drawing activities**—Students depict details of concepts explored in the *Beginning Building Thinking Skills* program (family members, jobs, food, vehicles, animals, and buildings).

- **Portfolio assessment**—Students' drawings and limited writing are gathered and evaluated.

- **Creating "big books"**—Drawings are collected to form individual or class "big books" to show students' understanding and growth.

- **Story telling**—Personal narratives and imaginative stories extend concept development in the *Beginning Building Thinking Skills* program

- **Telling Riddles**—Oral and written language activities feature humor and reasoning to figure out the answer to riddles.
- **Writing**—Students create sentences, definitions, paragraphs, and full stories about concepts featured in the *Beginning Building Thinking Skills* program.

**Follow-up activities at home**—Each verbal section contains suggestions for communicating and extending the thinking skills featured in the *Beginning Building Thinking Skills* program. These activities include asking parents to model the thinking in contexts related to family history, habits, and values. Parents reinforce the process and language of thinking and practice parenting habits that promote children's cognitive growth.

**Picture Book Extension**—Fiction and nonfiction books for primary students depict and explain important concepts. Lesson plans include identifying appropriate books and offer guidelines for discussing them. An extensive bibliography identifies books commonly available in general bookstores and school libraries. Multicultural books are identified for most concepts.

## Types of Graphic Organizers

Several graphic organizers are used in *Beginning Building Thinking Skills* activities. They may be used as bulletin board designs or patterns for organizing student drawings in "big books." Each diagram cues a different thinking process.

For additional graphic organizers and model lessons see *Organizing Thinking Book 1*, Sandra Parks and Howard Black (Critical Thinking Books and Software, Pacific Grove, CA, 1992).

**Central idea graphs** are used to prepare descriptions and definitions, to depict a main idea and supporting details, to depict parts of a given object, and to depict general classes and subclasses.

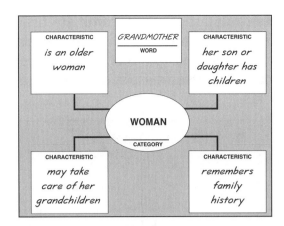

**Transitive Order graphs** are used to record the order or sequence of information.

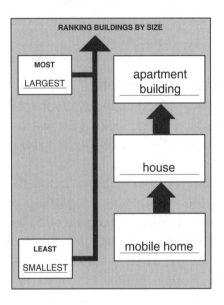

**Compare and contrast diagrams** are used to compare and contrast two terms or ideas, to organize thinking, and to clarify the meaning of terms.

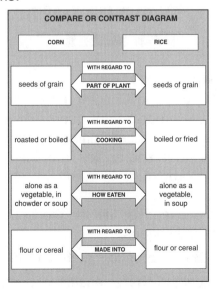

**Class relationship diagrams** are used to depict class membership and to depict class/subclass relationships. Students may depict members of a given class such as emergency vehicles.

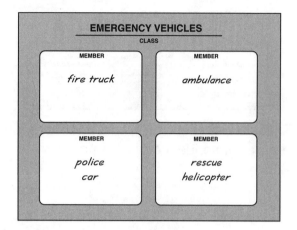

## Supplemental Materials

The following books and software published by Critical Thinking Books & Software may be used to extend the lessons in *Beginning Building Thinking Skills*.

- *Building Thinking Skills Book 1*—parallels the lessons in *Beginning Building Thinking Skills* and can be used to extend students' skills in all thinking processes.
- *Language Smarts Book A-1* and *B-1*—offer supplemental activities in Verbal Similarities and Differences, Verbal Sequences, and Verbal Classification
- *Organizing Thinking Book 1*—is an excellent resource in using graphic organizers.

## RATIONALE AND DESCRIPTION OF THINKING SKILLS

### Describing Shapes

The exercises in Chapter 1 help students express the properties of geometric figures. Students systematically name polygons, observe the sides and angles, and tell or write about the properties of common geometric figures.

Types of exercises include the following:
1. Naming shapes
2. Finding shapes to match a description
3. Describing characteristics of a shape

### Figural Similarities and Differences

Chapter 2 features activities to develop visual discrimination skills and to improve students' perception of congruence and similarity. The ability to discern similarities and differences is necessary before the learner can place objects in order, classify them, or make analogous comparisons.

Visual discrimination in its simplest forms involves recognizing geometric shapes and the appearance of letters. In elementary school mathematics programs, the concepts of congruence and similarity are involved in establishing geometric definitions and developing perceptions of area and volume.

Reading development requires the learner to recognize subtle differences in the shapes and sequences of letters or the appearance of whole words. Visual discrimination activities promote word decoding for students having reading difficulty.

Visual discrimination skills are fundamental to elementary science and mathematics instruction. Relational observations of rotation, reflection, size change, and shape change are basic observations in geometry, life sciences, and earth sciences.

In the Figural Similarities and Differences strand, students select the correct shape among subtly different ones. The learner evaluates whether or not a shape matches others or appears in a more complex design.

Types of exercises in this strand include the following:
1. Analyzing and matching shapes
2. Finding and combining shapes
3. Evaluating and producing equal shapes
4. Recognizing shapes necessary to complete a whole figure

### Figural Sequences

Chapter 3 provides exercises to develop visual discrimination and to promote sequential reasoning. Identifying sequences in figural form sharpens observational skills regarding change or alternation.

In the Figural Sequences strand, students demonstrate a variety of sequencing skills: adding or subtracting detail in figures; changing size, shape, or color of figures in a sequence; rotation and reflection of shapes; and rearrangement of figures in a sequence.

Types of exercises in this strand include the following:

1. Recognizing the next figure in a sequence

2. Producing the next figure in a sequence

## Figural Classification

Figural Classification exercises in chapter 4 help students develop the ability to group or organize objects by similar characteristics. Classification is a significant concept-building process, especially useful in developing science concepts.

Classification promotes visual discrimination, memory, and observation. A learner uses classification as an observational tool, by identifying similar or different characteristics, and systematically examining new examples. Classification is involved in assimilating new information and accommodating old categories to include new information or experiences.

The Figural Classification exercises increase in complexity and difficulty throughout the chapter:

1. Classifying by shape

2. Classifying by color

3. Classifying by shape and color

4. Completing or forming a class

5. Using diagrams to depict overlapping classes

## Describing Things

In chapter 5 students discuss and define the characteristics of key concepts in the elementary school curriculum such as family members, occupations, food, animals, vehicles, and buildings. Students practice using precise language to describe or define things they study.

Types of exercises include the following:

1. Matching a picture to a description

2. Describing people or objects shown in pictures

## Verbal Similarities and Differences

In chapter 6 students compare and contrast family members, occupations, foods, animals, vehicles, and buildings. Types of exercises in this chapter include the following:

1. Selecting similar words

2. Explaining how words are alike and how they are different

## Verbal Sequences

In chapter 7 verbal sequence exercises include distinguishing transitive order. Students rank objects or people being compared according to some characteristic (size, age, or order or frequency of occurrence.)

## Verbal Classifications

Chapter 8 features activities to improve students' conceptualization of class relationships and formation of clear definitions. Classification promotes the understanding and recall of the meaning of words. *Classes* are the categories in any definition of nouns. In the definition of *bicycle* as a "vehicle having two wheels," "vehicle" is the class and the words "two wheels" are the descriptors.

Verbal classification exercises feature detailed pictures and are appropriate for older students.

Types of exercises include the following:

1. Selecting and explaining common characteristics of a class

2. Explaining the exception to a class

3. Sorting words (pictures) into classes

## Verbal Analogies

The Verbal Analogies strand in chapter 9 features activities to introduce students to analogical relationships among concepts they study. The types of analogies include synonyms, antonyms, part of, kind of (classification), something used to, and association.

Analogy exercises include the following:

1. Naming the kind of analogy

2. Supplying the word (picture) to complete an analogy

## Recommendations for ESOL Teachers

• Use attribute blocks to form chains of blocks that are different from each other by one attribute.

• Start with concepts and words that students know.

• Insist that students use complete sentences when responding. Students whose language proficiency is underdeveloped are inclined to answer in single words or phrases. To realize the language acquisition benefits of these lessons, students should answer in complete sentences, expressing whole thoughts that are grammatically correct.

• Ask students to identify verbs associated with specific family members, animals, or jobs. For example: doctors treat, test, examine, record, listen, etc. List the verbs on a flip chart or chalkboard. Ask students to select verbs to create a sentence about what doctors do. Sentence strips with students' writing can be added to student picture displays that show the action described in the sentence.

• Ask students to identify adjectives associated with specific family members, animals, or jobs. For example: a butterfly is colorful, light, flowerlike, busy, beautiful, etc. List the adjectives on a flip chart or chalkboard. Ask students to select adjectives to create a sentence to describe a butterfly. Sentence strips with students' writing can be added to student picture displays that show the features described in the sentence.

• Practice vocabulary prior to the lesson by reading the topic-related picture book and/or actually examining the objects described in the lesson.

• Pairs of students may use "Think, Pair, Share" to discuss guided practice items, as needed.

• Make Thinking Process signs (describe, compare and contrast, sequence, classify, find an analogy, etc.) for use on bulletin boards and while conducting lessons.

• Review various types of thinking process lessons just prior to achievement testing in order to remind students of the language of thinking used on such tests, as well as the process of doing these thinking tasks quickly.

• Use attribute blocks to form chains of blocks that are different from each other by one attribute.

• Use picture cards to show the answer to riddles that the teacher or students create.

## EVALUATING BUILDING THINKING SKILLS INSTRUCTION

Implementation of the *Building Thinking Skills* program has been evaluated using many assessment procedures:

• Student performance on cognitive abilities tests

• Student performance on normed-referenced achievement tests

• Student performance on language proficiency tests

• Number of students placed in heterogeneous grouped classes, or advanced academic programs, as well as students' subsequent successful performance in gifted or academic excellence classes

### Cognitive Abilities Tests

Cognitive abilities tests indicate students' capabilities to perform thinking tasks that are related to school performance but do not require content knowledge. Such tasks include figural and verbal forms of tasks that require certain analysis skills. Because the *Building Thinking Skills* series is a cognitive development program that emphasizes language development, the figural and verbal subtests of cognitive abilities tests are closely correlated to *Building Thinking Skills* goals and activities.

The following cognitive abilities tests have been used in program effectiveness evaluation of thinking instruction using the *Building Thinking Skills* series:

- *Cognitive Abilities Test* (*Woodcock-Johnson*)
  Riverside Publishing Company
  425 Spring Lake Dr.
  Itasa, IL 60143
  800-323-9540 • 312-693-0325 (fax)

- *Developing Cognitive Abilities Test*
  American College Testronics (formerly American Testronics)
  P.O. Box 2270
  Iowa City, IA 52244
  800-533-0030 • 319-337-1578 (fax)

- *Test of Cognitive Skills*
  CTB-McGraw Hill
  P.O. Box 150
  Monterey, CA 93942-0150
  800-538-9547 • 800-282-0266 (fax)

- *Structure of Intellect Learning Abilities Test*
  S.O.I. Institute
  P.O. Box D
  Vida, OR 97488
  503-896-3936 • 503-896-3983 (fax)

- *WISC-III*
  Psychological Corporation
  Order Service Center
  P.O. Box 839954
  San Antonio, TX 78283-3954
  800-228-0752 • 800-232-1223 (fax)

**Norm-referenced Achievement Tests**

Composite scores on norm-referenced achievement tests are generally poor indicators of improved thinking skills. Some subtests do reflect the analysis skills addressed in *Building Thinking Skills* instruction. Program evaluation using this series has indicated substantial gains in subtests which measure reading comprehension and mathematics concepts. If achievement test information is used to report the effectiveness of *Building Thinking Skills* instruction, only those subtests should be monitored.

**Language Proficiency Tests**

Because one goal of the *Beginning Building Thinking Skills* program is language development, increased vocabulary can be shown on a variety of language tests. Tests commonly used to evaluate the effect of thinking instruction on language development include the following:

- *Peabody Picture Vocabulary Test*
  American Guidance Service
  4201 Woodland Rd.
  Circle Pines, MN 55014-1796
  800-328-5260 • 612-786-5603 (fax)

**Inclusion and Performance in Mainstream or Advanced Academic Programs**

The *Building Thinking Skills* series is commonly used to promote access to academic excellence programs or to prepare students to be successful in mainstream classes from special services programs (Chapter 1 classes, bilingual programs, ESOL classes, special education classes, or remedial programs). The key statistics for evaluating this goal are the number of students who gain access to programs, the speed with which the transition is accomplished, and the students' level of achievement when included in general or advanced classes.

# INSTRUCTIONAL RECOMMENDATIONS

- **Do description and similarities and differences exercises first.** To describe food, plants, animals, people, buildings, and vehicles, students must identify the significant characteristics of these items. To compare and contrast objects or organisms, students identify similarities and differences in significant characteristics. Both describing and comparing are required in sequencing, classifying, and reasoning analogously.

- **Use real objects or detailed pictures whenever possible.** To enhance students' observation skills and language acquisition, allow them to examine actual objects to replace or supplement the vivid pictures provided with the series.

- **Encourage peer discussion.** Program effectiveness evaluation of the *Building Thinking Skills* series suggests that the quality of student responses, their willingness to participate, and their attentiveness significantly improve when peers discuss their answers prior to full class discussion. Peer discussion is very effective in special education, bilingual, and Title I classes.

- **Conduct short exercises.** Do only a few activities in each session—lasting not more than 20 to 25 minutes. Discuss a few exercises with ample time for students to explain their thinking, rather than attempting to conduct additional lessons.

- **Identify and use students' background knowledge.** Use these lessons as diagnostic indicators of students' prior knowledge. Remember the language that students use in their descriptions. Use the same words to remind students of the thinking processes in subsequent social studies and science lessons.

- **Use *Beginning Building Thinking Skills* lessons before or after social studies or science activities.** The list of possible responses in each lesson plan has more answers than are commonly expected from students in grades K–2. Jot down unusual responses in the lessons for future use.

- **Examine concepts in mathematics, science, and social studies using the same thinking processes.** Use correct terms for the thinking process to cue students to use a similar process in other contexts. Use the same methods (peer and class discussion, observation of pictures or objects, graphic organizers, etc.) in other lessons.

- **Insist that students use complete sentences when responding**. Students whose language proficiency is underdeveloped are inclined to answer in single words or phrases. To realize the language acquisition benefits of these lessons, students should answer in complete sentences, expressing whole thoughts that are grammatically correct.

- ***Beginning Building Thinking Skills* lessons should not be given as homework assignments or as independent activities.** The lessons in *Beginning Building Thinking Skills* are designed to enhance cognitive development through discussion and observation. Independent practice exercises may be used to reinforce mastery or build confidence but should never be used as a substitute for class discussions. Experience suggests that kindergarten and first grade students require adult direction when attempting "independent practice" exercises.

- **Use graphic organizers to cue various thinking processes.** The following graphic organizers are featured: central idea (definition) graph, compare and contrast diagram, transitive order graph, and class relationship diagram. Each diagram cues a different thinking process.

# VOCABULARY AND SYNONYMS

Reinforce the language of thinking in thinking skills activities and in other lessons. The following list includes terms that teachers and students can use in *Building Thinking Skills* lessons, content lessons, and personal applications. Students may create a "thinking thesaurus" of the words and idioms that they use to describe their thinking. Encourage them to express their thinking using the terms below.

| WORD | SYNONYMS |
|------|----------|
| Analogies | comparisons, similarities |
| Appropriate | fitting, correct, proper, suitable |
| Arrange | place, order, rank, organize |
| Assemble | put together, gather, build, organize |
| Attribute | feature, characteristic |
| Category | classification, class, kind, type, form |
| Characteristic | attribute, traits |
| Chart | map, outline, graph, diagram, matrix |
| Class | group, set, category, kind, type, sort |
| Classification | arrangement, assortment, grouping |
| Combine | connect, put together, link, assemble, join |
| Common | familiar, ordinary, similar, have the same characteristic, frequently occurring |
| Compare | relate, match, find similarities |
| Confirm | prove, explain, agree, make sure, show, determine, check |
| Construct | build, create, compose, invent, put together, assemble |
| Contrasts | differs, is unlike |
| Decreasing | lessening, diminishing, shrinking, becoming smaller |
| Definition | meaning, explanation, description |
| Demonstrate | show, illustrate, enact, make clear |
| Describe | explain, clarify, give details |
| Detail | part, piece, feature |
| Determine | decide, find out, learn, conclude, figure out, show |

| WORD | SYNONYMS |
|------|----------|
| Diagram | graph, layout, outline, design |
| Differences | unlike, contrasts |
| Disassemble | separate, divide, take apart, dismantle, disconnect |
| Discuss | talk about, describe, explain, explore, express |
| Eliminate | remove, take out, erase, end |
| Enable | allow, approve, permit, make possible |
| Equal | same, matching, same size, evenly divided, |
| Examine | find the details, analyze, inspect, explore, investigate, look at, observe closely |
| False | not true, not real, untrue, unreal, not valid |
| Figural | pictured, drawn, geometric |
| Figure | picture, shape, structure, diagram, outline, drawing |
| Geometric | figural, having shape, many-sided |
| Graph | diagram, chart, outline |
| Hidden | unclear, not distinct, camouflaged |
| Identify | find, recognize, pick out, know, indicate, show, specify |
| Illustrate | draw, depict, show, represent, picture, portray, model |
| Interpret | convey, explain, make clear, define, show, tell another way |
| Locate | identify, place, find |
| Location | place, position, point |
| Matching | equal, making an equal pair, same |
| Matrix | chart, graph with rows and columns, grid |
| Member | belongs to a group or class |
| Observe | examine, look at carefully |

**BEGINNING BUILDING THINKING SKILLS LESSON PLANS**    **INTRODUCTION**

Order ................. rank, sequence, organization

Overlap ............. intersection, come together, belong to both

Part .................... piece, fragment, segment, section, detail

Pattern .............. arrangement, design, repetition

Point/position .... location, spot

Prepare ............ produce, create, arrange, ready, plan

Produce ............ make, create, assemble

Quality .............. characteristic, attribute, trait, standard

Rank ................. order, class, grade, type

Recognize ........ identify, be familiar with, verify, indicate

Relationship ..... tie, connection, how related or similar

Represent ........ show, depict, model

Select .............. pick out, identify, locate, decide

Sequence ......... steps, order, rank, consecutive arrangement, change

Series .............. group, succession, sequence, order

Set .................... group, category, collection, class, type

Shape .............. figure, form, pattern, outline, drawing

Significant ........ important, key, basic

Similarity .......... likeness, sameness

Solution ........... answer, result, outcome

Solve ............... figure out, think, find answer, find out why

Sort .................. group, classify, file, organize

Supply ............. provide, furnish, produce

Transparent ...... revealing, clear, see-through

True ................. real, accurate, precise

Verbal .............. spoken, expressed in words, oral

Visualize .......... imagine, picture in your mind, see

Whole .............. entire, complete, total

BEGINNING BUILDING THINKING SKILLS LESSON PLANS                                    INTRODUCTION

**Chapter Number**
**EXERCISES**

# GUIDE TO USING THE LESSON PLANS

## LESSON TITLE

> ### ANSWERS
> Lists exercises and pages covered in student book.
> **Guided Practice:** Provides answers to guided practice exercises.
> **Independent Practice:** Lists independent practice answers.

**LESSON PREPARATION**

### OBJECTIVE AND MATERIALS
OBJECTIVE: Explains for the teacher the thinking objective of the lesson.
MATERIALS: Lists materials or supplies for modeling the lesson

### SKILL LEVEL
Indicates the degree of concentration, dexterity, decoding, or writing required in the lesson.

### CURRICULUM APPLICATIONS
Lists content objectives which feature the skill or require it as a prerequisite.

### TEACHING SUGGESTIONS
Alerts the teacher to special vocabulary or concepts in the lesson. Guided practice should be followed by class discussion of the exercises, with the teacher clarifying significant terms and concepts. Discussion should also include student explanations, reasons for rejecting incorrect answers, and confirmation of correct responses.

**MODEL LESSON**

### LESSON

#### Introduction
- Indicates to the learner when he or she has seen or used a similar kind of learning.

#### Explaining the Objective to Students
   Q: Explains to the student what he or she will learn in the lesson.

#### Class Activity–the example
- Offers a concrete form of the thinking task (and/or illustrates the task by modeling). Students may also prepare models or materials similar to those suggested. When conducting the lesson, teachers should verbalize their own thinking process. This modeling provides cues to students for executing the thinking task skillfully.

#### GUIDED PRACTICE–the exercise
Allows the teacher to identify errors or omissions in students' processing. Guided practice should be followed by class discussion.

#### OPTIONAL INDEPENDENT PRACTICE
- Provides an optional additional practice exercise if needed.

#### THINKING ABOUT THINKING
Helps the student clarify and verbalize the thinking process: metacognition.

© 2000 CRITICAL THINKING BOOKS & SOFTWARE • WWW.CRITICALTHINKING.COM • 800-458-4849          XIX

## PERSONAL APPLICATION

Relates the skill to the learner's experience and cues the learner regarding possible future uses of the skill.

**LESSON EXTENSION**

**(VERBAL EXERCISES ONLY)**

## LANGUAGE INTEGRATION ACTIVITIES

- Drawing Activities
- Pre-instruction diagnosis of students' background
- Portfolio assessment
- Creating "big books"
- Storytelling
- Telling
- Writing

## FOLLOW-UP ACTIVITIES AT HOME

Asking parents to reinforce the concepts and thinking processes in *Beginning Building Thinking Skills* as important benefits for children and families:

1. Parents are asked to reinforce concepts that their children are learning in science and social studies.

2. Parents model the thinking process that their children are learning at school.

3. Suggestions model good parenting practices to help parents enrich their children's vocabularies and their thinking processes in ordinary conversation.

## PICTURE BOOK EXTENSION

Discussing picture books to extend the content and the thinking processes addressed in each *Beginning Building Thinking Skills* lesson serves several purposes:

1. To integrate language arts instruction with primary science and social studies concepts through thinking skills instruction.

2. To extend students' background knowledge of the content before or after the thinking activity, depending on the background level and language development of the class.

3. To practice and enhance students' observation skills.

4. To demonstrate the multicultural universality and diversity of family relationships, jobs, food, transportation, and vehicles.

5. To add humor or beauty to social studies and science instruction.

# TEACHING SUGGESTIONS FOR FIGURAL LESSONS

**MATERIALS**

- Figural lessons require one set of interlocking cubes and one set of attribute blocks for each cooperative learning group of four students. Since each attribute block set contains two blocks of each color, shape, and size, one set of blocks for every four students allows pairs of students to take turns placing and tracing the blocks. Students within each group may take turns holding up the correct block to answer questions. For most figural exercises, students will need a pencil and red, blue, and yellow crayons or fine markers.

- All figural lessons using attribute blocks feature outlines of Invicta Attribute Blocks, available from Addison Wesley, Jacob Way, Reading, MA 01867.

- While students may make paper attribute blocks, we find that unmounted paper shapes are easily lost or damaged. First- and second-grade students generally lack the manual dexterity to cut out these shapes accurately or easily. To create a set of sturdy attribute blocks, photocopy the Transparency Master 1 on page 325 on sheets of red, blue, or yellow paper. Mount each sheet on cardboard, laminate, and cut out the shapes.

- Interlocking cubes are outlines of Multilink or Unifix cubes. Multilinks are available from NES Arnold, 899-H, Airport Park Road, Glen Burnie, MD 21061-2557. Unifix cubes are available from Didax, 395 Main Street, P.O. Box 785, Rowley, MA 01969.

- Transparent attribute blocks may be used to introduce lessons on color, shape, and size. These manipulatives can be purchased from many school supply stores or from Learning Resources, 500 Greenview Ct., Vernon Hills, IL 60061. To make a set of transparent attribute blocks, photocopy the Transparency Master 1 on page 325 on sheets of red, blue, or yellow acetate film. Cut out the shapes and store them in a heavy envelope or transparent bag to prevent loss or damage.

- Each cooperative learning group may use a set of response cards, made from Transparency Masters 2–4 on pages 326–8. Fold, laminate, and cut apart the cards. Store each set in a heavy envelope or transparent bag to prevent loss or damage. Students within each cooperative learning group may take turns holding up the correct response card to show their group's answer.

- Figural exercises often require a transparency showing the example exercise. Photocopy the transparency master onto acetate film and store in clear sheet protectors to create a notebook of transparencies.

- Most kindergarten students cannot read sufficiently well to do exercises independently. Their distractibility may make it difficult for them to stay focused and/or to recall directions. Use the process modeled in the lesson introduction to complete the exercises.

## MODIFYING LESSONS BASED ON SKILL LEVEL

- Some first-grade students and most second-grade students can decode the terms in the student book well enough to work independently after guided practice exercises show them how to carry out the thinking task.

- Generally, kindergarten students find one page of exercises sufficient for one class session. Attempting additional exercises may strain their attention span.

- *Beginning Building Thinking Skills* lessons are carefully ungraded in order to allow flexible use with students who exhibit delayed skill development or limited English usage. These exercises are also generally appropriate for gifted preschool or kindergarten students. Decoding skills, writing proficiency, manual dexterity, and attention span are more significant than grade level in determining appropriateness.

- One of three skill levels is identified for each lesson:
  1. Requires no reading or writing skill development (typical of kindergarten students).
  2. Requires reading simple words and limited copying (typical of advanced kindergarten or first-grade students). Requires some manual dexterity or reasoning that is complex for primary students.
  3. Requires reading terms or short directions and writing short sentences (typical of second-grade students). Requires reasoning that is complex for primary students.

## MANAGING BLOCKS AND CUBES

### Managing attribute blocks

- Remove only the blocks needed for each lesson and distribute them to each work group. This preparation prevents distraction by students playing with or dropping unneeded blocks.

- Tracing the attribute blocks is more difficult and time consuming for kindergarten children than adults may expect. Give kindergarten students sufficient practice tracing attribute blocks in order to allow them to trace the shapes comfortably, accurately, and quickly before they do *Beginning Building Thinking Skills* exercises. Students should practice first with the large blocks and, once proficiency is gained, then trace the smaller blocks. Help students learn to shift the positions of their hands in order to hold the block steady as they trace its perimeter.

- Students who have motor difficulty or are developmentally not ready to trace can place blocks without tracing around them. The teacher can check accuracy. There are also rubber stamps of the basic geometric shapes that students can use to stamp in their answers. Although these stamps may not match the size of the attribute blocks used, students can still show their answers.

- Since the writing points of crayons and markers are broad, encourage students to trace the attribute blocks using a pencil first. Student pages contain a narrow shaded perimeter to give sufficient room to accommodate the imprecise drawing ability of kindergarten students.

BEGINNING BUILDING THINKING SKILLS LESSON PLANS                    FIGURAL TEACHING SUGGESTIONS

- Plan sufficient time in each lesson for students to trace and color their drawings. Since young children may have difficulty tracing the blocks accurately, they may express disappointment that their papers may seem messier than their usual drawings.

- After matching attribute blocks to the outlines on student pages, students should color the outline to match the block before following additional instructions.

## MANAGING BLOCKS AND CUBES

### Managing interlocking cubes

- All exercises using interlocking cubes feature only red, blue, and yellow cubes.

- For kindergarten or first-grade students unaccustomed to using manipulatives, students should work in pairs. One partner can check whether the cubes are correctly joined and moved about the page correctly. Students should take turns serving as the "checking" partner.

- Give kindergarten students sufficient practice joining interlocking cubes before they do *Beginning Building Thinking Skills* exercises. This practice builds manual dexterity and allows students to enjoy the patterns that they make.

- Although kindergarten students commonly enjoy doing exercises with interlocking cubes, their manual dexterity and inexperience in handling the cubes creates some frustration. Interlocking the cubes may prove to be more difficult for them than adults may expect. A partner can hold the cube construction steady while the other partner snaps new cubes in place. Sometimes the cube construction comes apart because of the pressure applied when snapping additional blocks in place. When that happens, in reassembling the construction a kindergarten child may join them incorrectly or add a new block to a wrong location. A partner can check that the figure has been built correctly.

- Kindergarten students may find it more comfortable to stand rather than sit while snapping or moving the cubes.

## DISCUSSING GEOMETRIC FIGURES

### Discussing geometric figures

- *Beginning Building Thinking Skills* lessons should supplement, not introduce, instruction about geometric shapes. Be sure that BBTS lessons are conducted *after* the terms and properties of various polygons have been carefully developed in your mathematics program.

- In many of these lessons, students' descriptive answers may provide memorable cues for reinforcing their perceptions and developing vocabulary. Celebrate and refine students' colorful language. Playful descriptions, if correct, can imprint concepts. For example:

  "A trapezoid is like a triangle with a haircut"

  "An oval is a smashed circle"

  "Some parallelograms look like lazy rectangles"

© 2000 CRITICAL THINKING BOOKS & SOFTWARE • WWW.CRITICALTHINKING.COM • 800-458-4849          XXIII

- Kindergarten and first-grade students commonly lack language for position or orientation and make up metaphors to describe these properties. An upright oval may be "standing up," a horizontal oval "lying down."

- Young children may not express dimensions accurately. Height may be "taller, shorter, longer up, farther up, up and down on the page, or higher." Width may be "fatter, skinnier, longer across, or sidewise."

- Young children enjoy using long words to describe shapes but often have difficulty pronouncing them. *Trapezoid* may get abbreviated to "trap." Give children extra practice in enunciating the l's in *parallelogram*. As with the names of dinosaurs, once young children become comfortable saying these terms, they do so joyfully with personal satisfaction in sounding so mature.

- A right triangle may be "straight up" or "leaning" to a child who thinks that the only "good" triangles are equilateral. Young children lack the language to describe the two equal sides of an isosceles triangle. Young children can find metaphors for *isosceles*, such as church steeple or pointed arrow.

- Children may describe the slanted sides of polygons as "broken," meaning that the child realizes that the slant results when a regular figure has been altered. Young children may describe the slant as a ramp or a hill.

- Integrate the geometry concepts in *Beginning Building Thinking Skills* with your language arts program by supplementing thinking lessons with whole language discussion of the picture books listed in the bibliography in the appendix, especially those books related to shapes.

# TEACHING SUGGESTIONS FOR VERBAL LESSONS

**THINK/PAIR/ SHARE**
- Using "THINK/PAIR/SHARE" in Guided Practice exercises promotes the quality and accuracy of students' responses. Program effectiveness evaluation suggests that bilingual students particularly gain confidence and willingness to participate when they have an opportunity to "rehearse" their comments with a partner. This diagram depicts one form of "THINK/PAIR/SHARE."

**THINK/PAIR/SHARE**

THINK ABOUT YOUR ANSWER

⬇

SELECT A PARTNER

⬇

LISTEN TO OR EXPLAIN ANSWERS

⬇

SWITCH ROLES

⬇

STATE YOUR ANSWER IN CLASS DISCUSSION, A WRITTEN ASSIGNMENT, OR A SPEECH.

**PHOTO CARDS**
- Photos are printed back to back to minimize storage. Each photo is numbered in the upper right corner. A list of the individual photos is included in this manual. Photo cards are referenced in the lessons by both subject and number.

- When viewing pictures, make sure that all students examine the pictures closely enough to see the details. Encourage students to cite details to support their answers. Young students, particularly bilingual students, may not know the terms to describe details in pictures, such as a duck's *bill* or a chicken's *beak*.

- Using more than one picture may be helpful when discussing food items. Food items may include a picture of the source of the food, such as the cow for milk or a tree branch for the apple.

- When discussing families, help students understand that all families are different. In some families, the "mother" of the household may be a grandmother or an aunt. In some Native American groups, cousins may be called brothers. This may create some confusion about identifying grandparents for teachers unfamiliar with Native American clans and the terms assigned to family relationships.

**DEDUCTIVE REASONING GAME**
- The "Twenty Questions" game may supplement or substitute for riddles. "Twenty Questions" is a deductive reasoning game whose goal is to guess the selected person or thing in fewer than twenty questions. The leader selects the item to be guessed and may answer only yes or no to questions that others ask. By some rules a questioner may continue asking questions until he or she receives a "no" answer. In some versions of the game, each student may ask only one question.

For example, to guess the selection "frog," the dialogue may proceed as follows:

Q. Is it an animal?
   A. Yes (This rules out plants, minerals, or manufactured goods).

Q. Is it a vertebrate?
   A. Yes (This rules out insects and other invertebrates).

Q. Is it warm-blooded?
A. No (This rules out birds and mammals).

Q. Does it change form from newborn to adult?
A. Yes (This rules out reptiles and fish).

Q. Is it a frog?
A. Yes.

- Some verbal exercises often feature graphic organizers. Photocopy the transparency master onto acetate film and store in clear sheet protectors to create a notebook of transparencies.

- Generally kindergarten students find one page of exercises sufficient for one class session. Attempting additional exercises may strain their attention span.

**LANGUAGE INTEGRATION ACTIVITIES**

- Supplemental language acquisition activities in *Beginning Building Thinking Skills* lesson plans include drawing activities, portfolio assessments, student-made big books, storytelling, riddles, and writing exercises.

- Conduct only one language integration activity for each *Beginning Building Thinking Skills* lesson, not one of each type.

    1. **Drawing activities**—Drawing allows primary students to express the details that they remember about concepts addressed in the *Beginning Building Thinking Skills* program (family members, jobs, food, vehicles, animals, and buildings). These drawings may be used to assess an individual student's background and understanding of concepts, as well as to evaluate the general level of social studies and science background within a specific class. Students' misconceptions, such as believing that oranges grow on the ground, may emerge from their drawings. This information informs the teacher about the degree of explanation that students may require.

    The graphic organizers used throughout the *Beginning Building Thinking Skills* program may serve as designs for organizing students' drawings into bulletin board displays. Visual displays depict the concepts and the thinking process used in the lessons. For example, to create a display for classifying buildings, you can organize students' drawings in this kind of display.

    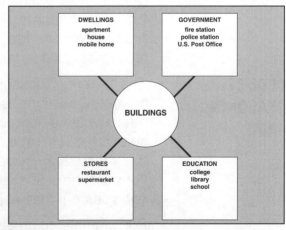

    2. **Portfolio assessment**—Since the social studies and science concepts developed in this series are addressed more than once during the school year, compare students' drawings made early in *Beginning Building Thinking Skills* instruction to drawings made after students

have analyzed and discussed these concepts. Details in students' drawings may show growth in students' abilities to conceptualize the ideas featured in thinking skills lessons.

3. **Creating "big books"**—Each student may create or contribute to a "big book" that shows what the individual student or the whole class has learned about family members, jobs, food, vehicles, animals, and buildings. Two types of "big books" may be created:

    - Personalized "big book" for each student. Save each student's drawings and assemble them to create a "big book" that describes each student's family members, jobs in his or her family, food that the family prefers, vehicles that the family uses or sees regularly, animals that the student has seen or wants to know more about, and buildings in the students' neighborhood. To use this collection for portfolio assessment purposes, teachers, parents, and students themselves evaluate the degree of detail and craftsmanship in later drawings compared to earlier ones.

    - Class "big book" describing what the class collectively knows about family members, jobs, food, vehicles, animals, and buildings. Create a "big book" for each category of concepts: family members, jobs, animals, food, vehicles, or buildings.

4. **Storytelling**—Several types of storytelling activities are described in *Beginning Building Thinking Skills* lessons. In some cases, students relate a personal narrative, such as a special event that his or her family enjoyed or buildings that he or she sees in the course of a day.

    Some storytelling experiences involve retelling traditional stories using a different building or vehicle instead of the one in the familiar story. Students may retell *Little Toot* as a story about a tractor, instead of a boat. This familiar story serves as a basic plot that is changed to describe conditions on land, rather than at sea, in which the little tractor must perform his act of courage and determination.

5. **Telling Riddles**—Oral language experiences include creating riddles about a family member, a job, a food, a vehicle, an animal, or a building. Students within each cooperative learning group may also play "Twenty Questions" about these concepts.

6. **Writing**—First- and second-grade students write sentences to create short descriptions that can be added to their drawings, if desired. Students may use graphic organizers to learn models for writing definitions and descriptions. They learn to state full, rich definitions using the following pattern.

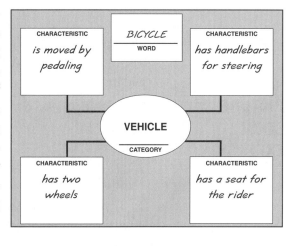

DEFINITION OF ANY NOUN = CATEGORY + CHARACTERISTICS
THAT DISTINGUISH IT FROM OTHERS IN THAT CATEGORY

The resulting definition may be stated:

A <u>bicycle</u> is a <u>vehicle</u> that has <u>two wheels, a driver's seat, handlebars, and is moved by pedaling.</u>

7. **Listening**—Some exercises feature Listening Tic Tac Toe. To create individual playing grids, photocopy the Transparency Master on page 336. Students select occupations, animals, vehicles, foods, and buildings from a list provided by the teacher and write a selection in each box. Each term may be used only once on any student's grid. Each student's playing grid should be different.

Make game slips from the terms on the word lists in the Transparency Master section. To play the game, draw a slip and state a description without naming the noun. Students listen to the description and cover the correct answer with a token if that term appears on their playing grid. The winner is the first student to have three answers in a row horizontally, vertically, or diagonally.

**FOLLOW-UP ACTIVITIES AT HOME**

- Communicating with parents about *Beginning Building Thinking Skills* instruction has important benefits for children and families:

  1. Parents are informed about the concepts that their children are learning in science and social studies and can reinforce these concepts.

  2. Parents are informed about the thinking process that their children are developing. This understanding assures parents that the thinking skills being taught are consistent with their values and serve an instructional purpose.

  3. Practicing thinking activities at home models good parenting practices to help parents enrich their children's vocabularies and their thinking processes.

- Parents are asked to model the thinking processes developed in the lesson and to reinforce the concepts that children learn. For example, parents identify two jobs that their children see regularly and describe something about the two jobs that is analogous (what workers do, vehicles they use, where they work, the clothes they wear, the equipment they use, etc.). Parents then describe the two jobs as an analogy ("A fire truck is parked in a fire station when it isn't used, like a tractor is parked in a barn when it is not used") and ask the child to describe another analogy about the two vehicles ("A firefighter drives a fire truck, like a farmer drives a tractor.")

**PICTURE BOOK EXTENSION**

- Discussing picture books to extend the content and the thinking processes addressed in *Beginning Building Thinking Skills* lessons serves several purposes:

  1. To integrate language arts activities with primary science and social studies concepts through thinking skills instruction.

  2. To extend students' background knowledge of the content before or after the thinking activity.

3. To promote students' observation skills.

4. To demonstrate the multicultural universality and diversity of family relationships, jobs, food, transportation, and vehicles.

5. To add humor or beauty to social studies and science instruction.

- Numerous examples of commonly available picture books are listed in the annotated bibliography in the appendix. Some books are also listed in each lesson. These picture books were selected because of the richness of their content, the quality of their illustrations, their depiction of concepts across cultures, and their appeal for young children. The list includes fiction and nonfiction books that depict various ethnic groups, books that are humorous, and books that are inspiring.

- The bibliography contains some pre-kindergarten books (wordless or pop-up books, and board books) to provide language stimulation for students whose English usage is underdeveloped. Some picture books commonly used in third or fourth grades are also recommended because they provide content enrichment or because they address rich human themes or ethnic diversity.

- Sample lesson plans recommend using picture books after the thinking skill activity. However, for students with limited background or developmental English usage, reading the book aloud and discussing it prior to the thinking activity provides additional information about the content. This discussion enhances students' thinking and promotes confidence in expressing both their thinking and their knowledge. The diagram on the previous page depicts the sequence for discussing the picture books.

**OPTIONAL SEQUENCES FOR INTEGRATING SCIENCE OR SOCIAL STUDIES CONCEPTS WITH LANGUAGE ARTS OBJECTIVES**

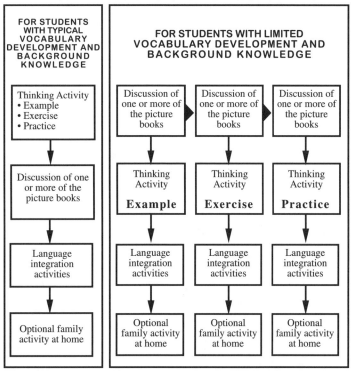

BEGINNING BUILDING THINKING SKILLS LESSON PLANS VERBAL TEACHING SUGGESTIONS

## METACOGNITIVE QUESTIONS

- Metacognitive questions extend the thinking process and content of the picture book.

  Q: Are there any new ideas about (a family member, job, food, vehicle, animal, or building featured in the lesson) that we learned from this story?

  Q. What ideas or details about (this family member, job, food, vehicle, animal, or building) did you get from the pictures?

  Q. Is this information true of most (family members, jobs, foods, vehicles, animals, or buildings)?

- After discussing each story, add new information about the concepts described in the story to the lists, posters, or graphic organizers used to discuss concepts in the thinking lesson.

## INTEGRATED UNITS

- For fully developed instructional units on the types of concepts in *Beginning Building Thinking Skills* (family, jobs, animals, vehicles, food, and buildings) see *Teaching Young Children through Themes*, Marjory J. Kostelnik, Goodyear Books, 1991.

xxx © 2000 CRITICAL THINKING BOOKS & SOFTWARE • WWW.CRITICALTHINKING.COM • 800-458-4849

BEGINNING BUILDING THINKING SKILLS LESSON PLANS                                    DESCRIBING SHAPES

## Chapter 1 | # DESCRIBING SHAPES
### (Student book pages 2–44)

## GENERAL INTRODUCTION

To remind students of the concept of shape:
- Take your students on a "shape walk" around the school grounds and ask them to identify various shapes. Make a list of the objects that show various shapes.
- Ask students to cut out pictures of objects that are circles, squares, rectangles, or triangles for a bulletin board display.
- Make a shape inventory of objects in the classroom.
- Reproduce and use the shape cards on pages 326–8 (see Transparency Masters)
- Cut an orange or grapefruit to show a circular cross-section.

### TEACHING SUGGESTIONS
- Ask students to discuss and explain their answers.
- Ask students to name the polygons as they discuss and explain their answers.
- Integrate these geometry concepts into your language arts program by discussing the picture books listed in the bibliography in the appendix.

### CURRICULUM APPLICATIONS
Language Arts: Develop visual discrimination for reading readiness; reinforce recognition of shape words and color words; reinforce concepts of large and small; understand position words (above, below, left, right, etc.).
Mathematics: Recognize and name geometric shapes; count the number of sides and corners.
Science: Recognize shapes of objects in nature such as leaves, shells, or insects.
Social Studies: Recognize geographic features on map puzzles.
Enrichment Areas: Recognize shapes of road signs; discern patterns in art.

## EXERCISES A-1 to A-2 | ## MATCHING BLOCKS TO SHAPES

**ANSWERS A-1 and A-2 — Student book pages 2–3**
**Guided Practice: A-1** Check to see that students have covered the shape with the correct block.
**Independent Practice: A-1** to **A-2** Check to see that students have covered the shape with the correct block.

## LESSON PREPARATION | ### SKILL LEVEL
This activity requires no reading or writing skill development (typical of kindergarten students).

© 2000 CRITICAL THINKING BOOKS & SOFTWARE • WWW.CRITICALTHINKING.COM • 800-458-4849          1

BEGINNING BUILDING THINKING SKILLS LESSON PLANS                                    DESCRIBING SHAPES

## OBJECTIVE AND MATERIALS

OBJECTIVE: Students will cover shape outlines with blocks.

MATERIALS: Large cardboard rectangle • red, blue, and yellow crayons or markers • the entire set of attribute blocks • transparencies of TM 1–2 on pages 325–6 • (Optional) Transparent attribute blocks. Project transparent attribute blocks to introduce the attributes of color, shape, and size

## TEACHING SUGGESTIONS

• Use attribute or pattern blocks to teach shape names. If you have transparent attribute or pattern blocks, use them with the overhead projector. Encourage students to use the names of shapes.

**MODEL LESSON**

## LESSON

### Introduction

• Identify squares, circles, and rectangles in your classroom or collect objects with these shapes.

• Hold up a square.
Q: What do we call this shape? (Encourage students to answer in complete sentences.)
   A: That shape is a square.

Q: Find a square in this room.
   A: Answers will vary.

• Hold up a large cardboard rectangle.
Q: What do we call this shape?
   A: That shape is a rectangle.

Q: Which objects in our classroom have this shape?
   A: Tables, desktops, door, windows, ceiling tiles, chalkboard, etc. (Ask students to use complete sentences such as: "A table is a rectangle.")

### Explaining the Objective to the Students

Q: You are going to practice finding blocks that match different shapes.

### Class Activity

• Using transparent attribute blocks, project a red circle. (You can also use a transparency of the lesson page.)
Q: What do we call this shape?
   A: The shape is a circle.

Q: Name objects that are circles.
   A: Tape rolls, bottle caps, can tops, round pillows, tops of cups, etc. (Ask students to use complete sentences such as: A roll of tape is a circle.)

• Repeat with a red square and a red triangle.

## GUIDED PRACTICE

EXERCISES: **A-1**

• Students will find and cover three or four shapes on page 2.

## INDEPENDENT PRACTICE

EXERCISES: **A-1** and **A-2**

2          © 2000 CRITICAL THINKING BOOKS & SOFTWARE • WWW.CRITICALTHINKING.COM • 800-458-4849

## THINKING ABOUT THINKING

Q: What did you pay attention to when you found the same shape?

1. I paid attention to whether the shape was round or not.

2. I looked at the number of sides.

3. I looked to see if the shape was large or small.

## PERSONAL APPLICATION

Q: When might you have to find shapes at home?

A: Making requests or giving directions (e.g., "Please hand me that round pillow, not the square one."), following the directions to assemble toys or models.

**EXERCISES A-3 to A-6**

# FINDING SHAPES—SELECT

**ANSWERS A-3 through A-6 — Student book page 4**
**Guided Practice: A-3** large or small square
**Independent Practice: A-4** large or small triangle; **A-5** large or small rectangle; **A-6** large or small hexagon

**LESSON PREPARATION**

### SKILL LEVEL

If the exercise is carefully directed, it requires little reading or writing skill development (typical of kindergarten students).

### OBJECTIVE AND MATERIALS

OBJECTIVE: Given the name of a shape, students will find the matching block. (First grade: Students will read a shape name and find a given shape.) MATERIALS: Attribute blocks (entire set) • transparency of student book page 4

### TEACHING SUGGESTIONS

• Use attribute blocks to teach or review polygon names. If you have transparent attribute blocks, use them with the overhead projector. Ask students to name the shapes or hold up the correct block as they discuss their answers.

• A set of shape cards can be produced using the transparency masters 2–4 on pages 326–8. To help children remember that the six-sided figure is a hexagon ask this question:

Q: What do the words *six* and *hexagon* have in common?

A: They both contain the letter *x*.

**MODEL LESSON**

### LESSON

**Introduction**

• To review the names of polygons, hold up a square.

Q: What do we call this shape?

A: That shape is a square.

Q: What objects in our classroom have this shape?

A: Answers will vary. (Ask students to use complete sentences, such as "The floor tiles are square.")

- Hold up a circle.
  Q: Name some things that are shaped like a circle.
    A: Tape rolls, bottle caps, can tops, round pillows, tops of cups, etc. (Ask students to use complete sentences such as: A roll of tape is a circle.)

### Explaining the Objective to Students

Q: In each exercise, you will read the name of a shape and find a block that has that name. (OR: In each exercise, I will read to you the name of a shape and you will find a block that has that name.)

### Class Activity

- Project a transparency of the lesson page 4.
  Q: Exercise **A-3** asks for a "square." Find a square and put it in the box.

- Check that all have found a square. Model the following activity by tracing around the projected image of the square on the chalkboard.
  Q: Trace around your square like I am doing. Color your drawing to match your block.
  Q: We will now finish exercises **A-4** through **A-6**.

- If students have difficulty with tracing, have them place the correct block in the box and check their work. It is also possible to have students use rubber stamps to print the correct shape.

## GUIDED PRACTICE
EXERCISES: **A-3**

- Check student answers. Give students sufficient time to complete these exercises.

## INDEPENDENT PRACTICE

- Assign exercises **A-4** through **A-6**.

- Kindergarten students may require teacher repetition of the directions to remember the task and keep pace.

## THINKING ABOUT THINKING

Q: What did you pay attention to when you looked for a shape?
1. I paid attention to whether or not the shape was round.

2. I looked at the number of sides.

## PERSONAL APPLICATION

Q: When do you need to find shapes at home?
  A: Examples include: Making requests (e.g., "Please hand me that small spoon, not the large one.") or giving directions; following the directions to assemble toys or models.

BEGINNING BUILDING THINKING SKILLS LESSON PLANS                          DESCRIBING SHAPES

**EXERCISES
A-7 to A-12**

# DESCRIBING SHAPES–SELECT A

**ANSWERS A-7 through A-12 — Student book pages 6–9**
**Guided Practice: A-7** 4 sides, 4 corners (square)
**Independent Practice: A-8** 4 sides, 4 corners (rectangle); **A-9** 6 sides,
6 corners (hexagon); **A-10** 4, 4; **A-11** 3, 3; **A-12** 6, 6

**LESSON
PREPARATION**

## SKILL LEVEL
If the exercise is carefully directed, it requires little reading or writing skill development (typical of kindergarten students). If students work independently, then some reading skill is required (typical of first-grade students).

## OBJECTIVE AND MATERIALS
OBJECTIVE: Students will count the sides and corners of a shape.
MATERIALS: Attribute blocks (entire set) • transparency of page 5 of the student book • transparent attribute blocks • blue and red crayons or markers

## TEACHING SUGGESTIONS
> Q: When students have finished **A-10** through **A-12**, ask "How are the number of sides of a block and the number of its corners related?"
>> A: If a shape has three sides, it has three corners also. (Any polygon has the same number of corners as it has sides.)

* Ask students to name the polygons as they discuss their answers.

* Integrate these geometry concepts into your language arts program by discussing the picture books listed in the bibliography in the appendix.

**MODEL LESSON**

## LESSON

### Introduction
> Q: You are going to count the sides and corners of attribute blocks. Let's practice counting to six.
>> A: Students count out loud.

### Explaining the Objective to Students
> Q: You are going to count the sides and corners of the large attribute blocks.

### Class Activity
> Q: What is the shape of our classroom?
>> A: Our classroom is a rectangle.

> Q: Let's count the sides of the classroom.

* Ask a student to stand in front of each of the walls of the room and ask them to count off from one.
>> A: Our classroom has four sides.

> Q: Let's count the corners of the classroom.

* Ask a student to stand in each corner of the room and count off starting with one.
>> A: Our room has four corners.

© 2000 CRITICAL THINKING BOOKS & SOFTWARE • WWW.CRITICALTHINKING.COM • 800-458-4849          5

**BEGINNING BUILDING THINKING SKILLS LESSON PLANS**                                    **DESCRIBING SHAPES**

- Project a transparency of student lesson page 5.
  Q: Name the shape.
    A: That shape is a triangle.

  Q: In your attribute block set, find a large triangle of any color.

- Allow students time to find the block.
  Q: Hold the triangle by a corner and keep holding that corner as you count. Hold tight and count the sides using a finger of your free hand.
  Q: How many sides did you feel?
    A: I touched three sides.

  Q: Now look at page 5. Take your red crayon and make a mark on each side of the triangle.
  Q: Now you are going to count the corners. Hold one side. Keep holding that same side and touch each corner with the finger of your free hand.
  Q: How many corners did you touch?
    A: I touched three corners.

  Q: Notice that the answers have circles around them. After counting sides and corners, you will circle the correct answers.

- Kindergarten modification:
  Q: Now take your blue crayon and circle each corner on the triangle. The first question on the page asks how many sides does this shape have? Notice that the answer has a circle around it—3. After counting sides and corners, you will circle the correct answers.

- Kindergarten students will require teacher repetition of the directions to remember the task and to keep pace.

## GUIDED PRACTICE
EXERCISES: **A-7**
- Read each set of directions and check students' answers. Give students sufficient time to complete these exercises.

## INDEPENDENT PRACTICE
- Assign exercises **A-8** through **A-12**. If students have difficulty with **A-10** through **A-12**, remind them to look back at pages 5–8.

## THINKING ABOUT THINKING
Q: What did you pay attention to when you followed directions?
1. I carefully listened to (or read) the directions.

2. I counted the number of sides.

3. I counted the number of corners.

## PERSONAL APPLICATION
Q: When do you need to name shapes at home?
  A: Making requests (e.g., "please hand me that round pillow, not the square one.")

6          © 2000 CRITICAL THINKING BOOKS & SOFTWARE • WWW.CRITICALTHINKING.COM • 800-458-4849

BEGINNING BUILDING THINKING SKILLS LESSON PLANS          DESCRIBING SHAPES

**EXERCISES A-13 to A-14**

# FINDING SHAPES—A

> ANSWERS A-13 through A-14 — Student book pages 10–1
> Guided Practice: **A-13** See below.
> Independent Practice: **A-14** See below.

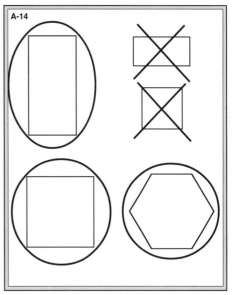

**LESSON PREPARATION**

**SKILL LEVEL**
If the exercise is carefully directed, it requires no reading or writing skill development (typical of kindergarten students). If students work independently, then some reading skill is required (typical of first-grade students).

**OBJECTIVE AND MATERIALS**
OBJECTIVE: Students will identify shapes as large or small.
MATERIALS: Attribute blocks (entire set) • transparent attribute blocks • transparency of student book page 10

**TEACHING SUGGESTIONS**
• In this lesson, only the attribute of size is identified. Use the terms *small* and *large* frequently so students become familiar with them.

**MODEL LESSON**

**LESSON**

**Introduction**

   Q: Name a large animal, building, or vehicle.
      A: An elephant is a large animal. Large building—skyscraper, tall office building, etc. Large vehicle—train, truck, jet. (Remind students to use complete sentences.)

   Q: Name a small animal, building, or vehicle.
      A: A mouse is a small animal. Small building—shed, garage, cottage, etc. Small vehicle—bicycle, motorcycle, small car, etc.

   Q: Large and small are words that describe the size of things. Give examples of using the words "large" and "small."
      A: I have a large drink or small drink, etc.

BEGINNING BUILDING THINKING SKILLS LESSON PLANS                                    DESCRIBING SHAPES

### Explaining the Objective to Students

Q: You will draw a circle around the shapes that are large and cross out the shapes that are small.

### Class Activity

• Project the transparency of page 10 and point to the large triangle at the top left.

Q: Name this shape.

A: That shape is a triangle.

Q: Is this triangle large or small?

A: It is a large triangle.

Q: There is a circle around the large triangle.

Q: How do you describe the other triangle?

A: That triangle is small.

Q: The small triangle has been crossed out.

Q: Look at the circle in the middle of the page. Is it large or small?

A: It is small.

Q: What will you do to the small circle?

A: I will cross it out.

Q: We will now finish the page by crossing out the small shapes and drawing a circle around the large shapes.

• Kindergarten students may require teacher repetition of the directions to remember the task and to keep pace.

### GUIDED PRACTICE
EXERCISES: **A-13**

• Check students' work as they complete the page.

### INDEPENDENT PRACTICE
• Assign exercises **A-14**

### THINKING ABOUT THINKING

Q: What did you pay attention to when you followed directions?

1. I carefully listened to the directions.

2. I looked at each shape to decide its size.

3. I marked the shape according to the directions.

### PERSONAL APPLICATION

Q: What other times is it necessary to follow oral or written directions?

A: Examples include: Doing crafts or sports activities involving order, assembling games or models, taking tests.

**EXERCISES
A-15 to A-26**

## FINDING SHAPES—B

**ANSWERS A-15 through A-26 — Student book pages 12–4**
**Guided Practice: A-15** any large circle; **A-16** any small circle

BEGINNING BUILDING THINKING SKILLS LESSON PLANS                                    DESCRIBING SHAPES

> **Independent Practice: A-17** any large square; **A-18** any small triangle;
> **A-19** any large triangle; **A-20** any small triangle; **A-21** any large rectangle;
> **A-22** any small rectangle; **A-23** any large hexagon; **A-24** any small
> hexagon; **A-25** any large rectangle; **A-26** any small circle

**LESSON PREPARATION**

### SKILL LEVEL

If the exercise is carefully directed, it requires little reading or writing skill development (typical of kindergarten students). However, tracing blocks can be difficult for kindergarten students. If students work independently, then some reading skill is required (typical of first grade students).

### OBJECTIVE AND MATERIALS

OBJECTIVE: Students will read two-word descriptions and then find large or small shapes from a set of attribute blocks. For kindergarten, the teacher will read the description to the students.

MATERIALS: Attribute blocks (entire set) • transparency of student book page 12

### TEACHING SUGGESTIONS

• In this lesson, only the attributes of shape and size are identified; color is not. Ask students to name the polygons as they discuss their answers.

• Integrate these geometry concepts into your language arts program by discussing the picture books listed in the bibliography in the appendix.

**MODEL LESSON**

### LESSON

**Introduction**

• Hold up a large circle.
  Q: What do we call this shape?
    A: That shape is a circle.

  Q: What objects in our classroom have this shape?
    A: Answers will vary. (Ask students to use complete sentences such as: "The top of the drinking glass is a circle.")

• Hold up a small and large circle of the same color.
  Q: I am holding up two circles. How are they different?
    A: One is small, and the other is large.

**Explaining the Objective to Students**

• There will be three possible correct answers to each of these exercises since color is not specified.
  Q: In each exercise, you will read the description of a shape and find a shape that fits that description. (In each exercise, you will find a shape that fits the description I read to you.)

**Class Activity**

• Project a transparency of page 12.
  Q: Exercise **A-15** asks for a "large circle." Find a large circle and put it in the box.

© 2000 CRITICAL THINKING BOOKS & SOFTWARE • WWW.CRITICALTHINKING.COM • 800-458-4849          9

BEGINNING BUILDING THINKING SKILLS LESSON PLANS                    DESCRIBING SHAPES

- Check that all students have found a large circle. Model the following process by drawing the projected image of the large circle on the chalkboard transparency.

  Q: Trace around your circle like I am doing. Color your drawing the same color as your block.

  Q: You may now finish the exercises on page 12.

- Kindergarten students may require teacher repetition of the directions to remember the task and to keep pace. Also, to reinforce the size difference you may have the students trace the large shape in one color and the small shape in a different color.

- If students have difficulty with tracing, have them simply place the correct blocks and then check their work.

### GUIDED PRACTICE
EXERCISES: **A-21** through **A-23**
- Ask students to discuss and explain their answers.

### INDEPENDENT PRACTICE
- Assign exercises **A-24** through **A-31**.

### THINKING ABOUT THINKING
Q: What did you pay attention to when you looked for a shape?
1. I read the description and paid attention to whether the shape was a circle or not.

2. If the shape was not a circle, I recalled how many sides the shape has.

3. I looked for a single shape with that number of sides.

4. I read the description again to see if I was asked to find a large or small shape and checked to see that I had picked the correct size.

### PERSONAL APPLICATION
Q: When do you need to find shapes at home?
A: Examples include: Making requests (e.g., "Hand me that round pillow, not the square one") or giving directions; following the directions to assemble toys or models.

**EXERCISE A-27**

## DESCRIBING SHAPES—SELECT B

> **ANSWERS A-27 — Student book page 15**
> **Guided Practice: A-27** see diagram next page

**LESSON PREPARATION**

### SKILL LEVEL
If the exercise is carefully directed, it requires some writing skill development (typical of advanced kindergarten students). If students work independently, then some reading and writing skill is required (typical of first grade students).

10          © 2000 CRITICAL THINKING BOOKS & SOFTWARE • WWW.CRITICALTHINKING.COM • 800-458-4849

BEGINNING BUILDING THINKING SKILLS LESSON PLANS　　　　DESCRIBING SHAPES

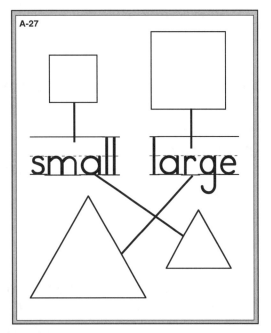

**OBJECTIVE AND MATERIALS**
OBJECTIVE: Students will identify shapes as large or small and trace over the size words and the names of the shapes. Kindergarten students may draw a line from the size word to the correct shape without tracing.
MATERIALS: Attribute blocks • transparent attribute blocks • transparency of student lesson page 15

**MODEL LESSON** | **LESSON**

**Introduction**
   Q: "Large" and "small" are words that describe the size of things.

**Explaining the Objective to Students**
   Q: In this lesson, you will trace over the words *large* and *small* and draw a line from each shape to the word that tells its size.

**Class Activity**
• Project the image of the lesson page and point to the small square at the top of the page.
   Q: Name this shape.
     A: That shape is a square.

   Q: Is this square large or small?
     A: It is a small square.

   Q: Draw a line from the small square to the word *small* that is below it. Trace over the word small. (This step can be eliminated.)
   Q: How do you describe the other square?
     A: That square is large.

   Q: Draw a line from the large square to the word *large.*
   Q: Name the two shapes at the bottom of the page.
     A: They are triangles.

BEGINNING BUILDING THINKING SKILLS LESSON PLANS                                      DESCRIBING SHAPES

Q: Draw lines from the triangles to the words that describe their size.

• Finish the guided practice.

• Kindergarten students may not be able to trace over the words. They may require teacher repetition of the directions to remember the task and to keep pace.

**GUIDED PRACTICE**
EXERCISES: **A-27**

• Check students' answers. Give students sufficient time to complete this exercises.

**INDEPENDENT PRACTICE**

• Assign rest of exercise **A-27**.

**THINKING ABOUT THINKING**

Q: What did you pay attention to when you looked at the shapes?
1. I decided if it was large or small.

2. I found the right word to describe the size of the shape.

3. I drew a line from the shape to the word.

**PERSONAL APPLICATION**

Q: What are some times when you need to identify the size of something?
A: When you are looking for a tool that is a certain size; when you are looking for something that needs to fit something else

**EXERCISES
A-28 to A-43**

# FINDING SHAPES—C

ANSWERS A-28 through A-43 — Student book pages 16–9
**Guided Practice: A-28** any large red block; **A-29** any small red block
**Independent Practice: A-30** any large blue block; **A-31** any small blue block; **A-32** any large yellow block; **A-33** any small yellow block; **A-34** any large red block; **A-35** any small blue block; **A-36–43** each has a single answer; check students' work

**LESSON
PREPARATION**

**SKILL LEVEL**
If the exercise is carefully directed, it requires little reading or writing skill development (typical of kindergarten students). If students work independently, then some reading skill is required (typical of first-grade students.)

**OBJECTIVE AND MATERIALS**
OBJECTIVE: Students will read three-word descriptions and first find large or small shapes of a particular color from a collection of attribute blocks, then find specific shapes of a particular color.
MATERIALS: Attribute blocks (entire set) • transparency of page 16 of the student book

**TEACHING SUGGESTIONS**

• In this lesson, the attributes of shape, size and color are used. Ask students to name the polygons as they discuss their answers.

12          © 2000 CRITICAL THINKING BOOKS & SOFTWARE • WWW.CRITICALTHINKING.COM • 800-458-4849

BEGINNING BUILDING THINKING SKILLS LESSON PLANS                    DESCRIBING SHAPES

- Integrate these geometry concepts into your language arts program by discussing the picture books listed in the bibliography in the appendix.

**MODEL LESSON** | **LESSON**

## Introduction

- This lesson may be presented in two parts: Part 1 **A-28** through **A-35**, and Part 2 **A-36** through **A-43**.

### LESSON—Part 1

#### Introduction

- Hold up a large red triangle attribute block.

  Q: Is this attribute block large or small?
    A: It is large.

  Q: What color is it?
    A: It is red.

  Q: Name this shape.
    A: It is a triangle.

  Q: Describe the attribute block by naming size, color, and shape.
    A: The attribute block is a large red triangle.

#### Explaining the Objective to Students

  Q: In each exercise, you will read the description of a shape and find a shape that fits the description. (For kindergarten: I will read to you a description of a shape, and you will find an attribute block that matches that description.)

#### Class Activity

- Project transparency of page 16.

  Q: Exercise **A-28** calls for a "large red shape." Find any large red attribute block and put it in the box.

- Check that all students have found a large red attribute block.

- Ask students to describe their shapes.

  Q: How many different large red shapes are in the set?
    A: There are five large red shapes. A large red square, a large red circle, a large red triangle, a large red rectangle, and a large red hexagon.

  Q: Fill each of the boxes on this and the next page with any of the five possible shapes.

#### GUIDED PRACTICE—Part 1

EXERCISES: **A-28** through **A-35**. Ask students to discuss and explain their answers.

#### INDEPENDENT PRACTICE—Part 1

- Assign exercises **A-36** through **A-43**.
  Kindergarten students may require teacher repetition of the directions to remember the task and to keep pace.

© 2000 CRITICAL THINKING BOOKS & SOFTWARE • WWW.CRITICALTHINKING.COM • 800-458-4849          13

BEGINNING BUILDING THINKING SKILLS LESSON PLANS                                    DESCRIBING SHAPES

**MODEL LESSON**

## LESSON—Part 2

### Introduction

- Up to this point, the shape was not specified. Pages 18 and 19 require students to find the correct block for all three attributes. Students will work in pairs.

  Q: Look at **A-36**. Notice that you have to find a large red square. What shape will you find?

  A: A large red square.

- Check that each pair of students has found a large red square.

  Q: Put your large red square in the box on the page. Trace around it and color the shape red.

- Repeat the procedure with the guided practice problems.

### GUIDED PRACTICE—Part 2
EXERCISES: **A-43** through **A-45**.

### INDEPENDENT PRACTICE—Part 2

- Assign exercises **A-46** through **A-49**.

### THINKING ABOUT THINKING

Q: What did you pay attention to when you found a shape?

1. In part 1, I looked for a shape that was both the correct size and color.

2. In part 2, I first looked for the specific shape that was named.

3. Then I made sure the block was the right size and color.

### PERSONAL APPLICATION

Q: When do you need to find shapes at home?

A: Examples include: Making requests (e.g., "hand me that round pillow, not the square one") or giving directions; following the directions to assemble toys or models.

**EXERCISES A-44 to A-45**

# IDENTIFYING SHAPES BY COLOR

> **ANSWERS A-44 through A-45 — Student book pages 20–1**
>
> **Guided Practice: A-44** Answers will vary because student groups may select different colors. Check students' work or ask student pairs to check each other's work.
>
> **Independent Practice: A-45** Answers will vary because student groups may select different colors. Check students' work or ask student pairs to check each other's work.

**LESSON PREPARATION**

### SKILL LEVEL

If the exercise is carefully directed, it requires little reading or writing skill development (typical of kindergarten students.) If students work independently, then some reading skill is required (typical of first-grade students).

14          © 2000 CRITICAL THINKING BOOKS & SOFTWARE • WWW.CRITICALTHINKING.COM • 800-458-4849

BEGINNING BUILDING THINKING SKILLS LESSON PLANS                                    DESCRIBING SHAPES

**OBJECTIVE AND MATERIALS**

OBJECTIVE: Students will learn to identify the words *red, blue,* and *yellow* by tracing the words and matching the words to a block having that color.

MATERIALS: Attribute blocks • transparent attribute blocks • transparency of lesson page 20

**TEACHING SUGGESTIONS**

• In this lesson color is introduced as an attribute.

**MODEL LESSON**   | **LESSON**

**Introduction**

Q: Find an object in the room that is red (or blue or yellow).

**Explaining the Objective to Students**

Q: You are going to learn to recognize the words for three colors and are going to identify the attribute block that matches each color.

**Class Activity**

• Project a transparency of the lesson page 20.
Q: Find an attribute block that matches each shape. Each block should be a different color.
Q: Color each shape the same color as the block you found.

• Allow students time to color the shapes.
Q: Trace over the first word at the top.

• Allow time for writing.
Q: Read the top word.
  A: The top word is *red.*

• Repeat the above steps for the words *blue* and *yellow.*
Q: Now that you have written the words *red, blue,* and *yellow,* find your red picture and draw a line from the red shape to the word *red.*

• Repeat the directions for *blue* and *yellow.*

• Check students' progress.
Q: You are now ready to do the next page on your own.

• Use the following lesson modifications for kindergarten students.
Q: Find an attribute block that matches each shape. Each block should be a different color.
Q: Color each shape the same color as the block you found.

• Allow students time to color the shapes.
Q: The first word at the top of the page is *red.* (You can have them trace over the word if they are able to.)
Q: Find the red shape that you colored. Now draw a line from the shape to the word *red.*

• Kindergarten students will probably need to have each word read to them.

**GUIDED PRACTICE**
EXERCISE: **A-44**

© 2000 CRITICAL THINKING BOOKS & SOFTWARE • WWW.CRITICALTHINKING.COM • 800-458-4849          15

BEGINNING BUILDING THINKING SKILLS LESSON PLANS                              DESCRIBING SHAPES

- Read each set of directions and check students' answers. Give students sufficient time to complete these exercises.

**INDEPENDENT PRACTICE**
- Assign exercise **A-45**.

**THINKING ABOUT THINKING**
Q: What did you pay attention to when you looked at the shapes?
1. I decided if it was red, blue or yellow.
2. I found the right word to describe the color of the shape.
3. I drew a line from the shape to the word.

**PERSONAL APPLICATION**
Q: When do you need to describe shapes by color at home?
A: Making requests or giving directions (e.g., "Hand me that red pillow, not the blue one"), preparing food

**EXERCISES A-46 to A-51**

# FOLLOWING DIRECTIONS—SELECT FIRST TO LAST

**ANSWERS A-46 through A-51 — Student book pages 22–3**
**Guided Practice: A-46–7** See below
**Independent Practice: A-48–51** See below

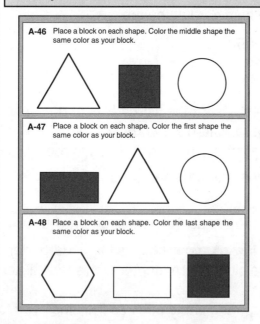
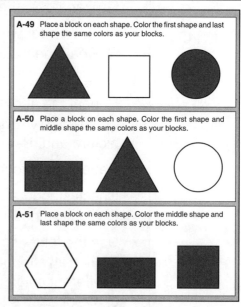

**LESSON PREPARATION**

**SKILL LEVEL**
If the exercise is carefully directed, it requires little reading or writing skill development (typical of kindergarten students). If students work independently, then some reading skill is required (typical of first grade students.)

**OBJECTIVE AND MATERIALS**
OBJECTIVE: Students will cover drawings with attribute blocks and then be asked to use the concepts first, middle, and last to identify and color certain blocks.

**BEGINNING BUILDING THINKING SKILLS LESSON PLANS**                    **DESCRIBING SHAPES**

MATERIALS: Attribute blocks (entire set) • transparency of page 22 of the student book

**TEACHING SUGGESTIONS**
- See the General Introduction on page 1.

**MODEL LESSON** | **LESSON**

**Introduction**

Q: Use the word *first* in a sentence.
　A: (Student name) came in first place. (Student name) was first in line. (Student name) sits in the first row.

- Repeat the sample questions using *middle* and *last.*

- Illustrate *first, middle,* and *last* by asking three children to line up.
　Q: Which student is in the first (or middle or last) position?
　　A: (Student name) is in the first (or middle or last) position.

**Explaining the Objective to Students**

Q: You will follow directions to place attribute blocks in a line. You will color the blocks in the first, middle, or last place in the line.

**Class Activity**

- Project a transparency of the lesson page 22. Uncover only one row at a time.
　Q: Name the first shape.
　　A: That shape is a triangle.

　Q: Name the middle shape.
　　A: That shape is a square.

　Q: Name the last shape.
　　A: That shape is a circle.

　Q: Using the words *first, middle,* or *last,* name the position of the square.
　　A: The square is in the middle position.

　Q: Using first, middle or last, name the position of the circle.
　　A: The circle is in the last position.

　Q: Look at **A-46**. Color the middle shape the same color as the block covering it.

- Check students' work, then repeat above with **A-47**.

- The following modifications can be made for kindergarten students: Using the attribute blocks, have students place them in the same order that you place them on the overhead. Then ask students to pick up the block in the middle as you do the same. Practice picking up blocks in different positions until the students are comfortable. Then display the transparency of page 22, uncovering only one row at a time.

- Check students' work, then assign independent practice.

- Kindergarten students may require continued repetition of the directions to remember the task and keep pace.

© 2000 CRITICAL THINKING BOOKS & SOFTWARE • WWW.CRITICALTHINKING.COM • 800-458-4849                    17

BEGINNING BUILDING THINKING SKILLS LESSON PLANS          DESCRIBING SHAPES

**GUIDED PRACTICE**
EXERCISES: **A-46** through **A-47**

**INDEPENDENT PRACTICE**
• Assign exercises **A-48** through **A-51**.

**THINKING ABOUT THINKING**
Q: What did you pay attention to when you followed directions?
1. I carefully listened to (or read) the directions.
2. I found the correct position.
3. I colored the block outline the same color as the attribute block I used to cover it.

**PERSONAL APPLICATION**
Q: When might you have to find the shapes at home?
A: Making requests or giving directions (e.g., "Please hand me that round pillow, not the square one."), following the directions to assemble toys or models.

**EXERCISES A-52 to A-56**

# FOLLOWING DIRECTIONS—SELECT FIRST TO THIRD

**ANSWERS A-52 through A-56 — Student book pages 24–5**
**Guided Practice: A-52–3** See below
**Independent Practice: A-54–6** See below

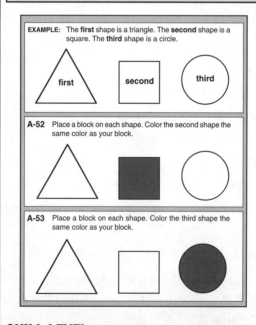
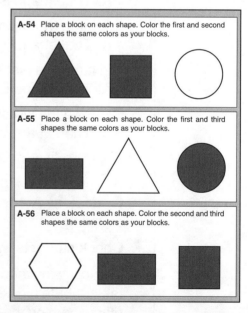

**LESSON PREPARATION**

**SKILL LEVEL**
If the exercise is carefully directed, it requires little reading or writing skill development (typical of kindergarten students). If students work independently, then some reading skill is required (typical of first grade students).

**OBJECTIVE AND MATERIALS**
OBJECTIVE: Students will cover drawings with attribute blocks and then be

BEGINNING BUILDING THINKING SKILLS LESSON PLANS                    DESCRIBING SHAPES

asked to use the concepts first, second, and third to identify and color certain blocks.

MATERIALS: Small attribute blocks • transparency of page 24 of the student book

## TEACHING SUGGESTIONS
- See the General Introduction on page 1.

**MODEL LESSON** | ## LESSON
### Introduction
Q: In the last lesson, you used "first, middle, and last." In this lesson, you will use the words *first, second,* and *third.*

Q: Give examples of sentences using the words *first, second,* and *third.*
  A: First base, second base, third base. First place, second place, third place. First grade, second grade, third grade.

- Illustrate first, second, and third by asking three or more children to line up.
Q: Which student is in the first (or second or third) position?
  A: (Student name) is in the first (or second or third) position.

### Explaining the Objective to Students
Q: You will follow directions to place attribute blocks in line. You will color blocks in the first, second, or third place in the line.

### Class Activity
- Project a transparency of student lesson page 24.
Q: Name the first shape.
  A: It is a triangle.

Q: Name the second shape.
  A: It is a square.

Q: Name the third shape.
  A: It is a circle.

Q: Using the words *first, second,* and *third,* name the position of the square.
  A: The square is in the second position.

Q: Using first, second, or third, name the position of the circle.
  A: The circle is in the third position.

- Kindergarten students may require teacher repetition of the directions to remember the task and keep pace.

### GUIDED PRACTICE
EXERCISES: **A-52** through **A-53**
- For kindergarten students, do one row at a time. The teacher can model on the overhead for the students.

### INDEPENDENT PRACTICE
- Assign exercises **A-54** through **A-56**.

© 2000 CRITICAL THINKING BOOKS & SOFTWARE • WWW.CRITICALTHINKING.COM • 800-458-4849          19

BEGINNING BUILDING THINKING SKILLS LESSON PLANS                                                        DESCRIBING SHAPES

**THINKING ABOUT THINKING**

Q: What did you pay attention to when you followed directions?

1. I carefully listened to (or read) the directions.

2. I found the correct position.

3. I colored the block outline the same color as the attribute block I used to cover it.

**PERSONAL APPLICATION**

Q: When might you have to understand the terms *first, second,* and *third*?

A: These words help me to understand my place in line, whose turn it is in a game, the names of grades in the school, etc.

**EXERCISES A-57 to A-61**

## FOLLOWING DIRECTIONS—SELECT LEFT OR RIGHT

**ANSWERS A-57 through A-61 — Student book pages 26–7**
**Guided Practice: A-57–8** See below
**Independent Practice: A-59–61** See below

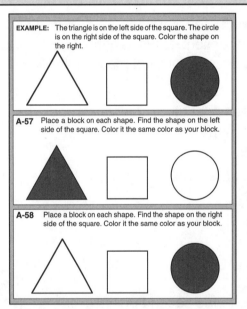 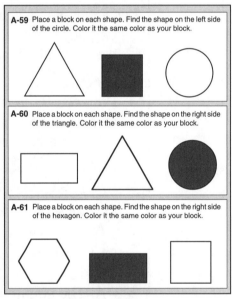

**LESSON PREPARATION**

**SKILL LEVEL**

If the exercise is carefully directed, it requires little reading or writing skill development (typical of kindergarten students). If students work independently, then some reading skill is required (typical of first grade students).

**OBJECTIVE AND MATERIALS**

OBJECTIVE: Students will cover drawings with attribute blocks and then be asked to use the concepts of left and right to identify and color certain blocks.
MATERIALS: Attribute blocks (entire set) • transparency of student page 26

**TEACHING SUGGESTIONS**

- See the General Introduction on page 1.

- Teachers need to model this activity on the overhead before doing the paper and pencil activities.

BEGINNING BUILDING THINKING SKILLS LESSON PLANS                    DESCRIBING SHAPES

**MODEL LESSON** | **LESSON**

### Introduction

Q: Use the word *left* (or right) in a sentence.

A: My pocket is on the left (right) side of my shirt. When I leave school, I make a left (right) turn at the corner. (Student name) is left-handed. (Name) plays left field in baseball.

### Explaining the Objective to Students

Q: You will follow directions to place attribute blocks in line. You will color a block that is located to the left or right of another block.

### Class Activity

• To practice left and right, ask students to raise one hand and then the other.

Q: Raise your right hand.

A: Hands down.

Q: Raise your left hand.

A: Hands down.

• Practice until the students are reasonably proficient.

• Ask three students to line up in a row facing the class. (A, B, C)

Q: Which student is on the left side?

A: (Student name—A) is on the left side.

Q: Which student is on the right side?

A: (Student name—C) is on the right.

Q: Which student is on the right side of (student name—A)?

A: (Student name—B) is on the right side of (name—A).

Q: Which student is on the left side of (student name—C)?

A: (Student name—B) is on the left side of (name—C).

• Project a transparency of student lesson page 26. Uncover only one row at a time.

Q: Name the shape that is on the left side of the square.

A: It is a triangle.

Q: Name the shape that is on the right side of the square.

A: It is a circle.

Q: Name the shape that is to the right of the triangle.

A: It is a square.

Q: Name the shape that is to the left of the circle.

A: It is a square.

### GUIDED PRACTICE

EXERCISES: **A-57** and **A-58**

• Read each set of directions and check students' answers. Give students sufficient time to complete these exercises.

© 2000 CRITICAL THINKING BOOKS & SOFTWARE • WWW.CRITICALTHINKING.COM • 800-458-4849          21

BEGINNING BUILDING THINKING SKILLS LESSON PLANS　　　　DESCRIBING SHAPES

**INDEPENDENT PRACTICE**
- Assign exercises **A-59** through **A-61**.
- Kindergarten students may require teacher repetition of the directions to remember the task and keep pace.

**THINKING ABOUT THINKING**
Q: What did you pay attention to when you followed directions?
1. I carefully listened to (or read) the directions.
2. I found the correct shape.
3. I colored the shape the same color as the attribute block covering it.

**PERSONAL APPLICATION.**
Q: When might you have to understand the terms *left* or *right*?
A: Answers may include: to find an object, to place an object in position, to follow marching instructions, to find the location of a city on a map.

**EXERCISES A-62 to A-65**

# FOLLOWING DIRECTIONS—SELECT TOP TO BOTTOM

**ANSWER A-62 through A-65 — Student book pages 28–9**
Guided Practice: **A-62–3** See below
Independent Practice: **A-64–5** See below

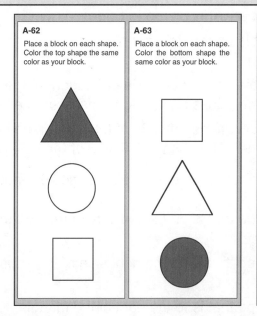
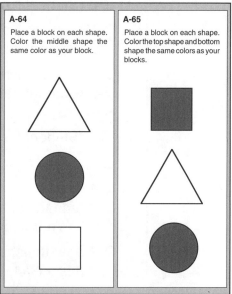

**LESSON PREPARATION**

**SKILL LEVEL**
If the exercise is carefully directed, it requires little reading or writing skill development (typical of kindergarten students). If students work independently, then some reading skill is required (typical of first-grade students).

**OBJECTIVE AND MATERIALS**
OBJECTIVE: Students will cover drawing with attribute blocks and then use the concepts of top and bottom to identify and color certain shapes.
MATERIALS: Small attribute blocks (entire set) • transparency of student lesson page 28

BEGINNING BUILDING THINKING SKILLS LESSON PLANS                                    DESCRIBING SHAPES

**TEACHING SUGGESTIONS**
- See the General Introduction on page 1.

MODEL LESSON | **LESSON**
- Play "Shape Up."
  Q: Find your favorite attribute block and hold it in your hand. When I say "shape up on top," raise your shape above your head. When I say "shape down on bottom," lower your arm to the side or front. When I say "put your shape in the middle," extend your arm straight out in front of you.

- Play the game until you are satisfied that your students have an understanding of "top," "middle," and "bottom."

**Introduction**
  Q: Give examples of using the words *top* and *bottom.*
   A: Top of the house, top shelf, bottom shelf, etc.

**Explaining the Objective to Students**
  Q: You will place attribute blocks in top, middle, and bottom positions. You will then color one of the blocks according to its position.

**Class Activity**
- Project a transparency of lesson page 28.
  Q: Name the shape that is in the top position.
   A: It is a triangle.

  Q: Name the shape that is in the middle.
   A: It is a circle.

  Q: Name the shape that is in the bottom position.
   A: It is a square.

  Q: Name the position of the triangle.
   A: It is on the top.

**GUIDED PRACTICE**
EXERCISES: **A-62** and **A-63**
- Read each set of directions and check students' answers. Give students sufficient time to complete these exercises.

**INDEPENDENT PRACTICE**
- Assign exercises **A-64** through **A-65**.

- Kindergarten students may require teacher repetition of the directions to remember the task and to keep pace.

**THINKING ABOUT THINKING**
  Q: What did you pay attention to when you followed directions?
   1. I carefully listened to (or read) the directions.

   2. I found the correct position.

   3. I colored the block shape the same color as the block covering it.

© 2000 CRITICAL THINKING BOOKS & SOFTWARE • WWW.CRITICALTHINKING.COM • 800-458-4849          23

BEGINNING BUILDING THINKING SKILLS LESSON PLANS                              DESCRIBING SHAPES

**PERSONAL APPLICATION**
Q: When might you have to understand the terms *top* or *bottom*?
A: Answers may include: to follow directions for finding an object, to follow directions for placing an object in position.

**EXERCISES A-66 to A-68**

# FOLLOWING DIRECTIONS—SELECT ABOVE OR BELOW

**ANSWERS A-66 through A-68 — Student book pages 30–1**
**Guided Practice: A-66** See below
**Independent Practice: A-67–8** See below

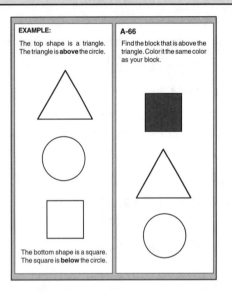 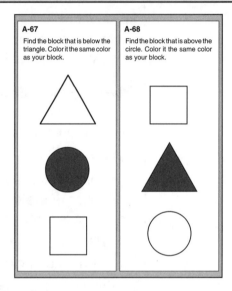

**LESSON PREPARATION**

### SKILL LEVEL
If the exercise is carefully directed, it requires little reading or writing skill development (typical of kindergarten students). If students work independently, then some reading skill is required (typical of first-grade students).

### OBJECTIVE AND MATERIALS
OBJECTIVE: Students will cover drawings with attribute blocks and then use the concepts of above and below to color a specific drawing based on its position.
MATERIALS: Attribute blocks (entire set) • transparency of student lesson page 30

### TEACHING SUGGESTIONS
• See the General Introduction on page 1.

**MODEL LESSON**

### LESSON
• Play a second version of "Shape Up."
Q: Find your favorite attribute block and hold it in your hand. When I say "shape above your head," raise the block above your head. When I say "shape below," lower your arm to your side.

• Play the game until you are satisfied that your students have an understanding of "above" and "below."

24    © 2000 CRITICAL THINKING BOOKS & SOFTWARE • WWW.CRITICALTHINKING.COM • 800-458-4849

**BEGINNING BUILDING THINKING SKILLS LESSON PLANS**                    **DESCRIBING SHAPES**

### Introduction

Q: Give examples using the words *above* and *below*.

A: The picture hung above the shelf. The basketball player jumped above the rim. The diver went below the surface of the water.

### Explaining the Objective to Students

Q: You will follow directions to place attribute blocks above or below one another.

### Class Activity

- Project a transparency of lesson page 30.

Q: Name the shape that is above the circle.

A: That shape is a triangle.

Q: Name the shape that is below the circle.

A: That shape is a square.

Q: Name the shape that is below the triangle.

A: It is a circle.

Q: Describe the position of the circle.

A: The circle is below the triangle and/or above the square.

Q: Exercise **A-66** asks you to find the shape above the triangle. What shape is above the triangle?

A: The square

Q: Color the square to match your attribute block.

### GUIDED PRACTICE

EXERCISES: **A-66**

- Read each set of directions and check students' answers. Give students sufficient time to complete these exercises.

### INDEPENDENT PRACTICE

- Assign exercises **A-67** through **A-68**.

- Kindergarten students may require teacher repetition of the directions to remember the task and to keep pace.

### THINKING ABOUT THINKING

Q: What did you pay attention to when you followed directions?

1. I carefully listened to (or read) the directions.

2. I found the correct position.

3. I colored the block shape the same color as the attribute block I used to cover it.

### PERSONAL APPLICATION

Q: When might you have to understand the terms *above* or *below*?

A: Answers may include: to follow directions for finding an object, to follow directions for placing an object in position.

© 2000 CRITICAL THINKING BOOKS & SOFTWARE • WWW.CRITICALTHINKING.COM • 800-458-4849          25

BEGINNING BUILDING THINKING SKILLS LESSON PLANS                    DESCRIBING SHAPES

**EXERCISES A-69 to A-74**

# FOLLOWING DIRECTIONS—SUPPLY ABOVE OR BELOW

**ANSWERS A-69 through A-74 — Student book pages 32–4**
**Guided Practice: A-69–70** See below
**Independent Practice: A-71–4** See below

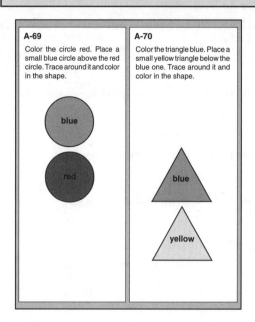
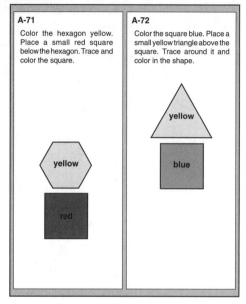

## LESSON PREPARATION

**SKILL LEVEL**
If the exercise is carefully directed, it requires little reading or writing skill development (typical of kindergarten students). If students work independently, then some reading skill is required (typical of first grade students).

**OBJECTIVE AND MATERIALS**
OBJECTIVE: Students will use the concepts of above and below to place an attribute block in a specific position in relation to another block.
MATERIALS: Attribute blocks (entire set) • transparency of lesson page 32 from the student book

**TEACHING SUGGESTIONS**
• See the General Introduction on page 1.

## MODEL LESSON

**LESSON**

### Introduction
   Q: Give examples using the words *above* and *below*.
      A: The picture hung above the shelf. The basketball player jumped above the rim. The diver went below the surface of the water.

### Explaining the Objective to Students
   Q: You will follow directions to place an attribute block above or below another one.

### Class Activity
• Project a transparency of the lesson page 32.
   Q: In exercise **A-69**, color the circle red.

26          © 2000 CRITICAL THINKING BOOKS & SOFTWARE • WWW.CRITICALTHINKING.COM • 800-458-4849

BEGINNING BUILDING THINKING SKILLS LESSON PLANS                                    DESCRIBING SHAPES

Q: Find a small blue circle and place it above the red circle.

• Check students' progress.
Q: Trace around the blue circle and then color your drawing blue.

• Check students' progress. Ask a student to demonstrate the activity on the overhead projector using transparent attribute blocks. If tracing is too difficult for students, have them simply place the block.
Q: Let's do exercise **A-70**. Color the triangle blue.

• Check students' progress.
Q: Find a small yellow triangle.
Q: Where should you place the triangle?
A: Below the blue triangle.

• Check students' progress.

**GUIDED PRACTICE**
EXERCISES: **A-69** and **A-70**

• Read each set of directions and check students' answers. Give students sufficient time to complete these exercises.

**INDEPENDENT PRACTICE**

• Assign exercises **A-71** through **A-74**.

• Kindergarten students may require teacher repetition of the directions to remember the task and to keep pace.

**THINKING ABOUT THINKING**
Q: What did you pay attention to when you followed directions using above or below?
1. I carefully listened to (or read) the directions.
2. I found a block that fit the directions.
3. I found the correct position and placed the block there.
4. I traced around the block and colored my drawing.

**PERSONAL APPLICATION**
Q: When might you have to understand the terms *above* or *below*?
A: Answers may include: to follow directions for finding an object, to follow directions for placing an object in position.

**EXERCISES A-75 to A-80**

# FOLLOWING DIRECTIONS—SUPPLY RIGHT OR LEFT

**ANSWERS A-75 through A-80 — Student book pages 35–6**
**Guided Practice: A-75–7** See next page
**Independent Practice: A-78–80** See next page

**LESSON PREPARATION**

**SKILL LEVEL**
If the exercise is carefully directed, it requires little reading or writing skill development (typical of kindergarten students). If students work independently, then some reading skill is required (typical of first-grade students).

© 2000 CRITICAL THINKING BOOKS & SOFTWARE • WWW.CRITICALTHINKING.COM • 800-458-4849          27

BEGINNING BUILDING THINKING SKILLS LESSON PLANS                                    DESCRIBING SHAPES

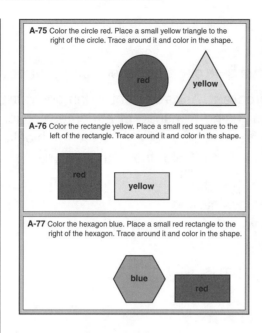
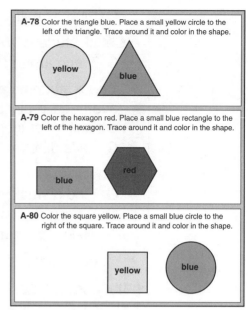

**OBJECTIVE AND MATERIALS**
OBJECTIVE: Students will use the concepts left and right to place a specific attribute block in relation to another attribute block.
MATERIALS: Attribute blocks (entire set) • transparency of page 35 of the student book

**TEACHING SUGGESTIONS**
• See the General Introduction on page 1.

**MODEL LESSON** | **LESSON**

**Introduction**
   Q: What are some examples of telling someone about left and right?
      A: My pocket is on the left (right) side of my shirt. When I leave school, I make a left (right) turn at the corner. (Student name) is left-handed. (Name) plays left field in baseball.

**Explaining the Objective to Students**
   Q: You will follow directions for placing an attribute block to the left or the right of another block.

**Class Activity**
• If necessary, review the practice lesson on left and right by asking students to raise one hand and then the other. Example—Raise your right hand, hands down. Raise your left hand, hands down. The teacher can also ask students to place themselves to the left or right of another student. Practice until students are reasonably proficient.

• Project a transparency of the student lesson page 35.
   Q: Look at exercise **A-75**. Color the circle red.

• Check students' progress.
   Q: Find a small yellow triangle. Place it on the right side of the red circle.

• Check students' progress.

BEGINNING BUILDING THINKING SKILLS LESSON PLANS                    DESCRIBING SHAPES

Q: Trace around the triangle and color the drawing yellow.

Q: Look at exercise **A-76**. Color the rectangle yellow.

- Check students' progress.

Q: Find a small red square. Place it on the left side of the yellow rectangle.

- Check students' progress.

Q: Trace around the square and color the drawing red.

## GUIDED PRACTICE
EXERCISES: **A-75** through **A-77**

- Kindergarten students may require teacher repetition of the directions to remember the task and to keep pace.

## INDEPENDENT PRACTICE
- Assign exercises **A-78** through **A-80**.

## THINKING ABOUT THINKING
Q: What did you pay attention to when you followed directions using right and left?

1. I carefully listened to (or read) the directions.

2. I found a block that fit the directions.

3. I found the correct position and placed the block there.

4. I traced around the block and colored my drawing.

## PERSONAL APPLICATION
Q: When might you have to understand the terms *right* and *left*?

A: Answers may include: to find an object, to place an object in position, to follow marching instructions, to find the location of a city on a map

**EXERCISES A-81 to A-85**

# NAMING SHAPES—SELECT AND WRITE–A

**ANSWERS A-81 through A-85 — Student book page 37**
**Guided Practice: A-81** This shape is a **circle**; **A-82** This shape is a **square.**
**Independent Practice: A-83** rectangle; **A-84** triangle; **A-85** hexagon

**LESSON PREPARATION**

## SKILL LEVEL
This activity requires both reading and writing skills (typical of first- and second-grade students). However, the activity can be done orally with kindergarten students. The teacher can also model writing the shape names on the overhead. Students can color the blocks or find matching attribute blocks.

## OBJECTIVE AND MATERIALS
OBJECTIVE: Students will identify a shape and find a matching attribute block, then find the name of the shape in a word box and write it on the line provided.

MATERIALS: Small attribute blocks • transparency of student lesson page 37

© 2000 CRITICAL THINKING BOOKS & SOFTWARE • WWW.CRITICALTHINKING.COM • 800-458-4849          29

BEGINNING BUILDING THINKING SKILLS LESSON PLANS                    DESCRIBING SHAPES

**MODEL LESSON**

## LESSON

### Introduction
- Hold up a large triangle or the triangle shape card.
  Q: What is this shape called?
    A: It is a triangle.

### Explaining the Objective to Students
  Q: You are going to trace over the names of the attribute blocks shown on the page.

### Class Activity
- Using transparent attribute blocks, project a circle.
  Q: What is this shape called?
    A: It is called a circle.

- Repeat with a square.
  Q: Find a small shape like this one.
  Q: What is the name of this shape?
    A: The shape is called a square.

  Q: Place a matching attribute block on shape number **A-81**. It is a circle. Trace over the word *circle* on the line.

### GUIDED PRACTICE
EXERCISES: **A-81** and **A-82**

- Give students sufficient time to complete these exercises. Ask students to discuss and explain their answers.

### INDEPENDENT PRACTICE
- Assign exercises **A-83** through **A-85**.

### THINKING ABOUT THINKING
  Q: What did you pay attention to when you named a shape?
  1. I paid attention to whether or not the shape was round.
  2. I counted the number of sides.
  3. I looked at whether or not the sides were the same length.
  4. I traced over the name for the shape.

### PERSONAL APPLICATION
  Q: When might you have to write names?
    A: When putting name tags or labels on objects or storage bins.

**EXERCISES A-86 to A-93**

## DESCRIBING SHAPES—SELECT AND WRITE–B

**ANSWERS A-86 through A-93 — Student book pages 38–40**
**Guided Practice: A-86** Shape 2 is a **small** rectangle. **A-87** Shape 3 is a small **square**.
**Independent Practice: A-88** small circle; **A-89** small hexagon; **A-90** large circle; **A-91** four, four; **A-92** three, three; **A-93** six, six

30                    © 2000 CRITICAL THINKING BOOKS & SOFTWARE • WWW.CRITICALTHINKING.COM • 800-458-4849

BEGINNING BUILDING THINKING SKILLS LESSON PLANS                                    DESCRIBING SHAPES

**LESSON PREPARATION**

### SKILL LEVEL

Some reading and writing skill is required (typical of first grade students). Activities can be done orally with kindergarten students. For activities **A-91** through **A-93**, kindergarten students can write the numerals.

### OBJECTIVE AND MATERIALS

OBJECTIVE: Students will write the size and name of specific attribute blocks; students will write the number of sides and corners a shape has.

MATERIALS: Attribute blocks (entire set) • transparencies of student lesson pages 38 and 40

### TEACHING SUGGESTIONS

- Kindergarten students have difficulty copying the words three, four, and five. This may be the first time that young children "read" or copy the words for numbers instead of expressing them as numerals. Give sufficient time and practice for student comfort and confidence.

- Prompt students to express the inference that a figure has the same number of sides and angles.

  Q: What do you find interesting about your sentences?

  A: Students may "count" the edge of the shape ("side, corner, side, corner,...") a preliminary observation to stating that a figure has the same number of sides and angles.

**MODEL LESSON**

### LESSON

### Introduction

- This lesson can be done in two parts, **A-86** to **A-90**, and **A-91** to **A-93**.

### Explaining the Objective to Students

Q: You will describe attribute blocks by size and shape. You will write the name of the block and whether it is large or small.

### Class Activity—Lesson 1

- Project a transparency of lesson page 38.

  Q: Compare shapes 1 and 2. Which is larger?

  A: Shape 2 is larger than shape 2.

  Q: Name shape 1.

  A: Shape one is a rectangle.

  Q: Notice in the example that the words *large rectangle* have been written. You will be writing two-word descriptions of shapes. Use the word box at the top of the page to help you spell the words correctly.

  Q: Look at **A-86**. Is shape 2 large or small?

  A: Shape 2 is small.

  Q: Write *small* on the lines above the word "size."

  Q: Look at **A-87**. Name shape 3.

  A: Shape 3 is a square.

  Q: Write *square* on the lines above the words "shape name."

© 2000 CRITICAL THINKING BOOKS & SOFTWARE • WWW.CRITICALTHINKING.COM • 800-458-4849          31

BEGINNING BUILDING THINKING SKILLS LESSON PLANS                    DESCRIBING SHAPES

**Class Activity—Lesson 2**
- Project a transparency of page 40.

  Q: Look at the example on the page. What shape is this?
    A: It is a rectangle.

  Q: How many sides does this shape have?
    A: It has four sides.

  Q: How many corners does this shape have?
    A: It has four corners.

  Q: The word four is written on both lines. A rectangle has four sides and four corners.

  Q: Using the words in the word box, you will write the word that tells how many sides and how many corners each shape has.

- Repeat the modeling with **A-91**.

**GUIDED PRACTICE**
EXERCISES: **A-86** and **A-87; A-91**
- Give students sufficient time to complete these exercises. Ask students to discuss and explain their answers.

**INDEPENDENT PRACTICE.**
- Assign exercises **A-82** through **A-90**; **A-92** and **A-93**

**THINKING ABOUT THINKING**
  Q: What did you pay attention to when you picked a word that described a shape?
    1. I looked at special features of the shape (square corners, equal sides, length of sides).

    2. I recalled the name of the shape.

    3. I named the shape and decided its size.

**PERSONAL APPLICATION**
  Q: When might you have to describe shapes at home?
    A: Making requests (e.g., "hand me that round pillow, not the square one") or giving directions, following directions to assemble toys or models.

**EXERCISES A-94 to A-98**

## DESCRIBING SHAPES—EXPLAIN (A)

**ANSWERS A-94 through A-98 — Student book pages 41–2**
**Guided Practice: A-94** This square has four sides and four corners (angles). **A-95** This rectangle has four sides and four corners (angles).
**Independent Practice: A-96** This triangle has three sides and three corners (angles). (One corner is square.) **A-97** This rectangle has four sides and four corners (angles). **A-98** This hexagon has six sides and six corners (angles).

32          © 2000 CRITICAL THINKING BOOKS & SOFTWARE • WWW.CRITICALTHINKING.COM • 800-458-4849

BEGINNING BUILDING THINKING SKILLS LESSON PLANS                    DESCRIBING SHAPES

**LESSON PREPARATION**

**SKILL LEVEL**

Requires reading terms or short directions and writing short sentences (typical of second-grade students). Kindergarten teachers can make a game using this page. Students pick an attribute block from a box and then describe it using a complete sentence. This activity is also good modeling for older students.

**OBJECTIVE AND MATERIALS**

OBJECTIVE: Students will name a shape and describe its number of sides and angles using a complete sentence.

MATERIALS: Photocopies and transparency of page 41 of the student lesson book.

**TEACHING SUGGESTIONS**

• Descriptions can be either oral or written depending on the writing skill of your students.

• Integrate these geometry concepts into you language arts program by discussing the picture books listed in the bibliography in the appendix.

• Introduce *angle* for *corner* if the term is appropriate for your students.

**MODEL LESSON**

**LESSON**

**Introduction**

Q: How many sides does the triangle have?
   A: The triangle has three sides.

Q: How many corners (angles) does it have?
   A: The triangle has three corners (angles).

Q: Put these ideas into a sentence.
A:  A triangle has three sides and three corners.

**Explaining the Objective to Students**

Q: You are going to describe shapes by naming the shape and telling how many sides and how many corners it has.

**Class Activity**

• Project page 41, exercise **A-94**.
   Q: Name this shape.
     A: It is a square.

   Q: How many sides does the square have?
     A: The square has four sides.

   Q: How many corners (angles) does it have?
     A: It has four corners (angles).

   Q: Put these ideas into a sentence.
     A: A square has four sides and four corners.

**GUIDED PRACTICE**

EXERCISE: **A-94** and **A-95**

• Give students sufficient time to complete this exercise. Ask students to discuss and explain their answers.

© 2000 CRITICAL THINKING BOOKS & SOFTWARE • WWW.CRITICALTHINKING.COM • 800-458-4849          33

BEGINNING BUILDING THINKING SKILLS LESSON PLANS — DESCRIBING SHAPES

### INDEPENDENT PRACTICE
- Assign exercises **A-96** through **A-98**.

### THINKING ABOUT THINKING
Q: What did you pay attention to when you described a shape?
1. I recalled the name of the shape.
2. I looked at special features of the shape (number of sides, length of sides, number of corners).
3. I named the shape and described its special features.

### PERSONAL APPLICATION
Q: When do you need to describe shapes?
A: Making requests or giving directions (e.g., "hand me that round pillow, not the square one"); following directions to assemble toys or models.

## DESCRIBING SHAPES—EXPLAIN (B)

**EXERCISES A-99 to A-101**

ANSWERS A-99 through A-101 — Student book pages 43–4
Guided Practice: **A-100** See below
Independent Practice: **A-101** See below

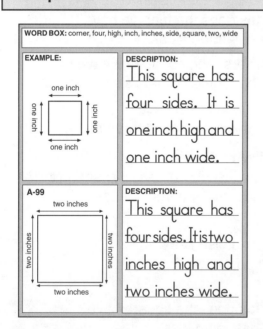
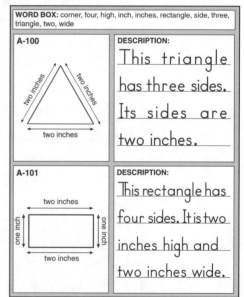

**LESSON PREPARATION**

### SKILL LEVEL
This activity requires reading terms or short directions and writing short sentences (typical of second-grade students). It can be done orally.

### OBJECTIVE AND MATERIALS
OBJECTIVE: Students will use dimensions to describe shapes either orally or in writing.
MATERIALS: Photocopies and transparency of student lesson page 43 • rulers.

BEGINNING BUILDING THINKING SKILLS LESSON PLANS                                    DESCRIBING SHAPES

## TEACHING SUGGESTIONS

• Remind students that the marks on a ruler show the length measure of an object. The units of measure are *inches*.

• Reinforce the following vocabulary emphasized in this lesson: *inches, rectangle, sides, triangle*. If appropriate to the vocabulary level of your students, introduce the term *dimension*.

• Integrate these geometry concepts into your language arts program by discussing the picture books listed under shapes in the bibliography.

**MODEL LESSON** | ## LESSON

### Introduction

Q: In other lessons, you have described shapes by name, color and size.

### Explaining the Objective to Students

Q: You will describe shapes by mentioning the length of the sides in your description.

### Class Activity

• Project the example on page 43. Cover the description.
   Q: What is this shape called?
   A: It is a square.

   Q: How many sides does it have?
   A: The square has four sides.

   Q: How high is the square?
   A: The square is one inch high.

   Q: How wide is the square?
   A: The square is one inch wide.

   Q: Put these ideas into a sentence.
   A: This square has four sides. It is one inch high and one inch wide.

• Uncover the description.

### GUIDED PRACTICE
EXERCISE: **A-99**

• Follow the same line of questioning with exercise **A-99**.
• Give students sufficient time to complete this exercise. Ask students to discuss and explain their answer.

### INDEPENDENT PRACTICE

• Assign exercises **A-100** to **A-101**.

### THINKING ABOUT THINKING

Q: What did you pay attention to when you described a shape?
   1. I recalled the name of the shape.
   2. I looked at special features of the shape (number of sides, length of sides, number of corners).
   3. I named the shape and described its special features.

© 2000 CRITICAL THINKING BOOKS & SOFTWARE • WWW.CRITICALTHINKING.COM • 800-458-4849          35

**PERSONAL APPLICATION**

Q: When do you need to describe shapes?

A: Making requests or giving directions (e.g., "hand me that round pillow, not the square one); following directions to assemble toys or models.

# Chapter 2 | FIGURAL SIMILARITIES AND DIFFERENCES

(Student book pages 46–94)

## GENERAL INFORMATION

### TEACHING SUGGESTIONS
- Ask students to name the polygons as they discuss and explain their answers. Remember the words that students use to describe their choices. Use these same words to remind students of the key characteristics of items in these lessons.
- Integrate these geometry concepts into your language arts program by discussing the picture books listed in the bibliography in the appendix.

### CURRICULUM APPLICATIONS
Language Arts: Use visual discrimination activities for reading readiness.
Mathematics: Identify similar figures; write numerals in the correct direction (5, 7, etc.).
Science: Recognize similarly shaped leaves, insects, or shells.
Social Studies: Match puzzle sections to geographic features on map puzzle.
Enrichment Areas: Recognize shapes of road signs; discern different patterns in art.

**EXERCISES B-1 to B-10**

## MATCHING SHAPES—A

> **ANSWERS B-1 through B-10 — Student book pages 46–50**
> Guided Practice: **B-1, B-2** see below
> Independent Practice: **B-3** through **B-10** see below and next page

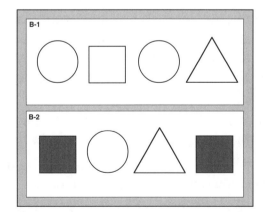 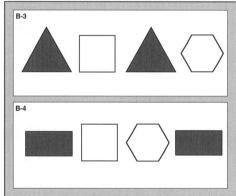

**LESSON PREPARATION**

### SKILL LEVEL
Requires no reading or writing skill development (typical of kindergarten students). Directions at the top of the page are read to the students, step by step.

© 2000 CRITICAL THINKING BOOKS & SOFTWARE • WWW.CRITICALTHINKING.COM • 800-458-4849    37

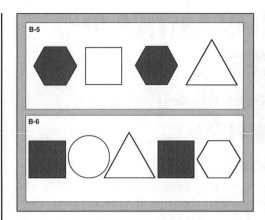
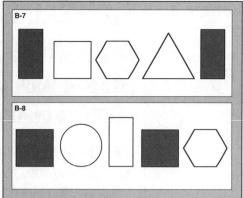
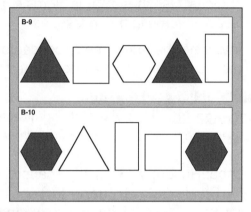

## OBJECTIVE AND MATERIALS

OBJECTIVE: Students will use attribute blocks to match shapes.
MATERIALS: Attribute blocks • transparency of student book page 46

## TEACHING SUGGESTIONS

- Ask students to name the polygons as they discuss and explain their answers.

**MODEL LESSON** | **LESSON**

### Introduction

Q: In the first chapter, you learned how to describe shapes. We learned three things about shapes by using attribute blocks. An attribute tells us something special about an object. What is one of the three special things about an attribute block that we can name or describe?
  A: We can name its shape.

Q: Name another special attribute to help us describe a block.
  A: We can describe the size of the block, whether it is large or small.

Q: What is the third thing we can describe about the attribute block?
  A: We can name the color of the attribute block.

Q: In this chapter, we will see how shapes are alike and how they are different. We will start by looking at shapes that match.

### Explaining the Objective to Students

Q: You are going to find matching shapes.

BEGINNING BUILDING THINKING SKILLS LESSON PLANS          FIGURAL SIMILARITIES AND DIFFERENCES

### Class Activity

- Arrange a group of four attribute blocks, including two of the same shape, in a row. The last block should match the first block in the row.
  Q: Which shape matches the first one?

- Ask a student to demonstrate.
    A: Student moves the first block to fit on top of the last block.

- Project the transparency of page 46.
  Q: Look at exercise **B-1**. Cover the shaded figure with a block that matches it. Color the picture the same color as the block.

- After students have colored the first shape, give these directions:
  Q: Slide the block along the row until you find the shape that matches it. Color the shape the same color as the block.

### GUIDED PRACTICE
EXERCISES: **B-2** and **B-3**
- Give students sufficient time to complete this exercise. Ask students to discuss and explain their answers.

### INDEPENDENT PRACTICE
- Assign exercises **B-4** through **B-10**.

### THINKING ABOUT THINKING
    Q: What did you pay attention to when you matched these shapes?
    1. I looked carefully at the first shape.

    2. I looked for a matching shape.

    3. I moved the block to check that the shapes matched.

### PERSONAL APPLICATION
    Q: When might you have to match shapes?
      A: Putting away toys or tools; matching building blocks; matching parts or sections from construction toys; putting away dishes or silverware.

**EXERCISES
B-11 to B-21**

# MATCHING SHAPES—B

> **ANSWERS B-11 through B-21 — Student book pages 51–3**
> **Guided Practice: B-11** through **B-13** see next page
> **Independent Practice: B-14** through **B-21** see next page

**LESSON PREPARATION**

### SKILL LEVEL
Requires no reading or writing skill development (typical of kindergarten students).

### OBJECTIVE AND MATERIALS
OBJECTIVE: Students will find the shape that matches the first shape in the row. They will match the drawings of shapes that are not attribute block shapes.
MATERIALS: Transparency of student page 51

© 2000 CRITICAL THINKING BOOKS & SOFTWARE • WWW.CRITICALTHINKING.COM • 800-458-4849          39

BEGINNING BUILDING THINKING SKILLS LESSON PLANS          FIGURAL SIMILARITIES AND DIFFERENCES

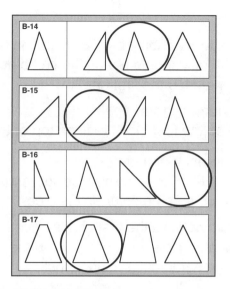
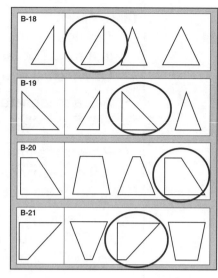

**TEACHING SUGGESTIONS**

- See the introduction to this chapter on page 37.

- Ask students to explain why the incorrect answers were eliminated. Remember the words that students use to describe their choices and use these same words to remind students of the key characteristics of figures in these lessons and in subsequent ones.

- In many of these lessons, students' descriptive answers may provide memorable cues for reinforcing their perceptions and developing vocabulary. Celebrate and refine students' colorful language. Playful descriptions, if correct, can imprint concepts. For example:
    "A trapezoid is like a triangle with a haircut."
    "An oval is a smashed circle."
    "Some parallelograms look like lazy rectangles."

- Kindergarten and first-grade students commonly lack language for position or orientation and make up analogies to describe these properties. An upright oval may be "standing up," a horizontal oval may be "lying down."

**MODEL LESSON** | **LESSON**

**Introduction**

Q: In the last lesson, we matched shapes that were exactly alike in size and shape. Find two objects in the room that are exactly alike.
   A: Answers vary. (Floor or ceiling tiles of the same size, tabletops of the same size, chalkboard panels, etc.)

Q: You have matched shapes using attribute blocks. In this lesson, you will use drawings instead of blocks.

**Explaining the Objective to Students**

Q: You are going to match a shape with one that looks like it.

**Class Activity**

- Project the Example square cut from the transparency of page 51.
    Q: You are going to look for a shape that is exactly like this shape.

BEGINNING BUILDING THINKING SKILLS LESSON PLANS                    FIGURAL SIMILARITIES AND DIFFERENCES

- Project the other three shapes.
  Q: Let's see which of these shapes matches the movable shape.

- Place the square over the first rectangle.
  Q: The rectangle is as tall as the square, but it is thinner.

- Move the square to cover the square shape.
  Q: The square is an exact match. It is just as tall and just as wide.

- Move the square to cover the last square shape.
  Q: These two pieces don't fit; the movable square is taller and wider. Notice that a circle is drawn around the larger square because it matches the Example square.

### GUIDED PRACTICE
EXERCISES: **B-11** through **B-13**.
- Give students sufficient time to complete these exercises. Ask students to discuss and explain their answers.

### INDEPENDENT PRACTICE
- Assign exercises **B-14** through **B-21**.

### THINKING ABOUT THINKING
Q: What did you pay attention to when you matched these figures?
1. I looked carefully at the details (size of the figure, length of the sides, size of the angle, pattern or color, similarity to some common object, etc.).
2. I matched equal parts. (side, angle, etc.)
3. I checked that all the sides and angles were the same.
4. I checked how those that didn't match were really different.

### PERSONAL APPLICATION
Q: When might you have to match shapes?
A: Putting away toys or tools; matching building blocks; matching parts or sections from construction toys; putting away dishes or silverware.

**EXERCISES B-22 to B-32**

# MATCHING SHAPES—C

> **ANSWERS B-22 through B-32 — Student book pages 54–6**
> **Guided Practice: B-22** through **B-24** see next page
> **Independent Practice: B-25** through **B-32** see next page

**LESSON PREPARATION**

### SKILL LEVEL
Requires no reading or writing skill development (typical of kindergarten students).

### OBJECTIVE AND MATERIALS
OBJECTIVE: From a group of four drawings, students will circle the two shapes that are the same in each row.
MATERIALS: Transparency of TM 5 page 329

BEGINNING BUILDING THINKING SKILLS LESSON PLANS         FIGURAL SIMILARITIES AND DIFFERENCES

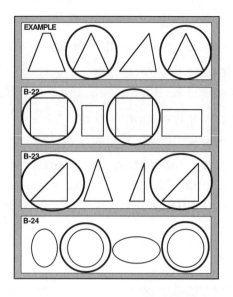
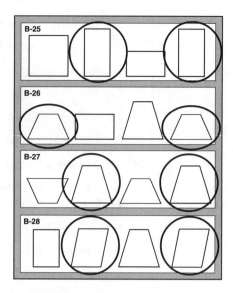
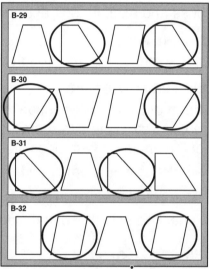

### TEACHING SUGGESTIONS
- Emphasize students' use of *equal* to explain the perception of matching shapes.

**MODEL LESSON**

### LESSON

#### Introduction
Q: You match shapes when you stack dishes on a shelf. You put all the small plates in one stack and the larger plates in another. In the previous lesson, you looked at a picture of a shape and found another shape like it. In this lesson, you will also match shapes that are exactly alike.

#### Explaining the Objective to Students
Q: You will pick out two shapes that are alike from a row of shapes.

#### Class Activity
- Project four triangles cut from the transparency of TM 5.
  Q: Let's test triangle 1 to see if it matches any of the other shapes.

- Move triangle 1 to each of the other triangles.

Q: How are triangles 1 and 2 alike?
A: They are about the same size. (They have the same height.)

Q: How are triangles 1 and 2 different?
A: Triangle 2 is wider than triangle 1.

- Move triangle 1 to triangle 3.
Q: How are triangles 1 and 3 alike?
A: They both have three sides and three corners.

Q: How are triangles 1 and 3 different?
A: Triangle 3 is shorter and wider than triangle 1.

- Move triangle 1 to triangle 4.
Q: How are triangles 1 and 4 alike?
A: They are the same width and the same height. Triangle 1 fits triangle 4 exactly.

Q: How are triangles 1 and 4 different?
A: They are exactly the same. They are not different.

Q: How are triangles 2 and 3 alike?
A: They are the same width (base).

Q: How are triangles 2 and 3 different?
A: Triangle 2 is taller than triangle 3.

## GUIDED PRACTICE
EXERCISES: **B-22** through **B-24**
- Give students sufficient time to complete these exercises. Ask students to discuss and explain their answers. Discuss <u>why</u> the incorrect answers were eliminated.

## INDEPENDENT PRACTICE
- Assign exercises **B-25** through **B-32**.

## THINKING ABOUT THINKING
Q: What did you pay attention to when you matched these figures?
1. I looked carefully at the details (size of the figure, length of the sides, size of the angle, pattern or color, similarity to some common object, etc.).

2. I matched equal parts (side, angle, etc.).

3. I checked that all the sides and angles are the same.

4. I checked how those that don't match are really different.

## PERSONAL APPLICATION
Q: When might you have to match shapes?
A: Putting away toys or tools; matching building blocks; matching parts or sections from construction toys; putting away dishes or silverware.

BEGINNING BUILDING THINKING SKILLS LESSON PLANS                FIGURAL SIMILARITIES AND DIFFERENCES

**EXERCISES B-33 to B-35**

# MATCHING SHAPES BY SHAPE AND COLOR

**ANSWERS B-33 through B-35 — Student book pages 57–9**
**Guided Practice: B-33** see below
**Independent Practice: B-34** through **B-35** see below

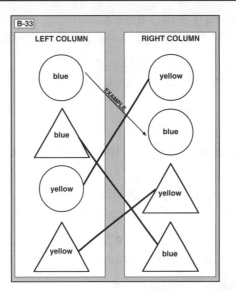
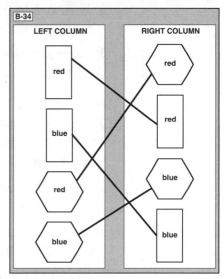
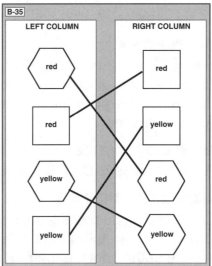

**LESSON PREPARATION**

**SKILL LEVEL**

Requires no reading or writing skill development (typical of kindergarten students).

**OBJECTIVE AND MATERIALS**

OBJECTIVE: Students will find matching shapes that are the same color.
MATERIALS: All small attribute blocks • transparency of student book page 57 • colored transparency markers or colored chalk

**TEACHING SUGGESTIONS**

- This lesson can also help with color recognition and following directions. Have the students color each shape the appropriate color and then match the shapes in each column.

44       © 2000 CRITICAL THINKING BOOKS & SOFTWARE • WWW.CRITICALTHINKING.COM • 800-458-4849

BEGINNING BUILDING THINKING SKILLS LESSON PLANS                    FIGURAL SIMILARITIES AND DIFFERENCES

**MODEL LESSON** | **LESSON**

**Introduction**

- Arrange a group of four attribute blocks: square, circle, triangle, square. Q: Which shape matches the first one?

- Ask a student to demonstrate—move the first square to fit on top of the last square.

**Explaining the Objective to Students**

  Q: From two groups of blocks, you will find the matching blocks that are the same shape and the same color.

**Class Activity**

- Project the transparency of page 57 on the chalkboard or overhead. Color the projected image to match the correct colors. Ask a student to draw lines connecting the shapes that are alike.

- Ask a student to place an attribute block on each of the shapes on page 57.
  Q: Draw a line connecting the two blue circles.
    A: Check students' work.

  Q: Now draw lines to connect the rest of the matching shapes.

**GUIDED PRACTICE**
EXERCISE: **B-33**

- Give students sufficient time to complete these exercises. Ask students to discuss and explain their answers.

**INDEPENDENT PRACTICE**

- Assign exercises **B-34** through **B-35**.

**THINKING ABOUT THINKING**

  Q: What did you pay attention to when you matched these figures?
  1. I looked carefully at the color and shape of each block in the left column.

  2. I looked for a block in the right column with the same shape and color.

  3. I checked how those that don't match are really different.

**PERSONAL APPLICATION**

  Q: When might you have to match shapes?
    A: Examples include putting away toys or tools; matching building blocks; matching parts or sections from construction toys; putting away dishes or silverware.

**EXERCISES**
**B-36 to B-38**

# MATCHING SHAPES—D

**ANSWERS B-36 through B-38 — Student book pages 60–2**
**Guided Practice: B-36** see next page
**Independent Practice: B-37** see next page, **B-38** see next page

© 2000 CRITICAL THINKING BOOKS & SOFTWARE • WWW.CRITICALTHINKING.COM • 800-458-4849          45

BEGINNING BUILDING THINKING SKILLS LESSON PLANS                    FIGURAL SIMILARITIES AND DIFFERENCES

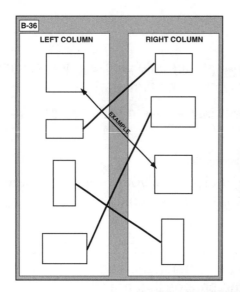
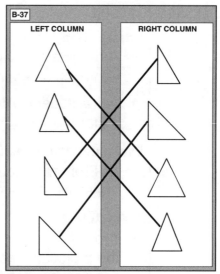
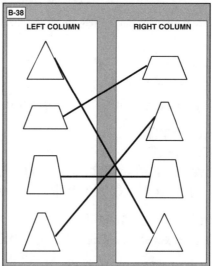

**LESSON PREPARATION**

**SKILL LEVEL**
Requires the concentration and visual discrimination typical of first-grade students. Can be used with kindergarten students.

**OBJECTIVE AND MATERIALS**
OBJECTIVE: Students will find matching attribute blocks or figures.
MATERIALS: Transparency of page 60 of the student book

**TEACHING SUGGESTIONS**
- This lesson is similar to the previous lesson and may be used as an extension of the matching attribute lesson or as a separate lesson. If this lesson is used separately, then review matching attribute blocks.

**MODEL LESSON**

**LESSON**

**Introduction**

Q: When you put eating utensils away, you put all the knives together, all the forks together, and all the spoons together. To do that you must see how shapes are alike.

BEGINNING BUILDING THINKING SKILLS LESSON PLANS                    FIGURAL SIMILARITIES AND DIFFERENCES

### Explaining the Objective to Students
Q: From two groups of shapes, you will find matching ones.

### Class Activity
• Project the transparency of page 60.
Q: Name the top shape in the left column.
  A: The top shape is a square.

Q: Ask a student to point to the matching square.
Q: Notice that a line connects the two squares. Name the second shape.
  A: The second shape is a rectangle.

Q: Find a rectangle in the right column and draw a line between the two rectangles.
  A: Check students' work.

Q: Now finish exercise **B-36**.

### GUIDED PRACTICE
EXERCISES: **B-36**
• Give students sufficient time to complete these exercises. Ask students to discuss and explain their answers.

### INDEPENDENT PRACTICE
• Assign exercises **B-37** to **B-38**.

### THINKING ABOUT THINKING
Q: What did you pay attention to when you matched these figures?
  1. I looked carefully at a shape in the left column.

  2. I looked for the same shape in the right column.

  3. I checked how the shapes that don't match are really different.

### PERSONAL APPLICATION
Q: When might you have to match shapes?
  A: Putting away toys or tools; matching building blocks; matching parts or sections from construction toys; putting away dishes or silverware.

**EXERCISES B-39 to B-44**

# WHICH SHAPE DOES NOT MATCH THE BLOCK?

**ANSWERS B-39 through B-44 — Student book pages 63–5**
**Guided Practice: B-39, B-40** see next page
**Independent Practice: B-41** through **B-44** see next page

**LESSON PREPARATION**

### SKILL LEVEL
Requires no reading or writing skill development (typical of kindergarten students)

### OBJECTIVE AND MATERIALS
OBJECTIVE: Students will find the shape that does not match a given block and color that shape.

© 2000 CRITICAL THINKING BOOKS & SOFTWARE • WWW.CRITICALTHINKING.COM • 800-458-4849          47

BEGINNING BUILDING THINKING SKILLS LESSON PLANS    FIGURAL SIMILARITIES AND DIFFERENCES

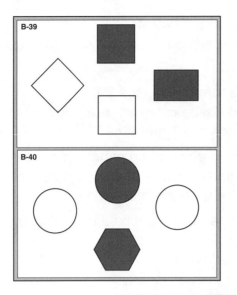
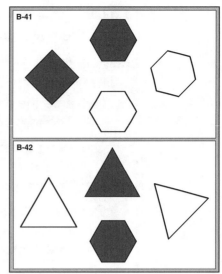
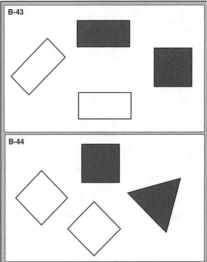

MATERIALS: Transparency of student lesson page 63 • colored chalk or transparency marker • small attribute blocks

**TEACHING SUGGESTIONS**
- Ask students to explain their answers. Ask them to explain how the shape outline they colored is different from the shape of the attribute block. Remember the words that students use to describe their choices. Use these same words to remind students of the key characteristics of figures in these lessons and in subsequent ones.

- Kindergarten students' limited language may result in phrases like: "some peaks have a straight up line and a slanted line (right triangle)," or "the oval is taller and skinnier than the circle."

**MODEL LESSON** | **LESSON**

**Introduction**

Q: Think of a time you needed to know that a shape did not match another shape.
　　A: Answers will vary. (Fitting puzzle pieces, putting objects or tools into their proper container or slot, etc.)

BEGINNING BUILDING THINKING SKILLS LESSON PLANS     FIGURAL SIMILARITIES AND DIFFERENCES

### Explaining the Objective to Students

Q: You have matched blocks and shapes. In this lesson, you will find the shape that is different from the attribute block. You will color the drawing of the shape that is different.

### Class Activity

• Project exercise **B-39** on student lesson page 63. Point to the shaded square at the top of the page.

Q: Find a small square attribute block of any color. Place it on the shaded square.

Q: Move your square around until you find the shape that does not match. A shape may be the same but may be turned in a different position. Be sure to move the block around to make sure whether or not it fits.

Q: What is the name of the shape in this group that does not belong?
  A: It is the rectangle.

Q: Why doesn't the rectangle belong.
  A: The other shapes in the group are all squares.

Q: Color the drawing of the rectangle. Why doesn't the rectangle match the square block?
  A: Its sides are not all equal in length. The height is shorter than the width. In the square, all the sides are the same length.

### GUIDED PRACTICE
EXERCISE: **B-40**

• Give students sufficient time to complete these exercises. Ask students to discuss and explain their answers.

### INDEPENDENT PRACTICE

• Assign exercises **B-41** through **B-44**.

### THINKING ABOUT THINKING

Q: What did you pay attention to when you matched these figures?

1. I moved my block to see if it fit the drawing.

2. I checked that all the sides and angles were the same.

3. I looked for the shape that did not match.

### PERSONAL APPLICATION

Q: When might you have to match shapes?
  A: Examples include putting away toys or tools; matching building blocks; matching parts or sections from construction toys; putting away dishes or silverware.

**EXERCISES
B-45 to B-55**

## WHICH SHAPE DOES NOT MATCH?

**ANSWERS B-45 through B-55 — Student book page 66–8**
**Guided Practice: B-45** through **B-47** see next page
**Independent Practice: B-46** through **B-55** see next page

© 2000 CRITICAL THINKING BOOKS & SOFTWARE • WWW.CRITICALTHINKING.COM • 800-458-4849     49

BEGINNING BUILDING THINKING SKILLS LESSON PLANS                    FIGURAL SIMILARITIES AND DIFFERENCES

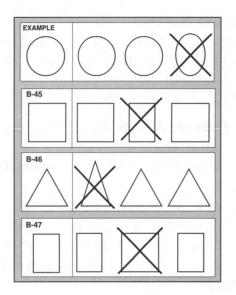 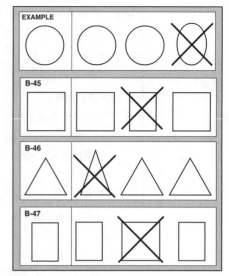

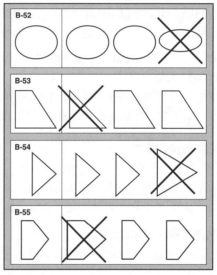

| LESSON PREPARATION | **SKILL LEVEL**<br>Requires no reading or writing skill development (typical of kindergarten students).<br><br>**OBJECTIVE AND MATERIALS**<br>OBJECTIVE: Students will find the shape that does not match a given shape.<br>MATERIALS: Transparency of page 66 of the student lesson book<br><br>**TEACHING SUGGESTIONS**<br>• Kindergarten students' limited language may result in phrases like: "some peaks have a straight up line and a slanted line (right triangle)," or "the oval is taller and skinnier than the circle." |
|---|---|
| **MODEL LESSON** | **LESSON**<br>**Introduction**<br>    Q: Think of a time you needed to know that a shape did not match another shape.<br>        A: Answers will vary. (Fitting puzzle pieces, putting objects or tolls into their proper container or slot, etc.) |

50          © 2000 CRITICAL THINKING BOOKS & SOFTWARE • WWW.CRITICALTHINKING.COM • 800-458-4849

BEGINNING BUILDING THINKING SKILLS LESSON PLANS                    FIGURAL SIMILARITIES AND DIFFERENCES

Q: You have used attribute blocks to find a block that did not match the others in the group. today you will use drawings of many different shapes.

## Explaining the Objective to Students

Q: In this lesson, you will find a shape that is different from the one in the box.

## Class Activity

• Cut out the Example shape from the transparency of page 66 and project the rest of the page.

Q: I have cut out the shape in the Example box and will move it over each of the shapes. Let's find the shape that is not like the circle.

• Move the circle from shape to shape.

Q: Notice that this circle matches the first two shapes. Why doesn't the circle match the last shape?

    A: It is an oval. The oval isn't perfectly round. It is taller and skinnier than the circle.

Q: Which shape must be crossed out?

    A: The last shape, the oval.

• Allow time for questions.

Q: Let's try **B-45**. Which shape doesn't match?

    A: The rectangle

Q: Why doesn't the rectangle match the square?

    A: A square has all sides the same length. This rectangle is taller than it is wide.

Q: Practice the next two activities on the page.

## GUIDED PRACTICE

EXERCISES: **B-46** and **B-47**

• For kindergarten students, repeat this pattern of questioning:

    1. Which shape doesn't match?

    2. Why doesn't it match?

    3. Which shape must be crossed out?

• Give students sufficient time to complete these exercises. Ask students to discuss and explain their answers.

## INDEPENDENT PRACTICE

• Assign exercises **B-48** through **B-55**.

## THINKING ABOUT THINKING

Q: What did you pay attention to when you matched these figures?

    1. I looked at the shape in the shape box.

    2. I checked that all sides and angles are the same.

    3. I looked for the shape that did not match.

© 2000 CRITICAL THINKING BOOKS & SOFTWARE • WWW.CRITICALTHINKING.COM • 800-458-4849            51

BEGINNING BUILDING THINKING SKILLS LESSON PLANS — FIGURAL SIMILARITIES AND DIFFERENCES

**PERSONAL APPLICATION**
Q: When might you have to match shapes?
A: Examples include putting away toys or tools, matching building blocks, matching parts or sections from construction toys, putting away dishes or silverware

**EXERCISES B-56 to B-60**

## COPYING A FIGURE

> **ANSWERS B-56 through B-60 — Student book pages 69–70**
> **Guided Practice: B-56** to **B-57** see below
> **Independent Practice: B-58** through **B-60** see below

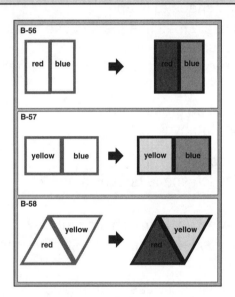
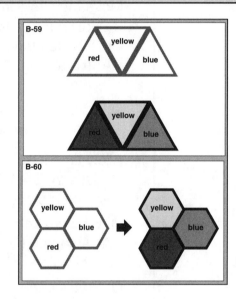

**LESSON PREPARATION**

**SKILL LEVEL**
Requires no reading or writing skill development (typical of kindergarten students). Teacher can read the color words to the students.

**OBJECTIVE AND MATERIALS**
OBJECTIVE: Students will use attribute blocks to reproduce a figure made with two or three blocks.
MATERIALS: Transparency of page 69 from student lesson book • set of small attribute blocks

**MODEL LESSON**

**LESSON**

**Introduction**
Q: When you work on a picture puzzle, you have to put pieces together. What do you look at to help you put the puzzle together?
A: Answers will vary. Desired response—I look at the picture on the box to see where the colors belong, and I match the pieces to the picture.

**Explaining the Objective to Students**
Q: We will make figures with attribute blocks by copying the "picture" of the figure.

BEGINNING BUILDING THINKING SKILLS LESSON PLANS                    FIGURAL SIMILARITIES AND DIFFERENCES

**Class Activity**

• Project a transparency of page 69.
    Q: In exercise **B-56**, name the smaller figures within the square.
        A: There are two rectangles inside the square. One is red, and the other
            is blue.

    Q: Find a small red and a small blue rectangle. Place them on the blank
    square. Make a drawing and color it like the figure you copied.

• Check students' work.
    Q: Repeat with exercise **B-57**.

• Check students' work. Then assign **B-58** through **B-60**.

**GUIDED PRACTICE**
EXERCISE: **B-56** and **B-57**

**INDEPENDENT PRACTICE**
• Assign exercises **B-58** through **B-60**.

**THINKING ABOUT THINKING**
    Q: What did you pay attention to when you copied these figures?
    1. I looked at the figure I needed to copy.

    2. I found the blocks that matched the shapes in the figure.

    3. I placed the blocks in the blank space.

**PERSONAL APPLICATION**
    Q: When might you have to copy figures?
        A: I copy figures and shapes in art and in math.

**EXERCISES
B-61 to B-66**

# MAKING A FIGURE

**ANSWERS B-61 through B-66 — Student book page 71**
**Guided Practice: B-61–2** check students' patterns
**Independent Practice: B-63** through **B-66** check students' patterns

**LESSON
PREPARATION**

**SKILL LEVEL**
Requires some reading skill development (typical of first-grade students). For
kindergarten students, the teacher may read the directions in each box.

**OBJECTIVE AND MATERIALS**
OBJECTIVE: Students will make a figure by placing the correct colored cubes
on the shape shown.
MATERIALS: Interlocking cubes (5 each of red, blue, and yellow) • transparency of page 71 from student lesson book

**MODEL LESSON**

**LESSON**

**Introduction**
    Q: In the previous lesson we copied drawings of figures by placing attribute
    blocks on them.

© 2000 CRITICAL THINKING BOOKS & SOFTWARE • WWW.CRITICALTHINKING.COM • 800-458-4849                    53

BEGINNING BUILDING THINKING SKILLS LESSON PLANS                FIGURAL SIMILARITIES AND DIFFERENCES

**Explaining the Objective to Students**
Q: Now we will make figures by placing interlocking cubes on drawings of them.

**Class Activity**
- Project a transparency of page 71.
  Q: Find one red and two yellow cubes.
  Q: Connect them like the ones shown in the drawing.
- Check students' work.
  Q: Repeat with exercise **B-62**.
- Check students' work. Then assign rest of exercises.

**GUIDED PRACTICE**
EXERCISES: **B-61** and **B-62**

**INDEPENDENT PRACTICE**
- Assign exercises **B-63** through **B-66**.

**THINKING ABOUT THINKING**
Q: What did you pay attention to when you made these figures?
1. I looked at the figure I needed to make.
2. I found the correct colored cubes that matched the squares in the figure.
3. I placed the cubes on top of the drawing.

**PERSONAL APPLICATION**
Q: When might you have to copy figures?
A: I copy shapes and figures in art and math.

**EXERCISES B-67 to B-69**

# MATCHING FIGURES WITH CUBES

**ANSWERS B-67 through B-69** — Student book pages 72–4
**Guided Practice: B-67** see below
**Independent Practice: B-68** through **B-69** see below and next page

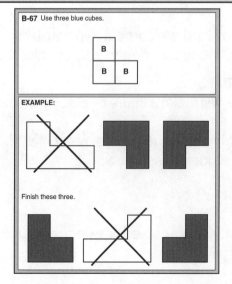
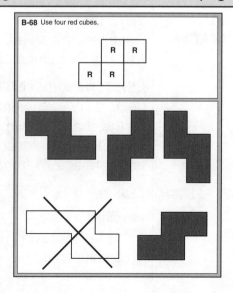

BEGINNING BUILDING THINKING SKILLS LESSON PLANS · FIGURAL SIMILARITIES AND DIFFERENCES

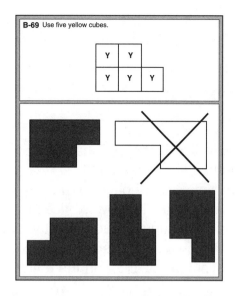

**LESSON PREPARATION**

**SKILL LEVEL**
Requires little or no reading or writing skill development (typical of kindergarten students).

**OBJECTIVE AND MATERIALS**
OBJECTIVE: Students will build a figure from cubes. They will find and color figures that match the one they built. They will cross out the figure that does not match.
MATERIALS: Transparency of page 72 of student lesson book • colored chalk or transparency marker • interlocking cubes (Unifix or Multilink®)

**TEACHING SUGGESTIONS**
• Ask students to explain their answers. Ask them to explain how the shape outline they colored is different from the shape they built. Remember the words that students use to describe their choices. Use these same words to remind students of the key characteristics of figures in these lessons and in subsequent ones.

**MODEL LESSON**

**LESSON**

**Introduction**
Q: We have been working with cubes to produce figures that had different designs. Find designs in this room.
  A: Answers vary.

Q: Today we will be looking at shapes that are not like the attribute shapes. The shapes will be made from cubes of the same color. They will not have a color pattern.

**Explaining the Objective to Students**
Q: In this lesson, you will make a shape with cubes. You will move your shape around like a puzzle piece and find all the outlines that match the shape you made. You will color the shapes that match your figure. You will make an "X" through the figures that do not match.

**Class Activity**
• Distribute 5 red, 5 yellow, and 5 blue cubes to each group. Project exercise

© 2000 CRITICAL THINKING BOOKS & SOFTWARE • WWW.CRITICALTHINKING.COM • 800-458-4849      55

BEGINNING BUILDING THINKING SKILLS LESSON PLANS                    FIGURAL SIMILARITIES AND DIFFERENCES

**B-67**. Point to the L-shaped figure at the top of the page.
Q: Make a shape that looks like this one.

• Allow time for construction. Demonstrate the following process:
Q: Slide your figure over the first drawing like I am doing. What do you notice?
  A: The drawing is larger than my figure.

Q: Notice that an "X" has been made through the drawing because the figures do not match.
Q: Notice that I have to turn my figure, but I can fit it inside the last two shapes in the top row. Notice those figures are shaded showing that they match the figure made with the cubes.
Q: Finish the exercise. Color the outline of the shapes that you can match and put an "X" through the outline of the shape that does not match.

• Allow students time to match their shapes and color the correct outlines. Ask for a volunteer to show the class which shape doesn't match.

**GUIDED PRACTICE**
EXERCISE: **B-67**
• Give students sufficient time to complete this exercise. Ask students to discuss and explain their answers.

**INDEPENDENT PRACTICE**
• Assign exercises **B-68** through **B-69.**

**THINKING ABOUT THINKING**
Q: What did you pay attention to when you matched these figures?
1. I moved my figure to see if it covered the drawing.

2. I checked that all sides and angles were the same.

3. I looked for the shape that did not match.

**PERSONAL APPLICATION**
Q: When might you have to match shapes?
A: Putting away toys or tools, matching building blocks, matching parts or sections from construction toys, putting away dishes or silverware

**EXERCISES B-70 to B-72**

## COMBINING ATTRIBUTE BLOCKS

**ANSWERS B-70 through B-72 — Student book pages 75–8**
**Guided Practice: B-70** See next page.
**Independent Practice: B-71** to **B-72** See next page.

**LESSON PREPARATION**

**SKILL LEVEL**
Requires no reading or writing skill development (typical of kindergarten students).

**OBJECTIVE AND MATERIALS**
OBJECTIVE: Students will decide which figures can be produced by combining two attribute blocks.

56                    © 2000 CRITICAL THINKING BOOKS & SOFTWARE • WWW.CRITICALTHINKING.COM • 800-458-4849

BEGINNING BUILDING THINKING SKILLS LESSON PLANS                    FIGURAL SIMILARITIES AND DIFFERENCES

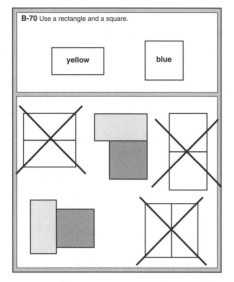
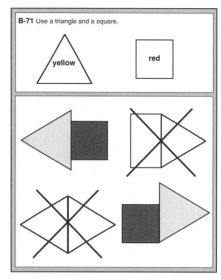
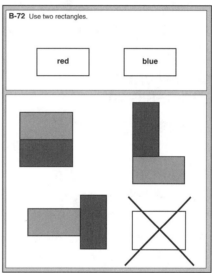

MATERIALS: Small attribute blocks • transparency of page 75 of student lesson book • colored chalk or transparency markers • projection attribute blocks

**TEACHING SUGGESTIONS**

Q: Identify things in the classroom that are *whole* objects made up of geometric shapes. Note how the part appears within the whole.
  A: Ceiling tiles, floor tiles, brick or concrete block walls, window panes, etc. are parts of this room.

**MODEL LESSON** | **LESSON**

**Introduction**

Q: This lesson is similar to the previous one. Today you will use attribute blocks instead of interlocking cubes.

**Explaining the Objective to Students**

Q: You will find the figures that can be covered with two attribute blocks. You will color the figures that can be covered and make an "X" through the ones that cannot.

© 2000 CRITICAL THINKING BOOKS & SOFTWARE • WWW.CRITICALTHINKING.COM • 800-458-4849          57

BEGINNING BUILDING THINKING SKILLS LESSON PLANS                    FIGURAL SIMILARITIES AND DIFFERENCES

**Class Activity**

- Project the transparency of page 75.
  Q: Find two attribute blocks—a small yellow square and a small blue square.
  Q: Move the blocks over your page and notice that the shaded examples can be covered with these two blocks.

- Model moving the blocks on the overhead. Give students time to work with the blocks.
  Q: Notice that two of the figures cannot be covered, and they have been crossed out. Why couldn't you make these two figures with the two squares?
    A: They are made from two rectangles.

- Ask a student to demonstrate the above on the overhead projector.
  Q: Now do exercise **B-70** and I'll check your work.

- For kindergarten students, go through each of the steps given in the directions.

**GUIDED PRACTICE**
EXERCISES **B-70**

**INDEPENDENT PRACTICE**
- Assign exercises **B-71** and **B-72**.

**THINKING ABOUT THINKING**
  Q: What did you pay attention to when you combined blocks?
  1. I found the two blocks to be combined.
  2. I moved the blocks over the figures to check that I could fit them on the diagram.
  3. I checked that my construction matched the figure.

**PERSONAL APPLICATION**
  Q: When do you need to combine objects?
    A: Examples include assembling toys, doing picture puzzles.

| EXERCISES B-73 to B-77 | # COMBINING INTERLOCKING CUBES |
|---|---|

> **ANSWERS B-73 through B-77 — Student book pages 79–81**
> **Guided Practice:** B-73 See next page.
> **Independent Practice B-74 to B-77** See next page.

**LESSON PREPARATION**

**SKILL LEVEL**
Requires some reading and manual skill development (typical of first-grade students). Can be used as enrichment for kindergarten students.

**OBJECTIVE AND MATERIALS**
OBJECTIVE: Students will use interlocking cubes to build combinations from a given set of cubes.

58                    © 2000 CRITICAL THINKING BOOKS & SOFTWARE • WWW.CRITICALTHINKING.COM • 800-458-4849

MATERIALS: 2 red, 2 blue, and 2 yellow cubes for each student • transparency of student book page 79

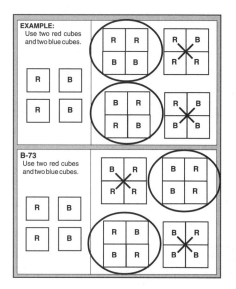
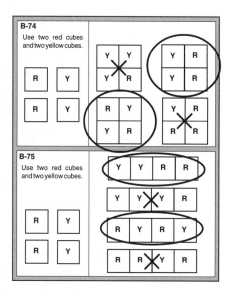
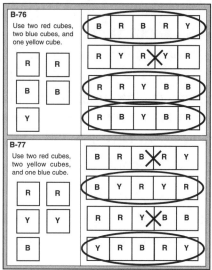

## TEACHING SUGGESTIONS

Q: Ask the students to identify objects in the classroom which are *wholes* made up of geometric shapes. Note how the part appears within the whole.
A: Ceiling tiles, floor tiles, brick or concrete block walls, window panes, etc.

**MODEL LESSON**

## LESSON

### Introduction

Q: Sometimes when you put a puzzle together, the parts don't look like you expect they should.

- Hold out 4 cubes: 2 red and 2 blue. Snap the cubes together in different arrangements.

### Explaining the Objective to Students

Q: In this exercise, you will build combinations of cubes. You will decide which combination you can build with a set of cubes.

BEGINNING BUILDING THINKING SKILLS LESSON PLANS                    FIGURAL SIMILARITIES AND DIFFERENCES

### Class Activity

- Using the 4 given cubes, ask the students to show that the circled items in the EXAMPLE on page 79 can be built.

  Q: Open your books to page 79 and build the cube combinations that are circled in the EXAMPLE.

- Give students time to build with the cubes.

  Q: Why are the two combinations on the right crossed out?

    A: They are made using 3 cubes of the same color and we have only 2 cubes of each color.

### GUIDED PRACTICE

EXERCISE: **B-73**

- Give students sufficient time to complete these exercises. Ask students to discuss and explain their answers.

### INDEPENDENT PRACTICE

- Assign exercises **B-74** through **B-75** to first-grade students.

- Assign exercises **B-74** through **B-77** to second-grade students.

### THINKING ABOUT THINKING

Q: What did you pay attention to when you combined cubes?

1. I found the correct colored cubes.

2. I moved the cubes over the figures to check that I could build the figure with the given cubes combined.

3. I checked that the colors matched the pattern.

4. I checked that my construction matched the figure.

### PERSONAL APPLICATION

Q: When do you need to combine objects?

   A: Examples include assembling toys, doing picture puzzles

**EXERCISES B-78 to B-86**

# COVERING SHAPES WITH EQUAL PARTS—BLOCKS

**ANSWERS B-78 through B-86 — Student book pages 82–5**
**Guided Practice: B-78 to B-80** See next page.
**Independent Practice: B-81** through **B-86** See next page.

**LESSON PREPARATION**

### SKILL LEVEL

Requires no reading or writing skill development (typical of kindergarten students).

### OBJECTIVE AND MATERIALS

OBJECTIVE: Students will use attribute blocks to cover a whole figure with equal parts.

MATERIALS: Attribute blocks • transparency of student lesson book page 82

BEGINNING BUILDING THINKING SKILLS LESSON PLANS    FIGURAL SIMILARITIES AND DIFFERENCES

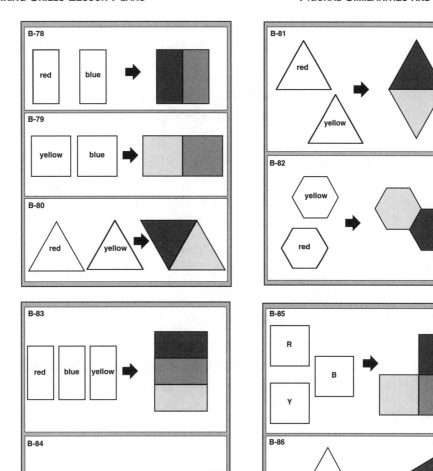

**TEACHING SUGGESTIONS**
Review the concepts of one-half and one-third, if appropriate for your class. Encourage students to use shape names when discussing their answers. Reinforce the names *rectangle, square, triangle,* and *trapezoid.*

**MODEL LESSON** | **LESSON**

**Introduction**
- Hold up a sheet of paper.
  Q: It is easy to fold a sheet of paper exactly in half. Note: First fold the paper vertically.

- Practice "whole" and "half" by alternately showing the unfolded whole and the folded half.
  Q: (Holding the unfolded sheet) This is a whole sheet of paper. (Fold the sheet.) What part of the sheet of paper can you see now?
    A: I can see one-half of the sheet of paper.

- Repeat until the students show an understanding of half and whole.

**BEGINNING BUILDING THINKING SKILLS LESSON PLANS**                    **FIGURAL SIMILARITIES AND DIFFERENCES**

- Hold up a second sheet of paper.
  Q: I can also fold a sheet of paper exactly in half a second way. (Fold the paper horizontally.)

### Explaining the Objective to Students
Q: You will use attribute blocks to cover figures. The attribute blocks are equal parts of the whole figure.

### Class Activity
- Distribute small attribute blocks (each pair of students needs: three small triangles of the same color, three small squares of another color, and three small rectangles of a third color).

- Project the transparency of page 82.

  Q: Open your books to page 82, exercise **B-78**. Cover the blank space with two rectangles.

- Give students time to work.

- On the transparency, draw a line in the figure to outline the two shapes.
  Q: Draw a line on the figure to outline the two shapes.
  Q: How has the figure been divided?
   A: The shape has been divided into equal parts.

  Q: What is each part called?
   A: Each part is one-half of the whole figure.

### GUIDED PRACTICE
EXERCISES: **B-79** and **B-80**
- Give students sufficient time to complete these exercises. Ask students to discuss and explain their answers.

### INDEPENDENT PRACTICE
- Assign exercises **B-81** through **B-86**.
- Use exercises **B-83—B-86** to introduce the concept of thirds if it is appropriate for your students.

### THINKING ABOUT THINKING
Q: What did you pay attention to when you combined blocks?
 1. I found the two blocks to be combined.

 2. I moved the blocks over the figure to check that I could fit them on the diagram.

 3. I checked that my construction matched the figure.

### PERSONAL APPLICATION
Q: When do you need to combine objects?
 A: Assembling toys, doing picture puzzles

BEGINNING BUILDING THINKING SKILLS LESSON PLANS                FIGURAL SIMILARITIES AND DIFFERENCES

**EXERCISES B-87 to B-92** | **COVERING SHAPES WITH EQUAL PARTS—CUBES**

**ANSWERS B-87 through B-92 — Student book pages 86–7**
**Guided Practice: B-87–8** See below
**Independent Practice: B-89–92** See below

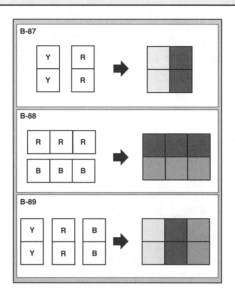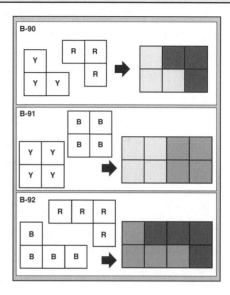

**LESSON PREPARATION**

**SKILL LEVEL**
Requires the manual skill and concentration typical of first-grade students. Can be used as an enrichment activity for advanced kindergarteners.

**OBJECTIVE AND MATERIALS**
OBJECTIVE: Students will use interlocking cubes to cover a whole figure with equal parts.
MATERIALS: Interlocking cubes (4 yellow, 4 blue, and 4 red per student) • transparency of page 86 of student lesson book

**TEACHING SUGGESTIONS**
Identify objects in the classroom which are whole designs made up of geometric shapes.
    Q: Which are the parts within the whole?
      A: Ceiling tiles, floor tiles, brick or concrete block walls, window panes, etc. are parts of this room.

**MODEL LESSON**

**LESSON**

**Introduction**
- Distribute two sheets of paper to each student. Hold up a sheet of paper.
  Q: You have two sheets of paper. Fold one of them to show how it can be divided into equal parts.
    A: Check students' work.

  Q: Fold the second sheet in a different way to divide it into equal parts.

**Explaining the Objective to Students**
    Q: In each exercise, you will build two equal shapes with interlocking cubes. You will practice covering a figure with these equal parts.

© 2000 CRITICAL THINKING BOOKS & SOFTWARE • WWW.CRITICALTHINKING.COM • 800-458-4849    63

BEGINNING BUILDING THINKING SKILLS LESSON PLANS   FIGURAL SIMILARITIES AND DIFFERENCES

**Class Activity**
- Each student needs twelve interlocking cubes: four blue cubes, four red cubes, and four yellow cubes.
  Q: Open your books to exercise **B-87** on page 86. Use interlocking cubes to build the two combinations at the top of the page.
- Give students time to build with the cubes.
  Q: Cover the blank square on the right with the two equal parts you made.
  Q: Remove the parts and draw a line down the middle of the square to show how you covered it. Color the square to match the cubes.

**GUIDED PRACTICE**
EXERCISES: **B-88**
- Give students sufficient time to complete these exercises. Ask students to discuss and explain their answers.

**INDEPENDENT PRACTICE**
- Assign exercises **B-89** through **B-92**.

**THINKING ABOUT THINKING**
  Q: What did you pay attention to when you covered the figure?
  1. I first combined the cubes to make two equal parts.
  2. I moved the parts over the figure to check that I could cover it with the cubes combined.
  3. I checked that my construction matched the figure.

**PERSONAL APPLICATION**
  Q: When do you need to combine objects?
  A: Assembling toys, doing picture puzzles

**EXERCISES B-93 to B-95**

## COMBINING SHAPES MADE WITH CUBES

> **ANSWERS B-93 through B-95 — Student book pages 88–90**
> **Guided Practice: B-93** see below
> **Independent Practice: B-94–5** see below and next page

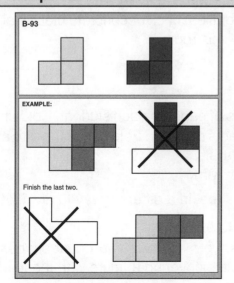

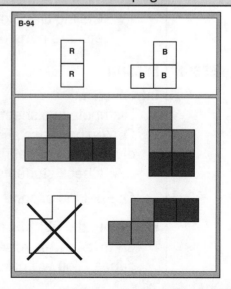

64   © 2000 CRITICAL THINKING BOOKS & SOFTWARE • WWW.CRITICALTHINKING.COM • 800-458-4849

BEGINNING BUILDING THINKING SKILLS LESSON PLANS                FIGURAL SIMILARITIES AND DIFFERENCES

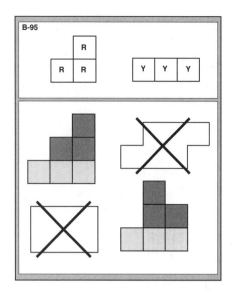

**LESSON PREPARATION**

**SKILL LEVEL**
Requires the manual skill and concentration typical of first-grade students.

**OBJECTIVE AND MATERIALS**
OBJECTIVE: Students will combine shapes made from interlocking cubes
MATERIALS: Transparency of student lesson book page 88 • 3 red, 3 blue, and 3 yellow interlocking cubes for each student

**TEACHING SUGGESTIONS**
Reinforce the terms *combining, constructed, construction*.

**MODEL LESSON**

**LESSON**

**Introduction**
   Q: Sometimes when you put a puzzle together, the pieces don't seem to fit. Sometimes the pieces need to be turned in order to make them fit.

• Build the two "L-shaped" figures shown at the top of page 88.
   Q: Notice that there are many ways that I can put these two shapes together.

**Explaining the Objective to Students**
   Q: In this lesson, you will build two shapes with interlocking cubes. You will practice putting those shapes together.

**Class Activity**
• Each student needs six interlocking cubes (3 blue and 3 red). Project transparency of page 88.
   Q: Open your books to exercise **B-93** on page 88 and build the two cube combinations shown at the top of the page.

• Give students time to build with the cubes.
   Q: Move your constructions to cover the shaded figure.
   Q: Since you can make that shape, the drawing has been shaded.
   Q: Move your constructions to the right and try to cover the drawing that has been crossed out. Why can't you make the figure that has an "X" through it?

© 2000 CRITICAL THINKING BOOKS & SOFTWARE • WWW.CRITICALTHINKING.COM • 800-458-4849        65

A: The lower part of the figure is a row of cubes without a "bend" or "L-shape."

Q: You will color the figures that you can make with your two constructions. You will draw an "X" through the ones you cannot make with your two constructions.

Q: Decide which of the two figures on the bottom of the page can be made by combining the two shapes.

- Allow activity time.

Q: Color the figure to show how you put the two shapes together to make it. Draw an "X" through the figures that you cannot make.

**GUIDED PRACTICE**
EXERCISE: **B-93**

**INDEPENDENT PRACTICE**
- Assign exercises **B-94** through **B-95**.

**THINKING ABOUT THINKING**
Q: What did you pay attention to when you covered the figure?
1. I used cubes to build the two shapes.
2. I moved my constructions over the figure to check if I could build the figure with my constructions.
3. I checked that my construction matched the figure.

**PERSONAL APPLICATION**
Q: When do you need to combine objects?
A: Assembling toys, doing picture puzzles

**EXERCISES B-96 to B-98**

## COMBINING SHAPES

**ANSWERS B-96 through B-98 — Student book pages 91–2**
**Guided Practice: B-96** See below
**Independent Practice: B-97** to **B-98** See below

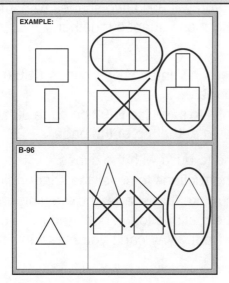
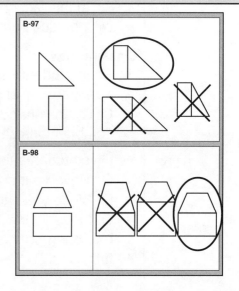

BEGINNING BUILDING THINKING SKILLS LESSON PLANS
FIGURAL SIMILARITIES AND DIFFERENCES

**LESSON PREPARATION**

**SKILL LEVEL**
Requires the concentration and visual discrimination typical of first grade students.

**OBJECTIVE AND MATERIALS**
OBJECTIVE: Students will see which figures can be made by combining shapes.
MATERIALS: Transparency of student book page 91

**MODEL LESSON**

**LESSON**

**Introduction**
Q: You have put blocks or cubes together in many ways. In these exercises, you will use drawings instead of blocks or cubes.

**Class Activity**
- Cut out shapes the same size as the ones in the example on page 96. Project the transparency of student book page 91. Ask a student to show which of the figures can be made by moving the paper cutouts around.

Q: Open your book to page 91 and follow the demonstration.

Q: Why was one figure crossed out?
    A: It was made from a rectangle that was wider than the one we were using.

Q: Do exercise **B-96**.
- Check students' work.

**GUIDED PRACTICE**
EXERCISE: **B-96**

**INDEPENDENT PRACTICE**
- Assign exercises **B-97** through **B-98**.

**THINKING ABOUT THINKING**
Q: What did you pay attention to when you combined shapes?
1. I looked carefully at two shapes to be combined.
2. I looked carefully at the parts of the figures to be made.
3. I imagined the parts stacked on top of the figure.
4. I decided if the parts fit.
5. If both parts fit I circled the figure.

**PERSONAL APPLICATION**
Q: When do you need to combine objects?
    A: Assembling toys, doing picture puzzles.

**EXERCISES B-99 to B-100**

# COMPARING SHAPES

**ANSWERS B-99 through B-100 — Student book pages 93–4**
**Guided Practice: B-99** See next page.
**Independent Practice: B-100** See next page.

© 2000 CRITICAL THINKING BOOKS & SOFTWARE • WWW.CRITICALTHINKING.COM • 800-458-4849
67

# BEGINNING BUILDING THINKING SKILLS LESSON PLANS
## FIGURAL SIMILARITIES AND DIFFERENCES

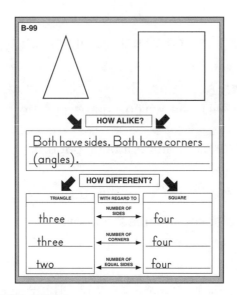
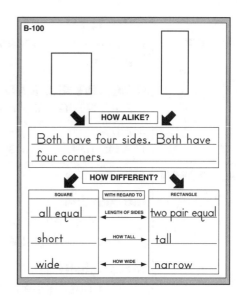

**LESSON PREPARATION**

**SKILL LEVEL**
Requires reading terms or short directions and writing short sentences (typical of second-grade students)

**OBJECTIVE AND MATERIALS**
OBJECTIVE: Students will use a graphic organizer to compare and contrast two shapes.
MATERIALS: Transparency of student lesson book page 93 • Transparency Master 6 page 330 (optional)

**TEACHING SUGGESTIONS**
- Students may use their fingers or rulers to confirm whether the figures are the same height.
- Students may name additional similarities: straight sides, same color. In **B-99** they may recognize that the figures do not have the same width.
- Reinforce the following terms: *triangle, rectangle, square, corners, tall, short, wide, narrow, sides,* and *equal* sides.
- To extend this lesson use the blank comparison graphic organizer Transparency Master 6. Us it to compare other shapes. Examples: rectangle and trapezoid, trapezoid and rhombus, trapezoid and parallelogram, etc.

**MODEL LESSON**

**LESSON**

**Introduction**
Q: We have compared attribute block shapes and shapes made from interlocking cubes.

**Explaining the Objective to Students**
- Project transparency of page 93.
  Q: Open your books to exercise **B-99** on page 93. Look at the two figures. What do both shapes have?
     A: Both shapes have straight sides.

  Q: This is one way that the shapes are alike. Write "Both shapes have

BEGINNING BUILDING THINKING SKILLS LESSON PLANS                    FIGURAL SIMILARITIES AND DIFFERENCES

straight sides" on the first line of the "How Alike" box.
Q: What else do both shapes have?
   A: Both shapes have corners (vertices).

Q: This is another way the shapes are alike. Write "Both shapes have corners" on the second line of the "How Alike" box.

- Point to the "How Different" box.
  Q: Finish the chart by answering how the shapes are different with regard to number of sides, corners, and number of equal sides.

- Give students sufficient time to complete these exercises. Ask students to discuss and explain their answers.

## INDEPENDENT PRACTICE
- Assign exercise **B-100.**

## THINKING ABOUT THINKING
Q: What did you pay attention to when you compared shapes?
   1. I paid attention to the important characteristics in the two shapes.

   2. I gave names to those characteristics.

   3. I combined the names and characteristics into a description.

   4. I checked to see that my description was complete.

## PERSONAL APPLICATION
Q: When do you need to describe shapes?
   A: When making requests or giving directions.

© 2000 CRITICAL THINKING BOOKS & SOFTWARE • WWW.CRITICALTHINKING.COM • 800-458-4849          69

**Chapter 3**

# FIGURAL SEQUENCES
## (Student book pages 96–115)

**EXERCISES C-1 to C-10**

## COPYING A SEQUENCE OF CUBES

**ANSWERS C-1 through C-10 — Student book pages 96–7**
**Guided Practice: C-1** through **C-3** Check students' work and/or ask student pairs to check each others' work.
**Independent Practice: C-4** through **C-10** Check students' work and/or ask student pairs to check each others' work.

**LESSON PREPARATION**

### SKILL LEVEL
These exercises require the manual skill and concentration typical of kindergarten or first-grade students. Kindergarten students may require teacher repetition of the directions to remember the task and keep pace. Some students may have difficulty fastening the cubes together. (See page xxii for suggestions to help students use interlocking cubes.)

### OBJECTIVE AND MATERIALS
OBJECTIVE: Students will build sequences with interlocking cubes.
MATERIALS: Interlocking cubes (6 red, 6 yellow, and 6 blue) • transparency of student lesson page 96 (optional)

### CURRICULUM APPLICATIONS
<u>Language Arts</u>: Identify letter patterns in decoding unfamiliar words.
<u>Mathematics</u>: Identify repeating geometric patterns.
<u>Science</u>: Identify repeating patterns in leaves, shells, and life cycles.
<u>Social Studies</u>: Identify latitude and longitude.
<u>Enrichment Areas</u>: Do art exercises involving patterns; identify repeating patterns in written music.

### TEACHING SUGGESTIONS
Reinforce the following vocabulary: *sequence, repeating, pattern, interlocking.*

**MODEL LESSON**

### LESSON

#### Introduction
Q: You create a sequence when you put objects of numbers in order like a chain. Some sequences are repeated many times, patterns that you can see in nature or man-made things. A sequence is part of a pattern. Patterns are all around us. Where in this room can you see examples of regular or repeating sequences?
   A: Examples might include fabric in clothing, brick or cement block walls, floor tiles, ceiling tiles, Venetian blinds, leaf arrangements on plants, etc.

#### Explaining the Objective to Students
Q: In this exercise, you will build a sequence of interlocking cubes.

© 2000 CRITICAL THINKING BOOKS & SOFTWARE • WWW.CRITICALTHINKING.COM • 800-458-4849          71

BEGINNING BUILDING THINKING SKILLS LESSON PLANS                    FIGURAL SEQUENCES

**Class Activity**

• Project the transparency of page 96. Uncover one row at a time. Build the sequence shown in exercise **C-1.**
  Q: Use your set of interlocking cubes to build a sequence like this one.

• Check that the students can duplicate the six-cube sequence.
  Q: The colors make a pattern. Describe the colors in the sequence.
    A: The colors are red, blue, red, blue, red, blue.

**GUIDED PRACTICE**
EXERCISES: **C-2** and **C-3**

• Give students sufficient time to complete these exercises. Ask students to discuss and explain their answers.
  Q: Describe the colors in the **C-2** sequence.
    A: The colors repeat the pattern red, blue, yellow, red, blue, yellow.

  Q: Describe the colors in the **C-3** sequence.
    A: The colors repeat the pattern two red, two blue, two red.

**INDEPENDENT PRACTICE**

• Assign exercises **C-4** through **C-10**.

**THINKING ABOUT THINKING**

  Q: What did you pay attention to when you copied a sequence of cubes?
  1. I looked carefully at the colors of the cubes.

  2. I found the cubes that matched the colors in the sequence.

  3. I arranged my cubes like the ones in the diagram.

  4. I checked that I had them in the right order.

**EXERCISES C-11 to C-25**

# WHICH CUBE COMES NEXT?/WHICH CUBE IS MISSING?

> **ANSWERS C-11 through C-25 — Student book pages 98–100**
> **Guided Practice: C-11** through **C-13** See next page.
> **Independent Practice: C-17** through **C-25** See next page.

**LESSON PREPARATION**

**SKILL LEVEL**
These exercises require the manual skill and concentration typical of kindergarten or first-grade students. Kindergarten students may require teacher repetition of the directions to remember the task and to keep pace. Some students may have difficulty fastening the cubes together. (See page xxii for suggestions to help students use interlocking cubes.)

**OBJECTIVE AND MATERIALS**
OBJECTIVE: Students will build sequences with interlocking cubes and find the missing cube(s) in the sequence.
MATERIALS: Interlocking cubes (6 red, 6 yellow, and 6 blue)

© 2000 CRITICAL THINKING BOOKS & SOFTWARE • WWW.CRITICALTHINKING.COM • 800-458-4849

BEGINNING BUILDING THINKING SKILLS LESSON PLANS                                    FIGURAL SEQUENCES

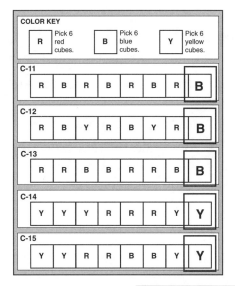
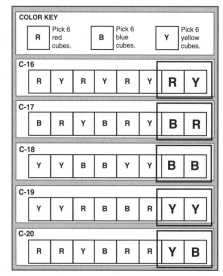
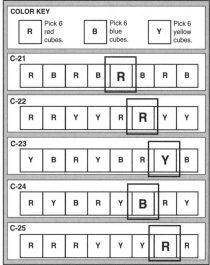

## TEACHING SUGGESTIONS

Reinforce the following terms: *repeating, pattern, interlocking, cube*

Remember the words that students use to describe their choices and use these same words to remind students of the key characteristics of items in these lessons and subsequent ones.

**MODEL LESSON** | **LESSON**

### Introduction

Q: Where in this room can you see patterns of regular or repeating sequences?
  A: Examples may include fabric in clothing, brick or cement block walls, floor tiles, ceiling tiles, Venetian blinds, leaf arrangements on plants, etc.

### Explaining the Objective to Students

Q: In this exercise, you will build a sequence of cubes and find the next cube in the sequence.

© 2000 CRITICAL THINKING BOOKS & SOFTWARE • WWW.CRITICALTHINKING.COM • 800-458-4849          73

BEGINNING BUILDING THINKING SKILLS LESSON PLANS                    FIGURAL SEQUENCES

**Class Activity**

• Build the sequence shown in exercise **C-11** on student page 98.
  Q: Use your cubes to build a sequence like this one.

• Check that students can duplicate a long sequence.
  Q: Say the sequence.
    A: Red, blue, red, blue, red, blue, red, ?

  Q: You can hear the sequence of "red, blue" repeating. So what cube comes next if the sequence stops at red?
    A: Blue comes next in the sequence.

## GUIDED PRACTICE
EXERCISE: **C-12** to **C-13**

• Give students sufficient time to complete these exercises. Ask students to discuss and explain their answers.
  Q: In exercise **C-12**, a sequence of three colors is repeated. What is that sequence?
    A: The sequence is red, blue, yellow, red, blue, yellow.

  Q: If the sequence stops at red, what color cube comes next?
    A: Blue follows red in the sequence because the sequence is red, blue, yellow.

  Q: In exercise **C-13**, there is a sequence of repeating colors. What is the sequence?
    A: The sequence repeats red, red, blue, blue.

  Q: If the sequence stops after one blue, what color cube comes next?
    A: Blue comes next because the sequence is two red cubes and then two blue cubes.

## INDEPENDENT PRACTICE

• Assign exercises **C-14** through **C-25**.
In exercises **C-21** through **C-25**, a colored cube is missing within the sequence, rather than at the end of the sequence. This page may be too difficult for kindergarten students.

## THINKING ABOUT THINKING

  Q: What did you pay attention to when you decided which cube came next?

  1. I looked carefully at the colors of the cubes.

  2. I looked for a sequence of color changes.

  3. I figured out what the next cube would be if the sequence continued.

  Q: When would you need to find the next item in a sequence?
    A: Examples include knitting, carving, weaving, art activities.

74          © 2000 CRITICAL THINKING BOOKS & SOFTWARE • WWW.CRITICALTHINKING.COM • 800-458-4849

BEGINNING BUILDING THINKING SKILLS LESSON PLANS                              FIGURAL SEQUENCES

**EXERCISES C-26 to C-31**

## WHAT GROUP COMES NEXT?

**ANSWERS C-26 through C-31 — Student book pages 101–3**
Guided Practice: **C-26** See below
Independent Practice: **C-27** through **C-31** See below

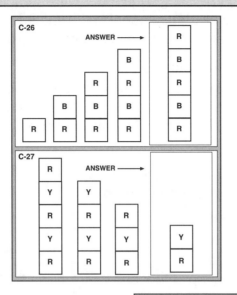
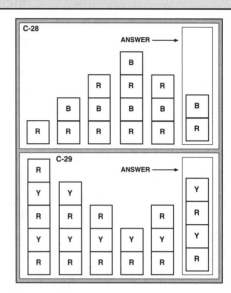
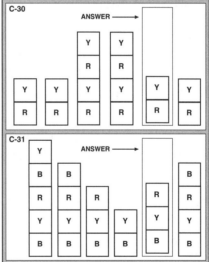

**LESSON PREPARATION**

### SKILL LEVEL
These exercises require the manual skill and concentration typical of kindergarten and first-grade students. Kindergarten students can do this activity with good modeling by the teacher.

### OBJECTIVE AND MATERIALS
OBJECTIVE: Students will complete vertical sequences of interlocking cubes.
MATERIALS: Interlocking cubes (6 red, 6 yellow, and 5 blue) • transparency of TM 7 on page 331.

### CURRICULUM APPLICATIONS
See introduction to chapter on page 71.

BEGINNING BUILDING THINKING SKILLS LESSON PLANS                                FIGURAL SEQUENCES

**MODEL LESSON**

**TEACHING SUGGESTIONS**
See introduction to chapter.

**LESSON**

**Introduction**
   Q: We have practiced making sequences with interlocking cubes. Next we are going to make stair step sequences. Sometimes the sequence is like going up the stairs and sometimes like going down the stairs.

**Explaining the Objective to Students**
   Q: In this exercise, you will build and draw the group of cubes that comes next in a sequence. (Kindergarten students who have difficulty with drawing the cubes can simply place them in the box.)

**Class Activity**
- Project TM 7 exposing only the top left section showing the "stairs" going up.
  Q: Build this set of stairs.

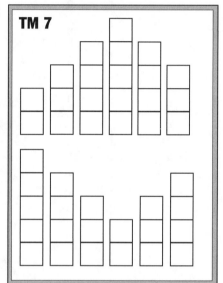

- Allow ample work time.
  Q: Describe these stairs.
     A: They are going up. One cube is added in each change.

- Expose the last two stairs.
  Q: Describe what is happening.
     A: The stairs are going back down. Once cube is taken away in each change.
  Q: Build these stairs and add another set of stairs that will continue the downward pattern.

- Project TM 7, exposing only the bottom left section showing the "stairs" going down.
  Q: Build this set of stairs.

- Allow ample work time.
  Q: Describe these stairs.
     A: They are going down.

- Expose the last two stairs.
  Q: Describe what is happening.
     A: The stairs are going back up.
  Q: Build these stairs and add another that will continue the upward stairs.

**GUIDED PRACTICE**
EXERCISES: **C-26** and **C-27**
- Repeat the above modeling for students as needed.
- Give students sufficient time to complete these exercises.

BEGINNING BUILDING THINKING SKILLS LESSON PLANS                    FIGURAL SEQUENCES

**INDEPENDENT PRACTICE**
- Assign exercises **C-28** through **C-31**.

**THINKING ABOUT THINKING**

Q: What did you pay attention to when you decided which figure came next?

1. I looked carefully at the number of cubes in each stack.

2. I looked for a sequence of changes.

3. I figured out what the next one would be if the sequence continued.

**EXERCISES C-32 to C-37**

# COPYING A SEQUENCE OF BLOCKS

> **ANSWERS C-32 through C-37 — Student book pages 104–6**
> **Guided Practice: C-32** and **C-33** Check students' sequences.
> **Independent Practice: C-34** through **C-37** Check students' sequences.

**LESSON PREPARATION**

**SKILL LEVEL**
These exercises require the manual skill and concentration typical of kindergarten students.

**OBJECTIVE AND MATERIALS**
OBJECTIVE: Students will build sequences of attribute blocks.
MATERIALS: Transparency of student lesson page 104 • small attribute blocks

**MODEL LESSON**

**LESSON**

**Introduction**

Q: We have built some sequences with cubes. Where in this room can you see examples of regular or repeating sequences?

A: Examples may include fabric in clothing, brick or cement block walls, floor tiles, ceiling tiles, Venetian blinds, leaf arrangements on plants.

**Explaining the Objective to Students**

Q: In this exercise, you will build a sequence of attribute blocks.

**Class Activity**
- Project the transparency of page 104, showing the first row. Build the sequence shown on **C-32**.
  Q: Use your set of attribute blocks to build a sequence like this one.

- Check that the students can duplicate the six-block sequence.
  Q: Describe the colors in this sequence.
  A: Three red shapes followed by three yellow shapes.

  Q: Describe the shapes in this sequence.
  A: The shapes repeat: circle, rectangle, square, circle, rectangle, square.

**GUIDED PRACTICE**
EXERCISE: **C-33**
- Give students sufficient time to complete this exercise. Ask students to

© 2000 CRITICAL THINKING BOOKS & SOFTWARE • WWW.CRITICALTHINKING.COM • 800-458-4849          77

discuss and explain their answers.

Q: Describe the colors in this sequence.
A: The colors repeat: red, yellow, blue, red, yellow, blue.

Q: Describe the shapes in this sequence.
A: The shapes repeat: square, circle, rectangle, square, circle, rectangle.

**INDEPENDENT PRACTICE**
- Assign exercises **C-34** through **C-37**.

**THINKING ABOUT THINKING**
Q: What did you pay attention to when you copied a sequence of blocks?
1. I looked carefully at the shapes and colors in the diagram.
2. I found the blocks that matched the shapes and colors in the diagram.
3. I arranged my blocks like the ones in the diagram.
4. I checked that I had them in the right order.

**PERSONAL APPLICATION**
Q: When do you need to follow a pattern?
A: Knitting, carving, weaving, art activities.

**EXERCISES C-38 to C-43**

# WHICH BLOCK COMES NEXT?

**ANSWERS C-38 through C-43 — Student book pages 107–9**
**Guided Practice: C-38** See below
**Independent Practice: C-39** through **C-43** See below

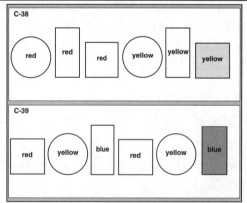
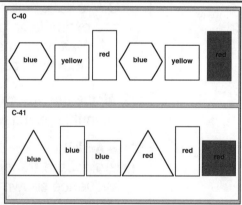
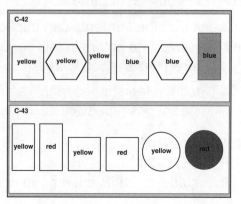

**BEGINNING BUILDING THINKING SKILLS LESSON PLANS**

**FIGURAL SEQUENCES**

**LESSON PREPARATION**

**SKILL LEVEL**
These exercises require the manual skill and concentration typical of kindergarten students. Kindergarten students may require teacher repetition of the directions to remember the task and keep pace.

**OBJECTIVE AND MATERIALS**
OBJECTIVE: Students will build sequences with attribute blocks and identify the next block in the sequence.
MATERIALS: Small attribute blocks

**MODEL LESSON**

**LESSON**

**Introduction**
> Q: Where can you see examples of regular or repeating patterns?
>> A: Examples may include patterns in clothing fabric, brick or cement block walls, floor tiles, ceiling tiles, Venetian blinds, leaf arrangements on plants, etc.

**Explaining the Objective to Students**
> Q: In this exercise, you will build a sequence of attribute blocks and then find the next block in the sequence.

**Class Activity**
• Build the sequence shown in exercise **C-38** on student page 107.
> Q: Use your set of blocks to build a sequence like this one.

• Check that the students can duplicate the five-block partial sequence.
> Q: What color comes next? Explain your answer.
>> A: A yellow block comes next because three red blocks are followed by three yellow blocks. (This is like exercise **C-32**.)

> Q: What shape comes next? Explain your answer.
>> A: A square comes next because the sequence of shapes is square, circle, rectangle.

**GUIDED PRACTICE**
EXERCISE: **C-38**
• Give students sufficient time to complete this exercise. Ask students to discuss and explain their answers.
> Q: What color comes next? Explain your answer.
>> A: A blue block comes next because the color sequence is red, yellow, blue. (This is like exercise **C-33**.)

> Q: What shape comes next? Explain your answer.
>> A: A rectangle comes next because the sequence of shapes is square, circle, rectangle.

**INDEPENDENT PRACTICE**
• Assign exercises **C-39** through **C-43**.

**THINKING ABOUT THINKING**
> Q: What did you pay attention to when you decided which block came next?

© 2000 CRITICAL THINKING BOOKS & SOFTWARE • WWW.CRITICALTHINKING.COM • 800-458-4849

BEGINNING BUILDING THINKING SKILLS LESSON PLANS                    FIGURAL SEQUENCES

1. I looked carefully at the colors of the blocks.

2. I looked for a sequence of changes of color and shape.

3. I figured out that what the next one would be if the sequence continued.

4. I checked that other blocks didn't fit the sequence.

**PERSONAL APPLICATION**

Q: When do you need to make or figure out the next thing in a pattern?
A: Knitting, carving, weaving, art activities.

**EXERCISES C-44 to C-48**

# DESCRIBING SEQUENCES OF CUBES

**ANSWERS C-44 through C-48 — Student book pages 110–2**
**Guided Practice: C-44** This sequence of colors is yellow, red, yellow, red, yellow.
**Independent Practice: C-45** This sequence of colors is red, yellow, blue, red, yellow, blue. **C-46** This sequence of colors is two red, two yellow, two red, two yellow. **C-47** This sequence of colors is yellow, blue, blue, yellow, blue, blue. **C-48** This sequence of colors is one blue, two red, and three yellow cubes.

**LESSON PREPARATION**

## SKILL LEVEL

Requires reading short directions and writing short sentences (typical of second-grade students). Kindergarten and first-grade students can do this activity orally.

## OBJECTIVE AND MATERIALS

OBJECTIVE: Students will observe and describe sequences.
MATERIALS: Transparency of student lesson page 110 • interlocking cubes

## CURRICULUM APPLICATIONS

Language Arts: Write observations.
Mathematics: Identify number sequences, simple bar graphs
Science: Recognize stages in the development of plants or animals
Social Studies: Develop a time line pattern
Enrichment Areas: Create art projects having repeated patterns

## TEACHING SUGGESTIONS

• Descriptions can be oral if appropriate for your students. Ask students to name the colors they used as they describe their sequences.

• Remember the words that students use to describe their choices and use these same words to remind students of the key characteristics of items in these lessons and subsequent ones.

**MODEL LESSON**

## LESSON

### Introduction

Q: Name the kinds of sequences we have seen.
A: Changing number and color of cubes, stacking cubes (stair steps)

80            © 2000 CRITICAL THINKING BOOKS & SOFTWARE • WWW.CRITICALTHINKING.COM • 800-458-4849

BEGINNING BUILDING THINKING SKILLS LESSON PLANS                    FIGURAL SEQUENCES

### Explaining the Objective to Students

Q: In this exercise, you will study a sequence, then write a description of that sequence.

### Class Activity

• Project transparency of page 110 or build a "red-blue" sequence of cubes.
  Q: Look at the first four cubes. How are they changing?
    A: Red, blue, red, blue

  Q: Look at the whole pattern. Are all the cubes changing in the same way?
    A: Yes, the red-blue sequence continues.

  Q: Count the number of red-blue changes. Write a description.

### GUIDED PRACTICE

EXERCISE: **C-44**

• Give students sufficient time to complete this exercise. Ask students to discuss and explain their answers.

### INDEPENDENT PRACTICE

• Assign exercises **C-45** through **C-48**.

### THINKING ABOUT THINKING

Q: What did you pay attention to in order to write your description?
  1. I looked carefully at the number and color of the cubes.

  2. I looked for a pattern of change.

  3. I wrote (or spoke) a description of what I observed.

### PERSONAL APPLICATION

Q: When do you need to describe a sequence?
  A: When giving instructions that involve a series of steps.

---

**EXERCISES C-49 to C-56**

## DESCRIBING SEQUENCES OF SHAPES

> **ANSWERS C-49 through C-56 — Student book pages 113–5**
> **Guided Practice: C-49** This sequence of large shapes is triangle, square, triangle, square.
> **Independent Practice: C-50** This sequence of shapes is small circle, large circle, small circle, large circle. **C-51** This sequence of shapes is large triangle, small triangle, large triangle, small triangle. **C-52** This sequence of small shapes is circle, triangle, circle, triangle. **C-53** This sequence of shapes is large square, small square, large square, small square. **C-54** This sequence of shapes is small triangle, small square, large triangle, large square. **C-55** This sequence of shapes is large triangle, large circle, small triangle, small circle. **C-56** This sequence of shapes is two large triangles, two small circles.

---

**LESSON PREPARATION**

### SKILL LEVEL

Requires reading short directions and writing short sentences (typical of second-grade students). Can be done orally with kindergarten and first grade.

© 2000 CRITICAL THINKING BOOKS & SOFTWARE • WWW.CRITICALTHINKING.COM • 800-458-4849          81

BEGINNING BUILDING THINKING SKILLS LESSON PLANS

FIGURAL SEQUENCES

## OBJECTIVE AND MATERIALS

OBJECTIVE: Students will write (or speak) a description of a sequence of changes in shapes.

MATERIALS: Transparency of student lesson page 113 • attribute blocks (optional)

## CURRICULUM APPLICATIONS

Language Arts: Write observations.

Mathematics: Identify number sequences, simple bar graphs

Science: Recognize stages in the development of plants or animals

Social Studies: Develop a time line pattern

Enrichment Areas: Create art projects having repeated patterns

## TEACHING SUGGESTIONS

• Descriptions can be oral if appropriate for your students. Ask students to name the colors they used as they describe their sequences.

• Remember the words that students use to describe their choices and use these same words to remind students of the key characteristics of items in these lessons and subsequent ones.

**MODEL LESSON**

## LESSON

### Introduction

Q: Patterns are all around us. Where in this room can you see examples of regular or repeating patterns?
  A: Patterns in clothing fabric, brick or cement block walls, floor tiles, ceiling tiles, Venetian blinds, leaf arrangements on plants, etc.

### Explaining the Objective to Students

Q: In this exercise, you will study a sequence, then write a description of that sequence.

### Class Activity

• Project transparency of page 113 or build the sequence with attribute blocks.
  Q: Describe the first two shapes of this sequence.
    A: Square then circle

  Q: Look at the next two figures. Are they changes in the same way?
    A: Yes, again the shapes are square followed by a circle.

  Q: You are ready to write a description.

## GUIDED PRACTICE

EXERCISE: **C-49**

• Give students sufficient time to complete this exercise. Ask students to discuss and explain their answers.

## INDEPENDENT PRACTICE

• Assign exercises **C-50** through **C-56**.

82       © 2000 CRITICAL THINKING BOOKS & SOFTWARE • WWW.CRITICALTHINKING.COM • 800-458-4849

**THINKING ABOUT THINKING**

Q: What did you pay attention to when you decided how to write your description?

1. I named the shape and looked carefully at its size.

2. I looked for a pattern of changes.

3. I wrote (or spoke) a description of what I observed.

**PERSONAL APPLICATION**

Q: When do you need to describe a sequence?

A: When giving instructions that involve a series of steps.

**Chapter 4**

# FIGURAL CLASSIFICATION
(Student book pages 118–180)

## GENERAL INFORMATION

### CURRICULUM APPLICATIONS
Language Arts: Decoding words as reading readiness; recognizing sentence types from punctuation marks; forming letters
Mathematics: Recognizing properties of polygons.
Science: Classifying natural objects by shape (leaves, fish, shells, etc.)
Social Studies: Identifying road signs from their shape
Enrichment Areas: Distinguishing note values in printed music

### PERSONAL APPLICATION
Q: When do you need to classify objects by shape, color, or size?
A: Sorting eating or cooking utensils, sorting construction toys or tools, sorting edge pieces from interior pieces in a picture puzzle, organizing objects or materials at home or in school

**EXERCISES D-1 to D-8**

## COMPARING ONE CHARACTERISTIC

ANSWERS D-1 through D-8 — Student book pages 118–20
**Guided Practice: D-1, D-2** See below.
**Independent Practice: D-3** through **D-8** See below and next page.

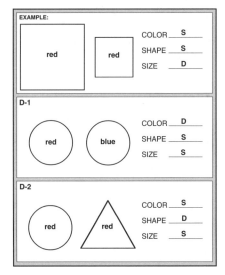
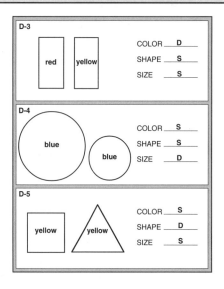

**LESSON PREPARATION**

### SKILL LEVEL
Requires some reading and writing skill development (typical of advanced kindergarten students). The activity can be modified to eliminate the writing (see Teaching Suggestions).

### OBJECTIVE AND MATERIALS
OBJECTIVE: Students will compare two attribute blocks by color, shape, and size.

© 2000 CRITICAL THINKING BOOKS & SOFTWARE • WWW.CRITICALTHINKING.COM • 800-458-4849

BEGINNING BUILDING THINKING SKILLS LESSON PLANS                FIGURAL CLASSIFICATION

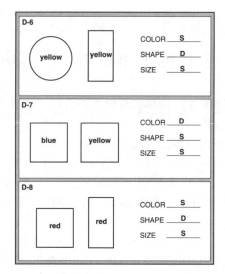

MATERIALS: Transparency of student lesson page 118 • washable transparency markers or colored chalk in three colors • attribute blocks (large and small red triangles, large and small blue circles, small red circle and rectangle, small yellow square and rectangle)

## TEACHING SUGGESTIONS

- Reinforce the following terms: *class, classify, classification, characteristics, attributes.*

- Kindergarten students who have difficulty with writing can circle the word if the attribute is the same for both shapes and cross out the word if the attribute is different for both shapes.

**MODEL LESSON** | **LESSON**

### Introduction

Q: We call ourselves a "class" of students. In this class, everyone is about the same age, meets in the same place, studies the same things, and has the same teacher. *Class* means more than just a school room; it also means <u>a group which has a common characteristic</u>. When we describe a group by using that characteristic, we are <u>classifying</u>.

### Explaining the Objective to Students

Q: In order to classify objects, it is necessary to find the characteristics of the objects. In this exercise, you will practice comparing the characteristics of two shapes that have one characteristic that is different.

### Class Activity

- On a flat surface or chalk rail, place a large red triangle and a large red square. On the chalkboard write

  COLOR: _____

  SHAPE: _____

  SIZE: _____

  Q: How are these shapes alike?
    A: They are both red. They are both large.

86        © 2000 CRITICAL THINKING BOOKS & SOFTWARE • WWW.CRITICALTHINKING.COM • 800-458-4849

BEGINNING BUILDING THINKING SKILLS LESSON PLANS                    FIGURAL CLASSIFICATION

- Write "S" for same on the "Color" and "Size" lines.
  Q: How are these shapes different?
    A: They are different shapes.

- Write "D" for different on the "Shape" line.

- On a flat surface or chalk rail, place a large red triangle and a large yellow triangle.
  Q: How are these shapes alike?
    A: They are both triangles. They are both large.

- Write "S" for same on the "Shape" and "Size" lines.
  Q: How are these shapes different?
    A: They are different colors.

- Write "D" for different on the "Color" line.

### GUIDED PRACTICE
EXERCISES: **D-1, D-2**
- Give students sufficient time to complete these exercises. Ask students to discuss and explain their answers.

### INDEPENDENT PRACTICE
- Assign exercises **D-3** through **D-8**.

### THINKING ABOUT THINKING
  Q: What did you pay attention to when you compared blocks?
  1. I looked to see if the blocks were the same color.
  2. I looked to see if the blocks were the same shape.
  3. I looked to see if the blocks were the same size.

### PERSONAL APPLICATION
See chapter introduction.

**EXERCISES
D-9 to D-23**

# CHANGING ONE CHARACTERISTIC—COLOR, SIZE, OR SHAPE

> **ANSWERS D-9 through D-23 — Student book pages 121–6**
> **Guided Practice: D-9** a small red or a yellow rectangle
> **Independent Practice: D-10** a small red or blue triangle; **D-11** a small red or blue square; **D-12** a small yellow or blue circle; **D-13** a small red or yellow hexagon; **D-14** a small red circle; **D-15** a large blue triangle; **D-16** a large yellow hexagon; **D-17** a small red square; **D-18** any small blue block that is not a circle; **D-19** any small yellow block that is not a triangle; **D-20** any small red block that is not a square; **D-21** any small yellow block that is not a rectangle; **D-22** any small blue block that is not a triangle; **D-23** any small red block that is not a hexagon

**LESSON
PREPARATION**

### SKILL LEVEL
Requires no reading or writing skill development (typical of kindergarten students).

© 2000 CRITICAL THINKING BOOKS & SOFTWARE • WWW.CRITICALTHINKING.COM • 800-458-4849          87

BEGINNING BUILDING THINKING SKILLS LESSON PLANS                    FIGURAL CLASSIFICATION

## OBJECTIVE AND MATERIALS

OBJECTIVE: Students will find attribute blocks that differ by one characteristic (color or shape).

MATERIALS: Transparency of student lesson page 121 • washable transparency markers or colored chalk in three colors • attribute blocks

## TEACHING SUGGESTIONS

* Reinforce the following terms: *class, classify, classification, characteristics, attributes.*

* Kindergarten students will need to be told which characteristic to change on each page.

* If students have difficulty tracing around a block, they can simply place an attribute block in the box.

**MODEL LESSON**

## LESSON

### Introduction

Q: You have practiced comparing the characteristics of two shapes. What characteristics of attribute blocks have you described?

    A: Attribute blocks have three characteristics: color, shape, and size.

### Explaining the Objective to Students

Q: In this lesson, you will find and trace around a block that is different from another block in just one way.

### Class Activity

* On a flat surface or chalk rail place a large yellow hexagon.

    Q: Describe this shape.

      A: It is a yellow hexagon.

    Q: Find another large hexagon of a different color.

      A: Either the large red or large blue hexagon.

    Q: Now find a different yellow shape.

      A: The (circle, square, rectangle, or triangle) is a different yellow shape.

    Q: Find a yellow hexagon of a different size.

      A: The small yellow hexagon is the same shape and color but a different size.

    Q: Notice the example on page 121. Find a block with the same size and shape, but with a different color. Why is the answer correct?

      A: The two small squares are different colors. One is red and the other is blue.

    Q: Is there another correct answer?

      A: Yes, a small yellow square.

    Q: You are now ready to try exercise **D-9**.

### GUIDED PRACTICE

EXERCISE: **D-9**

* Give students sufficient time to complete these exercises. Ask students to discuss and explain their answers.

88      © 2000 CRITICAL THINKING BOOKS & SOFTWARE • WWW.CRITICALTHINKING.COM • 800-458-4849

Q: What blocks are the same size and shape but different colors?
A: The small rectangles are the same size and shape but different colors: red and yellow.

### INDEPENDENT PRACTICE
- Assign exercises **D-10** through **D-23**.
Kindergarten students will need to be told which characteristic to change on each page.

### THINKING ABOUT THINKING
Q: What did you pay attention to in order to find a block with different characteristics?
1. I looked to find a block that fit the color characteristic.
2. I looked to find a block that fit the size characteristic.
3. I looked to find a block that fit the shape characteristic.

### PERSONAL APPLICATION
See the chapter introduction.

**EXERCISES D-24 to D-32**

## COMPARING TWO CHARACTERISTICS

ANSWERS D-24 through D-32 — Student book pages 127–9
**Guided Practice: D-24** See below.
**Independent Practice: D-25–32** See below and next page.

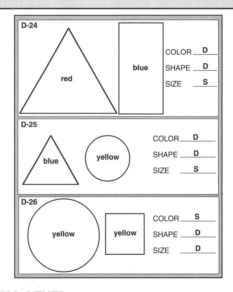
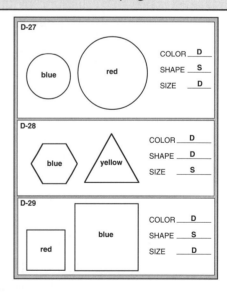

**LESSON PREPARATION**

### SKILL LEVEL
Requires some thinking skill development (typical of advanced kindergartners or first-grade students).

### OBJECTIVE AND MATERIALS
OBJECTIVE: Students will find an attribute block that differs from another in two characteristics (color and shape, size and shape, or size and color).
MATERIALS: Transparency of student lesson page 121 • washable transparency markers or colored chalk in three colors • attribute blocks

BEGINNING BUILDING THINKING SKILLS LESSON PLANS                    FIGURAL CLASSIFICATION

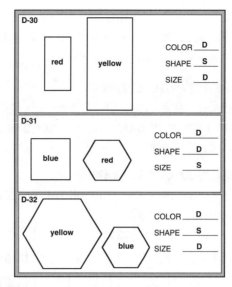

### TEACHING SUGGESTIONS
- Reinforce the following terms: *class, classify, classification, characteristics, attributes.*

**MODEL LESSON**

### LESSON
#### Introduction
Q: You have practiced finding a block that was different from another block in one way. Recall the different changes you found.
  A: I found blocks of the same size and shape, but a different color. I found blocks of the same size and color, but different shape. I found blocks of the same shape and color, but a different size.

#### Explaining the Objective to Students
Q: You will look at a block and then find another block that is different from the first block in two ways.

#### Class Activity
- Use the methodology of the two previous lessons indicating that now two characteristics are being changed.
  Q: In exercise **D-24**, describe the two blocks.
    A: A large red triangle and a large blue square.

  Q: How are these blocks alike?
    A: They are both large attribute blocks.

  Q: How are these blocks different?
    A: They are different colors and different shapes.

### GUIDED PRACTICE
EXERCISES: **D-25** and **D-26**
- Give students sufficient time to complete these exercises. Ask students to discuss and explain their answers.
  Q: In exercise **D-25**, describe the two blocks.
    A: A small blue triangle and a small yellow circle.

  Q: How are these blocks different?
    A: They are different colors and different shapes.

BEGINNING BUILDING THINKING SKILLS LESSON PLANS                    FIGURAL CLASSIFICATION

Q: In exercise **D-26**, describe the two blocks.
   A: A large yellow circle and a small yellow square.

Q: How are these blocks alike?
   A: They are both yellow attribute blocks.

Q: How are these blocks different?
   A: They are different sizes and shapes.

### INDEPENDENT PRACTICE
• Assign exercises **D-27** through **D-32**.

### THINKING ABOUT THINKING
Q: What did you pay attention to in order to find a block with different characteristics?
   1. I looked to find a block that didn't fit one characteristic.
   2. I looked to find a block that didn't fit a second characteristic.
   3. I made sure that the block was different in two ways.

**EXERCISES D-33 to D-47**

# CHANGING TWO CHARACTERISTICS

**ANSWERS D-33 through D-47 — Student book pages 130–5**
**Guided Practice: Example 1:** (possible answers) red square, yellow square, red circle, yellow circle, red rectangle, yellow rectangle, red hexagon, or yellow hexagon; **D-33** any blue or yellow block that is not a hexagon **Independent Practice: D-34** any red or blue block that is not a circle; **D-35** any yellow or blue block that is not a rectangle; **D-36** any red or yellow block that is not a square; **D-37** any red or blue block that is not a triangle; **Example 2:** large red square, large red rectangle, large red triangle, large red hexagon; **D-38** any small yellow block that is not a square; **D-39** any small blue block that is not a hexagon; **D-40** any large blue block that is not a triangle; **D-41** any small red block that is not a circle; **D-42** any small yellow block that is not a rectangle; **Example 3:** large red rectangle, large blue rectangle; **D-43** a small red or yellow triangle; **D-44** a small blue or yellow circle; **D-45** a large red or yellow square; **D-46** a small red or blue hexagon; **D-47** a small blue or yellow square

**LESSON PREPARATION**

### SKILL LEVEL
Requires some thinking skill development (typical of advanced kindergarteners or first-graders).

### OBJECTIVE AND MATERIALS
OBJECTIVE: Students will find an attribute block that differs from another in color and shape, size and shape, or size and color.
MATERIALS: Transparency of student page 130 • washable transparency markers or colored chalk in three colors • attribute blocks

### TEACHING SUGGESTIONS
• Reinforce the following terms: *class, classify, characteristics, attributes*.

© 2000 CRITICAL THINKING BOOKS & SOFTWARE • WWW.CRITICALTHINKING.COM • 800-458-4849          91

BEGINNING BUILDING THINKING SKILLS LESSON PLANS                    FIGURAL CLASSIFICATION

• Because there may be more than one correct answer, check several students' work to assess how well the class as a whole answers correctly. Ask students to check their answers with a partner to check for accuracy.

• Tracing of attribute blocks may be difficult for some kindergarten students. See page xxii of the introduction for suggestions on tracing. Also, students can simply place the correct blocks on the page and the teacher or a student partner can check their work.

**MODEL LESSON**

## LESSON

### Introduction

Q: You have practiced finding a block that was different from another block in two ways. Recall the different changes you found.
  A: I found blocks that were the same size, but a different shape and color. I found blocks that were the same color, but a different size and shape. I found blocks that were the same shape, but a different size and color.

### Explaining the Objective to Students

Q: You will look at a block and then find another block that is different from the first block in two ways.

### Class Activity

• Use the methodology of the previous lesson indicating that now two characteristics are being changed. Project transparency of page 130.
  Q: The example on page 130 asks you to change the color and shape of a blue triangle. Besides blue, what other attribute block colors are there?
  A: Red or yellow

Q: The example also asks you to change the shape. Besides triangles, what are the other attribute block shapes?
  A: Circle, hexagon, rectangle, and square.

Q: In exercise **D-33**, describe the block.
  A: It is a small red hexagon.

Q: Besides red, what other attribute block colors are there?
  A: The colors are blue and yellow.

Q: Name the shapes that are not hexagons.
  A: They are circles, rectangles, triangles, and squares.

Q: There are many attribute blocks that are different from the red hexagon in color and shape.

### GUIDED PRACTICE
EXERCISE: **D-33**

• Give students sufficient time to complete this exercise. Ask students to discuss and explain their answers.
  Q: In exercise **D-33**, what blocks are possible answers?
    A: A small blue circle, small blue rectangle, small blue square, small blue triangle, small yellow circle, small yellow rectangle, small yellow square, small yellow triangle

**BEGINNING BUILDING THINKING SKILLS LESSON PLANS**                    **FIGURAL CLASSIFICATION**

### INDEPENDENT PRACTICE
- Assign exercises **D-34** through **D-47**. Note: You may wish to use these exercises as three separate lessons: changing color and shape (**D-34–7**), changing size and shape (**D-38–42**), changing size and color (**D-43–7**).

### THINKING ABOUT THINKING
Q: What did you pay attention to in order to find a block with different characteristics?
  1. I looked to find a block that didn't fit one characteristic.
  2. I looked to find a block that didn't fit a second characteristic.
  3. I made sure that the block was different in two ways.

**EXERCISES D-48 to D-53**

# GROUPING BLOCKS BY SHAPE, COLOR, OR SIZE

> **ANSWERS D-48 through D-53 — Student book pages 136–8**
> **Guided Practice: D-48** all squares
> **Independent Practice D-49** all rectangles; **D-50** all blue blocks; **D-51** all red blocks; **D-52** all small blocks; **D-53** all small blocks

**LESSON PREPARATION**

### SKILL LEVEL
Requires no reading or writing skill development (typical of kindergarten students.)

### OBJECTIVE AND MATERIALS
OBJECTIVE: Students will follow directions to add more blocks that are the same shape, color, or size to form a group.
MATERIALS: Transparency of student page 136 • washable transparency markers or colored chalk in three colors • all small attribute blocks

### TEACHING SUGGESTIONS
- Tracing of attribute blocks may be difficult for some kindergarten students. See page xxii of the introduction for suggestions on tracing. Also, students can simply place the correct blocks on the page and the teacher or a student partner can check their work.

- For kindergarten students, tell them the attribute that they are looking for on each lesson page.

**MODEL LESSON**

### LESSON

#### Introduction
Q: In the previous lesson, you found a block that was different from another block in two ways. In this exercise, you will find two blocks that are different from another block in one way.

#### Explaining the Objective to Students
Q: In this lesson, you will find other blocks that are like a square or rectangle in one way. First you are asked to find blocks that are the same shape. Then you will find blocks that are the same color, and finally you will find blocks that are the same size.

© 2000 CRITICAL THINKING BOOKS & SOFTWARE • WWW.CRITICALTHINKING.COM • 800-458-4849                    93

BEGINNING BUILDING THINKING SKILLS LESSON PLANS                    FIGURAL CLASSIFICATION

## Class Activity

- Place a large red circle block on a flat surface or chalk rail.

  Q: Name this shape by describing its attributes.

  A: It is a large red circle.

  Q: Find two more blocks that are the same shapes as this large one.

  A: Answers vary (other circles such as a large yellow circle, a small yellow circle, etc.)

  Q: Place them with the large red circle.

- Ask a student to select two more circles and place them in the circles group.

  Q: Name this group of blocks.

  A: It is a group of circles.

- Remove the additional blocks and display only the large red circle.

  Q: What other blocks are the same color as this large red circle?

  A: Any red block that fits that group.

- Have a student pick two or more red blocks and place them with the red circle.

  Q: Name this group of blocks.

  A: It is a group of red blocks.

- Remove the additional blocks and display only the large red circle.

  Q: What other blocks are the same size as this large red circle?

  A: Other large blocks

- Ask a student to select two or more large blocks and place them with the red circle.

  Q: Name this group of blocks.

  A: A group of large blocks.

  Q: You will repeat this lesson with squares and rectangles. Try exercise **D-48**, and I will check your work. (Tell kindergarten students that they are to find two other blocks of the same <u>shape</u>.)

## GUIDED PRACTICE

EXERCISE: **D-48**

- Give students sufficient time to complete this exercise. Ask students to discuss and explain their answers.

## INDEPENDENT PRACTICE

- Assign exercises **D-49** through **D-53**.

- For kindergarten students, tell them the attribute that they are looking for on each lesson page.

## THINKING ABOUT THINKING:

Q: What did you pay attention to in order to find a block with the characteristics of the group?

1. I carefully listened to or read the directions.

2. I looked for other blocks of the same shape, color, or size.

3. I placed the blocks with the original block.

94             © 2000 CRITICAL THINKING BOOKS & SOFTWARE • WWW.CRITICALTHINKING.COM • 800-458-4849

BEGINNING BUILDING THINKING SKILLS LESSON PLANS                    FIGURAL CLASSIFICATION

**EXERCISES D-54 to D-62** | **DESCRIBING A GROUP—WHAT BELONGS?**

**ANSWERS D-54 through D-62 — Student book pages 139–41**
**Guided Practice: D-54** through **D-56** See below.
**Independent Practice: D-57** through **D-62** See below.

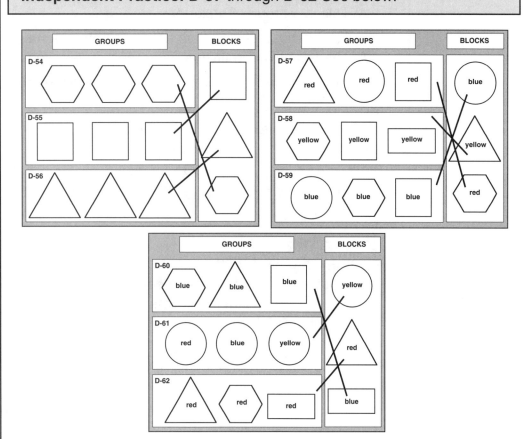

**LESSON PREPARATION**

**SKILL LEVEL**
Requires some thinking skill development (typical of mature kindergarten students).

**OBJECTIVE AND MATERIALS**
OBJECTIVE: Students will match a block with the group to which it belongs.
MATERIALS: Transparency of student page 139 • washable transparency markers or colored chalk in three colors • all small attribute blocks

**TEACHING SUGGESTIONS**
• Ask students to name the group and explain why the block they matched does not fit the group.

**MODEL LESSON** | **LESSON**

**Introduction**
Q: In the previous lesson, you were given an attribute block and asked to find others that were similar to it. The blocks were similar in shape, size, or color.

**Explaining the Objective to Students**
Q: You will match a block with a group of blocks.

© 2000 CRITICAL THINKING BOOKS & SOFTWARE • WWW.CRITICALTHINKING.COM • 800-458-4849      95

BEGINNING BUILDING THINKING SKILLS LESSON PLANS                    FIGURAL CLASSIFICATION

### Class Activity

- Project the transparency of page 139. Ask students to place a block on each of the single blocks on the right side of the page. Point to the top group of blocks.

   Q: Give a name to the group of blocks.
     A: This is a group of hexagons.

   Q: Which of the blocks on the right can belong to this group?
     A: The red hexagon fits into the group of hexagons.

   Q: Draw a line from the group of hexagons to the red hexagon.

- Point to group **D-55**.

   Q: Give a name to the group of blocks.
     A: This is a group of squares.

   Q: Find a block on the right which fits this group.
     A: The yellow square fits into the group of square blocks.

   Q: Draw a line from the group of squares.

### GUIDED PRACTICE

EXERCISE: **D-56** and **D-57**

- Give students sufficient time to complete this exercise. Ask students to discuss and explain their answers.

   Q: Name the **D-56** group.
     A: A group of triangles.

   Q: Which block belongs to this group?
     A: The blue triangle.

   Q: In exercises **D-54** through **D-56**, how were the groups alike?
     A: Each group of attribute blocks has the same shape.

   Q: How do you describe group **D-57**?
     A: A group of red attribute blocks.

   Q: Which block belongs to this group?
     A: The red hexagon belongs in the group of red blocks.

   Q: Draw a line from the red hexagon to the red group.

### INDEPENDENT PRACTICE

- Assign exercises **D-58** through **D-62**.

### THINKING ABOUT THINKING

   Q: What did you pay attention to in order to find a block with the characteristics of the group?

     1. I looked at all the blocks to see how they were alike in color or shape.

     2. I named the group by color or shape.

     3. I looked for another block that had the same color or shape.

### PERSONAL APPLICATION

See chapter introduction.

96          © 2000 CRITICAL THINKING BOOKS & SOFTWARE • WWW.CRITICALTHINKING.COM • 800-458-4849

BEGINNING BUILDING THINKING SKILLS LESSON PLANS          FIGURAL CLASSIFICATION

**EXERCISES D-63 to D-68**

# WHICH BLOCK DOES NOT BELONG?

> **ANSWERS D-63 through D-68 — Student book pages 142–4**
> **Guided Practice: D-63** The blue hexagon does not belong with a group of red blocks. See below.
> **Independent Practice: D-64** The yellow hexagon does not belong with a group of circles. **D-65** The red square does not belong with a group of hexagons. **D-66** The yellow circle does not belong with a group of blue blocks. **D-67** The blue rectangle does not belong with a group of squares. **D-68** The red square does not belong with a group of rectangles. (If your students realize that a square is a special rectangle then all these blocks are members of a group of rectangles.) See below.

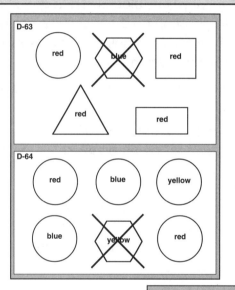
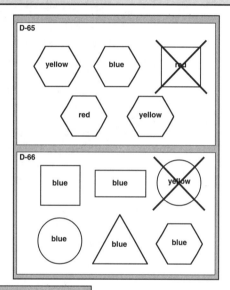
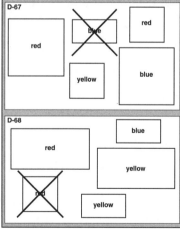

**LESSON PREPARATION**

**SKILL LEVEL**

Requires no reading or writing skill development (typical of kindergarten students).

**OBJECTIVE AND MATERIALS**

OBJECTIVE: Students will select the block that does not belong to the group.
MATERIALS: Transparency of student book page 142 • washable transparency markers or colored chalk in three colors • all small attribute blocks

© 2000 CRITICAL THINKING BOOKS & SOFTWARE • WWW.CRITICALTHINKING.COM • 800-458-4849

BEGINNING BUILDING THINKING SKILLS LESSON PLANS                    FIGURAL CLASSIFICATION

## TEACHING SUGGESTIONS
• Ask students to name the group and explain why the exception does not belong.

**MODEL LESSON**

## LESSON

### Introduction
Q: You have practiced finding a block that belonged to a group of blocks.

### Explaining the Objective to Students
Q: In this exercise, you will make a group of blocks and cross out the drawing of the shape that does not belong to the group.

### Class Activity
• Find a group of four small yellow blocks of different shapes and any small red block. Place this collection on a flat surface or chalk rail.
  Q: Which of these blocks doesn't belong with the others?
   A: The red block does not belong.

  Q: What characteristic is true of all the other blocks?
   A: They are all yellow blocks.

  Q: Why doesn't the red block belong?
   A: The red block does not belong because it's not yellow.

• Mark it with an "X."

• Place a group of small squares of three different colors and a small red triangle on a flat surface or chalk rail.
  Q: Which of these blocks doesn't belong with the others.
   A: The triangle does not belong.

  Q: What characteristic is true of all the other blocks?
   A: They are all squares.

  Q: Why doesn't the triangle belong?
   A: The triangle does not belong because it's not a square.

• Mark it with an "X."

### GUIDED PRACTICE
EXERCISES: **D-63**
• Give students sufficient time to complete these exercises. Ask students to discuss and explain their answers.
  Q: Name the group in exercise **D-63**.
   A: A group of red attribute blocks.

  Q: Which attribute block does not belong?
   A: The blue hexagon does not belong in a group of red blocks.

### INDEPENDENT PRACTICE
• Assign exercises **D-64** through **D-68**.

### THINKING ABOUT THINKING
Q: What did you pay attention to in order to find a block with the characteristics of the group?

98          © 2000 CRITICAL THINKING BOOKS & SOFTWARE • WWW.CRITICALTHINKING.COM • 800-458-4849

BEGINNING BUILDING THINKING SKILLS LESSON PLANS                    FIGURAL CLASSIFICATION

1. I looked to see how four of the blocks were alike.

2. I named the characteristics of the group. (Same color different shape, or same shape different color.)

3. I crossed out the drawing of the block that did not belong with the group.

**PERSONAL APPLICATION**
See chapter introduction.

**EXERCISES D-69 to D-74**

# DESCRIBING A GROUP—ADDING SHAPES

> **ANSWERS D-69 through D-74 — Student book pages 145–7**
> **Guided Practice: D-69** Add any yellow shape.
> **Independent Practice: D-70** Add any hexagon. **D-71** Add any triangle.
> **D-72** Add any yellow block. **D-73** Add any circle. **D-74** Add any red block.

**LESSON PREPARATION**

**SKILL LEVEL**
Requires no reading or writing skill development (typical of kindergarten students).

**OBJECTIVE AND MATERIALS**
OBJECTIVE: Students will make a group of blocks and then add another block that belongs to the group.
MATERIALS: Transparency of student page 145 • washable transparency markers or colored chalk in three colors • all small attribute blocks

**TEACHING SUGGESTIONS**
• Ask students to name the group and explain their addition. Students may draw any small shapes that correctly fit the classification, such as a trapezoid, a parallelogram, or a rhombus.

**MODEL LESSON**

**LESSON**

**Introduction**
Q: In the preceding exercise, you named a group of blocks and identified the block that did not belong to the group.

**Explaining the Objective to Students**
Q: You will make a group of blocks and then find another block that belongs to the group.

**Class Activity**
• Place a group of any four red blocks on a flat surface or chalk rail.
Q: Name this group of blocks.
  A: This is a group of red blocks.

Q: What other block can belong to this group?
  A: Any red block fits this group.

• Ask a student to select a red block and place it in the group.

• On a flat surface or chalk rail, place a group of squares of three different colors.

© 2000 CRITICAL THINKING BOOKS & SOFTWARE • WWW.CRITICALTHINKING.COM • 800-458-4849          99

BEGINNING BUILDING THINKING SKILLS LESSON PLANS FIGURAL CLASSIFICATION

Q: Name this group of blocks.
A: This is a group of squares.

Q: What other block can belong to this group?
A: Any square fits this group.

- Ask a student to select a square and place it in the group.

**GUIDED PRACTICE**

- Project a transparency of page 145 and model exercise **D-69**.
  Q: What do all the blocks in exercise **D-69** have in common?
  A: They are all yellow.

- Give students sufficient time to complete this exercise. Ask students to discuss and explain their answers.

**INDEPENDENT PRACTICE**

- Assign exercises **D-70** through **D-74**.

**THINKING ABOUT THINKING**

Q: What did you pay attention to in order to find a block with the characteristics of the group?

1. I looked at all the blocks to see how they were alike in color or shape.
2. I named the group by color or shape.
3. I looked for another block that had the same color or shape.

**EXERCISES D-75 to D-76**

## COMPLETE THE GROUP—WHAT BELONGS?

**ANSWERS D-75 through D-76 — Student book pages 148–9**
**Guided Practice: D-75** See below.
**Independent Practice: D-76** See below.

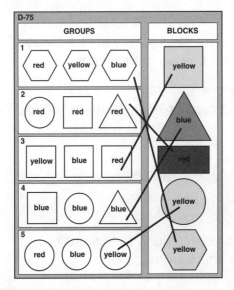
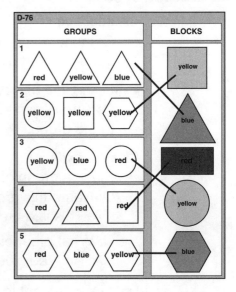

**LESSON PREPARATION**

**SKILL LEVEL**
Requires some thinking skill development (typical of advanced kindergarten students or first-grade students).

BEGINNING BUILDING THINKING SKILLS LESSON PLANS                    FIGURAL CLASSIFICATION

**OBJECTIVE AND MATERIALS**

OBJECTIVE: Students will match blocks to the group to which each belongs.
MATERIALS: Transparency of student page 148 • washable transparency markers or colored chalk in three colors • attribute blocks

**TEACHING SUGGESTIONS**

• Ask students to name the group and explain why the block they matched fits the group.

**MODEL LESSON**

**LESSON**

**Introduction**

Q: In the preceding exercise, you found another block that belonged to a group of blocks.

**Explaining the Objective to Students**

Q: In this activity, you will find the matching block for each of five groups.

**Class Activity**

• Project the transparency of **D-75** on page 148. Point to the top group.
Q: Name this group of blocks.
  A: A group of hexagons

Q: Which block on the right can belong to this group?
  A: The yellow hexagon fits into the group of hexagons.

Q: Draw a line from the group of hexagons to the yellow hexagon.

• Point to the second group.
Q: Name this group of blocks.
  A: This is a group of red blocks.

Q: Find a block on the right which fits this group.
  A: The red rectangle fits into the group of red blocks.

Q: Draw a line from the group of red blocks to the red rectangle.

**GUIDED PRACTICE**

• Assign group 3 of exercise **D-75**.

• Give students sufficient time to complete this exercise. Ask students to discuss and explain their answers.

**INDEPENDENT PRACTICE**

• Assign groups 4 and 5 of exercise **D-75** and all of **D-76**.

**THINKING ABOUT THINKING**

Q: What did you pay attention to in order to find a block with the characteristics of the group?
  1. I looked at all the blocks to see how they were alike in color or shape.

  2. I named the group by color or shape.

  3. I looked for another block that had the same color or shape.

© 2000 CRITICAL THINKING BOOKS & SOFTWARE • WWW.CRITICALTHINKING.COM • 800-458-4849          101

BEGINNING BUILDING THINKING SKILLS LESSON PLANS                FIGURAL CLASSIFICATION

**EXERCISES D-77 to D-80**

# SORTING BLOCKS BY COLOR OR SHAPE

**ANSWERS D-77 through D-80 — Student book pages 150–3**
**Guided Practice: D-77** See below.
**Independent Practice: D-78–80** See below.

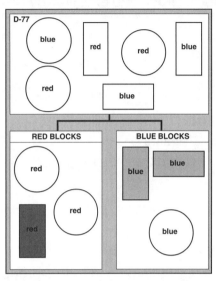
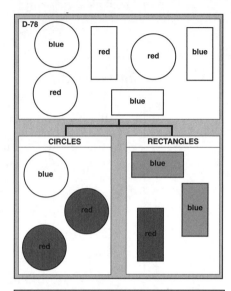
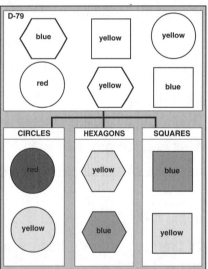
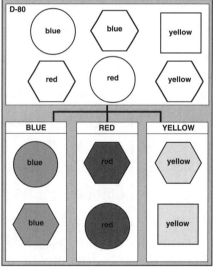

**LESSON PREPARATION**

**SKILL LEVEL**
Requires some reading skill development (typical of advanced kindergarten students).

**OBJECTIVE AND MATERIALS**
OBJECTIVE: Students will sort a group of blocks by color or by shape.
MATERIALS: Attribute blocks (small)

**TEACHING SUGGESTIONS**
- Ask students to explain their answers.
- If students have difficulty tracing the blocks, they can simply sort them into the proper boxes.

102     © 2000 CRITICAL THINKING BOOKS & SOFTWARE • WWW.CRITICALTHINKING.COM • 800-458-4849

BEGINNING BUILDING THINKING SKILLS LESSON PLANS

FIGURAL CLASSIFICATION

**MODEL LESSON** | **LESSON**

### Introduction

Q: In the previous lesson, you matched a block to a group of blocks.

### Explaining the Objective to Students

Q: In this exercise, you will sort blocks first by color and then by shape.

### Class Activity

*   On a flat surface or chalk rail, place one blue hexagon, two red hexagons, one red triangle, and two blue triangles.
    Q: Sort these blocks by color.

*   Give students time to sort the blocks.
    Q: Describe the red blocks.
       A: Two red hexagons and one red triangle

    Q: Describe the blue blocks.
       A: One blue hexagon and two blue triangles

*   Rearrange the same shapes on a flat surface or chalk rail.
    Q: Sort the blocks by shape.

*   Give students time to sort the blocks.
    Q: Describe the triangles.
       A: One is red and two are blue.

    Q: Describe the hexagons.
       A: Two are red and one is blue.

### GUIDED PRACTICE

EXERCISE **D-77**

*   Give students sufficient time to complete these exercises. Ask students to discuss and explain their answers.

### INDEPENDENT PRACTICE

*   Assign exercise **D-78** through **D-80**.

### THINKING ABOUT THINKING

Q: What did you pay attention to in order to sort the blocks?
1. I looked for blocks of the same color or blocks of the same shape.
2. I moved the blocks into their groups.

**EXERCISES D-81 to D-85**

## FIND THE ONE THAT DOESN'T BELONG

**ANSWERS D-81 through D-85 — Student book pages 154–6**
**Guided Practice: D-81** See next page.
**Independent Practice: D-82–5** See next page.

**LESSON PREPARATION**

### SKILL LEVEL

Requires no reading or writing skill development (typical of kindergarten students).

© 2000 CRITICAL THINKING BOOKS & SOFTWARE • WWW.CRITICALTHINKING.COM • 800-458-4849

103

BEGINNING BUILDING THINKING SKILLS LESSON PLANS          FIGURAL CLASSIFICATION

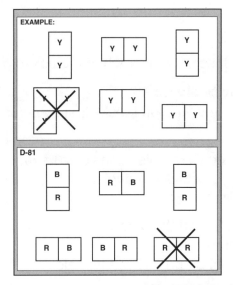

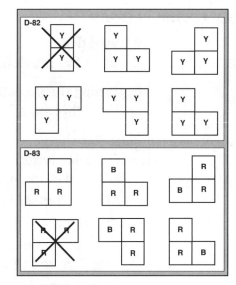

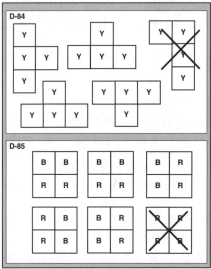

## OBJECTIVE AND MATERIALS
OBJECTIVE: Students will build a group of figures with cubes and find which figure does not belong to the group.
MATERIALS: Interlocking cubes (15 each yellow, red, and blue for each 2 students) • transparency of student page 154

## TEACHING SUGGESTIONS
- Remember the words that students use to describe their choices and use these same words to remind students of the key characteristics of items in these lessons and subsequent ones.

**MODEL LESSON**

### LESSON

#### Introduction
Q: In the previous lesson, you sorted a collection of blocks by color or shape.

#### Explaining the Objective to Students
Q: In this exercise, you will make figures with interlocking cubes and then find the figure that does not belong to the group.

104    © 2000 CRITICAL THINKING BOOKS & SOFTWARE • WWW.CRITICALTHINKING.COM • 800-458-4849

BEGINNING BUILDING THINKING SKILLS LESSON PLANS                                    FIGURAL CLASSIFICATION

**Class Activity**

• Distribute the interlocking cubes.
  Q: Build the six combinations of interlocking cubes shown in the example on page 154.

• Give students time to build the combinations.
  Q: How are all the figures alike?
    A: They are all made with yellow cubes.

  Q: How are five of the figures alike?
    A: They are made from two cubes.

  Q: Which combination does not belong with the others?
    A: The figure made with three cubes.

  Q: That figure has been crossed out.

**GUIDED PRACTICE**

EXERCISE: **D-81**

• Give students sufficient time to complete these exercises. Ask students to discuss and explain their answers.
  Q: In exercise **D-81**, cross out the figure that doesn't belong.
  Q: How are all the figures alike?
    A: They are all made with cubes.

  Q: How are five of the figures alike?
    A: They are made from one red and one blue cube.

  Q: Which combination does not belong with the others?
    A: The figure made with two red cubes.

  Q: Did you cross out the drawing of the red two-cube figure?

**INDEPENDENT PRACTICE**

• Assign exercises **D-82** through **D-85**.

**THINKING ABOUT THINKING**

  Q: What did you pay attention to in finding the figure that did not match?
  1. I looked at the number of cubes used and their colors.

  2. I found the figure that had the wrong number of cubes or the wrong colors.

**EXERCISES
D-86 to D-89**

# SORTING CUBE FIGURES

> **ANSWERS D-86 through D-89 — Student book pages 157–60**
> **Guided Practice: D-86** See next page.
> **Independent Practice: D-87** to **D-89** See next page.

**LESSON
PREPARATION**

**SKILL LEVEL**

Requires some reading skill development (typical of first-grade students).

**OBJECTIVE AND MATERIALS**

OBJECTIVE: Students will construct figures from interlocking cubes and then sort them by shape or by color.

© 2000 CRITICAL THINKING BOOKS & SOFTWARE • WWW.CRITICALTHINKING.COM • 800-458-4849                    105

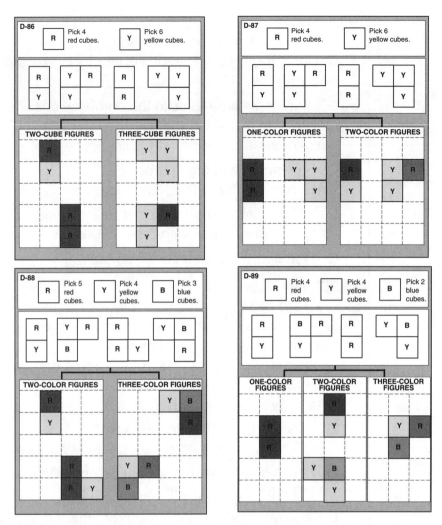

MATERIALS: Interlocking cubes (6 yellow, 6 red, and 6 blue for each 2 students)

## CURRICULUM APPLICATIONS

<u>Language Arts</u>: Classify words by letter pattern, recognize prefixes and suffixes
<u>Mathematics</u>: Classify numbers by place value, sort geometric shapes
<u>Science</u>: Classify natural objects (leaves, fish, shells, etc.) by pattern.
<u>Social Studies</u>: Use a legend to distinguish topographical features on a map (mountains, coastal plains, deserts, etc.), interpret graphs
<u>Enrichment Areas</u>: Classify color families in art, classify music by sound or rhythm pattern (classical, rock and roll, jazz, opera, etc.)

## TEACHING SUGGESTIONS

- Remember the words that students use to describe their choices and use these same words to remind students of the key characteristics of items in these lessons and subsequent ones.

## MODEL LESSON | LESSON

### Introduction

Q: In the previous lesson, you found the cube figure that did not belong in a group.

BEGINNING BUILDING THINKING SKILLS LESSON PLANS                FIGURAL CLASSIFICATION

**Explaining the Objective to Students**
Q: In this exercise, you will build a group of cube figures and then sort the figures by shape or color.

**Class Activity**
- Distribute the interlocking cubes.
  Q: Build the six figures of interlocking cubes shown in exercise **D-86**.

- Give students time to build the figures.
  Q: Sort the figures into two groups: those made from two cubes and those made from three cubes.

- Give students time to sort the figures.
  Q: Now that you have finished sorting your figures, color your drawings to match your answer.

**GUIDED PRACTICE**
EXERCISE: **D-86**
- Using the same figures, sort them by color in exercise **D-87**.

- Give students sufficient time to complete this exercise. Ask students to discuss and explain their answers.

**INDEPENDENT PRACTICE**
- Assign exercises **D-88** through **D-89**.

**THINKING ABOUT THINKING**
Q: What did you pay attention to when you classified the figures?
1. I looked carefully at the details to decide how they are alike (color or shape).
2. I checked to be sure that all the figures have the same characteristic(s).
3. I moved members of the same class into their answer boxes.

**PERSONAL APPLICATION**
Q: Where else might you use classifying something by pattern or color?
A: Sorting art materials, fabrics, or puzzle pieces; sorting laundry by color

**EXERCISES D-90 to D-91**

# FORMING GROUPS

**ANSWERS D-90 and D-91 — Student book pages 161–3**
**Guided Practice: D-90** See next page.
**Independent Practice: D-91** See next page.

**LESSON PREPARATION**

**SKILL LEVEL**
Requires some thinking skill development (typical of advanced first graders or second-grade students).

**OBJECTIVE AND MATERIALS**
OBJECTIVE: Students will use rings to sort blocks by color or shape.
MATERIALS: Transparency of student book pages 161 and 162 • small attribute blocks • two <u>movable</u> circles, hoops, or large rings of some type

© 2000 CRITICAL THINKING BOOKS & SOFTWARE • WWW.CRITICALTHINKING.COM • 800-458-4849          107

BEGINNING BUILDING THINKING SKILLS LESSON PLANS                                    FIGURAL CLASSIFICATION

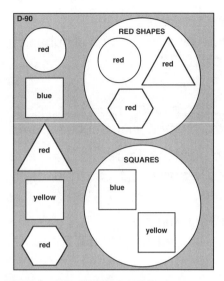
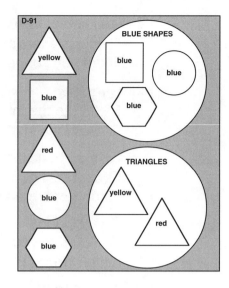

**CURRICULUM APPLICATIONS**
<u>Language Arts</u>: Classifying words into various categories based on word formation rather than meaning (e.g., double consonants words, "ie" words, "-ance" words, etc.).
<u>Mathematics</u>: Doing attribute block exercises, sorting geometric shapes.
<u>Science</u>: Sorting natural objects into overlapping classes.
<u>Social Studies</u>: Interpreting graphic information, using a legend to read a map.
<u>Enrichment Areas</u>: Classifying musical instruments into different types (marching band/orchestra).

**TEACHING SUGGESTIONS**
• Encourage discussion; remember the words that students use to describe their choices and use these same words to remind students of the key characteristics of items in these lessons and subsequent ones.

**MODEL LESSON** | **LESSON**

**Introduction**
Q: You have practiced forming groups in many ways. You have sorted attribute blocks and shapes made from interlocking cubes. You have grouped objects by size, by shape, and by color.

**Explaining the Objective to Students**
Q: In this exercise, you will use grouping circles to sort attribute blocks into groups according to color and shape.

**Class Activity**
• Project a transparency of page 161 and/or place one ring representing yellow shapes and one representing rectangles on a table. Select the attribute blocks that match the ones in the exercise.

• Point to the ring representing yellow shapes.
   Q: This group or class will be yellow shapes.

• Point to the ring representing rectangles.
   Q: This group or class will be rectangles. We will pick out some blocks and put each one into the class that <u>best</u> describes it.

108                © 2000 CRITICAL THINKING BOOKS & SOFTWARE • WWW.CRITICALTHINKING.COM • 800-458-4849

BEGINNING BUILDING THINKING SKILLS LESSON PLANS                    FIGURAL CLASSIFICATION

- Pick up the blue rectangle.
  Q: Which class should this shape fit in, the yellow class or the rectangle class?
    A: The blue rectangle belongs in the rectangle ring.

- Put the block in the rectangle ring. Continue until all five blocks have been placed.

### GUIDED PRACTICE
EXERCISE: **D-90**
- Project the transparency of page 162 and model exercise **D-90**.

- Give students sufficient time to complete this exercise. Ask students to discuss and explain their answers.
  Q: Name the blocks you placed in the grouping circle labeled "red shapes."
    A: The red circle, red rectangle, and the red hexagon belong in the grouping circle labeled "red shapes."

  Q: Name the blocks you placed in the grouping circle labeled "squares."
    A: The blue square and the yellow square belong in the grouping circle labeled "squares."

### INDEPENDENT PRACTICE
- Assign exercises **D-91**.
  Q: Name the blocks you placed in the grouping circle labeled "blue shapes."
    A: The blue square, blue circle, and blue hexagon belong in the grouping circle labeled "blue shapes."

  Q: Name the blocks you placed in the grouping circle labeled "rectangles."
    A: The yellow rectangle and the red rectangle belong in the grouping circle labeled "rectangles."

### THINKING ABOUT THINKING
  Q: What did you pay attention to when you classified the blocks?
  1. I looked at the shape and color of each block.
  2. I checked the sorting circles to see where the block belonged.
  3. I placed the block in the correct sorting circle.

### PERSONAL APPLICATION
  Q: Where else might you use classifying something by shape or color?
    A: Finding art materials, fabrics, or puzzle pieces; sorting laundry by color; stacking items in the kitchen or closet

**EXERCISES
D-92 to D-94**

# FORMING OVERLAPPING GROUPS

> **ANSWERS D-92 through D-94 — Student book pages 165–7**
> **Guided Practice: D-92** See next page.
> **Independent Practice: D-93–4** See next page.

© 2000 CRITICAL THINKING BOOKS & SOFTWARE • WWW.CRITICALTHINKING.COM • 800-458-4849          109

BEGINNING BUILDING THINKING SKILLS LESSON PLANS                    FIGURAL CLASSIFICATION

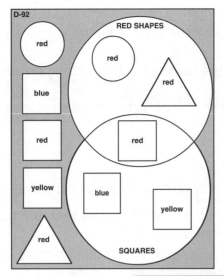
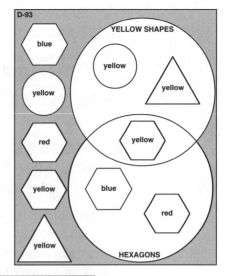
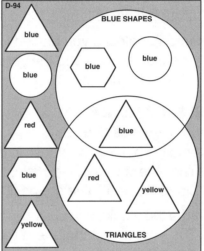

**LESSON PREPARATION**

**SKILL LEVEL**
Requires some thinking skill development (typical of mature first-graders or second-grade students).

**OBJECTIVE AND MATERIALS**
OBJECTIVE: Students will sort attribute blocks according to both color and shape.
MATERIALS: Transparencies of student book page 164 and 165 • attribute blocks • two <u>movable</u> circles, hoops, or large rings of some type

**CURRICULUM APPLICATIONS**
See previous lesson on Forming Groups.

**TEACHING SUGGESTIONS**

- Encourage discussion; remember the words that students use to describe their choices and use these same words to remind students of the key characteristics of items in these lessons and subsequent ones.

**MODEL LESSON**

**LESSON**

**Introduction**

Q: In the last lesson, you sorted blocks by color or by shape. You put the

BEGINNING BUILDING THINKING SKILLS LESSON PLANS                    FIGURAL CLASSIFICATION

blocks having the same color in one grouping circle and the blocks having the same shape in another circle.

### Explaining the Objective to Students

Q: In this exercise, you will sort <u>some</u> shapes using one characteristic and <u>other</u> shapes using two characteristics.

### Class Activity

• Project a transparency of page 164 and/or place one ring or circle representing yellow shapes and one representing rectangles on a table. Select the attribute blocks that match the ones in the exercise.

• Point to the ring representing yellow shapes.
Q: This group or class will be yellow shapes.

• Point to the ring representing rectangles.
Q: This group or class will be rectangles. We will pick out some blocks and put each one into the class that <u>best</u> describes it.

• Pick up the blue rectangle.
Q: Which class should this shape fit in, the yellow class or the rectangle class?
  A: The blue rectangle belongs in the rectangle grouping circle.

• Put the shape into the rectangle grouping circle. <u>Saving the yellow rectangle until last</u>, continue until all other figures have been placed. Hold up the yellow rectangle.
Q: Where does this one belong?
  A: The yellow rectangle belongs in the yellow group (or in the rectangle circle).

Q: Yes, it is yellow (or a rectangle), but that doesn't describe its shape (color), does it?
  A: No, put it in the rectangle (yellow) circle.

Q: Yes, it is a rectangle (yellow), but that doesn't describe its color (shape), does it? We have a real problem here. We have one block and two places to put it. Where can we put a block to show that it is <u>both</u> yellow and a rectangle?

• Students may try to move it back and forth between the yellow class and the rectangle class or place it in the space between the two grouping circles. Encourage students to move the rings. If they do not move the rings, you should then move the rings so that they overlap as shown on page 165.
Q: Does this show the different classes? Are all of the shapes in the rectangle group rectangles? Are all of the shapes in the yellow group yellow? Is the yellow rectangle part of both circles? We call this a diagram of <u>overlapping</u> <u>classes</u>. Overlapping means that some of the shapes or objects fit into more than one class.

### GUIDED PRACTICE

• Project transparency of page 165 and model exercise **D-92**.

© 2000 CRITICAL THINKING BOOKS & SOFTWARE • WWW.CRITICALTHINKING.COM • 800-458-4849                    111

BEGINNING BUILDING THINKING SKILLS LESSON PLANS                    FIGURAL CLASSIFICATION

- When students have had sufficient time to complete these exercises, check their answers by discussion. It is important that students notice and talk about where each figure does not fit, and why, as well as where each figure does fit, and why.

**INDEPENDENT PRACTICE**
- Assign exercises **D-93** and **D-94**.

**THINKING ABOUT THINKING**
   Q: What did you pay attention to when you classified the blocks?
   1. I looked at the shape and color of each block.
   2. I checked to be sure that any block added to the grouping circle had the same characteristic(s).
   3. If a block has the characteristics of both groups, it belongs in the overlapping part of the diagram (intersection).

**PERSONAL APPLICATION**
   Q: When might you need to know if something fits into more than one class?
      A: Finding books or materials in a library, locating products in a grocery store, finding different uses for tools or materials (e.g., using one side of a claw hammer to drive in nails and the other side to pull them out).

**EXERCISES D-95 to D-100**

# OVERLAPPING CLASSES — MATRIX A

> **ANSWERS D-95 through D-100 — Student book pages 169–71**
> **Guided Practice: D-95–6** See below.
> **Independent Practice: D-97** through **D-100** See below and next page.

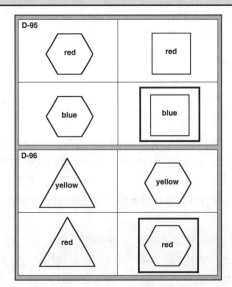
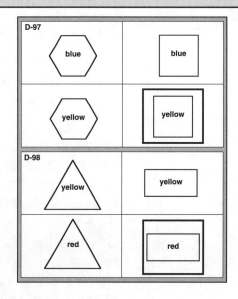

112    © 2000 CRITICAL THINKING BOOKS & SOFTWARE • WWW.CRITICALTHINKING.COM • 800-458-4849

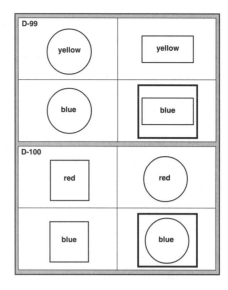

**LESSON PREPARATION**

**SKILL LEVEL**
Requires some thinking skill development (typical of advanced first-graders or second-grade students).

**OBJECTIVE AND MATERIALS**
OBJECTIVE: Students will use a matrix diagram to classify blocks by two characteristics.
MATERIALS: Transparencies of student book pages 168 and 169 • washable transparency marker • all small attribute blocks

**CURRICULUM APPLICATIONS**
Language Arts: Obtaining information from graphs, tables, or schedules.
Mathematics: Making and using arithmetic charts.
Science: Classifying objects or organisms by more than one characteristic (eye color/hair color, for example).
Social Studies: Making a graph or chart of survey results, using matrices to depict data.
Enrichment Areas: Comparing works of art, elements of design, or pieces of music.

**TEACHING SUGGESTIONS**
- Encourage students to use precise vocabulary when describing shape and pattern. Remember the words that students use to describe their choices and use these same words to remind students of the key characteristics of items in these lessons and subsequent ones.

**MODEL LESSON**

**LESSON**

**Introduction**
Q: In the last lesson, we learned that some figures could be classified by more than one characteristic. The overlapping circles diagram that we used to show that relationship is also sometimes called a Venn Diagram.

**Explaining the Objective to Students**
Q: In this exercise, all of the blocks can be classified by two characteristics. To do that, you will use a diagram called a matrix.

**BEGINNING BUILDING THINKING SKILLS LESSON PLANS**                    **FIGURAL CLASSIFICATION**

## Class Activity

*   Project the transparency of page 168

    Q: What do you call the long posts that hold up the roof of a porch?
      A: The posts that hold up a roof are called columns.

    Q: Columns go up and down. What do the blocks in Column 1 have in common?
      A: The blocks in column 1 have the same shape; they are circles.

    Q: What do the blocks in Column 2 have in common?
      A: The blocks in Column 2 have the same shape; they are squares.

    Q: Rows go across. What do the blocks in Row 1 have in common?
      A: The blocks in Row 1 have the same color; they are red.

    Q: What do the blocks in Row 2 have in common?
      A: The blocks in Row 2 have the same color; they are blue.

*   Project the transparency of page 169, exercise **D-95**.

    Q: What do the blocks in Column 1 have in common?
      A: They are the same shape. They are both hexagons.

    Q: If the blocks in a column have the same color, what should the blocks in Column 2 have in common?
      A: The blocks should be squares.

    Q: What do the blocks in Row 1 have in common?
      A: They are red.

    Q: If the blocks in a row have the same shape, what should the blocks in Row 2 have in common?
      A: They should be blue.

    Q: What block belongs in the missing space?
      A: A blue square.

## GUIDED PRACTICE
EXERCISE: **D-96**

*   Give students sufficient time to complete these exercises. Ask students to discuss and explain their answers.

    Q: What do the blocks in Column 1 have in common?
      A: They are the same shape. They are both triangles.

    Q: If the blocks in a column have the same shape, what should the blocks in Column 2 have in common?
      A: The blocks should be hexagons.

    Q: What do the blocks in Row 1 have in common?
      A: They are yellow.

    Q: If the blocks in a row have the same color, what should the blocks in Row 2 have in common?
      A: They should be red.

    Q: What block belongs in the missing space?
      A: A red hexagon

BEGINNING BUILDING THINKING SKILLS LESSON PLANS     FIGURAL CLASSIFICATION

### INDEPENDENT PRACTICE
• Assign exercises **D-97** through **D-100**.

### THINKING ABOUT THINKING
Q: What did you pay attention to when you classified the figures?
1. I looked carefully at the Row and Column headings.
2. I checked to be sure that any figure added to the matrix has the characteristics of both the Row and the Column.

### PERSONAL APPLICATION
Q: When do you need to complete or read a matrix?
A: Using or making charts and schedules, solving puzzles by filling in clues.

**EXERCISES D-101 to D-104**

## OVERLAPPING CLASSES—MATRIX B

**ANSWERS D-101 through D-104 — Student book pages 172–4**
**Guided Practice: D-101** See below.
**Independent Practice: D-102–4** See below.

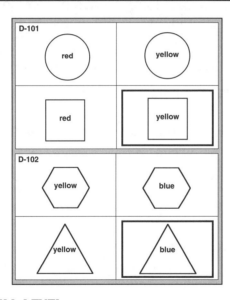
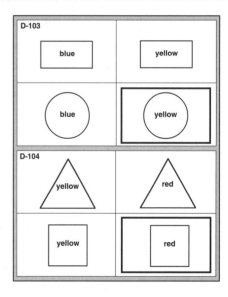

**LESSON PREPARATION**

### SKILL LEVEL
Requires some thinking skill development (typical of advanced first-graders or second-grade students).

### OBJECTIVE AND MATERIALS
OBJECTIVE: Students will use a matrix diagram to classify blocks by two characteristics and find the block that completes the matrix.
MATERIALS: Transparencies of student lesson pages 172 and 173 • washable transparency marker • all small attribute blocks

### CURRICULUM APPLICATIONS
See previous lesson.

BEGINNING BUILDING THINKING SKILLS LESSON PLANS                    FIGURAL CLASSIFICATION

## TEACHING SUGGESTIONS
- Encourage students to use precise vocabulary when describing shape and pattern. Remember the words students use to describe their choices and use these same words to remind students of the key characteristics of items in these lessons and subsequent ones.

**MODEL LESSON**

## LESSON

### Introduction
Q: In the last lesson, we learned about columns and rows and a diagram called a matrix. In those lessons, the columns represented shapes and the rows represented columns.

### Explaining the Objective to Students
Q: In this exercise, the columns represent colors and the rows represent shapes. You will find the attribute block that completes each matrix.

### Class Activity
- Project the transparency of student lesson page 172.
  Q: What do you call the up and down groups?
    A: Those groups are called columns.

  Q: What do the blocks in Column 1 have in common?
    A: The blocks in Column 1 have the same color; they are red.

  Q: What do the blocks in Column 2 have in common?
    A: The blocks in Column 2 have the same color; they are blue.

  Q: Rows go across the page. What do the blocks in Row 1 have in common?
    A: The blocks in Row 1 have the same shape; they are circles.

  Q: What do the blocks in Row 2 have in common?
    A: The blocks in Row 2 have the same shape; they are squares.

- Project the transparency of page 173, exercise **D-101**.
  Q: What do the blocks in Column 1 have in common?
    A: They are the same color. They are both red.

  Q: If the blocks in a column have the same color, what should the blocks in Column 2 have in common?
    A: The blocks should both be yellow.

  Q: What do the blocks in Row 1 have in common?
    A: They are circles.

  Q: If the blocks in Row 1 have the same shape, what should the blocks in Row 2 have in common?
    A: They should both be squares.

  Q: What block belongs in the missing space?
    A: A yellow square.

## INDEPENDENT PRACTICE
- Assign exercises **D-102** through **D-104**.

**116**        © 2000 CRITICAL THINKING BOOKS & SOFTWARE • WWW.CRITICALTHINKING.COM • 800-458-4849

BEGINNING BUILDING THINKING SKILLS LESSON PLANS                    FIGURAL CLASSIFICATION

**THINKING ABOUT THINKING**

Q: What did you pay attention to when you classified the figures?

1. I looked carefully at the Row and Column headings.

2. I checked to be sure that any figure added to the matrix has the same characteristics of both the Row and Column.

**PERSONAL APPLICATION**
See previous lesson.

**EXERCISES D-105 to D-107**

## OVERLAPPING CLASSES—MATRIX C

**ANSWERS D-105 through D-107 — Student book pages 175–8**
Guided Practice: **D-105** See below.
Independent Practice: **D-106–7** See below.

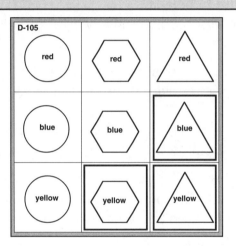

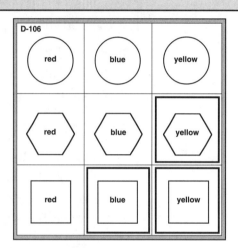

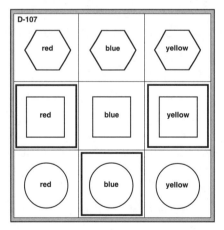

**LESSON PREPARATION**

**SKILL LEVEL**
Requires some thinking skill development (typical of advanced first-graders and second-grade students).

**OBJECTIVES AND MATERIALS**
OBJECTIVE: Students will use a matrix diagram to classify blocks by two characteristics.

© 2000 CRITICAL THINKING BOOKS & SOFTWARE • WWW.CRITICALTHINKING.COM • 800-458-4849      117

BEGINNING BUILDING THINKING SKILLS LESSON PLANS                    FIGURAL CLASSIFICATION

MATERIALS: Transparencies of student lesson pages 175 and 176 • washable transparency marker • all small attribute blocks

**TEACHING SUGGESTIONS**
Encourage students to use precise vocabulary when describing shape and pattern. Remember the words that students use to describe their choices and use these same words to remind students of the key characteristics of items in these lessons.

**MODEL LESSON**

**LESSON**

**Introduction**
Q: In the last two lessons, we learned about columns and rows and a diagram called a matrix. In those lessons, there were two columns and two rows in each matrix.

**Explaining the Objective to Students**
Q: You will solve matrix problems involving three columns and three rows.

**Class Activity**
• Project the transparency of student lesson page 175.
Q: Columns go up and down. What do the blocks in Column 1 have in common?
  A: The blocks in Column 1 have the same shape. They are circles.

Q: What do the blocks in Column 2 have in common?
  A: The blocks in Column 2 have the same shape. They are squares.

Q: What do the blocks in Column 3 have in common?
  A: The blocks in Column 3 have the same shape. They are hexagons.

Q: Rows go across the page. What do the blocks in Row 1 have in common?
  A: The blocks in Row 1 have the same color. They are red.

Q: What do the blocks in Row 2 have in common?
  A: They are the same color, blue.

Q: What do the blocks in Row 3 have in common?
  A: They are the same color, yellow.

• Project the transparency of student page 176, exercise **D-105**.
Q: Columns go up and down. What do the blocks in Column 1 have in common?
  A: The blocks in Column 1 have the same shape. They are circles.

Q: What do the blocks in Column 2 have in common?
  A: They are the same shape. They are hexagons.

Q: What do the blocks in Column 3 have in common?
  A: They have the same shape. They are triangles.

Q: Rows go across the page. What do the blocks in Row 1 have in common?
  A: The blocks in Row 1 have the same color. They are red.

118          © 2000 CRITICAL THINKING BOOKS & SOFTWARE • WWW.CRITICALTHINKING.COM • 800-458-4849

BEGINNING BUILDING THINKING SKILLS LESSON PLANS          FIGURAL CLASSIFICATION

Q: What do the blocks in Row 2 have in common?
    A: They have the same color. They are blue.

Q: What do the blocks in Row 3 have in common?
    A: They have the same color. They are yellow.

Q: If Row 2 represents blue blocks and Column 3 represents triangles, what block belongs in Row 2, Column 3?
    A: A blue triangle belongs in Row 2, Column 3.

Q: If Row 3 represents yellow blocks and Column 2 represents hexagons, what block belongs in Row 3, Column 2?
    A: A yellow hexagon.

Q: Describe the block that belongs in Row 3, Column 3.
    A: A yellow triangle belongs in Row 3, Column 3 because Row 3 is for yellow shapes and Column 3 is for triangles.

## GUIDED PRACTICE
EXERCISE **D-106**
• Give students sufficient time to complete this exercise. Ask students to discuss and explain their answers.

## INDEPENDENT PRACTICE
• Assign exercise **D-107**.

## THINKING ABOUT THINKING
Q: What did you pay attention to when you classified the figures?
1. I looked carefully at the Row and Column headings.

2. I checked to be sure that any figure added to the matrix has the characteristics of both the Row and Column.

**EXERCISES D-108 to D-112**

# DESCRIBING CHARACTERISTICS

**ANSWERS D-108 through D-112 — Student book pages 179–80**
**Guided Practice: D-108** ALIKE: *Both are small squares.* DIFFERENT: *The squares are different colors.*
**Independent Practice: D-109** ALIKE: *Both are small blue blocks.* DIFFERENT: *The blocks have different shapes and the square is larger than the circle.* **D-111** ALIKE: *Both are small squares.* DIFFERENT: *The blocks are different in shape and color.* **D-112** ALIKE: *No characteristics are the same.* DIFFERENT: *The blocks are different in shape, size, and color.*

**LESSON PREPARATION**

## SKILL LEVEL
Requires reading directions and writing short sentences (typical of second-grade students or mature first graders).

## OBJECTIVE AND MATERIALS
OBJECTIVE: Students will describe how two attribute blocks are alike and how they are different.

© 2000 CRITICAL THINKING BOOKS & SOFTWARE • WWW.CRITICALTHINKING.COM • 800-458-4849          119

**BEGINNING BUILDING THINKING SKILLS LESSON PLANS**                    **FIGURAL CLASSIFICATION**

MATERIALS: Transparency of student book page 179 • washable transparency markers or colored chalk in three colors • attribute blocks (small blocks: red circle, blue circle, yellow and blue squares and triangles, large red circle and red square)

## CURRICULUM APPLICATIONS
See the lesson **Comparing One Characteristic** on page 85.

## TEACHING SUGGESTIONS
- The descriptions may be either oral or written. The descriptions may be different from those given in the answers above.

**MODEL LESSON**

## LESSON

### Introduction
Q: You have classified blocks in many ways.

### Explaining the Objective to Students
Q: In this lesson you will look at two blocks and describe how they are alike and different.

### Class Activity

- Project transparency of student book page 179 covering the answers
  Q: How are these two blocks alike?
    A: They are both red and are circles.

  Q: How are these two red circles different?
    A: The first circle is larger than the second.

- Expose the answers
  Q: The answers have been written. Look at exercise D-108, decide how the blocks are alike and how they are different, and then write your answers on the blank lines.

## GUIDED PRACTICE
EXERCISE **D-108**
- Give students sufficient time to complete this exercise. Ask students to discuss and explain their answers.

## INDEPENDENT PRACTICE
- Assign exercise **D-109** through **D-112**.

## THINKING ABOUT THINKING
Q: What did you pay attention to in order to find a block with different characteristics?
  1. I looked to see if the blocks were the same shape.

  2. I looked to see if the blocks were the same color.

  3. I looked to see if the blocks were the same size.

  4. I wrote how the blocks were alike and how they were different.

## PERSONAL APPLICATION
See the lesson **Comparing One Characteristic** on page 85.

**120**                 © 2000 CRITICAL THINKING BOOKS & SOFTWARE • WWW.CRITICALTHINKING.COM • 800-458-4849

**Chapter 5**

# DESCRIBING PEOPLE AND THINGS

**EXERCISE
E-1**

## DESCRIBING FAMILY MEMBERS—SELECT

---
**ANSWERS E-1**
E-1 **Example:** grandmother
E-1 **Exercise:** toddler boy
E-1 **Practice:** girl
---

**LESSON
PREPARATION**

### OBJECTIVE AND MATERIALS

OBJECTIVE: Students will select the picture that fits a description of a family member.
MATERIALS: The following pictures are used in this lesson: *baby (1), boy (5), girl (4), grandmother (8), mother (6), toddler boy (3), toddler girl (2)*

### CURRICULUM APPLICATIONS

<u>Social Studies</u>: Examine roles of family members and cite examples of interdependence; distinguish between a family's wants and needs; identify how human needs are met within the family in different cultures; examine the roles of various family members in the celebration of holidays and traditions across cultures; explore the rights and responsibilities of various family members

### TEACHING SUGGESTIONS

• Students may not commonly use the term "toddler." Explain how the word was derived: the ages and capabilities that one usually associates with a toddler. Students may realize that the term "toddler," like "baby," may refer to children of either gender.

• Model and encourage students to express the following process for identifying a family member that someone has described:
  1. Recall the important characteristics of the family member (the person's age, gender, relationship to other members of the family, roles, my feelings about him or her, interests or experiences that make that person special.)
  2. Find the important characteristics in the pictures.
  3. Check that the other pictures of people don't show those important characteristics as well.

• If there are children in your class who live in foster homes, conduct discussion of family members cautiously in order to avoid the conflict and confusion discussing families creates for these children.

**MODEL LESSON**

### LESSON

**Introduction**

• Select a student without identifying whom you have chosen. Describe him or her to the class in three to five sentences.

© 2000 CRITICAL THINKING BOOKS & SOFTWARE • WWW.CRITICALTHINKING.COM • 800-458-4849          121

BEGINNING BUILDING THINKING SKILLS LESSON PLANS                    DESCRIBING PEOPLE AND THINGS

Q: Whom did I describe?

A: Responses will vary

Q: What clues let you know whom I described?

A: Students cite height, coloring, behavior, what each student adds to the class, and personality.

**Explaining the Objective to the Students**

Q: In this lesson, we will identify the characteristics that are important to discuss when you describe the members of a family.

**Class Activity**

• Display the following pictures:

**E-1 Example:** *girl, grandmother, mother*

Q: I will describe a family member. Select the picture that fits the description. This family member is an older woman whose son or daughter is a father or mother. Sometimes she takes care of her grandchildren. She remembers events and places that younger members of the family don't know about. She helps her grandchildren understand that they are loved and special. She may live nearby or far away.

Q: What do we call this family member?

A: This family member is a grandmother.

• Ask students to decide with their partners which picture depicts a grand-mother. Confirm the answer with the whole class.

Q: What clues let you know that the person in this picture is the grandmother?

A: The woman looks older, about the same age as students' own grandmothers or grandmothers they know.

Q: Why don't the other family members fit the description?

A: The girl is too young to be a grandmother; she may be someone's granddaughter. The mother looks too young to have grown children.

**Guided Practice**

• Display the following pictures:

**E-1 Exercise** *baby, boy, toddler boy*

Q: I will describe a family member. Select the picture that fits the description. This child is one or two years old. He is not as tall as a sink. His mother can lift him, but he is too heavy to carry very far. He is learning to talk and can walk by himself. He has some teeth and can eat many foods by himself, if someone cuts it into little pieces. He knows his family and where to find things in his house.

Q: What do we call this family member?

A: This family member is a toddler or a toddler boy.

Q: What clues let you know that the person in this picture is the toddler?

A: The child is about the right height compared to other objects. Students may remember what a sister, brother, or friend could and could not do at the age and height of the toddler in the picture. The

122          © 2000 CRITICAL THINKING BOOKS & SOFTWARE • WWW.CRITICALTHINKING.COM • 800-458-4849

picture and the description fit a child who is able to do more than a baby but less than a school-age child.

Q: Why don't the other family members fit the description?

A: A baby is smaller and lighter to lift; the larger child looks harder to lift. A baby can't talk or walk. A toddler can't ride a bicycle or play baseball.

**Optional Independent Practice**

• If students need additional practice, display the following pictures:
**E-1 Practice** *baby, girl, toddler girl*

Q: I will describe a family member. Select the picture that fits the description. This child is old enough to go to school. She can read some books and solve some mathematics problems. She has friends and shares her toys and belongings with them. She may know how to swim, roller skate, or ride a bicycle.

Q: What do we call this family member?

A: This family member is a girl or daughter.

Q: What clues let you know that the person in this picture is the girl?

A: The girl looks old enough to go to school. She probably knows how to do some games or sports, like swimming or baseball. She probably has some chores that she regularly does at home.

Q: Why do the other family members not fit the description?

A: The baby and the toddler are too young to do any of these activities. Both are smaller than a school-age child.

**Thinking About Thinking**

Q: What did you look for to pick the family member that was described?

A: Age, gender, relationships to other family members, roles, interests or experiences that make them special.

**Personal Application**

Q: When is it important to describe family members well?

A: To relate incidents that happen at home, to explain how each family member helps the family meet its needs, to introduce family members to friends, to tell or write stories about family members.

**LANGUAGE ARTS EXTENSION**

**LANGUAGE INTEGRATION ACTIVITIES**

• Drawing: Each student may draw a member of his or her family and label the person's family role. Students' drawings may be used to create a "big book" describing the families and the culture of the whole class or assembled as a "big book" for each student. See page xxvii for directions.

• Storytelling: Ask students to describe to a partner a special event that his or her family enjoyed. Ask the storyteller to relate how each family member contributed to the event.

• Telling: Select a magazine picture of a family member. Ask students to create a riddle that they will tell to a partner.

BEGINNING BUILDING THINKING SKILLS LESSON PLANS                    DESCRIBING PEOPLE AND THINGS

## FOLLOW-UP ACTIVITIES AT HOME

• Students may take home the family tree diagram and ask their parents to help them fill in names to show family relationships. They may draw pictures of family members in the boxes to create a family drawing. Individual drawings may be organized by the family into a poster-size family tree diagram. Use the family tree diagram furnished on page 332.

• Encourage students to explain how family needs are met if the family member being described is not present in the home, i.e., extended families, single-parent families, etc. Students may describe non-family members who fulfill the traditional roles of family members.

## PICTURE BOOK EXTENSION

• Language experiences with picture books extend this lesson and demonstrate how family members across cultures meet family needs. While discussing picture books, ask the following questions.
Q: Are there any new ideas about (grandmothers, toddlers, or girls) that we learned from this story?
Q: What ideas or details about (grandmothers, toddlers, or girls) did you get from the pictures?
Q: Is this information true of most (grandmothers, toddlers, or girls)?

After discussing each story, ask students to add new information about the characteristics of the family member described in the story to the lists, posters, or graphic organizers that you may have used when discussing the concepts in this lesson.

## SUPPLEMENTAL PICTURE BOOKS

• These books feature the family members discussed in this lesson. Descriptions of these and additional books on topics in this lesson are listed in the extended bibliography at the end of this manual.

### Girl
*I Want to Be,* Thylias Moss
*My Mama Had A Dancing Heart,* Libba Moore Gray
*When I Was Young on the Mountain,* Cynthia Rylant

### Grandmother
*A Busy Day For A Good Grandmother,* Margaret Mahy
*Dance in My Red Pajamas,* Edith Thacher Hurd
*Grandma According to Me,* Karen Magnuson Bell
*Something Special for Me,* Vera Williams

### Toddler
*Baby Says,* John Steptoe
*Glorious Angels,* Walter Dean Myers
*I Can,* Helen Oxenbury
*When I Was Young: A Four Year Old's Memoir of Her Youth,* Jamie Lee Curtis

124            © 2000 CRITICAL THINKING BOOKS & SOFTWARE • WWW.CRITICALTHINKING.COM • 800-458-4849

BEGINNING BUILDING THINKING SKILLS LESSON PLANS                    DESCRIBING PEOPLE AND THINGS

## EXERCISE E-2

# DESCRIBING FAMILY MEMBERS—EXPLAIN

---

**ANSWERS E-2**

**E-2 Example:** Baby—A baby is less than a year old and might be boy or girl. He or she must be dressed and fed milk or soft food. A baby may have tiny teeth or no teeth at all. He or she needs diapers. A baby learns to sit, crawl, play, smile, talk, and walk. He or she must be cared for by an adult.

**E-2 Exercise** Grandfather—This is an older man whose son or daughter is a father or mother. Sometimes he takes care of his grandchildren. He remembers events and places that younger members of the family don't know about. He helps his grandchildren understand that they are loved and special. Some grandfathers live nearby; others live far away.

**E-2 Practice:** Father—This man is old enough to have children. Some fathers live in the same house as their children; others don't. A father works for money for the family. Sometimes fathers work at home. Fathers teach their children how to do things, like riding a bike, or how to behave in different situations.

---

## LESSON PREPARATION

### OBJECTIVE AND MATERIALS

OBJECTIVE: Students will describe family members pictured in photographs.
MATERIALS: The following pictures are used in this lesson: *baby (1), father (7), grandfather (9)* • transparency of TM 9 on page 333

### CURRICULUM APPLICATIONS

Social Studies: Examine roles of family members and cite examples of interdependence, distinguish between a family's wants and needs, identify how human needs are met within the family in different cultures, examine the roles of various family members in the celebration of holidays and traditions across cultures, explore the rights and responsibilities of various family members.

### TEACHING SUGGESTIONS

- Model the following process for students and encourage them to use it when identifying a family member that someone has described:
    1. Recall the important characteristics of the family member (the person's age, sex, relationships to other members of the family, roles, interests or experiences that make them special.)

    2. Check that I describe all those important characteristics.

    3. Check that I have given enough details to keep the family member that I am describing from being confused for another relative.

- If there are children in your class who live in foster homes, conduct discussion of family members cautiously in order to avoid the conflict and confusion discussing family members creates for these children.

- To reinforce students' responses, you may draw a web diagram to record their answers. For a blank web diagram, see Transparency Master 9 on page 333.

---

© 2000 CRITICAL THINKING BOOKS & SOFTWARE • WWW.CRITICALTHINKING.COM • 800-458-4849                    125

BEGINNING BUILDING THINKING SKILLS LESSON PLANS — DESCRIBING PEOPLE AND THINGS

**MODEL LESSON** | **LESSON**

**Introduction**

Q: In the last lesson, we selected a family member who fit a specific description. What did you think about in order to figure out which family member was being described?

A: Age, gender, relationships to other members of the family, roles, interests or experiences that make him or her special.

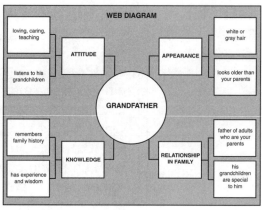

**Explaining the Objective to Students**

Q: In this lesson, we will describe family members shown in photographs.

**Class Activity**

• Display the following picture:

**E-2 Example:** *baby*

Q: Describe this family member.

A: A baby is less than a year old and might be a boy or a girl. He or she must be dressed and fed milk or soft food. A baby may have tiny teeth or no teeth at all. He or she needs diapers. A baby learns to sit, crawl, play, smile, talk, and walk. He or she must be cared for by an adult.

Q: What details do you describe to explain that the person in this picture is a baby?

A: His age (younger than a year old), his small size (compared to the stuffed toy), what his body looks like (his legs are still curved and don't look strong enough for walking), what he wears, what he can do.

**Guided Practice**

• Display the following picture:

**E-2 Exercise:** *grandfather*

Q: Describe this family member.

A: A grandfather is an older man whose son or daughter is a father or mother. Sometimes he takes care of his grandchildren. He remembers events and places that younger members of the family don't know about. He helps his grandchildren understand that they are loved and special. Some grandfathers live nearby; others live far away.

Q: What details do you describe to explain that the person in this picture is a grandfather?

A: His age and actions suggest that he may be an adult's father.

**Optional Independent Practice**

• If students need additional practice, display the following picture:

**E-2 Practice:** *father*

126 © 2000 CRITICAL THINKING BOOKS & SOFTWARE • WWW.CRITICALTHINKING.COM • 800-458-4849

Q: Describe this family member.
A: A father is old enough to have children. Some fathers live in the same house as their children; others don't. A father works for money for the family. Sometimes fathers work at home. Fathers teach their children how to do things, like riding a bike, or how to behave in different situations.

Q: What details do you describe to explain that the person in this picture is a father?
A: His age, his relationship to children, what he does to help children grow up healthy and safe, how he contributes to the family.

**Thinking About Thinking**

Q: What characteristics do you discuss to describe a member of a family?
A: Age, gender, relationships to other members of the family, roles, interests or experiences that make them special.

**Personal Application**

Q: When is it important to describe family members well?
A: To relate incidents that happen at home, to explain how each family members helps the family meet its needs, to introduce family members to friends, to tell or write stories or journals about family members.

**LANGUAGE ARTS EXTENSION**

**LANGUAGE INTEGRATION ACTIVITIES**

- Drawing: Each student may draw a member of his or her family and label the person's family role. Students' drawings may be used to create a "big book" describing the families and the culture of the whole class or assembled as a "big book" for each student. See page xxvii for directions

- Telling: Select a magazine picture of a family member role. Ask students to create a riddle that they will tell or write for a partner.

- Storytelling: Ask students to describe to a partner a special event that his or her family enjoyed. Ask the storyteller to relate how each family member discussed in this lesson contributed to the event.

- First/Second Grade Language Activity: For each item, list students' responses and ask students to read the list aloud or write sentences to create a short description that can be added to students' drawings.

**FOLLOW-UP ACTIVITIES AT HOME**

- Students may take home the family tree diagram (TM 8 on page 332) and ask parents to help them fill in the names to show family relationships. Students may draw pictures of family members in the boxes to create a family drawing, or individual drawings may be organized by the teacher into a poster-size family tree diagram.

- Encourage students to explain how family needs are met if the family member being described is not present in the home, i.e., extended families, single-parent families, etc. Students may describe non-family members who fulfill the traditional roles of family members.

BEGINNING BUILDING THINKING SKILLS LESSON PLANS                    DESCRIBING PEOPLE AND THINGS

## PICTURE BOOK EXTENSION

• Language experiences with picture books extend this lesson and demonstrate how family members across cultures meet family needs. After discussing any of the picture books, ask the following questions:

Q: Are there any new ideas about (babies, grandfathers, or fathers) that we learned from this story?

Q: What ideas or details about (babies, grandfathers, or fathers) did you get from the pictures?

Q: Is this information true of most (babies, grandfathers, or fathers)?

## SUPPLEMENTAL PICTURE BOOKS

• These books feature the family members discussed in this lesson. Descriptions of these and additional books on topics in this lesson are listed in the extended bibliography at the end of this manual.

### Baby

*Babies,* Toppers Series, Nicola Baxter
*Happy Birth Day,* Robie Harris
*The Baby's Catalogue,* Janet and Allan Ahlberg
*Welcoming Babies,* Margy Burns Knight

### Grandfather

*Grandfather's Love Song,* Reeve Lindbergh
*Now One Foot, Now the Other,* Vera Williams
*The Red Barn,* Eve Bunting

### Father

*I Love My Father Because,* Laurel Porter-Gaylord
*Owl Moon,* Jane Yolen

**EXERCISE E-3**

## DESCRIBING JOBS—SELECT

> **ANSWER E-3**
> **E-3 Example**: farmer
> **E-3 Exercise**: teacher
> **E-3 Practice**: police officer

**LESSON PREPARATION**

## OBJECTIVE AND MATERIALS

OBJECTIVE: Students will select the picture that fits a description of a person's job.

MATERIALS: The following pictures are used in this lesson: *barber (23), construction worker (10), farmer (12), firefighter (16), mail carrier (13), nurse (14), pilot (17), police officer (18), teacher (15)*

## CURRICULUM APPLICATIONS

Health: Identify people who produce and distribute food.

Social Studies: Define *consumer* as a user of goods and services; identify how a family depends upon products and services to meet its needs; identify some job roles in the home, school, and community; cite examples of community needs and services; recognize the differences between producing and selling goods; examine how jobs are similar and different across

128          © 2000 CRITICAL THINKING BOOKS & SOFTWARE • WWW.CRITICALTHINKING.COM • 800-458-4849

BEGINNING BUILDING THINKING SKILLS LESSON PLANS                    DESCRIBING PEOPLE AND THINGS

cultures; understand how community helpers are an example of interdependence.

**TEACHING SUGGESTIONS**

• Students may not commonly use the term *occupation*. Discuss with students the common synonyms for *job, livelihood, career, work,* etc.

• Model the following process for identifying a job that someone has described, and encourage students to use this process.

  1. Recall the important characteristics of the job.

  2. Find the important characteristics in the pictures (activities, goods or services, training, equipment, etc.).

  3. Check that the other pictures of jobs don't show those important characteristics as well.

**MODEL LESSON** | **LESSON**

**Introduction**

• Select a student and ask the student to describe in three or four sentences the job of one of his or her family members. Ask the class to name the job that has been described.

Q: What clues let you know what job (<u>student's name</u>) was describing?

  A: Answers will vary, but generally include the goods or services shown in the pictures, what consumer seeks these goods or services, work location, training, special clothes they wear, tools they use, and tasks that a person having this job would do.

**Explaining the Objective to Students**

Q: In this lesson, we will identify the important characteristics that you discuss when you describe certain jobs.

**Class Activity**

• Display the following pictures:

  **E-3 Example** *construction worker, cook, farmer*

  Q: I will describe one of the jobs and ask you to select the picture that fits the description. This person grows fruits or vegetables or raises animals for us to eat. He cares for large fields with lots of trees or plants. He must be sure that his plants or animals have enough water and food to grow healthy and large. He checks his crops or his animals to prevent pests (weeds, insects, or disease). He uses large machines, such as tractors, plows, and sprayers to grow large amounts of food. He has learned about plants and animals from other farmers, by growing up on a farm, or by going to school for a long time. He must keep good records about how his crops or animals grow and how to sell them for a good price.

  Q: What do we call a person who has this job?

    A: Farmer.

• Ask students to decide with their partners which picture has been described. Confirm the answer with the whole class.

  Q: What clues let you know that the person in this picture is the farmer?

© 2000 CRITICAL THINKING BOOKS & SOFTWARE • WWW.CRITICALTHINKING.COM • 800-458-4849          129

BEGINNING BUILDING THINKING SKILLS LESSON PLANS          DESCRIBING PEOPLE AND THINGS

A: His clothing, surroundings, tools, and vehicle let us know that he works outside where food grows.

Q: Why don't the other pictures fit this description?

A: The cook prepares food, but does not tend the plants or animals that produce food. The construction worker does not grow food, but may eat the food that the farmer grows.

## Guided Practice

• Display the following pictures:

**E-3 Exercise** *mail carrier, nurse, teacher*

Q: I will describe one of the jobs and ask you to select the picture that fits the description (teacher). This person helps boys and girls learn things they need to know: how to read, write, draw, play music, and get along with other people. She helps students learn to use numbers and shapes and to understand our city, our country, and nature. She works with the children from early morning to the middle of the afternoon. When the children leave, she checks their work and plans what they will do on the next day. She understands how children learn and how to explain things to them easily. She uses books, maps, computers, pictures, and a chalkboard to help children understand ideas. She went to school a long time to learn how to do this well.

Q: What do we call a person who has this job?

A: Teacher.

Q: What clues let you know that the person in this picture is the teacher?

A: Her surroundings, actions, and tools let us know that she works in a classroom.

Q: Why don't the other pictures fit this description?

A: A mail carrier works outdoors for much of his or her day and doesn't work with children. A nurse may help children get well but teaches them only about health, not how to read and write.

## Optional Independent Practice

• If students need additional practice, display the following pictures:

**E-3 Practice** *firefighter, pilot, police officer*

Q: I will describe one of the jobs and ask you to select the picture that fits the description. This law enforcement officer protects people and property and helps prevent crime. He or she sometimes rides in a car or on a motorcycle, wears a uniform, and has a badge to let people know that he or she is an official. He or she studies laws and learns how to keep himself or herself and other people safe.

Q: What do we call a person who has this job?

A: Police officer.

Q: What clues let you know that the person in this picture is the police officer?

A: His uniform, equipment, and badge show that this is a police officer.

Q: Why don't the other pictures fit this description?

130          © 2000 CRITICAL THINKING BOOKS & SOFTWARE • WWW.CRITICALTHINKING.COM • 800-458-4849

BEGINNING BUILDING THINKING SKILLS LESSON PLANS                    DESCRIBING PEOPLE AND THINGS

A: The pilot and the firefighter wear uniforms, but do not enforce laws. The pilot flies an airplane; the firefighter answers fire alarms in a fire truck.

### Thinking About Thinking

Q: What did you look for when you picked out the job that was described?

A: Goods or services, what consumer seeks these goods or services, work location, training, how he or she spends his/her time, and tools he or she uses. Name the actions shown in the pictures and other tasks that a person having this job would do.

Q: What do you discuss to describe a consumer?

A: The goods or services that people want or need, how often the goods and services are needed or obtained.

### Personal Application

Q: When is it important to describe people or jobs well?

A: To relate incidents that happen at home, to explain what friends or family members do for a living, to describe commercials, to describe businesses or services to a newcomer.

**LANGUAGE ARTS EXTENSION**

## LANGUAGE INTEGRATION ACTIVITIES

• Drawing: Each student may draw a farmer, a teacher, or a police officer. Label the drawing with a description of that job. Students' drawings may be used to create a "big book." See page xxvii for directions.

• Telling: Each student should select or draw a picture of a worker performing his or her job. Ask students to create a riddle that they will tell or write for a partner called "I am this worker's customer!" From the riddle, students must identify the job.

• Telling: Ask students within each cooperative learning group to play "Twenty Questions" about a job.

• Drama: Collect or construct hats from different professions and articles used in the jobs. Ask students to role-play a worker and a customer seeking goods or services from this worker.

• Encourage students to give examples from their local community where the jobs described in this lesson are performed. Identify examples of local jobs performed by individuals from various ethnic backgrounds.

## FOLLOW-UP ACTIVITIES AT HOME

• Ask parents to describe their jobs. They should then ask the child to describe their parents' jobs to another family member or friend.

## PICTURE BOOK EXTENSION

• Language experiences with picture books extend this lesson and demonstrate how various occupations provide goods and services to meet people's needs. After discussing any of the picture books, ask the following questions:

© 2000 CRITICAL THINKING BOOKS & SOFTWARE • WWW.CRITICALTHINKING.COM • 800-458-4849          131

BEGINNING BUILDING THINKING SKILLS LESSON PLANS                    DESCRIBING PEOPLE AND THINGS

Q: Are there any new ideas about (<u>farmers, teachers, or police officers</u>) that we learned from this story?

Q: What ideas or details about (<u>farmers, teachers, or police officers</u>) did you get from the pictures?

Q: Is this information true of most (<u>farmers, teachers, or police officers</u>)?

After discussing each story, ask students to add new information about the characteristics of the job described in the story to the lists, posters, or graphic organizers that you may have used when discussing the pictures.

## SUPPLEMENTAL PICTURE BOOKS

- These books feature the workers discussed in this lesson. Descriptions of these and additional books on topics in this lesson are listed in the extended bibliography at the end of this manual.

**Farmer**

*Family Farm,* Thomas Locker
*Farm Morning,* David McPhail
*If It Weren't for Farmers,* Allan Fowler
*If You Are Not From the Prairie...,* David Bouchard

**Police Officer**

*Officer Buckle and Gloria,* Peggy Rathman Calde

**Teacher**

*Miss Malarkey Doesn't Live in Room 101,* Judy Fincher
*My Great Aunt Arizona,* Gloria Houston
*My Teacher's Secret Life,* Stephen Krensky
*My Teacher Is My Best Friend,* P. K. Hallinan

**EXERCISE E-4**

# DESCRIBING JOBS—EXPLAIN

**ANSWERS E-4**

**E-4 Example:** Doctor—A doctor helps people feel better and can decide what medicine or treatment a person needs in order to heal. He or she works in offices or hospitals and at times wears special clothing. A doctor must study and go to school for a long time to learn how people's bodies work. He or she uses a thermometer to take people's temperature and uses other equipment such as scales, microscopes, stethoscopes, cotton, needles, blood pressure gauge, etc.

**E-4 Exercise:** Pilot—A pilot controls the speed and direction of an airplane. He is the driver of the plane. He and other specially trained airplane workers sit in the cockpit (driving section) and look out of a windshield like the one in cars. He has to learn how a plane operates and how to read the dials and lights that show that the plane is safe and operating correctly. He must know the correct direction to steer the plane where it must go. A pilot wears a special uniform.

**E-4 Practice:** Mail carrier—A mail carrier wears a uniform and delivers letters, bills, advertisements, magazines, and packages to homes and places of business.

BEGINNING BUILDING THINKING SKILLS LESSON PLANS          DESCRIBING PEOPLE AND THINGS

**LESSON PREPARATION**

## OBJECTIVE AND MATERIALS
OBJECTIVE: Students will describe people who work at certain jobs.
MATERIALS: The following pictures are used in this lesson: *doctor (19), mail carrier (13), pilot (17)*

## CURRICULUM APPLICATIONS
<u>Health</u>: Identify people who work in the medical profession
<u>Social Studies</u>: Define consumer as a user of goods and services; identify how a family depends upon products and services to meet its needs; identify some job roles in the home, school, and community; cite examples of community needs and services; recognize the differences between producing and selling goods; examine how jobs are similar and different across cultures; understand how community helpers are an example of interdependence.

## TEACHING SUGGESTIONS
• Students may not commonly use the term "occupation." Discuss with students the common synonyms for jobs—livelihood, career, work, etc.

• Model and encourage students to express the following process for describing a job.
  1. Recall the important characteristics of the kind of job. (Picture in my mind what someone doing that job does and looks like.)
  2. Check that I describe all those important characteristics (activities, goods or services, training, equipment, etc.).
  3. Check that I have given enough details to keep the kind of job that I am describing from being confused with another kind of job.

• To reinforce students' responses, use a web diagram to record their answers (Transparency Master 9 on page 333).

**MODEL LESSON**

## LESSON
### Introduction
Q: Think about a time that you had to describe someone's job. Tell your partner the details that describe that person's work.

• Give students a few minutes to exchange descriptions with a partner. To describe a job, students cite where one works, the activities of the job, training, clothing, equipment that is needed for the job, etc.

### Explaining the Objective to Students
Q: In this lesson, you will look at a photograph and describe the job the person is doing.

### Class Activity
• Display the following picture:
  **E-4 Example:** *doctor*
  Q: Describe this person's job.
    A: A doctor helps people feel better and can decide what medicine or treatment a person needs in order to heal. He or she works in offices or hospitals and at times wears special clothing. A doctor must study

© 2000 CRITICAL THINKING BOOKS & SOFTWARE • WWW.CRITICALTHINKING.COM • 800-458-4849          133

and go to school for a long time to learn how people's bodies work. He or she uses a thermometer to take people's temperature, and uses scales, microscopes, stethoscopes, cotton, needles, blood pressure gauge, etc.

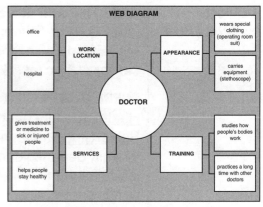

Q: What details do you describe to explain that the person in this picture is a doctor?

   A: His surroundings, tools, clothing, and actions show that he works in a hospital or office, helping people heal.

**Guided Practice**
- Display the following picture:

   **E-4 Exercise:** *pilot*

   Q: Describe this person's job.

      A: A pilot controls the speed and direction of an airplane. He is the driver of the plane. He and other specially trained airplane workers sit in the cockpit (driving section) and look out of a windshield like ones in cars. He has to learn how a plane operates and how to read the dials and lights that show that the plane is safe and operating correctly. He must know the correct direction to steer the plane where it must go. A pilot wears a special uniform.

   Q: What details do you describe to explain that the person in this picture is a pilot?

      A: His surroundings, equipment, and clothing show that he is a flyer. He works in a cockpit where he controls the equipment that operates the plane like a driver drives an automobile.

**Optional Independent Practice**
- If students need additional practice, display the following picture:

   **E-4 Practice:** *mail carrier*

   Q: Describe this person's job.

      A: A mail carrier is a government employee who wears a uniform with the symbol of the U. S. Postal Service on it. He or she delivers letters, bills, advertisements, magazines, and packages to homes and places of business.

   Q: What details do you describe to explain that the person in this picture is a mail carrier?

      A: His surroundings, clothing, and actions show that he works in a post office, preparing for his deliveries, or walks outside taking mail from place to place.

### Thinking About Thinking

Q: What characteristics do you discuss to describe someone's job?

A: Does the job provide goods or services, what consumer seeks these goods or services, work location, training, how they spend their time, and tools they use.

Q: What characteristics do you discuss to describe a consumer?

A: Students may name the goods or services that customers want or need, how goods and services are secured, or how often they are needed.

### Personal Application

Q: When is it important to describe people or jobs well?

A: To relate incidents that happen at home; to explain what friends or family members do for a living; to describe commercials; to describe businesses or services to a newcomer.

## LANGUAGE ARTS EXTENSION

## LANGUAGE INTEGRATION ACTIVITIES

* Drawing: Each student may draw a doctor, a pilot, or a mail carrier. Label the drawing with a description of that job. Students' drawings may be used to create a "big book." See page xxvii for directions.

* Telling: Each student should select or draw a picture of a worker performing his or her job. Ask students to create a riddle that they will tell or write for a partner called "I am this worker's customer!" From the riddle students must identify the job.

* Drama: Collect or construct hats from different professions and articles used in the job. Ask students to enact the worker and the customer seeking goods or services from these workers.

* Ask students within each cooperative learning group to play "Twenty Questions" about a job.

* First/Second Grade Language Activity: For each item, list students' responses and ask students to read the list aloud or write sentences to create a short description that can be added to students' drawings.

* Encourage students to give examples from their local community of the locations where the jobs described in this lesson are performed. Identify examples of local jobs performed by individuals from various ethnic backgrounds.

## FOLLOW-UP ACTIVITIES AT HOME

* Ask parents to describe their jobs. They should then ask the child to describe their parents' jobs to another family member or friend.

## PICTURE BOOK EXTENSION

* Language experiences with picture books extend this lesson and demonstrate how various occupations provide goods and services to meet people's needs. After discussing any of the picture books ask the following questions:

BEGINNING BUILDING THINKING SKILLS LESSON PLANS                    DESCRIBING PEOPLE AND THINGS

Q: Are there any new ideas about (pilots, doctors, or mail carriers) that we learned from this story?

Q: What ideas or details about (pilots, doctors, or mail carriers) did you get from the pictures?

Q: Is this information true of most (pilots, doctors, or mail carriers)?

After discussing each story, ask students to add new information about the characteristics of the job described in the story to the lists, posters, or graphic organizers that you may have used when discussing the pictures.

### SUPPLEMENTAL PICTURE BOOKS

• These books feature the workers discussed in this lesson. Descriptions of these and additional books on topics in this lesson are described in the extended bibliography at the end of this manual.

**Pilot**

*I Am A Pilot,* Cynthia Benjamin
*Nobody Owns the Sky,* Reeve Lindbergh

**Doctor**

*Going To the Doctor,* T. Barry Brazelton
*Going to the Doctor: Mister Rogers Neighborhood Series,* Fred Rogers

**Mail Carrier**

*The Jolly Postman,* Janet and Allan Ahlberg

**EXERCISE E-5**

# DESCRIBING FOODS—SELECT

**ANSWERS: E-5**
**E-5 Example:** bread
**E-5 Exercise:** carrot
**E-5 Practice:** potato

**LESSON PREPARATION**

### OBJECTIVE AND MATERIALS
OBJECTIVE: Students will select the picture that fits a description of a food.
MATERIALS: The following pictures are used in this lesson: *green beans (84), bread (73), butter (74), carrots (82), cheese (75), peas (85), potato (86), onions (83), oranges (93)*

### CURRICULUM APPLICATIONS
Health: Recognize foods that provide good nutrition.
Science: Identify, illustrate, and describe the parts of a plant: root, stem, and leaf; give three ways plants are important to people; recognize examples of common animals as being fish, birds, or mammals.

### TEACHING SUGGESTIONS
• Use fresh vegetables to supplement this lesson. Whenever possible select vegetables that are still intact with the stalks, root hairs, and leaves that are usually removed at the supermarket. For example, young children may not realize that the portion of the carrot that we eat is the root. Showing them the green tops and root hairs lets them realize how the food has been

136                    © 2000 CRITICAL THINKING BOOKS & SOFTWARE • WWW.CRITICALTHINKING.COM • 800-458-4849

BEGINNING BUILDING THINKING SKILLS LESSON PLANS                    DESCRIBING PEOPLE AND THINGS

changed before it gets to the customer and helps them to understand that the root holds valuable nutrients for the plant and for the person eating it.

- Use pictures and encourage students to give examples of the same foods prepared differently in various ethnic backgrounds. Provide pictures of ethnic foods from magazines or cookbooks or secure samples of ethnic foods using food mentioned in the lesson. Assist students in describing and pronouncing the names of ethnic foods. Discuss how its preparation and combination with other foods affects its appearance and taste.

- Young children and some adults do not realize that a peanut is not a nut like almonds or pecans. It is a fruit that contains a seed within a hard covering. Peanuts are actually tiny brown pods attached to the roots.

- "Beans" and "peas" are used interchangeably to describe legumes. Commonly, "bean" means that one eats the whole pod, including the seed portion, such as green beans. Seeds are commonly called "peas," such as black-eyed peas or green peas. However, the seed portion can be also be called beans, such as black beans, garbanzo beans, or lima beans. Trying to distinguish between beans and peas is probably not useful.

- If students have not seen dough rise, demonstrate this process or allow them to watch kitchen staff prepare bread. Give examples of different ingredients that make bread rise: yeast, baking powder, etc. Name breads that don't rise. Encourage students to describe types of bread from other cultures which have different size, shape and color, and which are made with different ingredients or by different preparation.

- Second grade science texts offer the scientific definition of fruit which applies to foods commonly called vegetables (tomatoes, squash, cucumbers, pumpkins, etc.). Clarify students' use of the term fruit in appropriate contexts: "vegetable" in cookbooks and grocery stores, "fruit" in scientific discussion of parts of a plant.

- Model and encourage students to express the following process for identifying a food that someone has described:
  1. Recall the important characteristics of the food. (What it looks like, its taste, how it's prepared, when it is usually eaten, etc.)
  2. Find the important characteristics in the pictures. (I will look for or try to recall whether it is a plant or animal product, its color, shape, flavor and size, how it is prepared, when it is commonly eaten, and special ways different groups of people prepare it.)
  3. Check that the other pictures of food don't show those important characteristics as well.

- For second grade classes, discuss basic nutrients the food contains: fats, protein, carbohydrates, vitamins, minerals and water.

**MODEL LESSON** | **LESSON**

**Introduction**

Q: Select a food that you ate for breakfast and bring a sample or the

© 2000 CRITICAL THINKING BOOKS & SOFTWARE • WWW.CRITICALTHINKING.COM • 800-458-4849          137

package to class. Describe the food to the class.

Q: What clues let you know what food I was describing?

  A: The kind of food (fruit, bread, meat, drink, etc.), where one gets it, or how it is prepared.

### Explaining the Objective to Students

Q: In this lesson, we will identify the important characteristics that you discuss when you describe certain foods.

### Class Activity

* Display the following pictures
  **E-5 Example:** _bread,_ butter, cheese

* I will describe one of the foods. Select the picture that fits the description. This food is made by mixing flour, water, salt, and oil or butter. The dough seems light because yeast or baking powder makes tiny bubbles in the dough. This food is usually white or light brown, and is not as sweet as desserts. The bakery often slices it so that we can use it for toast or sandwiches.

  Q: What do we call this food?

    A: This food is bread.

* Ask students to decide with their partners which picture has been described.

  Q: What clues let you know that the food in this picture is bread?

    A: It looks like loaves of bread that are sliced and used for sandwiches or toast (same size, shape, and color).

  Q: Why don't the other foods fit this description?

    A: Butter and cheese are made from milk and melt if heated.

### Guided Practice

* Display the following pictures:
  **E-5 Exercise:** _carrot_, onion, orange

* I will describe one of the foods. Select the picture that fits the description. This orange vegetable can be eaten cooked or served raw in a salad. It can be sliced, chopped, or eaten whole. The part that we eat is the root of the plant. It is pulled out of the ground by grabbing the green leaves that stick up above the surface. Rabbits and horses also like to eat it.

  Q: What do we call this food?

    A: This food is a carrot.

  Q: What clues let you know that the food in this picture is the carrot?

    A: Its color, shape, where it grows on the plant, and how it is prepared and eaten show that it is a carrot.

  Q: Why don't the other foods fit this description?

    A: We eat the root part of the onion, but onions are white or purple. Oranges are fruit, not roots.

BEGINNING BUILDING THINKING SKILLS LESSON PLANS                    DESCRIBING PEOPLE AND THINGS

### Optional Independent Practice
- If students need additional practice, display these three pictures:

**E-5 Practice:** *beans, peas, potato*

Q: I will describe one of the foods. Select the picture that fits the description. We eat the white part of the large, brown skinned, root (tuber) of this plant. This part of the plant is eaten boiled, mashed, pan fried, french fried, or baked.

Q: Which of these pictures matches the description?
  A: Potato is the food described.

Q: What clues let you know that the food in this picture is a potato?
  A: The part of the plant that we eat and how it is prepared show that this food is a potato.

Q: Why do the other foods not fit this description?
  A: Beans and peas are part of the seed pod. Peas are usually not baked or fried because they have to be cooked in water. Some beans are baked or fried but do not grow underground.

### Thinking About Thinking
Q: What did you look for when you picked out the food that was described?
  A: Whether the food is a plant or animal product is the primary question. If it is a plant product, describe what kind—tree, vine, or small bush. Identify what part we eat—seed, fruit, leaf, stem, or root. Describe its color, shape and size. If it is an animal product, identify the kind of animal that produces it, and how it is prepared. For plant or animal food products, describe how it is cooked, seasoned, and served at specific meals.

### Personal Application
Q: When is it important to describe food accurately?
  A: To order food in the school cafeteria or in a restaurant; to remind a friend or family member about food that he or she has been asked to bring home from the grocery store; to understand or relate a doctor's diet recommendations; to help someone who doesn't understand English well to request food that he or she wants.

**LANGUAGE ARTS EXTENSION**

### LANGUAGE INTEGRATION ACTIVITIES
- Drawing: Select a picture of a food or allow students to find or draw a picture of food. Ask students to create a riddle about food that they will tell or write for a partner.

- Telling: Ask students within each cooperative learning group to play "Twenty Questions" about a food.

- First/Second Grade Language Activity: For each item, list students' responses and ask students to read the list aloud or write sentences to create a short description that can be added to students' drawings, if desired.

© 2000 CRITICAL THINKING BOOKS & SOFTWARE • WWW.CRITICALTHINKING.COM • 800-458-4849          139

BEGINNING BUILDING THINKING SKILLS LESSON PLANS                    DESCRIBING PEOPLE AND THINGS

**FOLLOW-UP ACTIVITIES AT HOME**
- Ask parents to describe food they enjoy or have just purchased. They should then ask the child to describe the food to another family member or friend.

**PICTURE BOOK EXTENSION**
- Language experiences with picture books extend this lesson and demonstrate how food meets our needs and is prepared differently in various cultures. After discussing any of the pictures books, ask the following questions

  Q: Are there any new ideas about (bread, carrots, or potatoes) that we learned from this story?

  Q: What ideas or details about (bread, carrots, or potatoes) did you get from the pictures?

  Q: Is this information true of most (bread, carrots, or potatoes)?

  After discussing each story, ask students to add new information about the characteristics of the food described in the story to the lists, posters, or graphic organizers that you may have used when discussing the pictures.

**SUPPLEMENTAL PICTURE BOOKS**
- These books feature the food discussed in this lesson. Descriptions of these and additional books on topics in this lesson are listed in the extended bibliography at the end of this manual.

**Bread**
> *Bread, Bread, Bread,* Ann Morris
> *If It Weren't for Farmers,* Allan Fowler
> *The Unbeatable Bread,* Lyn Littlefield Hoops

**Carrot**
> *The Carrot Seed,* Ruth Kraus
> *Tops and Bottoms,* Janet Stevens
> *Vegetables, Vegetables!,* Fay Robinson

**Potato**
> *Jamie O'Rourke and the Big Potato: An Irish Folktale,* Tomie DePaola
> *Potatoes ,* Easy Readers series, Ann Burckhardt
> *The Amazing Potato,* Milton Meltzer

**EXERCISE E-6**

# DESCRIBING FOODS—EXPLAIN

**ANSWERS E-6**

**E-6 Example:** *ham*—This meat is made by adding salt and water to pork (the meat of a pig) and treating it (smoking) to prevent it from spoiling. It is usually baked in large pieces or fried in large slices. We usually eat ham in sandwiches, soups, or in large pieces for dinner or breakfast.

**E-6 Exercise:** *grapes*—This fruit grows in bunches on a vine. The soft, sweet, green or purple berry can be eaten whole, made into jelly, or squeezed into juice. Many bunches of berries grow on each vine.

**E-6 Practice:** *celery*—This vegetable has leaves and a stalk. The stalk

140                     © 2000 CRITICAL THINKING BOOKS & SOFTWARE • WWW.CRITICALTHINKING.COM • 800-458-4849

BEGINNING BUILDING THINKING SKILLS LESSON PLANS                    DESCRIBING PEOPLE AND THINGS

> of this plant can be eaten raw (without cooking it). Some people add celery to soup or stews to give it flavor. Celery is moist and crunchy to eat and can be dipped into sauces.

**LESSON PREPARATION**

## OBJECTIVE AND MATERIALS
OBJECTIVE: Students will describe a food pictured in a photograph.
MATERIALS: The following pictures are used in this lesson: *celery (87), grapes (94), ham (76)* • transparency of TM 9 on page 333

## CURRICULUM APPLICATIONS
<u>Health</u>: Recognize food that provides good nutrition for proper growth and functions of the body; identify a variety of foods.
<u>Science</u>: Identify the parts of a plant: root, stem, and leaf; recognize that there are many kinds of plants; recognize the major physical differences between plants and animals; investigate the importance of seeds; identify ways plants are important to people; recognize examples of common animals such as being fish, birds, or mammals.

## TEACHING SUGGESTIONS
• Use fresh vegetables to supplement this lesson. Whenever possible select intact vegetables that still have the stalks, root hairs, and leaves that are usually removed at the supermarket. For example, young children may not realize that we eat the stalk portion of celery. Showing them the green tops and base lets them realize how the food has been changed before it gets to the customer.

• Use pictures and encourage students to give examples of the same foods prepared differently in various ethnic backgrounds. Provide pictures of ethnic foods from magazines or cookbooks or secure samples of ethnic foods using the type of food mentioned in the lesson. Assist students in describing and pronouncing the names of ethnic foods. Discuss how their preparation and combination with other foods affects its appearance and taste.

• Young children may not know the difference between bacon, pork, and ham. Discuss how meat is processed differently to produce different flavor in each type of meat.

• Model and encourage students to express the following process for describing a food.
  1. Recall the important characteristics of this kind of food. (What it looks like, tastes like, how it's prepared, when it is usually eaten, etc.)
  2. Check that I describe all those important characteristics.
  3. Check that I have given enough details to keep the kind of food I am describing from being confused for another kind of food.

• For second grade classes, discuss basic nutrients the food contains: fats, protein, carbohydrates, vitamins, minerals and water.

• To reinforce students' responses, use a web diagram to record their answers (Transparency Master 9 on page 333).

© 2000 CRITICAL THINKING BOOKS & SOFTWARE • WWW.CRITICALTHINKING.COM • 800-458-4849          141

BEGINNING BUILDING THINKING SKILLS LESSON PLANS                    DESCRIBING PEOPLE AND THINGS

**MODEL LESSON** | **LESSON**
**Introduction**
- Ask a student to describe to the class a food that he or she ate for breakfast.
  Q: What clues let you know what food was described?
    A: The kind of food (fruit, bread, meat, drink, etc.), where one gets it, or how it is prepared.

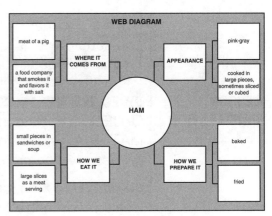

**Explaining the Objective to Students**
  Q: In this lesson, we will describe the main characteristics of certain foods.

**Class Activity**
- Display the following picture:
  **E-6 Example:** *ham*
  Q: Describe this food.
    A: This meat is made by adding salt and water to pork (the meat of a pig) and treating it (smoking) to prevent it from spoiling. It is usually baked in large pieces or fried in large slices. We usually eat ham in sandwiches, soups, or in large pieces for dinner or breakfast.

  Q: What details do you describe to explain that the food in this picture is ham?
    A: The size of pieces we cook and eat, along with information about what animal the meat comes from and how it is processed tell that this meat is different from others.

**Guided Practice**
- Display the following picture:
  **E-6 Exercise:** *grapes*
  Q: Describe this food.
    A: This fruit grows in bunches on a vine. The soft, sweet, green or purple berry can be eaten whole, made into jelly, or squeezed into juice. Many bunches of berries grow on each vine.

  Q: What details do you describe to explain that the food in this picture is grapes?
    A: The color, shape, appearance of the grapes, along with information about its use to flavor jelly or produce juice tells that these berries are grapes.

**Optional Independent Practice**
- If students need additional practice, select the following picture and ask students to describe the food.
- Display the picture:
  **E-6 Practice:** *celery*

142          © 2000 CRITICAL THINKING BOOKS & SOFTWARE • WWW.CRITICALTHINKING.COM • 800-458-4849

Q: Describe this food.
   A: This vegetable has leaves and a stalk. The stalk of this plant can be eaten raw (without cooking it). Some people add celery to soup or stews to give it flavor. Celery is moist and crunchy to eat and can be dipped into sauces.

Q: What details do you describe to tell that the food in this picture is celery?
   A: The part of the plant that we eat, how it is prepared, how it feels and sounds when we eat it show that this food is celery.

### Thinking About Thinking

Q: What did you look for when you picked out the food that was described?
   A: Whether the food is a plant or animal product is the primary question. If it is a plant product, describe what kind—tree, vine, or small bush. Identify what part we eat—seed, fruit, leaf, stem, or root. Describe its color, shape, and size. If it is an animal product, identify the kind of animal that produces it or is butchered for it, and how it is prepared. For plant or animal food products, describe how it is cooked, seasoned, and served at specific meals.

### Personal Application

Q: When is it important to describe food accurately?
   A: To order food in the school cafeteria or in a restaurant; to remind a friend or family member about food that he or she has been asked to bring home from the grocery store; to understand or relate a doctor's diet recommendations; to help someone who doesn't understand English well to request food that he or she wants.

**LANGUAGE ARTS EXTENSION**

## LANGUAGE INTEGRATION ACTIVITIES

- Drawing: Select a picture of a food or allow students to find or draw a picture of food. Ask students to create a riddle about food that they will tell or write for a partner.

- Telling: Ask students within each cooperative learning group to play "Twenty Questions" about a food.

- First/Second Grade Language Activity: For each item, list students' responses and ask students to read the list aloud or write sentences to create a short description that can be added to students' drawings, if desired.

## FOLLOW-UP ACTIVITIES AT HOME

- Ask parents to describe the food they enjoy or have just purchased. They should then ask the child to describe the food to another family member or friend.

## PICTURE BOOK EXTENSION

- Language experiences with picture books extend this lesson and demonstrate how food meets family needs and is prepared differently in various cultures. After discussing any of the pictures books, ask the following questions:

BEGINNING BUILDING THINKING SKILLS LESSON PLANS                    DESCRIBING PEOPLE AND THINGS

Q: Are there any new ideas about (<u>celery, grapes, or ham</u>) that we learned from this story?

Q: What ideas or details about (<u>celery, grapes, or ham</u>) did you get from the pictures?

Q: Is this information true of most (<u>celery, grapes, or ham</u>)?

After discussing each story, ask students to add new information about the characteristics of the food described in the story to the lists, posters, or graphic organizers that you may have used when discussing the pictures.

### SUPPLEMENTAL PICTURE BOOKS

- These books feature the food discussed in this lesson. Descriptions of these and additional books on topics in this lesson are listed in the extended bibliography at the end of this manual.

**Celery**

*The Celery Stalks at Midnight,* James Howe

**Ham**

*Green Eggs and Ham,* Dr. Seuss
*Meat,* Elizabeth Clark

**Grapes**

*Freedom's Fruit*, William H. Hooks
*We Love Fruit,* Fay Robinson

**EXERCISE E-7**

# DESCRIBING VEHICLES—SELECT

**ANSWERS E-7**
**E-7 Example:** ambulance
**E-7 Exercise:** bus
**E-7 Practice:** bicycle

**LESSON PREPARATION**

### OBJECTIVE AND MATERIALS

OBJECTIVE: Students will select a picture that fits a description of a vehicle.
MATERIALS: The following pictures are used in this lesson: *airplane (27), ambulance (24), bicycle (30), city bus (28), car (31), police car (25), school bus (32), train (29), pickup truck (26)*

### CURRICULUM APPLICATIONS

<u>Social Studies</u>: Identify how a family depends on transportation to meet its needs; identify some jobs in the home, school, and community; cite examples of community needs and services; understand how community helpers are an example of interdependence.

### TEACHING SUGGESTIONS

- Model and encourage students to express the following process for identifying a vehicle that someone has described:

  1. Recall the important characteristics of the vehicle.

  2. Find the important characteristics in the pictures.

  3. Check which picture shows those important characteristics.

144          © 2000 CRITICAL THINKING BOOKS & SOFTWARE • WWW.CRITICALTHINKING.COM • 800-458-4849

BEGINNING BUILDING THINKING SKILLS LESSON PLANS                    DESCRIBING PEOPLE AND THINGS

4. Check that the other pictures of vehicles don't show those important characteristics as well.

**MODEL LESSON**

## LESSON

### Introduction

• Without naming it, in three to five sentences describe a vehicle not in the example. Ask the class to identify the vehicle that was described.

Q: What clues let you know what vehicle was described?

A: Students cite number of wheels, how many people or what kind of cargo it carries, where it goes, whether one has to pay to ride it, etc.

### Explaining the Objective to Students

Q: In this lesson, we will identify the main characteristics that you discuss when you describe a vehicle.

### Class Activity

• Display the following pictures:

**E-7 Example:** _ambulance_, _police car, truck_

Q: I will describe one of the vehicles. Select the picture that fits the description. This vehicle carries emergency equipment, gives treatment to people in need, and carries sick or injured people to the hospital. It contains medicine, tables for moving people, and bandages. Emergency workers use its machines to help doctors understand what the patient needs and to keep people safe on the trip to the hospital. It can go fast in traffic because flashing lights and sirens warn people to get out of the way. It doesn't stop for signs or lights on its trip to the hospital.

• Ask students to decide with their partners which picture has been described. Confirm the answer with the whole class.

A: An ambulance

Q: What clues let you know that the vehicle in this picture is an ambulance?

A: The square, truck-like shape allows room in the rear for the patient, the equipment, and emergency workers. The lights, the siren, and the markings alert drivers that it is an emergency vehicle that will not stop for traffic signals.

Q: Why don't the other pictures fit the description?

A: The police car has lights and sirens, but does not look like a truck and has no room for a patient. A truck is not an emergency vehicle with lights, sirens, and emergency equipment.

### Guided Practice

• Display the following pictures:

**E-7 Exercise:** _airplane,_ _bus_, _train_

Q: I will describe one of the vehicles. Select the picture that fits the description. This vehicle is much taller and longer than a car and carries lots of people. Some travel the same streets around the city many times each day. Some carry passengers from one city to another. People usually pay to ride on them. Some are used by anyone who pays the fare. Some

© 2000 CRITICAL THINKING BOOKS & SOFTWARE • WWW.CRITICALTHINKING.COM • 800-458-4849                    145

are operated by companies for their employees or customers.

Q: What do we call this vehicle?
  A: A bus

Q: What clues let you know that the vehicle in this picture is the bus?
  A: The size, route, fare and how people make use of the vehicle show that the vehicle is the bus.

Q: Why don't the other vehicles fit the description?
  A: Airplanes and trains do not run on streets.

**Optional Independent Practice**
• Display the following pictures:
  **E-7 Practice:** _bicycle_, car, school bus

• Q: I will describe one of the vehicles. Select the picture that fits the description. This vehicle has two wheels and handle bars. The driver pedals it to make it go. It is usually ridden by only one person. Children often ride to school on one.
  Q: What do we call this vehicle?
    A: A bicycle

  Q: What clues let you know that the vehicle in this picture is the bicycle?
    A: The number of wheels, parts, who rides it, and how it moves show that this vehicle is a bicycle.

  Q: Why don't the other vehicles fit the description?
    A: The other vehicles run by a motor and cannot be driven by children.

**Thinking About Thinking**
  Q: What did you look for when you picked out the vehicle that was described?
    A: Its size, purpose, where it is driven, how it looks, who owns or uses it, what kind of equipment it has, and when it is used.

**Personal Application**
  Q: When is it important to describe vehicles accurately?
    A: To describe deliveries, to describe traffic, to give directions

**LANGUAGE ARTS EXTENSION**

**LANGUAGE INTEGRATION ACTIVITIES**
• Drawing: Select a picture of a vehicle or allow students to find or draw a picture of a vehicle. Ask students to create a riddle that they will tell or write for a partner.

• Telling: Ask students within each cooperative learning group to play "Twenty Questions" about a vehicle.

• First/Second Grade Language Activity: For each item, list students' responses and ask students to read the list aloud or write sentences to create a short description that can be added to students' drawings, if desired.

BEGINNING BUILDING THINKING SKILLS LESSON PLANS                    DESCRIBING PEOPLE AND THINGS

**FOLLOW-UP ACTIVITIES AT HOME**

• Ask parents to describe the vehicles they own or use in their work. They should then ask the child to describe these vehicles to another family member or friend.

**PICTURE BOOK EXTENSION**

• Language experiences with any of the following books extend this lesson and demonstrate how various vehicles meet individual family needs After discussing any of the picture books ask the following questions:

Q: Are there any new ideas about (ambulances, buses, or bicycles) that we learned from this story?

Q: What ideas or details about (ambulances, buses, or bicycles) did you get from the pictures?

Q: Is this information true of most (ambulances, buses, or bicycles)?

• After discussing each story, ask students to add new information about the characteristics of the various vehicles described in the story to the lists, posters, or graphic organizers that you may have used when discussing the pictures.

**SUPPLEMENTAL PICTURE BOOKS**

• These books feature the vehicles discussed in this lesson. Descriptions of these and additional books on topics in this lesson are listed in the extended bibliography at the end of this manual.

**Ambulance**

*Emergency,* Snap Shot series
*Emergency Vehicles,* Dayna Wolhart

**Bicycle**

*Amazing Bikes,* Trevor Lord
*Hello, Two Wheeler,* Jane Mason
*How Is A Bicycle Made?* Henry Horenstein

**Bus**

*Is There Room on the Bus,* Helen Piers and Hannah Giffard
*The Wheels on the Bus,* Paul Zelinsky
*Where's That Bus,* Eileen Brown

**EXERCISE E-8**

# DESCRIBING VEHICLES—EXPLAIN

**ANSWERS E-8**

**E-8 Example:** train—A train is a line of railroad cars that are joined together. The first railroad car, called a locomotive, has an engine that is very strong and pulls the cars. Trains can travel only on railroad tracks. Trains are used to carry people or things from one place to another. Passenger trains usually run on a regular schedule.

**E-8 Exercise:** helicopter—A helicopter flies straight up and down or across in the air. It can land in very small places. It has large blades that spin quickly to give it speed to rise into the air. A helicopter does not carry as many passengers as most airplanes. It can carry one to twelve people.

© 2000 CRITICAL THINKING BOOKS & SOFTWARE • WWW.CRITICALTHINKING.COM • 800-458-4849          147

BEGINNING BUILDING THINKING SKILLS LESSON PLANS                    DESCRIBING PEOPLE AND THINGS

> It is sometimes used to rescue people at sea or to get accident victims to help quickly by flying over traffic.
> **E-8 Practice:** ship—A ship is a large boat that carries people and goods long distances. Some, like ocean liners, carry large numbers of people and are like a large floating hotel. Some ships carry freight, like cars or oil. Some ships are used by the navy for defense, such as aircraft carriers. Ships have huge engines that turn huge propellers that push the ship through the water.

**LESSON PREPARATION**

## OBJECTIVE AND MATERIALS

OBJECTIVE: Students will look at a photograph of a vehicle and describe it.
MATERIALS: The following pictures are used in this lesson: *helicopter (38), ship (35), train (29)* • transparency of TM 9 on page 333

## CURRICULUM APPLICATIONS

Social Studies: Identifying how a family depends upon transportation to meet its needs; identifying some jobs in the home, school, and community; citing examples of community needs and services; understanding how community helpers are an example of interdependence.

## TEACHING SUGGESTIONS

* Although boats are generally smaller than ships, it may not be useful to make this distinction. Use common terms such as ferry boat.

* Students may not commonly use the term *vehicle*. Discuss with them synonyms for vehicle (means of transportation). Convey the concept that a vehicle is propelled by an engine within it, such as a car or airplane, or by some force that is applied to it, such as a person pedaling or wind pushing sails.

* Model and encourage students to express the following process for describing a vehicle:
  1. Recall the important characteristics of the kind of vehicle. (Picture in my mind what it looks like, what it is used for, how it moves, etc.)
  2. Check that I describe all those important characteristics.
  3. Check that I have given enough details to keep the vehicle I am describing from being confused for another kind of vehicle.

* To reinforce students' responses, use a web diagram to record their answers (Transparency Master 9 on page 333).

**MODEL LESSON**

## LESSON

### Introduction

* Ask a student to describe a vehicle in three to five sentences without naming what it is. Ask the class to identify the vehicle that the student has described.
  Q: What details let you know what vehicle was described?
  A: Number of wheels, how many people or what kind of cargo it carries, where it goes, whether one has to pay to ride it, etc.

148              © 2000 CRITICAL THINKING BOOKS & SOFTWARE • WWW.CRITICALTHINKING.COM • 800-458-4849

### Explaining the Objective to Students
Q: In this lesson, we will describe the important characteristics of vehicles.

### Class Activity
- Display the following picture:
  
  **E-8 Example:** *train*
  
  Q: Describe this vehicle.
  
  A: A train is a line of railroad cars that are joined together. The first railroad car, called a locomotive, has an engine that is very strong and pulls the cars. Trains can travel only on railroad tracks. Trains are used to carry people or things from one place to another. Passenger trains usually run on a regular schedule
  
  Q: What details do you describe to explain that the vehicle in this picture is a train?
  
  A: The vehicle's size, shape, and uses, and its need for tracks show that it is a train.

### Guided Practice
- Display the following picture:
  
  **E-8 Exercise:** *helicopter*
  
  Q: Describe this vehicle.
  
  A: A helicopter flies straight up and down or across in the air. It can land in very small places. It has large blades that spin quickly to give it speed to rise into the air. A helicopter does not carry as many passengers as most airplanes. It can carry one to twelve people. It is sometimes used to rescue people at sea or to get accident victims to help quickly by flying over traffic.

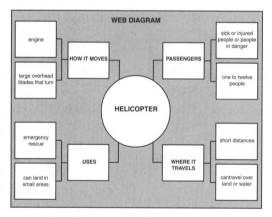

  Q: What details do you describe to explain that the vehicle in this picture is a helicopter?
  
  A: The vehicle's size, purposes, and operation, and the position of its propellers show that this vehicle is a helicopter.

### Optional Independent Practice
- Display the following picture:
  
  **E-8 Practice:** *ship*
  
  Q: Describe this vehicle.
  
  A: A ship is a large boat that carries people and goods long distances. Some, like ocean liners, carry large numbers of people. Some ships carry freight, such as cars or oil. Some ships are used by the navy for defense, such as aircraft carriers. Ships have huge engines that turn large propellers that push the ship through the water.
  
  Q: What details do you describe to tell that the vehicle in this picture is a ship?

A: Its size, the distances that it travels over water, and what it carries shows that this vehicle is a ship.

**Thinking About Thinking**

Q: What kind of characteristics did you discuss to describe vehicles?

A: Its size, purpose, where it is driven, who uses it, how it moves, how it looks, what kind of equipment it has, and when it is used.

**Personal Application**

Q: When is it important to describe vehicles accurately?

A: To describe deliveries; to describe traffic; to give directions.

**LANGUAGE ARTS EXTENSION**

## LANGUAGE INTEGRATION ACTIVITIES

• Drawing: Select a picture of a vehicle or allow students to find or draw a picture of food. Ask students to create a riddle that they will tell or write for a partner.

• Telling: Ask students within each cooperative learning group to play "Twenty Questions" about a vehicle.

• First/Second Grade Language Activity: For each item, list students' responses and ask students to read the list aloud or write sentences to create a short description that can be added to students' drawings, if desired.

• Create a bulletin board of pictures of different kinds of ships/boats by type. Discuss how the purpose of the ship or boat affects its size, shape, and appearance.

• Use a highly detailed drawing of a vehicle and identify how its parts contribute to the operation and purpose of the vehicle. Discuss how the vehicle is propelled.

## FOLLOW-UP ACTIVITIES AT HOME

• Ask parents to describe the vehicles they own or use in their work. They should then ask the child to describe these vehicles to another family member or friend.

## PICTURE BOOK EXTENSION

• Language experiences with any of the following books extend this lesson and demonstrate how various vehicles meet individual family needs. After discussing any of the picture books ask the following questions:

Q: Are there any new ideas about (helicopters, ships, or trains) that we learned from this story?

Q: What ideas or details about (helicopters, ships, or trains) did you get from the pictures?

Q: Is this information true of most (helicopters, ships, or trains)?

• After discussing each story, ask students to add new information about the characteristics of the various vehicles described in the story to the lists, posters, or graphic organizers that you may have used when discussing the pictures.

BEGINNING BUILDING THINKING SKILLS LESSON PLANS                    DESCRIBING PEOPLE AND THINGS

## SUPPLEMENTAL PICTURE BOOKS
- These books feature the vehicles discussed in this lesson. Descriptions of these and additional books on topics in this lesson are listed in the extended bibliography at the end of this manual.

**Helicopter**
*Aircraft,* Ian Graham
*Budgie, the Little Helicopter*, Sarah Ferguson
*Emergency Vehicles,* Dayna Wolhart

**Ship**
*Ships and Boats,* Dorling Kindersley
*Ships,* Richard Humble

**Train**
*Freight Train,* Peter Brady
*Freight Train,* Donald Crews
*The Little Engine That Could,* Watty Piper
*Trains,* Dorling Kindersley

**EXERCISE E-9**

# DESCRIBING ANIMALS—SELECT

**ANSWERS E-9**
**E-9 Example:** snake
**E-9 Exercise:** horse
**E-9 Practice:** spider

**LESSON PREPARATION**

### OBJECTIVE AND MATERIALS
OBJECTIVE: Students will select a picture that fits a description of an animal.
MATERIALS: The following pictures are used in this lesson: *camel (58), horse (64), fish (57), frog (55), giraffe (59), lizard (68), snake (69), spider (60), turtle (61)*

### CURRICULUM APPLICATIONS
<u>Science</u>: Identify living things as plants or animals; state what animals need to live and grow; recognize that needs of different kinds of animals are similar; recognize examples of common animals as fish, amphibians, reptiles, insects, birds, or mammals.

### TEACHING SUGGESTIONS
- For young children "cold-blooded" or "warm-blooded" may be new terms. Explain the effect of this difference on the survival needs of animals.

- The terms "backbone" or "vertebra" may be new concepts. Discuss with students the significance and function of a backbone.

- Model and encourage students to express the following process for identifying an animal that someone has described:
  1. Recall the important characteristics of the animal.

  2. Find the important characteristics in the pictures.

  3. Check that the other pictures of animals don't show those important characteristics as well.

© 2000 CRITICAL THINKING BOOKS & SOFTWARE • WWW.CRITICALTHINKING.COM • 800-458-4849          151

BEGINNING BUILDING THINKING SKILLS LESSON PLANS                    DESCRIBING PEOPLE AND THINGS

**MODEL LESSON** | **LESSON**

## Introduction

- In three to five sentences, describe an animal that the class has studied or seen recently. Ask students to name the animal that has been described.

    Q: What clues let you know which animal I was describing?

    A: Students cite type, coloring, behavior, how it moves, where it lives, what it eats or what animals eat it.

## Explaining the Objective to Students

Q: In this lesson, we will identify the main characteristics that you would discuss when you describe animals.

## Class Activity

- Display the following pictures:

    **E-9 Example:** *frog, snake, fish*

    Q: I will describe one of the animals. Select the picture that fits the description. This animal is long and thin, has a backbone, and is cold-blooded. Its babies hatch from eggs and look like the adult when they are born. It moves on its belly by moving many small muscles, making it seem to slide along the ground. It is covered with shiny scales. Some kinds are dangerous to people. Some can live near water; others can live in the desert. They eat small animals.

    Q: What do we call this animal?

    A: A snake

- Ask students to decide with their partners which picture has been described. Confirm the answer with the whole class. Encourage students to use as many verbs as possible to describe how the snake moves.

    Q: What clues let you know that the animal in this picture is a snake?

    A: Its shape, its habitat, what it eats, how it moves, and its skin covering show that this animal is a snake.

    Q: Why don't the other animals fit the description?

    A: A frog is a tadpole when it is born and does not look like an adult frog. A fish has to live in water.

## Guided Practice

- Display the following pictures:

    **E-9 Exercise:** *camel, horse, giraffe*

    Q: I will describe one of the animals. Select the picture that fits the description. This animal has a backbone and is warm-blooded. The babies look similar to their parents when they are born. It has a mane on its head and a long tail. It eats grass and hay. It lives on a farm. What do we call this animal?

    A: Horse

    Q: What clues let you know that the animal in this picture is the horse?

    A: Its size, appearance, where it lives, and coloring show that this animal is a horse.

152          © 2000 CRITICAL THINKING BOOKS & SOFTWARE • WWW.CRITICALTHINKING.COM • 800-458-4849

**BEGINNING BUILDING THINKING SKILLS LESSON PLANS**　　　　**DESCRIBING PEOPLE AND THINGS**

Q: Why don't the other animals fit the description?
　A: Camels have a hump on their back and no mane; giraffes have a long tail and a very long neck.

**Optional Independent Practice**
- Display the following pictures:
**E-9 Practice:** *lizard, spider, turtle*

Q: I will describe one of the animals. Select the picture that fits the description. This animal has eight legs. It is cold-blooded. It doesn't have a backbone; instead its body looks like several parts which are connected. Its babies hatch from tiny eggs and look like the adult. This animal makes webs out of a thin thread which they make from their bodies. The webs become their home and a trap for flies and other insects which they eat.

Q: What do we call this animal?
　A: A spider

Q: What clues let you know that the animal in this picture is the spider?
　A: The number of legs, appearance, behavior, and what it eats show that it is the spider.

Q: Why don't the other animals fit the description?
　A: Lizards and turtles are reptiles with four legs. Neither lizards nor turtles spin webs.

**Thinking About Thinking**

Q: What did you look for when you picked out the animal that was described?
　A: Students often answer: body structure, color, size, warm- or cold-blooded, whether it has a backbone, whether it hatches or gives live birth, where it lives, how it moves, what it eats.

**Personal Application**

Q: When is it important to describe animals well?
　A: To describe trips to the zoo, television shows, books and pictures.

**LANGUAGE ARTS EXTENSION**

**LANGUAGE INTEGRATION ACTIVITIES**
- Drawing: Ask students to draw a picture of a horse, a snake, or a spider. Students may write or tell short descriptions of the animal.

- *What Animal Am I? An Animal Guessing Game,* Iza Trapani. This book models animal riddles with pictures. Select a picture of an animal or allow students to find or draw a picture of food. Ask students to create a riddle that they will tell or write for a partner.

- Drama: Ask students to use animal puppets to act out "Brown bear, brown bear, what do I see?" for various animals discussed in the lesson.

- Telling: Ask students within each cooperative learning group to play "Twenty Questions" about an animal.

© 2000 CRITICAL THINKING BOOKS & SOFTWARE • WWW.CRITICALTHINKING.COM • 800-458-4849　　　153

BEGINNING BUILDING THINKING SKILLS LESSON PLANS                    DESCRIBING PEOPLE AND THINGS

### FOLLOW-UP ACTIVITIES AT HOME

• Ask parents to describe the animals they have seen or pets they own. They should then ask the child to describe these animals to another family member or friend.

### PICTURE BOOK EXTENSION

• Language experiences with any of the following books extend this lesson. After discussing any of the picture books ask the following questions:

Q: Are there any new ideas about (horses, snakes, or spiders) that we learned from this story?

Q: What ideas or details about (horses, snakes, or spiders) did you get from the pictures?

Q: Is this information true of most (horses, snakes, or spiders)?

• After discussing each story, ask students to add new information about the characteristics of the animal described in the story to the lists, posters, or graphic organizers that you may have used when discussing the pictures.

### SUPPLEMENTAL PICTURE BOOKS

• Descriptions of these and additional books on topics in this lesson are listed in the extended bibliography at the end of this manual.

**Lizards**

*Lizard in the Sun,* Joanne Ryder
*Lizard's Song,* George Shannon
*Amazing Lizards,* Trevor Smith

**Spiders**

*Amazing Spiders,* Alexandra Parsons
*Spiders,* I. Polendorf
*Spiders Are Not Insects*

**Turtles**

*And Still the Turtle Watched,* Sheila MacGill Callahan
*Box Turtle at Long Pond,* William T. George
*Into the Sea,* Brenda Z. Guiberson
*Turtles Take Their Time,* Rookie Read About Science series,

**EXERCISE E-10**

# DESCRIBING ANIMALS—EXPLAIN

**ANSWERS E-10**

**E-10 Example:** turkey—A turkey is a large bird with brownish feathers and a bare head and neck. It looks like a chicken but is bigger. This bird has a backbone and is warm-blooded. It lays eggs. Many people in the United States eat turkey for Thanksgiving dinner.

**E-10 Exercise:** ostrich—The ostrich is a large bird that can't fly but can run very fast on its two long legs. It has a long neck, is warm-blooded, has feathers, and lays large eggs. It eats grass, fruit, insects, and small animals. It lives in dry climates.

**E-10 Practice:** zebra—A zebra looks like a horse. It is white with black stripes. It has a backbone and is warm-blooded. It eats grass and leaves. Zebras live in Africa. The baby zebras look like their parents.

154              © 2000 CRITICAL THINKING BOOKS & SOFTWARE • WWW.CRITICALTHINKING.COM • 800-458-4849

| | |
|---|---|
| **LESSON PREPARATION** | **OBJECTIVE AND MATERIALS**<br>OBJECTIVE: Students will look at a photograph of an animal and describe it.<br>MATERIALS: The following pictures are used in this lesson: *ostrich (62), turkey (67), zebra (63)* • transparency of TM 9 on page 333<br><br>**CURRICULUM APPLICATIONS**<br><u>Science</u>: Identify living things as plants or animals; state what animals need to live and grow; recognize that needs of different kinds of animals are similar; recognize examples of common animals; recognize examples of common animals: fish, birds, or mammals.<br><br>**TEACHING SUGGESTIONS**<br>• For young children "cold-blooded" or "warm-blooded" may be new terms. Explain the effect of this difference on the survival needs of animals. Similarly, the terms "backbone" or "vertebra" may be new concepts. Discuss with students the significance and function of a backbone.<br><br>• Model and encourage students to express the following process for describing an animal.<br>   1. Recall the important characteristics of this kind of animal (Picture in my mind what it looks like, warm- or cold- blooded, whether it has a backbone, whether it hatches eggs or gives live birth, where it lives, how it moves, what it eats, etc.)<br>   2. Check that I describe all the important characteristics.<br>   3. Check that I have given enough details to keep the kind of animal I am describing from being confused with other kinds of animals.<br><br>• First/Second Grade Language Activity: For each item, list students' responses and ask students to read the list aloud or write sentences to create a short description that can be added to students' drawings.<br><br>• To reinforce students' responses, use a web diagram to record their answers (Transparency Master 9 on page 333). See the Guided Practice. 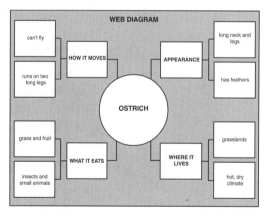 |
| **MODEL LESSON** | **LESSON**<br>**Introduction**<br>• Ask a student to describe to the class in three to five sentences an animal that they have studied or seen recently.<br><br>• Ask the class to name the animal that has been described.<br>   Q: What details let you know which animal was described?<br>      A: Type, coloring, behavior, how it moves, where it lives, what it eats or what animals eat it. |

BEGINNING BUILDING THINKING SKILLS LESSON PLANS                    DESCRIBING PEOPLE AND THINGS

### Explaining the Objective to Students

Q: In this lesson, we will discuss the main characteristics used to describe animals.

### Class Activity

• Display the following pictures:

**E-10 Example:** *turkey*

Q: Describe this animal.

A: A turkey is a large bird with brownish feathers and a bare head and neck. It looks like a chicken but is bigger. This bird has a backbone and is warm-blooded. It lays eggs. Many people in the United States eat turkey for Thanksgiving dinner.

Q: What details do you describe to explain that the animal in this picture is the turkey?

A: Its size, shape, body features, and when it is eaten.

### Guided Practice

• Display the following picture:

**E-10 Exercise:** *ostrich*

Q: Describe this animal.

A: The ostrich is a large bird that can't fly but can run very fast on its two long legs. It has a long neck, is warm-blooded, has feathers, and lays large eggs. It eats grass, fruit, insects, and small animals. It lives in dry climates.

Q: What details do you describe to explain that the animal in this picture is the ostrich?

A: Its shape and body features.

### Optional Independent Practice

• Display the following picture:

**E-10 Practice:** *zebra*

Q: Describe this animal.

A: A zebra looks like a horse. It is white with black stripes. It has a backbone and is warmblooded. It eats grass and leaves. Zebras live in Africa. The baby zebras look like their parents.

Q: What details do you describe to explain that the animal in this picture is the zebra?

A: Its size, markings, and where it is found.

### Thinking About Thinking

Q: What kind of characteristics did you discuss to describe an animal?

A: Body structure, color, size, warm- or cold- blooded, whether it has a backbone, whether it hatches or gives live birth, where it lives, how it moves, what it eats.

### Personal Application

Q: When is it important to describe animals well?

A: To describe trips to the zoo, television shows, books and pictures.

BEGINNING BUILDING THINKING SKILLS LESSON PLANS                    DESCRIBING PEOPLE AND THINGS

**LANGUAGE
ARTS
EXTENSION**

## LANGUAGE INTEGRATION ACTIVITIES

- Drawing: Ask students to draw a picture of a turkey, an ostrich, or a zebra. Students may write or tell short descriptions of the animal.

- *What Animal Am I? An Animal Guessing Game,* Iza Trapani (Whispering Coyote Press, Danvers, MA, 1992). This book models animal riddles with pictures. Select a picture of an animal or allow students to find or draw a picture of food. Ask students to create a riddle that they will tell or write for a partner.

- Drama: Ask students to use animal puppets to act out "Brown bear, brown bear, what do I see?" for various animals discussed in the lesson.

- Telling: Ask students within each cooperative learning group to play "Twenty Questions" about a food.

- Create a bulletin board of pictures of different kinds of animals by class. Discuss how each animal reproduces, whether it is warm or cold blooded, and other special characteristics:
  1. Birds: egg-laying, warm-blooded vertebrates with wings
  2. Fish: egg-laying, cold-blooded vertebrates with gills
  3. Reptiles: egg-laying, cold-blooded vertebrates with dry skin
  4. Amphibians: egg-laying, cold-blooded vertebrates with moist skin
  5. Mammals: baby grows inside mother's body; warm-blooded vertebrates with hair

## FOLLOW-UP ACTIVITIES AT HOME

- Ask parents to describe the animals they have seen or pets they own. They should then ask the child to describe these animals to another family member or friend.

## PICTURE BOOK EXTENSION

- Language experiences with any of the following books extend this lesson. After discussing any of the picture books ask the following questions:
  Q: Are there any new ideas about (ostriches, turkeys, or zebras) that we learned from this story?
  Q: What ideas or details about (ostriches, turkeys, or zebras) did you get from the pictures?
  Q: Is this information true of most (ostriches, turkeys, or zebras)?

- After discussing each story, ask students to add new information about the characteristics of the animal described in the story to the lists, posters, or graphic organizers that you may have used when discussing the pictures.

## SUPPLEMENTAL PICTURE BOOKS

- These books feature the animals discussed in this lesson. Descriptions of these and additional books on topics in this lesson are listed in the extended bibliography at the end of this manual.

### Ostriches

*Lion and the Ostrich Chicks, and Other African Folk Tales,* Bryan Ashley

© 2000 CRITICAL THINKING BOOKS & SOFTWARE • WWW.CRITICALTHINKING.COM • 800-458-4849          157

BEGINNING BUILDING THINKING SKILLS LESSON PLANS                    DESCRIBING PEOPLE AND THINGS

*Ostriches,* New True series, E.U. Lepthien
*The Cuckoo Child,* Dick King-Smith

**Turkey**
*Birds We Know,* M. Friskey
*Turkeys That Fly and Turkeys That Don't*

**Zebra**
*African Animals,* J. W. Purcell
*Greedy Zebra,* Mwenye Hadithi and Adrienne Kennaway
*Zebras,* E. U. Lepthien

**EXERCISE E-11**

# DESCRIBING BUILDINGS—SELECT

**ANSWERS E-11**
**E-11 Example:** mobile home
**E-11 Exercise:** fire station
**E-11 Practice:** restaurant

**LESSON PREPARATION**

## OBJECTIVE AND MATERIALS
OBJECTIVE: Students will select a picture that fits a description of a building.
MATERIALS: The following pictures are used in this lesson: *apartment building (50), barn (42), farm (47), fire station (45), gas station (41), house (53), mobile home (44), police station (46), restaurant (48),* and *supermarket (49).*

## CURRICULUM APPLICATIONS
Social Studies: Identify how a family depends on the products and services produced or housed in buildings; cite the role buildings play in providing community needs and services.

## TEACHING SUGGESTIONS
• Encourage students to give examples from their local community of the locations where the buildings described in this lesson are located.

• Young students may need to be reminded of synonyms for "house"— dwelling, home, shelter, etc.

• Model and encourage students to express the following process for identifying a building that someone has described:
1. Recall the important characteristics of the building.

2. Find the important characteristics in the pictures.

3. Check that the other pictures of buildings don't show those important characteristics as well.

**MODEL LESSON**

## LESSON

### Introduction
• Select a familiar building and describe it to the class in three to five sentences. Ask the class to name the building that has been described.
Q: What clues let you know what building I was describing?
  A: Students cite size, location, what it is used for, etc.

158                  © 2000 CRITICAL THINKING BOOKS & SOFTWARE • WWW.CRITICALTHINKING.COM • 800-458-4849

**BEGINNING BUILDING THINKING SKILLS LESSON PLANS**　　　　　**DESCRIBING PEOPLE AND THINGS**

### Explaining the Objective to Students

Q: In this lesson, we will identify the main characteristics that you would discuss when you describe a building.

### Class Activity

* Display the following pictures:

**E-11 Example:** *barn, house, mobile home*

Q: I will describe one of these buildings. Select the picture that fits the description. This building can be moved on wheels, so that it can be pulled by a car or truck. Some can be as big as a small house. Some people use this building as their permanent home. Other people live in one while traveling or on vacation. This building may be used as an office or as a classroom for a school that runs out of space.

Q: What do we call this building?

　A: A mobile home

* Ask students to decide with their partners which picture has been described. Confirm the answer with the whole class.

Q: What clues let you know that the building in this picture is a mobile home?

　A: The size, use, and number of people who live in one show that this building is the mobile home.

Q: Why don't the other buildings fit the description?

　A: A barn is not a home for people. Neither a barn nor a house is moveable.

### Guided Practice

* Display the following pictures:

**E-11 Exercise:** *fire station, gas station, police station*

Q: I will describe one of the buildings. Select the picture that fits the description. Firefighters and their equipment are located in a large building with a large open area that looks like a garage and is used to store the fire truck. Firefighters usually spend the night in this building while they are on duty. Firefighters spend time there getting their equipment ready, exercising, and practicing rescue skills.

Q: What do we call this building?

　A: A fire station

Q: What clues let you know that the building in this picture is the fire station?

　A: The size, purpose, who stays there, and what is stored there shows that this building is a fire station.

Q: Why don't the other buildings fit the description?

　A: A police station does not require such large doors and storage area for large vehicles. A gas station is a business that sells fuel, not a community emergency service.

---

© 2000 CRITICAL THINKING BOOKS & SOFTWARE • WWW.CRITICALTHINKING.COM • 800-458-4849　　　159

BEGINNING BUILDING THINKING SKILLS LESSON PLANS                    DESCRIBING PEOPLE AND THINGS

**Optional Independent Practice**
- Display the following pictures:

  **F-11 Practice:** *farm, restaurant, supermarket*

  Q: I will describe one of the buildings. Select the picture that fits the description. This business is a place where people sometimes go to eat. Customers may sit at a table or a counter. Someone usually takes an order of what you would like to eat, gets food from the cooks, and brings it to you. You must pay for the food before you leave.

  Q: What do we call this building?
  - A: A restaurant

  Q: What clues let you know that the building in this picture is a restaurant?
  - A: The people who are workers or customers, the activities in the building, and the furniture show that this building is a restaurant.

  Q: Why don't the other buildings fit the description?
  - A: A farm and a supermarket also sell food, but people do not always sit down and eat prepared food in those buildings.

**Thinking About Thinking**

  Q: What did you look for when you picked out the building that was described?
  - A: Size, purpose, who lives or works there, how it is constructed, its design, its materials, its usual location (rural, downtown, suburbs).

  Q: What will you pay attention to whenever you pick a building that fits a description?
  1. Recall the important characteristics of the building.
  2. Find the important characteristics in the pictures.
  3. Check which picture shows those important characteristics.
  4. Check that the other pictures of buildings don't show those important characteristics as well.

**Personal Application**

  Q: When is it important to describe buildings well?
  - A: To describe trips, to give directions, to find places

**LANGUAGE ARTS EXTENSION**

**LANGUAGE INTEGRATION ACTIVITIES**
- Drawing: Ask students to draw a picture of a mobile home, a fire station, or a restaurant. Students may write or tell short descriptions of the building.

- Telling: Select a picture of a building or allow students to find or draw a picture of a building. Ask students to create a riddle that they will tell or write for a partner.

- Ask students within each cooperative learning group to play "Twenty Questions" about a building.

**FOLLOW-UP ACTIVITIES AT HOME**
- Ask parents to describe the buildings they see or use. They should then ask the child to describe these buildings to a family member or friend.

160          © 2000 CRITICAL THINKING BOOKS & SOFTWARE • WWW.CRITICALTHINKING.COM • 800-458-4849

BEGINNING BUILDING THINKING SKILLS LESSON PLANS                              DESCRIBING PEOPLE AND THINGS

**PICTURE BOOK EXTENSION**
- Language experiences with any of the following books extend this lesson. After discussing any of the picture books, ask the following questions:

  Q: Are there any new ideas about (mobile homes, fire stations, or restaurants) that we learned from this story?

  Q: What ideas or details about (mobile homes, fire stations, or restaurants) did you get from the pictures?

  Q: Is this information true of most (mobile homes, fire stations, or restaurants)?

- After discussing each story, ask students to add new information about the characteristics of the building described in the story to the lists, posters, or graphic organizers that you may have used when discussing the pictures.

**SUPPLEMENTAL PICTURE BOOKS**
- These books feature the buildings discussed in this lesson. Descriptions of these books, and additional books on topics in this lesson, are listed in the extended bibliography at the end of this manual.

**Fire Station**
> *Fire Fighters,* R. Broekel
> *The Fire Station,* Robert Munsch and Michael Martchenko

**Mobile Home**
> *Homes*, Nicola Baxter
> *Someplace Else,* Carol Saul

**Restaurant**
> *The Frog Goes to Dinner,* Mercer Mayer
> *The Paper Crane,* Molly Bang

**EXERCISE E-12**

# DESCRIBING BUILDINGS—EXPLAIN

> **ANSWERS E-12**
>
> **E-12 Example:** apartment building—An apartment building is bigger than a house and has many families living in it. Each family lives in a group of rooms called an apartment. This building contains many apartments. Halls and stairs are used by all the families in the apartment building.
>
> **E-12 Exercise:** post office—A post office is a place where people pay to send, or mail, letters and packages. They also pick up mail if they rent a post office box. In large cities, the post office workers sort the mail and send it to other post offices. In small towns, a post office may look like a small store or be a section of the store. The post office is owned by the national government; people pay a small fee to have the mail delivered.
>
> **E-12 Practice:** library—A library is a large building where people go to read or borrow books. Books, magazines, videotapes, and audiotapes are stored on library shelves. Most libraries are owned by the government of the town or county. You usually don't pay to use a library.

© 2000 CRITICAL THINKING BOOKS & SOFTWARE • WWW.CRITICALTHINKING.COM • 800-458-4849          161

BEGINNING BUILDING THINKING SKILLS LESSON PLANS — DESCRIBING PEOPLE AND THINGS

**LESSON PREPARATION**

**OBJECTIVE AND MATERIALS**
OBJECTIVE: Students will look at a photograph of a building and describe it.
MATERIALS: The following pictures are used in this lesson: *apartment building (50), library (40), post office (51)* • transparency of TM 9 on page 333

**CURRICULUM APPLICATIONS**
Social Studies: Identify how a family depends upon products and services to meet its needs; cite examples of community needs and services; identify jobs within the community and understand how community helpers are an example of interdependence.

**TEACHING SUGGESTIONS**

- Encourage students to give neighborhood examples of the buildings described in this lesson.

- Use a highly detailed drawing of a building and identify how its parts contribute to the structure and purpose of the building.

- Model and encourage students to express the following process for describing a building:
    1. Recall the important characteristics of this kind of building. (What one looks like, its purpose, who lives or works there, how it is constructed, etc.)
    2. Check that I describe all those important characteristics.
    3. Check that I have given enough details to keep the building I am describing from being confused for other kinds of buildings.

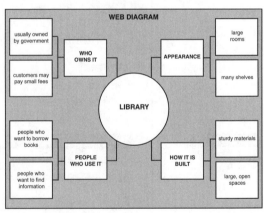

- To reinforce students' responses, use a web diagram to record their answers (Transparency Master 9 on page 333). See Independent Practice.

**MODEL LESSON**

**LESSON**

**Introduction**

- Ask a student to describe a building to the class in three to five sentences. Ask the class to name the building that has been described.
    Q: What details do you describe to tell what building was described?
        A: Size, location, what it is used for, etc.

**Explaining the Objective to Students**

Q: In this lesson, we will discuss the important characteristics to describe buildings.

**Class Activity**

- Display the following picture:
    **E-12 Example:** *apartment building*

162 © 2000 CRITICAL THINKING BOOKS & SOFTWARE • WWW.CRITICALTHINKING.COM • 800-458-4849

Q: Describe this building.
A: An apartment building is bigger than a house and has many families living in it. Each family lives in a group of rooms called an apartment. This building contains many apartments. Halls and stairs are used by all the families in the apartment building.

Q: What details do you describe to explain that the building in this picture is the apartment building?
A: The size, the number of people who live there, and how it is arranged describe it as an apartment building.

## GUIDED PRACTICE
• Display the following picture:
**E-12 Exercise:** *post office*

Q: Describe this building.
A: A post office is a place where people pay to send, or mail, letters and packages. They may also pick up mail if they rent a post office box. In large cities, the post office workers sort the mail and send it to other post offices. In small towns, a post office may look like a small store or take up a section of the store. The national government owns the post office; people pay a small fee to have the mail delivered.

Q: What details do you describe to explain that the building in this picture is the post office?
A: The size, what people do there, and how it is arranged show that it is a post office.

## Optional Independent Practice
• Display the following picture:
**E-12 Practice:** *library*

Q: Describe this building.
A: A library is a large building where people go to read or borrow books. Books, magazines, videotapes, and audiotapes are stored on library shelves. Most libraries are owned by the government of the town or county. You usually don't pay to use a library.

Q: What details do you describe to explain that the building in this picture is the library?
A: What people do there, its furniture, and the number of books on the shelves show that it is a library.

## Thinking About Thinking
Q: What kind of characteristics did you discuss to describe a building?
A: Size, purpose, who lives or works there, how it is constructed, its design, its materials, its usual location (rural, downtown, suburbs). Who owns or operates it.

## Personal Application
Q: When is it important to describe buildings well?
A: To describe trips to give directions, to find places

© 2000 CRITICAL THINKING BOOKS & SOFTWARE • WWW.CRITICALTHINKING.COM • 800-458-4849      163

BEGINNING BUILDING THINKING SKILLS LESSON PLANS · DESCRIBING PEOPLE AND THINGS

**LANGUAGE ARTS EXTENSION**

## LANGUAGE INTEGRATION ACTIVITIES
- Drawing: Ask students to draw a picture of an apartment building, a post office, or a library. Students may write or tell short descriptions of the building.
- Telling: Select a picture of a building or allow students to find or draw a picture of building. Ask students to create a riddle that they will tell or write for a partner.

- Ask students within each cooperative learning group to play "Twenty Questions" about a building.

- First/Second Grade Language Activity: For each item, list students' responses and ask students to read the list aloud or write sentences to create a short description that can be added to students' drawings, if desired.

- Create a bulletin board of pictures of different kinds of buildings by class. Discuss how each is used and other special characteristics:

## FOLLOW-UP ACTIVITIES AT HOME
- Ask parents to describe the buildings they see or use. They should then ask the child to describe these buildings to a family member or friend.

## PICTURE BOOK EXTENSION
- Language experiences with any of the following books extend this lesson. After discussing any of the picture books ask the following questions:
  Q: Are there any new ideas about (apartment buildings, post offices, or libraries) that we learned from this story?
  Q: What ideas or details about (apartment buildings, post offices, or libraries) did you get from the pictures?
  Q: Is this information true of most (apartment buildings, post offices, or libraries)?

- After discussing each story, ask students to add information about the characteristics of the buildings described in the story to the lists, posters, or graphic organizers you may have used when discussing the pictures.

## SUPPLEMENTAL PICTURE BOOKS
- These books feature the buildings discussed in this lesson. Descriptions of these and additional books on topics in this lesson are provided in the extended bibliography at the end of this manual.

### Apartment Building
*Homes,* Nicola Baxter
*Russell and Elisa,* Johanna Hurwitz
*Tar Beach,* Faith Ringgold

### Library
*Check It Out: The Book About Libraries,* Gail Gibbons
*The Library,* Sarah Stewart

### Post Office
*Hi,* Gio Coalson
*Will Goes to the Post Office,* Olof and Lena Landstrom

164 © 2000 CRITICAL THINKING BOOKS & SOFTWARE • WWW.CRITICALTHINKING.COM • 800-458-4849

BEGINNING BUILDING THINKING SKILLS LESSON PLANS          VERBAL SIMILARITIES AND DIFFERENCES

**Chapter 6**

# DESCRIBING SIMILARITIES AND DIFFERENCES

**EXERCISE F-1**

## SIMILAR FAMILY MEMBERS—SELECT

**ANSWERS F-1**
**F-1 Example:** mother
**F-1 Exercise:** baby

**LESSON PREPARATION**

### OBJECTIVE AND MATERIALS
OBJECTIVE: Students will use photographs to compare family members.
MATERIALS: The following pictures are used in this lesson: *baby (1), father (7), girl (4), grandmother (8), grandfather (9), mother (6), toddler boy (3), toddler girl (2).*

### CURRICULUM APPLICATIONS
<u>Social Studies</u>: Examine roles of family members and cite examples of interdependence; distinguish between a family's wants and needs; identify how human needs are met within the family in different cultures; identify some common rules in the home, school, and community; examine the roles of various family members in the celebration of holidays and traditions across cultures; explore the rights and responsibilities of various family members.

### TEACHING SUGGESTIONS
* Model and encourage students to express the following process for identifying a family member that someone has described:
  1. Recall the important characteristics of the family members. (Age, gender, relationships to other members of the family, roles, feelings about them, interests or experiences that make them special).

  2. Look for similar characteristics in the other family members.

  3. Select the family member that has most of the same characteristics.

  4. Check to see that none of the other family members fits the important characteristics better than the one I selected.

* Young children may not commonly use the terms *gender* to mean male or female or *relative* to mean someone in one's family. Encourage students to use these terms and to find synonyms for them.

* If there are children in your class who live in foster homes, conduct discussion of family members cautiously in order to avoid the conflict and confusion discussing family members creates for these children.

**MODEL LESSON**

### LESSON
#### Introduction
* Ask each student to describe to a partner in three to five sentences the responsibilities of a family member. After pairs of students have the

© 2000 CRITICAL THINKING BOOKS & SOFTWARE • WWW.CRITICALTHINKING.COM • 800-458-4849          165

opportunity to discuss a family member, ask a few students to report what they said to their partner to describe the family member.

### Explaining the Objective to Students

Q: In this lesson, we will identify people in a family that are most like others in the family.

### Class Activity

• Display the following pictures, placing the first to the left of the other three:
**F-1 Example:** *grandmother, father, mother, toddler boy*

Q: Here you see a picture of a grandmother. Tell your partner all the important things that you would need to say about a grandmother.

Q: What information about a grandmother is needed in order to describe the family member?

> A: A grandmother is an older woman whose son or daughter is a father or mother. Sometimes grandmothers take care of their grandchildren. Grandmothers remember events and places that younger members of the family may not know.

Q: Which person has most of the same important characteristics as a grandmother?

> A: A mother is a woman who has a son or daughter. Usually mothers take care of their children. Mothers help children get food, keep them clean and safe, and teach children how to take care of themselves. Mothers show a child that he or she is loved and special.

Q: What clues let you know that a mother is most like a grandmother?
> A: Age, their care of children

Q: How are the father and toddler boy different from the mother and grandmother?

> A: The father and the toddler boy are males. The toddler is a child; the mother and grandmother are adults.

### Guided Practice

• Display the following pictures, placing the first to the left of the other three:
**F-1 Exercise** *toddler girl, baby, father, grandfather*

Q: Tell your partner all the important things that you need to say about a toddler to find a picture of a similar family member.

> A: Toddlers are one to two years old. They can still be lifted and carried, but not for a long distance. They are learning to talk and walk by themselves (toddle). Toddlers have some teeth and can eat many foods by themselves if it is cut into small pieces. Toddlers can recognize their family and know where to find things in their home.

Q: What family member has most of the same characteristics as the toddler?

> A: A baby is less than a year old and might be boy or girl. He or she must be dressed and fed milk or soft food. A baby may have tiny teeth or no teeth at all. He or she needs diapers. A baby learns to sit, crawl, play, smile, talk, and walk. He or she must be cared for by an adult.

Q: What clues let you know that a baby is most like a toddler?
A: Small size, need to be carried

Q: How are the other members unlike the toddler and baby?
A: The father and grandfather are adults much older than the baby or toddler.

### Thinking About Thinking

Q: What characteristics do you discuss to compare family members?
A: How they are related, their ages, gender, and roles, feelings about them, interests, experiences that make them special

### Personal Application

Q: When is it important to compare family members well?
A: To relate incidents that happen at home; to explain how each family members helps the family meet its needs; to introduce family members to friends; to tell or write stories or journal entries about family members.

**LANGUAGE ARTS EXTENSION**

### LANGUAGE INTEGRATION ACTIVITIES

• Drawing: Each student may draw a member of his or her family and label the person's family role. Students' drawings may be used to create a "big book" describing the families and the culture of the whole class or assembled as a "big book" for each student. See page xxvii for directions.

• Encourage students to explain how family needs are met if the family member being described is not present in the home, i.e., extended families, single-parent families, etc. Students may describe non-family members who fulfill the traditional roles of family members.

### FOLLOW-UP ACTIVITIES AT HOME

• Students may take home the family tree diagram (TM 8 on page 332) and ask their parents to help them fill in the names to show family relationships. They may draw pictures of family members in the boxes to create a family drawing. Individual drawings may be organized by the teacher into a poster-size family tree diagram. Use the diagram furnished on page 332 or the family history forms found in genealogy books for children, such as *My First Family Tree Book,* Catherine Bruzzone (Ideals Children's Books, Nashville Tennessee, 1991).

### PICTURE BOOK EXTENSION

• Language experiences with picture books extend this lesson and demonstrate how family members across cultures meet family needs. After discussing any of the picture books ask the following questions:
Q: Are there any new ideas about (mothers or babies) that we learned from this story?
Q: What ideas or details about (mothers or babies) did you get from the pictures?
Q: Is this information true of most (mothers or babies)?

© 2000 CRITICAL THINKING BOOKS & SOFTWARE • WWW.CRITICALTHINKING.COM • 800-458-4849         167

BEGINNING BUILDING THINKING SKILLS LESSON PLANS                    VERBAL SIMILARITIES AND DIFFERENCES

After discussing each story, ask students to add new information about the family member described in the story to lists, posters, or graphic organizers that you may have used when discussing the pictures.

### SUPPLEMENTAL PICTURE BOOKS

• These books feature the family members discussed in this lesson. Descriptions of these and additional books on topics in this lesson are listed in the extended bibliography at the end of this manual.

**Baby**

*Babies,* Nicola Baxter
*Happy Birth Day,* Robie Harris
*The Baby's Catalogue,* Janet and Allan Ahlberg
*Welcoming Babies,* Margy Burns Knight
*Welcome Little Baby,* Aliki

**Mother**

*Abbeville Anthology of Mother/Daughter Tales,* Josephine Evetts-Sacker
*Families,* Nicola Baxter
*Mom Goes To Work,* Libby Gleason
*My Mama Had A Dancing Heart,* Libba Moore Gray
*Tell Me A Story, Mother,* Angela Johnson

**EXERCISE F-2**

# SIMILAR FAMILY MEMBERS—EXPLAIN

**ANSWERS F-2**

**F-2 Example:** Father and grandfather: Both are men. Both are fathers. They help children learn to take care of themselves and show their children that they are loved and special.

**F-2 Exercise:** Toddler boy and toddler girl: Toddlers are one to two years old. They can still be lifted and carried, but not for a long distance. They are learning to talk and walk by themselves (toddle). Both have some teeth and can eat many foods by themselves if it is cut into small pieces. Toddlers can recognize their family and know where to find things in their home.

**LESSON PREPARATION**

### OBJECTIVE AND MATERIALS

OBJECTIVE: Students will look at photographs of family members and explain how they are alike.

MATERIALS: The following pictures are used in this lesson: *father (7), grandfather (9), toddler boy (3), toddler girl (2)* • transparency masters of TM 8 on page 332 and TM 10 on page 334 (optional) • photocopies of TM 8 to send home (optional)

### CURRICULUM APPLICATIONS

Social Studies: Examine roles of family members and cite examples of interdependence; identify how a family depends upon products and services to meet its needs; distinguish between a family's wants and needs; identify how human needs are met within the family in different cultures; examine the roles of various family members in the celebration of holidays and traditions across cultures; explore the rights and responsibilities of various family

168        © 2000 CRITICAL THINKING BOOKS & SOFTWARE • WWW.CRITICALTHINKING.COM • 800-458-4849

members; examine how values of cooperation, respect, and resolving disputes within the family parallel good citizenship in the community.

**TEACHING SUGGESTIONS**

- Model and encourage students to express the following process for identifying a family member that someone has described:
  1. Recall the important characteristics of the two family members. (age, gender, relationships to other members of the family, roles, feelings about them, interests or experiences that make them special).
  2. Find the important characteristics in the pictures.
  3. Explain the important characteristics of both family members.

- Young children may not commonly use the terms *gender* to mean male or female or *relative* to mean someone in one's family. Encourage students to use these terms and to find synonyms for them.

- If there are children in your class who live in foster homes, conduct discussion of family members cautiously in order to avoid the conflict and confusion discussing family members creates for these children.

- To reinforce students' responses, you may draw a compare or contrast diagram to record their answers. For a blank compare or contrast diagram see Transparency Master 10 on page 334.

**MODEL LESSON** | **LESSON**

**Introduction**

Q: We have practiced selecting a family member that is similar to another particular one.

**Explaining the Objective to Students**

Q: In this lesson, we will explain how people in a family are alike

**Class Activity**

- Display the following pair of pictures:
  **F-2 Example** *father, grandfather*.
  Q: How are these two family members alike?
    A: Both are men. Both are fathers. They help children learn to take care of themselves and show their children that they are loved and special.

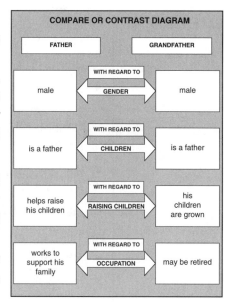

- Encourage students to keep answering until they have identified the key characteristics to discuss when comparing family members.

  Q: What characteristics did you pay attention to when explaining how these family members are alike?

A: Their adult age, their gender, their relationship to other people in the family, their role in helping children.

### Guided Practice
- Display the following pictures.
  **F-2 Exercise:** *toddler boy, toddler girl*
  Q: How are these family members alike?
    A: Toddlers are two years old or younger. They can still be lifted and carried, but not for a long distance. They are learning to talk and walk by themselves (toddle). Both have some teeth and can eat many foods by themselves if it is cut into small pieces. Toddlers can recognize their family and know where to find things in their home.

  Q: What characteristics did you pay attention to when explaining how these family members are alike?
    A: Their young age, their size, their relationship to other people in the family, what they know, and what they are just learning to do.

### Thinking About Thinking
Q: What will you think about anytime you have to explain how two family members are alike?
    A: Their age, gender, relationships to other members of the family, roles, feelings about them, interests or experiences that make them special.

### Personal Application
Q: When is it important to compare family members well?
    A: To relate incidents that happen at home; to explain how each family members helps the family meet its needs; to introduce family members to friends; to tell or write about family members.

**LANGUAGE ARTS EXTENSION**

### LANGUAGE INTEGRATION ACTIVITIES
- Drawing: Each student may draw a father, grandfather, or toddler in his family. Label the drawing with a description of that family member. Students' drawings may be used to create "big books." See page xxvii for directions.

- Encourage students to explain how family needs are met if a family member is not present in the home, i.e. extended families, single parent families, etc. Students may describe non-family members who fulfill the traditional roles of family members.

- Ask students to relate to a partner a description of a special event that his or her family enjoyed. Ask the storyteller to relate how each family member contributed to the event.

### FOLLOW-UP ACTIVITIES AT HOME
- Students may take home the family tree diagram and ask their parents to help them fill in the names to show family relationships. They may draw pictures of family members in the boxes to create a family drawing, or

BEGINNING BUILDING THINKING SKILLS LESSON PLANS                    VERBAL SIMILARITIES AND DIFFERENCES

individual drawings may be organized by the teacher into a poster-size family tree diagram. Use the family tree diagram furnished on page 332.

## PICTURE BOOK EXTENSION

• Language experiences with picture books extend this lesson. After discussing any of the picture books ask the following questions:

Q: Are there any new ideas about (fathers, grandfathers, toddlers) that we learned from this story?

Q: What ideas or details about (fathers, grandfathers, toddlers) did you get from the pictures?

Q: Is this information true of most (fathers, grandfathers, toddlers)?

After discussing each story, ask students to add new information about the family member described in the story to lists, posters, or graphic organizers that you may have used when discussing the pictures.

## SUPPLEMENTAL PICTURE BOOKS

• These books feature the family members discussed in this lesson. Descriptions of these and additional books on topics in this lesson are listed in the extended bibliography at the end of this manual.

### Grandfather

*Grandfather's Love Song,* Reeve Lindbergh
*Now One Foot, Now the Other,* Vera Williams
*The Red Barn,* Eve Bunting

### Father

*Daddy, Daddy Be There,* Candy Dawson Boyd and Floyd Cooper
*Fishing with Dad,* Michael Rosen
*I Love My Father Because,* Laurel Porter-Gaylord
*Owl Moon,* Jane Yolen

### Toddler

*Baby Says,* John Steptoe
*Glorious Angels,* Walter Dean Myers
*I Can,* Helen Oxenbury
*When I Was Young: A Four Year Old's Memoir of Her Youth,* Jamie Lee
   Curtis

**EXERCISE F-3**

# SIMILAR JOBS—SELECT

> **ANSWERS F-3**
> **F-3 Example:** doctor
> **F-3 Exercise:** grocer

**LESSON PREPARATION**

## OBJECTIVE AND MATERIALS

OBJECTIVE: Students will select the person whose job is most like another job.
MATERIALS: The following pictures are used in this lesson: dentist *(20)*, doctor *(19)*, farmer *(12)*, grocer *(22)*, nurse *(14)*, pilot *(17)*, police officer *(18)*.

## CURRICULUM APPLICATIONS

Social Studies: Classify likenesses and differences of people; identify how a

© 2000 CRITICAL THINKING BOOKS & SOFTWARE • WWW.CRITICALTHINKING.COM • 800-458-4849          171

BEGINNING BUILDING THINKING SKILLS LESSON PLANS                    VERBAL SIMILARITIES AND DIFFERENCES

family depends upon products and services to meet its needs; cite examples of community needs and services; identify jobs within the community and understand how community helpers are an example of interdependence.

## TEACHING SUGGESTIONS

• Students may not commonly use the term "occupation." Discuss with students the common synonyms for jobs—livelihood, career, work, etc.

• Model and encourage students to express the following process for comparing jobs:
   1. Describe the characteristics of this job.
   2. Look for similar characteristics in the other jobs.
   3. Select the job that has most of the same characteristics.
   4. Check to see that none of the other jobs fits the important characteristics better than the one I selected.

**MODEL LESSON**

## LESSON

### Introduction

• Ask each student to describe to a partner in three to five sentences the occupation of a family member. After pairs of students have the opportunity to discuss jobs, ask a few students to report what they said to their partner to describe the job.
Q: We have practiced describing jobs.

### Explaining the Objective to Students

• In this lesson, we will identify a job that is most like another one.

### Class Activity

• Display the following pictures, placing the first to the left of the other three:
**F-3 Example:** _dentist_, nurse, _doctor_, police officer
Q: Here you see a picture of a dentist. What should you say about a dentist to describe that job?
   A: Dentists clean and fix teeth. They go to school for a long time to learn how to keep teeth healthy. They use special tools or medicines to treat tooth and gum disease or injuries to our teeth. They wear special clothes, work in offices, and can be male or female.

Q: Which job has most of the same important characteristics as a dentist?
   A: Doctors help us keep our bodies healthy. They go to school for a long time to learn how all the parts of our bodies work, what healthy bodies need, and how to treat injuries or illnesses. They use special tools or medicines.

Q: What clues let you know that a doctor is most like a dentist?
   A: Both provide a health service to our community; must have special training, tools or supplies, wear special clothes, and work in offices or hospitals. Both can be male or female.

Q: How are the other jobs different from the dentist's?
   A: The nurse uses medical tools, but assists a doctor. The police officer enforces laws and does not treat illness and injury.

172                    © 2000 CRITICAL THINKING BOOKS & SOFTWARE • WWW.CRITICALTHINKING.COM • 800-458-4849

### Guided Practice

- Display the following pictures, placing the first to the left of the other three.
  **F-3 Exercise:** _farmer, grocer,_ nurse, pilot

  Q: What clues let you know that a grocer is most like a farmer?
  - A: Both provide food, can be male or female, work with people and have special tools to help them do their work. Farmers grow food which is then sold to grocers to sell in their stores.

  Q: How are the other jobs different from the farmer's?
  - A: The nurse and pilot provide services. Neither sells or produces food.

### Thinking About Thinking

Q: What characteristics do you discuss to describe someone's job?
- A: Whether the job provides goods or service. The usual location of the job. The training required to learn the job. The tasks the worker performs and the tools he or she uses.

Q: What characteristics do you discuss to describe a consumer?
- A: The consumer's wants and needs. The goods or service needed, who provides the goods or services, how often the goods or services are needed, and how they are obtained.

### Personal Application

Q: When is it important to understand how jobs are alike?
- A: To suggest or recognize jobs that are similar to ones you already understand; to explain a job to someone who is unfamiliar with it.

**LANGUAGE ARTS EXTENSION**

### LANGUAGE INTEGRATION ACTIVITIES

- Drawing: Each student may draw a member of his or her family and label the person's job. Students' drawings may be used to create a "big book" describing different jobs or assembled as a "big book" for each student. See page xxvii for directions.

### FOLLOW-UP ACTIVITIES AT HOME

- Ask parents to describe their jobs. They should then ask the child to describe parents' jobs to another family member or friend.

### PICTURE BOOK EXTENSION

- Language experiences with picture books extend this lesson. After discussing any of the picture books ask the following questions:
  Q: Are there any new ideas about (dentists, doctors, farmers, grocers) that we learned from this story?
  Q: What ideas or details about (dentists, doctors, farmers, grocers) did you get from the pictures?
  Q: Is this information true of most (dentists, doctors, farmers, grocers)?

- After discussing each story, ask students to add new information about the jobs described in the story to lists, posters, or graphic organizers that you may have used when discussing the pictures.

BEGINNING BUILDING THINKING SKILLS LESSON PLANS          VERBAL SIMILARITIES AND DIFFERENCES

## SUPPLEMENTAL PICTURE BOOKS

- These books feature the workers discussed in this lesson. Descriptions of these and additional books on topics in this lesson are listed in the extended bibliography at the end of this manual.

**Dentist**

*Doctor DeSoto,* William Steig
*Going to the Dentist: Mister Rogers Neighborhood Series,* Fred Rogers
*My Dentist,* Rockwell Harlow

**Doctor**

*Going To the Doctor,* T. Barry Brazelton
*Going to the Doctor: Mister Rogers Neighborhood Series,* Fred Rogers

**Farmer**

*Family Farm,* Thomas Locker
*Farm Morning,* David McPhail
*If It Weren't for Farmers,* Allan Fowler
*If You Are Not From the Prairie...,* David Bouchard

**Grocer**

*A Busy Day at Mr. Kang's Grocery Store,* Alice Flanagan
*Eats,* Arnold Adoff
*The Potato Man,* Megan McDonald

**EXERCISE F-4**

# SIMILAR JOBS—EXPLAIN

**ANSWERS F-4**

**F-4 Example:** Firefighter and police officer. They both offer a community service involving safety, require special training regarding law and investigation, have special equipment and uniforms

**F-4 Exercise:** Mail carrier and police officer. Both work for the government. Both wear special uniforms. Both walk or ride through neighborhoods on a regular route.

**LESSON PREPARATION**

## OBJECTIVE AND MATERIALS

OBJECTIVE: Students will explain how two jobs are alike.
MATERIALS: The following pictures are used in this lesson: *firefighter (16), mail carrier (13), police officer (18)* • transparency of TM 10 on page 334
CURRICULUM APPLICATIONS
Social Studies: Classify likenesses and differences of people; identify how a family depends on products and services to meet its needs; identify some job rules in the home, school, and community; cite examples of community needs and services; identify jobs within the community and understand how community helpers are an example of interdependence.

## TEACHING SUGGESTIONS

- Model and encourage students to express the following process for comparing jobs:
  1. Recall the important characteristics of one job (the goods or service they provide, training, how they spend their time, what tools they use).

174          © 2000 CRITICAL THINKING BOOKS & SOFTWARE • WWW.CRITICALTHINKING.COM • 800-458-4849

2. Find the important characteristics in the picture.

3. Check which important characteristics are also true for the other job.

4. List the important characteristics of both jobs.

- To reinforce students' responses you may draw a compare or contrast diagram to record their answers. For a blank compare or contrast diagram see Transparency Master 10 on page 334

**MODEL LESSON** | **LESSON**

### Introduction
Q: We have practiced selecting a job that is similar to another particular one.

### Explaining the Objective to Students
Q: In this lesson, we will explain how people who work at certain jobs are alike.

### Class Activity
- Display the following pair of pictures:
  **F-4 Example:** *firefighter, police officer*
  Q: How are these two jobs alike?
  A: Both offer a service to the community. Both help keep us, our homes and belongings safe from harm. Both wear uniforms and use special tools and vehicles in their jobs. Men and women perform this job. Both jobs may be dangerous. Both find out/investigate information to prevent harm.

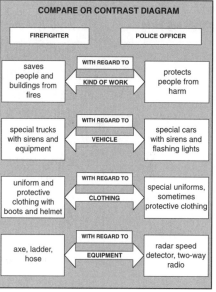

Q: What characteristics did you pay attention to when explaining how these jobs are alike?
  A: They both offer a community service involving safety, require special training regarding law and investigation, have special equipment and uniforms.

### Guided Practice
- Display the following pictures:
  **F-4 Exercise:** *mail carrier, police officer*
  Q: How are these jobs alike?
  A: Both work for the government. Both wear special uniforms. Both walk or ride through neighborhoods on a regular route.

  Q: What characteristics did you pay attention to when explaining how these jobs are alike?
  A: They both have special equipment and uniforms, follow a route, provide a service to the community.

**Thinking About Thinking**

Q: What will you think about anytime you have to explain how two jobs are alike?

A: The usual location of the job. The training required to learn the job. The tasks the worker performs and the tools they use. Whether the job provides goods or services.

Q: What characteristics do you discuss to describe a consumer?

A: The consumer's wants and needs. The goods or service needed, who provides the goods or services, how often the goods or services are needed, and how are they obtained.

**Personal Application**

Q: When is it important to understand how jobs are alike?

A: To suggest or recognize jobs that are similar to ones you already understand; to explain a job to someone who is unfamiliar with it.

**LANGUAGE ARTS EXTENSION**

**LANGUAGE INTEGRATION ACTIVITIES**

• Drawing: Each student may draw a firefighter, a police officer, or a mail carrier. Ask students to write or tell a description of the job. Students' drawings may be used to create a "big book." See page xxvii for directions.

**FOLLOW-UP ACTIVITIES AT HOME:**

• Ask parents to describe their jobs. They should then ask the child to describe a similar job.

**PICTURE BOOK EXTENSION**

• Language experiences with picture books extend this lesson. After discussing any of the picture books ask the following questions:

Q: Are there any new ideas about (mail carriers, firefighters, police officers) that we learned from this story?

Q: What ideas or details about (mail carriers, firefighters, police officers) did you get from the pictures?

Q: Is this information true of most (mail carriers, firefighters, police officers)?

After discussing each story, ask students to add new information about the jobs described in the story to lists, posters, or graphic organizers that you may have used when discussing the picture

**SUPPLEMENTAL PICTURE BOOKS**

• These books feature the workers discussed in this lesson. Descriptions of these and additional books on topics in this lesson are listed in the extended bibliography at the end of this manual.

**Firefighter**

*Fire Fighters,* R. Broekel

*"Fire! Fire!" Said Mrs. McGuire,* Bill Martin Jr. and Richard Egielski

**Mail Carrier**

*The Jolly Postman,* Janet and Allan Ahlberg

*Who Does This Job?,* Pat Upton

BEGINNING BUILDING THINKING SKILLS LESSON PLANS                VERBAL SIMILARITIES AND DIFFERENCES

**Police Officer**
*Officer Buckle and Gloria,* Peggy Rathman Calde

**EXERCISE
F-5**

# SIMILAR FOODS—SELECT

**ANSWERS F-5**
**F-5 Example:** Apple and orange. Both fruits grow on trees, taste sweet, and are made into juice and jelly. We eat the soft part of the fruit, but not the seeds.
**F-5 Exercise:** Cheese and butter. Both are solid food animal products that are made from milk. Both are stored in the refrigerator and found in the dairy case at the supermarket. Both melt at high temperatures and are used to add flavor to sandwiches or vegetables. Both are good for building strong bones and teeth.
**F-5 Practice:** Beans and peas: Both are small, round seeds; grow in pods on vines; are eaten as cooked vegetables.

**LESSON
PREPARATION**

## OBJECTIVE AND MATERIALS
OBJECTIVE: Students will identify foods that are alike.
MATERIALS: The following pictures are used in this lesson: *apple (92), bacon (77), green beans (84), butter (74), cheese (75), carrots (82), corn (88), eggs (78), onion (83), orange (93), peas (85), rice (89)*

## CURRICULUM APPLICATIONS
Health: Recognize food that provides good nutrition for proper growth and functions of the body.
Science: Identify the parts of a plant: root, stem, and leaf; recognize that there are many kinds of plants; identify living things as plants or animals; recognize the major physical differences between plants and animals; investigate the importance of seeds, identify how plants are important to people; recognize examples of common animals as being fish, birds, or mammals.

## TEACHING SUGGESTIONS
* Many young children do not know how butter and cheese are made. Films, books, and pictures may help them understand these processes. Explain how various cheeses get their flavors.

* Note: Beans and peas are seeds that grow in pods. Some bean or pea pods are eaten whole, including the bean or pea seed that is inside. Because the terms are used interchangeably, trying to distinguish between beans and peas is probably not useful.

* Second-grade science texts offer the scientific definition of fruit, which also applies to foods commonly called vegetables (tomatoes, squash, cucumbers, pumpkins, etc.). Clarify students' use of the term *fruit* in appropriate contexts: "vegetable" in cookbooks and grocery stores, "fruit" in scientific discussion of parts of a plant.

* Provide pictures of ethnic foods from magazines or cookbooks or secure samples of ethnic foods using the type of food mentioned in the lesson. Assist students in describing and pronouncing the names of ethnic foods.

© 2000 CRITICAL THINKING BOOKS & SOFTWARE • WWW.CRITICALTHINKING.COM • 800-458-4849                177

**BEGINNING BUILDING THINKING SKILLS LESSON PLANS**　　　　**VERBAL SIMILARITIES AND DIFFERENCES**

- For second grade use, discuss basic nutrients the food contains: fats, protein, carbohydrates, vitamins, minerals and water.

- Model and encourage students to express the following process for identifying a food that is similar to another one.

    1. Describe the characteristics of this food : Color, size, shape; whether it has leaves or a hard skin; what part we eat; whether it is a fruit, vegetable, meat, grain, or seed.

    2. Look for similar characteristics in the other food.

    3. Select the food that has most of the same characteristics.

    4. Check that the other pictures of food don't show those important characteristics as well.

**MODEL LESSON**

## LESSON

### Introduction

- Ask each student to describe a food to a partner in three to five sentences. After pairs of students have the opportunity to discuss a food, ask a few students to report what they said to their partner to describe it.
Q: We have described foods.

### Explaining the Objective to Students

Q: In this lesson, we will identify a food that is most like another one.

### Class Activity

- Display the following pictures, placing the first to the left of the other three.
**F-5 Example:** *apple, carrot, onion, orange*
Q: Tell your partner all the important things that you would need to say about an apple in order to find a similar food.
    A: Apples are a fruit that grows on trees. They taste sweet and are made into juice and jelly. We eat the soft part of the fruit, but not the core or the seeds. Apples have a thin red or green peel that we usually eat along with the fruit.

Q: Which food on the right is most like the one on the left?
    A: Oranges are a fruit that grows on trees. They taste sweet and are made into juice and jelly. We eat the soft part of the fruit, but not the seeds. Oranges have a thick peel that we don't eat.

Q: What clues let you know that orange is most like the apple?
    A: Both fruit grows on trees, taste sweet, and are made into juice and jelly. We eat the soft part of the fruit, but not the seeds.

Q: How are the other foods different from apples?
    A: Carrots and onions are both vegetables that grow around the root. They are not very sweet and do not have seeds.

### GUIDED PRACTICE

- Display the following pictures, placing the first to the left of the other three.
**F-5 Exercise:** *cheese, bacon, butter, eggs*
Q: Explain which food is most like cheese.

178　　　© 2000 CRITICAL THINKING BOOKS & SOFTWARE • WWW.CRITICALTHINKING.COM • 800-458-4849

A: Cheese and butter are solid food animal products that are made from milk. Both are stored in the refrigerator and found in the dairy case at the supermarket. Both melt at high temperatures and are used to add flavor to sandwiches or vegetables. Both are good for building strong bones and teeth.

Q: How are the other foods different from cheese?
A: Bacon is made from the meat of a pig and not a dairy product. Eggs come from chickens.

## OPTIONAL INDEPENDENT PRACTICE

* Display the following pictures, placing the first to the left of the other three.
**F-5 Practice:** _beans, corn, peas, rice_

Q: Explain which food is most like beans.
A: Both are seeds that grow in pods on vines and are eaten as vegetables in salad or soups. Both are small and either round or oval in shape. There are many different types of bean: green, yellow, kidney, lima, black, etc. Peas are small, round and green. Both must be cooked to be digested.

Q: What clues let you know that beans are most like the peas?
A: Both are small, round seeds; grow in pods on vines; are eaten as cooked vegetables.

Q: How are the other foods different from beans?
A: Corn and rice do not grown in pods on vines.

### Thinking About Thinking

Q: What kind of characteristics did you discuss to describe food?
A: If the food is a plant product, describe the kind of plant that produces it—tree, vine, or small bush. Identify the part of the plant that we eat—seed, fruit, leaf, stem, or root. Describe the food's color, shape, and size. If it is an animal product, describe the kind of animal that produces it and how it is prepared. For any food products, students describe how food is cooked, seasoned, and served at certain meals.

## PERSONAL APPLICATION

Q: When is it important to understand how different foods are alike?
A: To suggest or recognize foods that are similar to ones you already enjoy, to explain a certain food to someone who is unfamiliar with it.

**LANGUAGE ARTS EXTENSION**

## LANGUAGE INTEGRATION ACTIVITIES

* Drawing: Ask students to draw a picture of an apple, an orange, cheese, butter, beans, or peas. Students may write or tell short descriptions of the food. They may create a riddle about food that they will tell or write for a partner.

* Telling: Ask students within each cooperative learning group to play "Twenty Questions" about a food.

* First/Second Grade Language Activity: For each item, list students' responses and ask students to read the list aloud or write sentences to

create a short description that can be added to students' drawings, if desired.

## FOLLOW-UP ACTIVITIES AT HOME

- Ask parents to describe the food that the family eats or has just purchased. They should then ask the child to describe a similar food.

## PICTURE BOOK EXTENSION

- Language experiences with picture books extend this lesson. After discussing any of the picture books ask the following questions:

  Q: Are there any new ideas about (<u>apples, oranges, cheese, butter, peas, or beans</u>) that we learned from this story?

  Q: What ideas or details about (<u>apples, oranges, cheese, butter, peas, or beans</u>) did you get from the pictures?

  Q: Is this information true of most (<u>apples, oranges, cheese, butter, peas, or beans</u>)?

- After discussing each story, ask students to add new information about the characteristics of the food described in the story to the lists, posters, or graphic organizers that you may have used when discussing the pictures.

## SUPPLEMENTAL PICTURE BOOKS

- These books feature the food discussed in this lesson. Descriptions of these books and additional books on topics in this lesson are listed in the extended bibliography at the end of this manual.

**Apples**

*Apples*, Easy Readers series, Ann Burckhardt
*Apples of Your Eye*, Allan Fowler
*Johnny Appleseed,* Steven Kellogg

**Beans**

*Growing Colors*, Bruce McMillan
*Jack and the Beanstalk,* Paul Galdone
*Vegetables, Vegetables!*, Fay Robinson

**Butter**

*Butter,* Wake

**Cheese**

*The Old Man Who Loved Cheese*, Garrison Keillor

**Orange**

*An Orange for A Belly Button,* Harou Fukami
*Citrus Fruit,* Wake
*Each Orange Had Eight Slices,* Paul Giganti
*We Love Fruit,* Fay Robinson

**Peas**

*No Peas For Nellie,* Chris Demarest
*Peas,* Nicholas Heller
*The Pea Patch Jig,* Thatcher Hurd

BEGINNING BUILDING THINKING SKILLS LESSON PLANS                    VERBAL SIMILARITIES AND DIFFERENCES

**EXERCISE F-6**

# SIMILAR FOODS—EXPLAIN

> **ANSWERS F-6**
> **F-6 Example:** corn and rice. Both are grains, must be cooked, can be eaten alone, cooked in soups, or made into flour.
> **F-6 Exercise:** ham and bacon. Both are meat from pigs, may be cooked various ways, may be added to soup or eaten as a meat dish for breakfast, lunch or dinner.
> **F-6 Practice:** peach and orange. Both are fruit that grows on trees, are juicy, taste sweet, have seeds, and are made into jelly and juice.

**LESSON PREPARATION**

## OBJECTIVE AND MATERIALS

OBJECTIVE: Students will explain how two foods are alike.
MATERIALS: The following pictures are used in this lesson: *bacon (77), corn (88), ham (76), orange (93), peach (96), rice (89)* • transparency of TM 10 on page 334

## CURRICULUM APPLICATIONS

Health: Recognize food that provides good nutrition for proper growth and functions of the body; identify a variety of foods.
Science: Identify the parts of a plant: root, stem, and leaf; recognize that there are many kinds of plants; identify living things as plants or animals; recognize the major physical differences between plants and animals; investigate the importance of seeds, identify how plants are important to people; recognize examples of common animals as being fish, birds, or mammals.

## TEACHING SUGGESTIONS

* Model and encourage students to express the following process for identifying a food that is similar to another one.
  1. Recall the important characteristics of this food: color, size, shape; whether it has leaves or a hard skin; what part we eat; whether it is a fruit, vegetable, meat, grain, or seed
  2. Find the important characteristics in the pictures.
  3. List the important characteristics of both foods.
  4. Check to be sure that no important characteristics of the two foods have been left out.

* Provide pictures of ethnic foods from magazines or cookbooks or secure samples of ethnic foods using the type of food mentioned in the lesson. Assist students in describing and pronouncing the names of ethnic foods.

* Second-grade science texts offer the scientific definition of fruit which applies to foods commonly called vegetables (tomatoes, squash, cucumbers, pumpkins, etc.). Clarify students' use of the term *fruit* in appropriate contexts: "vegetable" in cookbooks and grocery stores, "fruit" in scientific discussion of parts of a plant.

* For second-grade classes, discuss basic nutrients the food contains: fats, protein, carbohydrates, vitamins, minerals and water.

© 2000 CRITICAL THINKING BOOKS & SOFTWARE • WWW.CRITICALTHINKING.COM • 800-458-4849          181

- To reinforce students' responses, you may draw a compare or contrast diagram to record their answers. For a blank compare or contrast diagram see Transparency Master 10 on page 334.

**MODEL LESSON** | **LESSON**

### Introduction
Q: We have practiced selecting a food that is similar to another particular one.

### Explaining the Objective to Students
Q: In this lesson, we will explain how foods are alike.

### Class Activity
- Display the following pictures.
  **F-6 Example:** *corn, rice*
  Q: Explain how are these foods alike.
     A: Both are grains (seeds that grow on grass plants). They can be roasted and eaten as cereal or cooked and eaten as a starch. Both can be cooked in soup or stews or can be ground and made into flour. Both are used in many cultures to make bread and as ingredients in other dishes.

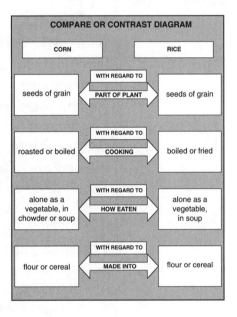

  Q: What characteristics did you pay attention to when explaining how these foods are alike?
     A: What type of food, how eaten, how used

### Guided Practice
- Display the following pictures:
  **F-6 Exercise:** *ham, bacon*
  Q: Explain how these foods are alike.
     A: Both are meat from pigs that has been processed to prevent spoilage and to give it a different flavor. Both must be cooked before being eaten. Both may be broiled, fried or cooked in a microwave oven. Both may be added to soup or eaten as a meat dish or in a sandwich. Both may be eaten for breakfast, lunch or dinner.

  Q: What characteristics did you pay attention to when explaining how these foods are alike?
     A: What kind of food, how cooked and used, how eaten

### Optional Independent Practice
- Display the following pictures:
  **F-6 Practice:** *peach, orange*
  Q: Explain how these foods are alike.

A: Both are orange fruit that grows on trees. Both are juicy and taste sweet. Both have seeds. Both are made into jelly and juice or nectar.

Q: What characteristics did you pay attention to when explaining how these foods are alike?

A: How they grow, how they taste, if they have seeds, and how they are used.

### Thinking About Thinking

Q: What kind of characteristics did you discuss to describe food?

A: If the food is a plant product, describe the kind of plant that produces it—tree, vine, or small bush. Identify the part of the plant that we eat—seed, fruit, leaf, stem, or root. Describe the food's color, shape, and size. If it is an animal product, describe the kind of animal that produces it and how it is prepared. For any food products, students describe how food is cooked, seasoned, and served at specific meals.

### PERSONAL APPLICATION

Q: When is it important to understand how different foods are alike?

A: To recognize foods that are similar to ones you already enjoy; to explain a particular food to someone who is unfamiliar with it, a friend or a younger child.

**LANGUAGE ARTS EXTENSION**

### LANGUAGE INTEGRATION ACTIVITIES

• Drawing: Ask students to draw a picture of corn, rice, an orange, a peach, bacon or ham. Students may write or tell short descriptions of the food. They may create a riddle about a food that they may tell or write for a partner.

• Ask students within each cooperative learning group to play "Twenty Questions" about a food.

• First/Second Grade Language Activity: For each item, list students' responses and ask students to read the list aloud or write sentences to create a short description that can be added to students' drawings, if desired.

### FOLLOW-UP ACTIVITIES AT HOME

• Ask parents to describe the food they eat or have just purchased. They should then ask the child to describe a similar food.

### PICTURE BOOK EXTENSION

• Language experiences with picture books extend this lesson. After discussing any of the picture books ask the following questions:

Q: Are there any new ideas about (bacon, corn, ham, orange, peach, rice) that we learned from this story?

Q: What ideas or details about (bacon, corn, ham, orange, peach, rice) did you get from the pictures?

Q: Is this information true of most of these foods?

BEGINNING BUILDING THINKING SKILLS LESSON PLANS                    VERBAL SIMILARITIES AND DIFFERENCES

- After discussing each story, ask students to add new information about the characteristics of the food described in the story to the lists, posters, or graphic organizers that you may have used when discussing the pictures.

### SUPPLEMENTAL PICTURE BOOKS
- These books feature the food discussed in this lesson. Descriptions of these books and additional books on topics in this lesson are listed in the extended bibliography at the end of this manual.

**Bacon**

*Don't Forget the Bacon,* Pat Hutchins

**Corn**

*Corn,* Ann Burckhardt
*Corn Is Maise: The Gift of the Indians,* Aliki

**Ham**

*Green Eggs and Ham,* Dr. Seuss
*Meat,* Elizabeth Clark

**Orange**

*An Orange for a Belly Button,* Harou Fukami
*Citrus Fruit,* Wake
*Each Orange Had Eight Slices,* Paul Giganti
*We Love Fruit,* Fay Robinson

**Peach**

*I Will Tell You A Story of A Peach Stone*, Nathan Zimelman
*James and the Giant Peach,* Roald Dahl
*We Love Fruit,* Fay Robinson

**Rice**

*Chicken Soup With Rice,* Maurice Sendak
*Everybody Cooks Rice,* Noral Dooley
*Rice,* Lynne Merrison
*The Rajah's Rice: A Mathematical Folktale From India*, David Barry

**EXERCISE F-7**

# SIMILAR VEHICLES—SELECT

**ANSWERS F-7**
**F-7 Example:** ambulance and fire truck
**F-7 Exercise:** helicopter and airplane
**F-7 Practice:** ship and boat

**LESSON PREPARATION**

### OBJECTIVE AND MATERIALS
OBJECTIVE: Students will select a vehicle that is most like another.
MATERIALS: The following pictures are used in this lesson: *airplane (27), ambulance (24), motorboat (36), school bus (32), car (31), fire truck (37), helicopter (38), pickup truck (26), police car (25), ship (35), train (29)*

### CURRICULUM APPLICATIONS
Social Studies: Identify how a family depends upon transportation to meet its needs; identify some jobs in the home, school, and community; cite examples

184          © 2000 CRITICAL THINKING BOOKS & SOFTWARE • WWW.CRITICALTHINKING.COM • 800-458-4849

BEGINNING BUILDING THINKING SKILLS LESSON PLANS                    VERBAL SIMILARITIES AND DIFFERENCES

of community needs and services; understand how community helpers are an example of interdependence.

**TEACHING SUGGESTIONS**
- Model and encourage students to express the following process for identifying a vehicle that is similar to another.
  1. Describe the characteristics of this vehicle (Its size, purpose, where it is driven, how it looks, what kind of equipment it has, and when it is used).
  2. Look for similar characteristics in the other vehicles.
  3. Select the vehicle that has most of the same characteristics.
  4. Check that the other pictures of vehicles don't show those important characteristics as well.

- Young students may not realize that generally a ship is any large boat. However, trying to distinguish between a ship and a boat is probably not useful, since the term "boat" may sometimes apply to a large vessel, such as a fishing boat or a ferry boat.

**MODEL LESSON** | **LESSON**

**Introduction**
- Ask each student to describe a vehicle to a partner in three to five sentences. After pairs of students have the opportunity to discuss a vehicle, ask a few students to report what they said to their partner to describe the vehicle.

**Explaining the Objective to Students**
Q: We have practiced describing vehicles. In this lesson, we will identify vehicles that are most alike.

**Class Activity**
- Display the following pictures, placing the first to the left of the other three:
**F-7 Example:** _ambulance_, car, _fire truck_, pickup truck
Q: Tell your partner all the important things that you need to say about an ambulance to find a similar vehicle.
   A: An ambulance is a vehicle that is used to bring a sick or injured person to the hospital. It contains special equipment and medical supplies that help keep a person alive on the trip. It is equipped with a siren and flashing lights that let people know it is going to an emergency or to the hospital.

Q: Which vehicle on the right is most like an ambulance?
   A: A fire truck is a vehicle that carries ladders and other equipment or tools a firefighter uses to fight and put out fires. Most fire trucks have a machine that pumps water or chemicals used to put out fires. Fire trucks have lights and sirens that let people know when they are going to a fire. This vehicle is used during an emergency or when people are in danger and need help.

© 2000 CRITICAL THINKING BOOKS & SOFTWARE • WWW.CRITICALTHINKING.COM • 800-458-4849          185

BEGINNING BUILDING THINKING SKILLS LESSON PLANS                    VERBAL SIMILARITIES AND DIFFERENCES

Q: What clues let you know that a fire truck is most like an ambulance?
   A: Both are emergency vehicles which have sirens. Both help people who are in danger.

Q: How are the other vehicles different from an ambulance?
   A: The car and pickup truck are not emergency vehicles with sirens. They can be used to help people in danger, but their primary purpose is to transport people or cargo.

## Guided Practice

- Display the following pictures, placing the first to the left of the other three:
  **F-7 Exercise:** _helicopter,_ _airplane,_ bus, police car

Q: Tell your partner all the important things that you need to say about a helicopter to find a similar vehicle.
   A: A helicopter flies straight up and down or across in the air. It can land in very small places. It has large blades that spin quickly to give it speed to rise into the air. A helicopter does not carry as many passengers as most airplanes. It can carry one to twelve people.

Q: Which vehicle on the right is most like a helicopter?
   A: An airplane is a vehicle that can fly. It has two wings or one or more engines that either turn propellers or compress air to jet propel it. Large airplanes can carry people, packages, and other things from one place to another.

Q: What clues let you know that a helicopter is most like an airplane?
   A: Both fly and can carry passengers through the air.

Q: How are the other vehicles different from a helicopter?
   A: A bus or police car cannot fly.

## Optional Independent Practice

- Display the following pictures with the first to the left of the other three:
  **F-7 Practice:** _ship,_ _motorboat,_ train, pickup truck

Q: Tell your partner all the important things that you need to say about a ship to find a similar vehicle.
   A: A ship is a large boat that carries people and goods long distances. Some, like ocean liners, carry large numbers of people and are like a large floating hotel. Some carry freight, like cars or oil. Some are used by the navy for defense, such as aircraft carriers. Ships have huge engines that turn huge propellers that push the ship through the water.

Q: Which vehicle on the right is most like a ship?
   A: A boat is a vehicle that is used to travel on water. Some boats are moved by oars, paddles, motors, or wind blowing on sails. Boats can be used to move people, things, or animals from one place to another. Boats can be large or small. People use boats to have fun or as equipment to do a job.

Q: What clues let you know that a ship is most like a boat?
   A: Both float and can carry passengers across the water.

186          © 2000 CRITICAL THINKING BOOKS & SOFTWARE • WWW.CRITICALTHINKING.COM • 800-458-4849

Q: How are the other vehicles different from a ship?
A: A train or truck cannot float.

• Young students may not realize that generally a ship is any large boat. However, trying to distinguish between a ship and a boat is probably not useful, since the term "boat" may sometimes apply to a large vessel, such as a fishing boat or a ferry boat.

**Thinking About Thinking**
Q: What kind of characteristics did you discuss to describe a vehicle?
A: Its size, purpose, where it is driven, who owns or uses it, how it is propelled, how it looks, and what kind of equipment it has.

**Personal Application**
Q: When is it important to describe vehicles accurately?
A: To describe deliveries; to describe traffic; to give directions.

## LANGUAGE ARTS EXTENSION

## LANGUAGE INTEGRATION ACTIVITIES

• Drawing: Select a picture of a vehicle or allow students to find or draw a picture of a vehicle. Ask students to create a riddle that they will tell or write for a partner.

• Telling: Ask students within each cooperative learning group to play "Twenty Questions" about a vehicle.

• First/Second Grade Language Activity: For each item, list students' responses and ask students to read the list aloud or write sentences to create a short description that can be added to students' drawings, if desired.

## FOLLOW-UP ACTIVITIES AT HOME:

• Ask parents to describe the vehicles they own or use on their job. They should then ask the child to describe a similar vehicle.

## PICTURE BOOK EXTENSION

• Language experiences with picture books extend this lesson. After discussing any of the picture books ask the following questions:
Q: Are there any new ideas about (fire trucks, airplanes, or boats) that we learned from this story?
Q: What ideas or details about (fire trucks, airplanes, or boats) did you get from the pictures?
Q: Is this information true of most (fire trucks, airplanes, or boats)?
After discussing each story, ask students to add new information about the vehicle described in the story to lists, posters, or graphic organizers that you may have used when discussing the pictures.

## SUPPLEMENTAL PICTURE BOOKS

• These books feature the vehicles discussed in this lesson. Descriptions of these books and additional books on topics in this lesson are listed in the extended bibliography at the end of this manual.

BEGINNING BUILDING THINKING SKILLS LESSON PLANS          VERBAL SIMILARITIES AND DIFFERENCES

**Airplane**

*Airplanes,* Eye Opener series
*Airport*, Byron Barton
*Bored—Nothing to Do,* Peter Spier
*Flying,* Donald Crews

**Boat**

*Boats on the River,* Marjorie Flack
*Ships and Boats,* Eye Opener series
*Little Toot,* Hardie Gramatky

**Fire Truck**

*Emergency Vehicles*, Dayna Wolhart
*Fire Fighters,* R. Broekel
*Fire Trucks,* Peter Brady

**EXERCISE F-8**

# SIMILAR VEHICLES—EXPLAIN

**ANSWERS F-8**

**F-8 Example:** Bus and train: Both are large vehicles that can carry many passengers. Both are powered by large engines. Many buses and trains have long distance routes. Both operate on schedules that tell when and where the bus or train will arrive. Both require a ticket or a fare.

**F-8 Exercise:** Bicycle and motorcycle: Both are small two-wheeled vehicles that have handlebars for steering and a seat for the driver. They can safely carry one person. Both are small and can maneuver in traffic. They use little or no fuel. They are both open vehicles with no covering to protect the driver. They cannot carry large loads.

**F-8 Practice:** Ship and airplane: Both carry large numbers of passengers. Both have large engines and are expensive to build. Both require several people performing different jobs to get them to their destination safely. Both run on schedules and require tickets. Some people use them for work, others travel on them for recreational trips. Both are used to move people and cargo from one place to another. The person in charge is called a captain. The direction of the wind can make either go faster or slower.

**LESSON PREPARATION**

## OBJECTIVE AND MATERIALS

OBJECTIVE: Students will explain how two vehicles are alike.
MATERIALS: The following pictures are used in this lesson: *airplane (27), bicycle (30), city bus (28), motorcycle (33), ship (35), train (29)* • transparency of TM 10 on page 334

## CURRICULUM APPLICATIONS

<u>Social Studies</u>: Identifying how a family depends upon transportation to meet its needs; identifying some jobs in the home, school, and community; citing examples of community needs and services; understanding how community helpers are an example of interdependence.

188          © 2000 CRITICAL THINKING BOOKS & SOFTWARE • WWW.CRITICALTHINKING.COM • 800-458-4849

## TEACHING SUGGESTIONS
- Model and encourage students to express the following process for comparing vehicles:
  1. Recall the important characteristics of the vehicle (size, shape, type, use)
  2. Find the important characteristics in the other picture.
  3. List the important characteristics of both vehicles.
  4. I will check to be sure that I don't leave out anything important or interesting about the two vehicles.

- To reinforce students' responses you may draw a compare or contrast diagram to record their answers. For a blank compare or contrast diagram see Transparency Master 10 on page 334.

**MODEL LESSON**

## LESSON

### Introduction
Q: We have practiced selecting a vehicle that is similar to another particular one.

### Explaining the Objective to Students
Q: In this lesson, we will explain how two vehicles are alike.

### Class Activity
- Display the following pictures:
  **F-8 Example:** *bus, train*
  Q: Discuss in pairs as many ideas as they can think of to describe how the two items are alike.
  A: Both are large vehicles that can carry many passengers. Both are powered by large engines. Many buses and trains have long distance routes. Both operate on schedules that tell when and where the bus or train will arrive. Both require a ticket or a fare.

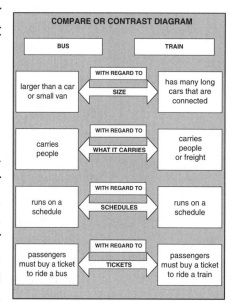

### Guided Practice
- Display the following pictures:
  **F-8 Exercise:** *bicycle, motorcycle*
  Q: How are these vehicles alike?
  A: Both are small two-wheeled vehicles that have handle bars for steering and a seat for the driver. They can safely carry one person. Both are small and can maneuver in traffic. They use little or no fuel. They are both open vehicles with no covering to protect the driver. They cannot carry large loads.

BEGINNING BUILDING THINKING SKILLS LESSON PLANS                    VERBAL SIMILARITIES AND DIFFERENCES

### Optional Independent Practice
- Display the following pictures:
  **F-8 Practice:** *ship, airplane*
  Q: How are these vehicles alike?
  > A: Both carry large numbers of passengers. Both have large engines and are expensive to build. Both require several people performing different jobs to get them to their destination safely. Both run on schedules and require tickets. Some people use them for work, others travel on them for recreational trips. Both are used to move people and cargo from one place to another. The person in charge is called a captain. The direction of the wind can make either go faster or slower.

### Thinking About Thinking
> Q: What characteristics did you pay attention to when explaining how these vehicles are alike?
> > A: Its size, purpose, where it is driven, who owns or uses it, how it is propelled, how it looks, what kind of equipment it has, and when it is used.

### Personal Application
> Q: When is it important to describe vehicles accurately?
> > A: To describe deliveries; to describe traffic; to give directions.

**LANGUAGE ARTS EXTENSION**

### LANGUAGE INTEGRATION ACTIVITIES
- Drawing: Select a picture of a vehicle or allow students to find or draw a picture of a vehicle. Ask students to create a riddle that they will tell or write for a partner.

- Telling: Ask students within each cooperative learning group to play "Twenty Questions" about a vehicle.

- First/Second Grade Language Activity: For each item, list students' responses and ask students to read the list aloud or write sentences to create a short description that can be added to students' drawings, if desired.

### FOLLOW-UP ACTIVITIES AT HOME:
- Ask parents to describe the vehicles they own or use at work. They should then ask the child to describe these vehicles to another family member or friend.

### PICTURE BOOK EXTENSION
- Language experiences with picture books extend this lesson. After discussing any of the picture books ask the following questions:
  Q: Are there any new ideas about (buses, trains, ships, airplanes, bicycles or motorcycles) that we learned from this story?
  Q: What ideas or details about (buses, trains, ships, airplanes, bicycles or motorcycles) did you get from the pictures?
  Q: Is this information true of most (buses, trains, ships, airplanes, bicycles or motorcycles)?

190          © 2000 CRITICAL THINKING BOOKS & SOFTWARE • WWW.CRITICALTHINKING.COM • 800-458-4849

BEGINNING BUILDING THINKING SKILLS LESSON PLANS                    VERBAL SIMILARITIES AND DIFFERENCES

- After discussing each story, ask students to add new information about the characteristics of the vehicle described in the story to the lists, posters, or graphic organizers that you may have used when discussing the pictures.

## SUPPLEMENTAL PICTURE BOOKS

- These books feature the vehicles discussed in this lesson. Descriptions of these and additional books on topics in this lesson are listed in the extended bibliography at the end of this manual.

**Airplane**

*Airplanes,* Eye Opener series
*Airport,* Byron Barton
*Bored—Nothing to Do,* Peter Spier

**Bicycle**

*Amazing Bikes,* Trevor Lord
*Hello, Two Wheeler,* Jane Mason
*How Is A Bicycle Made?* Henry Horenstein

**Bus**

*Is There Room on the Bus?,* Helen Piers and Hannah Giffard
*The Wheels on the Bus,* Paul Zelinsky
*Where's That Bus,* Eileen Brown

**Motorcycle**

*Dirt Bike Racer,* Matt Christopher
*The Mouse and the Motorcycle,* Beverly Cleary

**Ship**

*Ships and Boats,* Eye Opener series
*Ships,* Richard Humble

**Train**

*Freight Train,* Peter Brady
*Freight Train,* Donald Crews
*The Little Engine That Could,* Watty Piper
*Trains,* Eye Opener series

**EXERCISE F-9**

# SIMILAR ANIMALS—SELECT

**ANSWERS F-9**
**F-9 Example:** zebra and horse
**F-9 Exercise:** chicken and turkey
**F-9 Practice:** lizard and turtle

**LESSON PREPARATION**

## OBJECTIVE AND MATERIALS

OBJECTIVE: Students will select an animal that is most like another.
MATERIALS: The following pictures are used in this lesson: *camel (58), chicken (65), frog (55), giraffe (59), horse (64), lizard (68), ostrich (62), owl (66), spider (60), turkey (67), turtle (61), zebra (63).*

## CURRICULUM APPLICATIONS

Science: Identify living things as plants or animals; recognize that plants and

© 2000 CRITICAL THINKING BOOKS & SOFTWARE • WWW.CRITICALTHINKING.COM • 800-458-4849          191

BEGINNING BUILDING THINKING SKILLS LESSON PLANS                                    VERBAL SIMILARITIES AND DIFFERENCES

animals reproduce their own kind; recognize the major physical differences between plants and animals; state what animals need to live and grow; recognize that needs of different kinds of animals are similar; recognize examples of common animals as being fish, birds, or mammals.

**TEACHING SUGGESTIONS**
- For young children "cold-blooded" or "warm-blooded" may be new terms. Explain the effect of this difference on the survival needs of animals.
- The terms "backbone" or "vertebra" may be new concepts. Discuss with students the significance and function of a backbone.

- Model and encourage students to express the following process for identifying an animal that is similar to another.
  1. Describe the characteristics of this animal.
  2. Look for similar characteristics in the other animals.
  3. Select the animal that has most of the same characteristics.
  4. Check that the other pictures of animals don't show those important characteristics as well.

**MODEL LESSON** | **LESSON**

**Introduction**
- Ask each student to describe an animal to a partner in three to five sentences. After pairs of students have the opportunity to discuss an animal, ask a few students to report what they said to their partner to describe it.

**Explaining the Objective to Students**
Q: We have described animals. In this lesson, we will identify animals that are alike.

**Class Activity**
- Display the following pictures, placing the first to the left of the other three:
**F-9 Example:** _zebra,_ camel, giraffe, _horse_
Q: Here you see a picture of a zebra. Tell your partner all the important things that you need to say about a zebra to find a similar animal.
  A: A zebra is a large mammal with four legs with hooves, a mane, and a tail. It eats hay or grass. A zebra looks like a horse with stripes.

Q: Which animal on the right is most like a zebra?
  A: A horse

Q: What clues let you know that a horse is most like a zebra?
  A: A horse is a large mammal with four legs with hooves, a mane, and a tail. It eats hay or grass. People ride them to get from one place to another. They can also be used to pull heavy loads. Most people ride them today for fun. Most horses are tame, but some are wild.

Q: How are the other animals different from a zebra?
  A: A camel has humps and no stripes. A giraffe has a long neck and spots, instead of stripes.

192                    © 2000 CRITICAL THINKING BOOKS & SOFTWARE • WWW.CRITICALTHINKING.COM • 800-458-4849

BEGINNING BUILDING THINKING SKILLS LESSON PLANS                    VERBAL SIMILARITIES AND DIFFERENCES

Q: What clues let you know that a horse is most like a zebra?
   A: The number of legs, size, shape, appearance, behavior, and what it eats tell us that a horse is like a zebra.

### Guided Practice

• Display the following pictures with the first to the left of the other three:
**F-9 Exercise:** *chicken, ostrich, owl, turkey*

Q: Here you see a picture of a chicken. Tell your partner all the important things that you need to say about a chicken to find a similar animal.
   A: A chicken is a bird with feathers. It has a backbone, is warm-blooded, and lays eggs. Chickens are raised by farmers to be sold as food. Many people often enjoy eating chicken.

Q: Which animal on the right is most like a chicken?
   A: A turkey

Q: What clues let you know that a turkey is most like a chicken?
   A: A turkey is a large bird with reddish-brown feathers and a bare neck and head. It looks like a chicken but is bigger. The bird has a backbone and is warm-blooded. It lays eggs. Turkeys are raised by farmers to be sold as food. Many people in the United States eat turkey on Thanksgiving Day.

Q: How are the other animals different from a chicken?
   A: An owl is a small bird, but it is not used for food. An ostrich is a large bird that has longer legs and can move much faster than a chicken.

Q: What clues let you know that a turkey is most like a chicken?
   A: Both are feathered, warm-blooded animals that lay eggs. Both are used as food by people.

### Optional Independent Practice

• Display the following pictures, placing the first to the left of the other three:
**F-9 Practice:** *lizard, frog, spider, turtle*

Q: Here you see a picture of a lizard. Tell your partner all the important things that you need to say about a lizard to find a similar animal.
   A: A lizard has four legs and a long tail. Its body is long and scaly. It is a cold-blooded animal (reptile). Most lizards like to eat insects. They live in places where the temperature is usually warm most of the time. The skin of the lizard can be used to make leather, which can be used to make shoes, boots or wallets.

Q: Which animal on the right is most like a lizard?
   A: A turtle

Q: What clues let you know that a turtle is most like a lizard?
   A: A turtle is a reptile. It is a cold-blooded animal with a low, wide body, and four short legs. Its body is covered by a hard shell. When it gets scared, a turtle pulls its head and legs inside its shell. A turtle has a sharp-edged jaw but no teeth. A turtle can live on land or in salt or fresh water.

© 2000 CRITICAL THINKING BOOKS & SOFTWARE • WWW.CRITICALTHINKING.COM • 800-458-4849    193

Q: How are the other animals different from a lizard?
A: A spider is a kind of bug (an arachnid) with eight legs and two body parts. Spiders spin webs. A frog is a cold-blooded animal (an amphibian) with webbed feet and no tail that lives near or in water. It has strong back legs for hopping.

Q: What clues let you know that a turtle is most like a lizard?
A: Both have four legs and a hard shell or body covering. Both are cold-blooded animals and live where the temperature is usually warm most of the time. Both lay eggs.

**Thinking About Thinking**

Q: When is it important to understand how different animals are alike?
A: To understand how similar animals living in the same environment get the food, water, air, and safety that they need to survive.

Q: What kind of characteristics did you discuss to describe an animal?
A: Body structure, warm- or cold-blooded, whether it has a backbone, whether it hatches or gives live birth, where it lives, how it moves, what it eats.

**Personal Application**

Q: When is it important to understand how animals are alike?
A: To understand the needs of animals that we find at the zoo or the pet store, to care for pets properly.

**LANGUAGE ARTS EXTENSION**

**LANGUAGE INTEGRATION ACTIVITIES**

- *What Animal Am I? An Animal Guessing Game,* Iza Trapani. This book models animal riddles with pictures. Select a picture of an animal or allow students to find or draw a picture of food. Ask students to create a riddle that they will tell or write for a partner.

- Ask students to use animal puppets to act out "Brown bear, brown bear, what do I see?" for various animals discussed in the lesson.

- Telling: Ask students within each cooperative learning group to play "Twenty Questions" about a food.

- First/Second Grade Language Activity: For each item, list students' responses and ask students to read the list aloud or write sentences to create a short description that can be added to students' drawings.

- Create a bulletin board display of pictures of different kinds of animals by class. Discuss how each animal reproduces, whether it is warm or cold blooded, and other special characteristics:
    1. Birds: egg-laying, warm-blooded vertebrates with wings
    2. Fish: egg-laying, cold-blooded vertebrates with gills

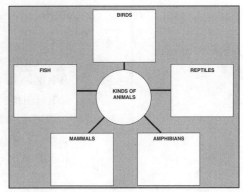

3. Reptiles: egg-laying, cold-blooded vertebrates with dry skin.

4. Amphibians: egg-laying, cold-blooded vertebrates with moist skin

5. Mammals: Baby grows inside mother's body; warm-blooded vertebrates with hair.

## FOLLOW-UP ACTIVITIES AT HOME

• Ask parents to describe the animals they have seen. They should then ask the child to describe these animals to another family member or friend. If the family has pets ask the child to describe them.

## PICTURE BOOK EXTENSION

• The books listed below relate to the answers to this lesson. After discussing any of the picture books ask the following questions:

Q: Are there any new ideas about (horses, turkeys, or turtles) that we learned from this story?

Q: What ideas or details about (horses, turkeys, or turtles) did you get from the pictures?

Q: Is this information true of most (horses, turkeys, or turtles)?

• After discussing each story, ask students to add new information about the characteristics of the family member described in the story to the lists, posters, or graphic organizers that you may have used when discussing the pictures.

## SUPPLEMENTAL PICTURE BOOKS

• These books feature the animals discussed in this lesson. Descriptions of these and additional books on topics in this lesson are listed in the extended bibliography at the end of this manual.

**Horse**

*Horses,* New True series, K. Jacobsen
*Horses, Horses, Horses,* Allan Fowler
*Horses and Ponies,* Usborne/EDC,
*The Black Stallion Picture Book,* Walter Farley

**Turkey**

*Birds We Know,* M. Friskey
*Turkeys That Fly and Turkeys That Don't,* Rookie Read About Science series

**Turtle**

*Box Turtle at Long Pond,* William T. George
*Into the Sea,* Brenda Z. Guiberson
*Reptiles,* New True series, L. Ballard
*Turtles Take Their Time,* Rookie Read About Science series

BEGINNING BUILDING THINKING SKILLS LESSON PLANS • VERBAL SIMILARITIES AND DIFFERENCES

## EXERCISE F-10

## SIMILAR ANIMALS—EXPLAIN

**ANSWERS F-10**

**F-10 Example:** Lizard and snake. Both are cold-blooded, have backbones and scaly bodies. Their babies are hatched from eggs. They both belong to the reptile family. Both lizards and snakes eat insects.

**F-10 Exercise:** Ostrich and turkey. Both are large, feathered, warm-blooded animals with backbones. Their babies are hatched from eggs. Both eat grain.

**F-10 Practice:** Fish and frog. Both are cold-blooded animals that have a backbone. Both eat insects. Their babies are hatched from eggs, can live in water, and have gills for breathing. The baby frog starts out as a tadpole living in the water and looks like a fish.

## LESSON PREPARATION

### OBJECTIVE AND MATERIALS
OBJECTIVE: Students will compare animals.
MATERIALS: The following pictures are used in this lesson: *fish (57), frog (55), lizard (68), ostrich (62), snake (69), turkey (67)* • transparency of TM 10 on page 334

### CURRICULUM APPLICATIONS
<u>Science</u>: Recognize that plants and animals reproduce their own kind; recognize the major physical differences between plants and animals; state what animals need to live and grow; recognize that needs of different kinds of animals are similar; recognize examples of common animals as being fish, birds, or mammals.

### TEACHING SUGGESTIONS

• For young children "cold-blooded" or "warm-blooded" may be new terms. Explain the effect of this difference on the survival needs of animals. Similarly, the terms "backbone" or "vertebra" may be new concepts. Discuss with students the significance and function of a backbone.

• Model and encourage students to express the following process for identifying how two animals are alike.
  1. Recall the important characteristics of the animals.
  2. Find the important characteristics in the pictures.
  3. List the important similar characteristics of the two animals.
  4. I will check to be sure that I don't leave out anything important or interesting about the two animals.

• To reinforce students' responses, you may draw a compare or contrast dia-

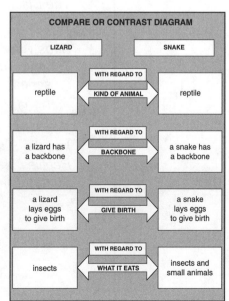

196 © 2000 CRITICAL THINKING BOOKS & SOFTWARE • WWW.CRITICALTHINKING.COM • 800-458-4849

BEGINNING BUILDING THINKING SKILLS LESSON PLANS                    VERBAL SIMILARITIES AND DIFFERENCES

gram to record their answers. For a blank compare or contrast diagram see Transparency Master 10 on page 334.

**MODEL LESSON** | **LESSON**

### Introduction

Q: We have practiced selecting an animal that is similar to a particular one.

### Explaining the Objective to Students

Q: In this lesson, we will explain how animals are alike.

### Class Activity

• Display the following pictures:

**F-10 Example:** *lizard, snake*

Q: How are these animals alike?

A: Both are cold-blooded, have backbones, and scaly bodies. Their babies are hatched from eggs. They both belong to the reptile family. Both lizards and snakes eat insects.

Q: What characteristics did you pay attention to when explaining how these animals are alike?

A: Whether they are warm- or cold-blooded, how they reproduce, what kind of skin they have, what family they belong to, what they eat.

### Guided Practice

• Display the following pictures.

**F-10 Exercise:** *ostrich, turkey*

Q: How are these animals alike?

A: Both are large, feathered, warm-blooded animals with backbones. Their babies are hatched from eggs. Both eat grain.

### Optional Independent Practice

• Display the following pictures:

**F-10 Practice:** *fish, frog*

Q: How are these animals alike?

A: Both are cold-blooded animals that have a backbone. Both eat insects. Their babies are hatched from eggs, can live in water, and have gills for breathing. The baby frog starts out as a tadpole living in the water. It looks like a fish but loses its gills as it grows up.

### Thinking About Thinking

Q: What kind of characteristics did you discuss to describe an animal?

A: Body structure, whether it is warm- or cold- blooded, whether it has a backbone, whether it hatches or gives live birth, where it lives, how it moves, what it eats.

Q: Why is it important to understand how different animals are alike?

A: To understand how similar animals living in the same environment get the food, water, air, and safety that they need to survive.

### Personal Application

Q: When is it important to understand how different animals are alike?

© 2000 CRITICAL THINKING BOOKS & SOFTWARE • WWW.CRITICALTHINKING.COM • 800-458-4849          197

BEGINNING BUILDING THINKING SKILLS LESSON PLANS                    VERBAL SIMILARITIES AND DIFFERENCES

A: To understand the needs of animals that we find at the zoo or the pet store; to care for pets; to explain the needs of pets or the characteristics of animals to a friend or younger child.

**LANGUAGE ARTS EXTENSION**

## LANGUAGE INTEGRATION ACTIVITIES

• Drawing: Ask students to draw a picture of a fish, a frog, a lizard, an ostrich, a snake, or a turkey. Students may write to tell short descriptions of the animal.

• *What Animal Am I? An Animal Guessing Game,* Iza Trapani. This book models animal riddles with pictures. Select a picture of an animal or allow students to find or draw a picture of an animal. Ask students to create a riddle that they will tell or write for a partner.

• Drama: Ask students to use animals puppets to act our "Brown bear, brown bear, what do I see?" for various animals discussed in the lesson.

• Telling: Ask students within each cooperative learning group to play "Twenty Questions" about a food.

• First/Second Grade Language Activity: For each item, list students' responses and ask students to read the list aloud or write sentences to create a short description that can be added to students' drawings, if desired.

## FOLLOW-UP ACTIVITIES AT HOME:

• Ask parents to describe the animals they have seen. They should then ask the child to describe similar animals to another family member or friend. If the family has pets ask the child to describe them.

## PICTURE BOOK EXTENSION

• The books listed below relate to the answers to this lesson. After discussing any of the picture books ask the following questions:
Q: Are there any new ideas about (fish, frogs, lizards, ostriches, snakes, or turkeys) that we learned from this story?
Q: What ideas or details about (fish, frogs, lizards, ostriches, snakes, or turkeys) did you get from the pictures?
Q: Is this information true of most (fish, frogs, lizards, ostriches, snakes, or turkeys)?

## SUPPLEMENTAL PICTURE BOOKS

• These books feature the animals discussed in this lesson. Descriptions of these and additional books on topics in this lesson are listed in the extended bibliography at the end of this manual.

**Fish**

*Crinkleroot's 25 Fish Every Child Should Know,* Jim Arnosky
*Fishes,* Brian Wildsmith
*Life in a Pond,* Allan Fowler
*My Visit to the Aquarium,* Aliki
*Swimmy,* Leo Lionni

198            © 2000 CRITICAL THINKING BOOKS & SOFTWARE • WWW.CRITICALTHINKING.COM • 800-458-4849

BEGINNING BUILDING THINKING SKILLS LESSON PLANS | VERBAL SIMILARITIES AND DIFFERENCES

**Frogs**
*Amazing Frogs and Toads,* Barry Clarke
*Frog,* Michael Chinery
*Frog, Where Are You,* Mercer Mayer
*In The Great Meadow, Skid Crease*
*The Fascinating World of Frogs and Toads,* Barron's Educational Series

**Lizards**
*Lizard in the Sun,* Joanne Ryder
*Lizard's Song,* George Shannon
*Reptiles,* L. Ballard

**Ostrich**
*African Animals,* J. W. Purcell
*Birds We Know,* M. Friskey
*Ostriches,* E.U. Lepthien
*The Cuckoo Child,* Dick King-Smith

**Snakes**
*A Snake in the House,* Faith McNulty
*It's Best to Leave a Snake Alone,* Rookie Read About Science series
*Reptiles,* L. Ballard

**Turkey**
*Birds We Know,* New True series, M. Friskey
*Turkeys That Fly and Turkeys That Don't,* Rookie Read About Science series

## EXERCISE F-11

# SIMILAR BUILDINGS—SELECT

---

**ANSWERS F-11**
**F-11 Example:** house and apartment building
**F-11 Exercise:** police station and fire station
**F-11 Practice:** library and post office

---

## LESSON PREPARATION

### OBJECTIVE AND MATERIALS
OBJECTIVE: Students will identify similar buildings.
MATERIALS: The following pictures are used in this lesson: *apartment building (50), farm (47), fire station (45), library (40), garage (53), hospital (39), house (53), playground (52), police station (46), post office (51), supermarket (49)*

### CURRICULUM APPLICATIONS
Social Studies: Identify how a family depends upon the products and services produced or housed in buildings; cite the role buildings play in providing community needs and services.

### TEACHING SUGGESTIONS
* "Dwellings" or "residences" are abstract concepts for most young children. Since they have heard these terms several times in previous exercises, students should begin to use them independently, if they have frequent practice doing so. Dwellings can refer to homes for animals, as well as

© 2000 CRITICAL THINKING BOOKS & SOFTWARE • WWW.CRITICALTHINKING.COM • 800-458-4849        199

BEGINNING BUILDING THINKING SKILLS LESSON PLANS                    VERBAL SIMILARITIES AND DIFFERENCES

people; residences refers only to people. Use the terms "dwellings" or "residences" often in these activities and in other contexts and encourage students to do so. Acknowledge students' unprompted use of these terms.

- Model and encourage students to express the following process for identifying a building that is similar to another.
    1. Describe the characteristics of this building.
    2. Look for similar characteristics in the other buildings
    3. Select the building that has most of the same characteristics
    4. Check that the other pictures of buildings don't show those important characteristics as well.

**MODEL LESSON**

## LESSON

### Introduction

- Ask each student to describe a building to a partner in three to five sentences. After pairs of students have the opportunity to discuss a building, ask a few students to report what they said to their partner to describe it.

### Explaining the Objective to Students

Q: We have described buildings. In this lesson, we will identify a building that is most like another.

### Class Activity

- Display the following pictures, placing the first to the left of the other three:
  **F-11 Example:** *house,* *farm, playground,* *apartment building*
  Q: Tell your partner all the important things that you need to say about a house to find a similar building.
    A: A house is a building where one or two families live. Families sleep, prepare their food, store their belongings, and stay safe and warm in houses.

  Q: Which building on the right is most like a house?
    A: An apartment building

    A: An apartment building is a building where many families live. Families sleep, prepare their food, store their belongings, and stay safe and warm in apartment buildings.

  Q: How are the other buildings different from a house?
    A: A farm is a place where people raise animals and plants, but a farm is not necessarily the home of the farmer. A playground is a place people go to play and have fun, but is not a dwelling.

  Q: What clues let you know that an apartment building is most like a house?
    A: Both are places where families sleep, prepare their food, store their belongings, and stay safe and warm.

### Guided Practice

- Display the following pictures with the first to the left of the other three.

200        © 2000 CRITICAL THINKING BOOKS & SOFTWARE • WWW.CRITICALTHINKING.COM • 800-458-4849

BEGINNING BUILDING THINKING SKILLS LESSON PLANS                    VERBAL SIMILARITIES AND DIFFERENCES

**F-11 Exercise:** _police station_, _garage_, _fire station_, _supermarket_

Q: Here you see a picture of a police station. Tell your partner all the important things that you need to say about a police station to find a similar building.

   A: A police station is the place where police officers meet and keep their equipment.

Q: Which building on the right is most like a police station?

   A: A fire station is the place where firefighters keep their equipment and stay until they are called to put out a fire.

Q: How are the other buildings different from a police station?

   A: A garage is a building used to store vehicles, not an office for community helpers and storage space for safety equipment. A supermarket is a place people go to buy food.

Q: What clues let you know that a fire station is most like a police station?

   A: Both are place where people who provide protection go to work and keep their vehicles and equipment.

## Optional Independent Practice

• Display the following pictures with the first to the left of the other three:

**F-11 Practice:** _library_, _hospital_, _post office_, _apartment building_

Q: Here you see a picture of a library. Tell your partner all the important things that you need to say about a library to find a similar building.

   A: A library is a building where people get free information about their interests. They may read or borrow books, magazines, or tapes. Libraries are usually operated by the government.

Q: Which building on the right is most like a library?

   A: A post office is a place where people send or pick up letters and packages. The cost of using the post office is very small because it is operated by the government.

Q: What clues let you know that a post office is most like a library?

   A: Both are buildings where people get information at little or no cost because most libraries and all post offices are operated by the government.

## Thinking About Thinking

Q: What kind of characteristics did you discuss to describe a building?

   A: Size, purpose, who lives or works there, color, design, its materials, its usual location, who owns the building.

## Personal Application

Q: When is it important to understand how buildings are alike?

   A: To describe trips; to follow directions; to find places

**LANGUAGE ARTS EXTENSION**

## LANGUAGE INTEGRATION ACTIVITIES

• Drawing: Select a picture of a building or allow students to find or draw a picture of building.

© 2000 CRITICAL THINKING BOOKS & SOFTWARE • WWW.CRITICALTHINKING.COM • 800-458-4849    201

- Telling: Ask students to create a riddle about a building to tell or write for a partner.

- Telling: Ask students within each cooperative learning group to play "Twenty Questions" about a building.

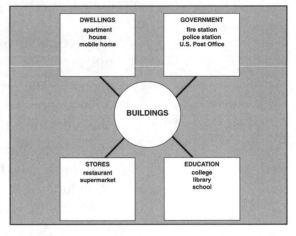

- First/Second Grade Language Activity: For each item, list students' responses and ask students to read the list aloud or write sentences to create a short description that can be added to students' drawings, if desired.

- Create a bulletin board display of pictures of different kinds of buildings (see sample on right). Discuss how each is used and other special characteristics.

**FOLLOW-UP ACTIVITIES AT HOME**
- Ask parents to describe the buildings they see or use. They should then ask the child to describe these buildings to another family member or friend.

- On family trips around the local community and when visiting other cities, parents should ask their child to identify the types of buildings and to name the goods or services that are provided there.

**PICTURE BOOK EXTENSION**
- After discussing any of the picture books ask the following questions:
  Q: Are there any new ideas about (apartment buildings, fire stations, or post offices) that we learned from this story?
  Q: What ideas or details about (apartment buildings, fire stations, or post offices) did you get from the pictures?
  Q: Is this information true of most (apartment buildings, fire stations, or post offices)?

- After discussing each story, ask students to add new information about the characteristics of the family member described in the story to the lists, posters, or graphic organizers that you may have used when discussing the pictures.

**SUPPLEMENTAL PICTURE BOOKS**
- These books feature the buildings discussed in this lesson. Descriptions of these and additional books on topics in this lesson are listed in the extended bibliography at the end of this manual.

**Apartment Building**
*Homes*, Nicola Baxter
*Russell and Elisa*, Johanna Hurwitz
*Tar Beach*, Faith Ringgold

**Fire Station**
*Fire Fighters,* R. Broekel
*The Fire Station,* Robert Munsch and Michael Martchenko

**Post Office**
*Hi,* Gio Coalson
*Will Goes to the Post Office,* Olof and Lena Landstrom

**EXERCISE F-12**

## SIMILAR BUILDINGS—EXPLAIN

**ANSWERS F-12**

**F-12 Example:** Restaurant and supermarket: both are places people go to get food. People who work there help customers buy the food they want. Customers have to pay before taking food out. People can buy prepared food in both stores. Both contain refrigerators, freezers, and clean shelves to keep food fresh and safe to eat.

**F-12 Exercise:** Barn and garage: both are buildings used to store vehicles and other equipment or animals.

**F-12 Practice:** Fire station and gas station: both contain equipment needed to repair vehicles.

**LESSON PREPARATION**

### OBJECTIVE AND MATERIALS

OBJECTIVE: Students will explain how two buildings are alike.

MATERIALS: The following pictures are used in this lesson: *barn (42), fire station (45), garage (53), gas station (41), restaurant (48),* and *supermarket (49)* • transparency of TM 10

### CURRICULUM APPLICATIONS

<u>Social Studies</u>: Identify how a family depends upon products and services to meet its needs, cite examples of community needs and services, identify jobs within the community and understand how community helpers are an example of interdependence.

### TEACHING SUGGESTIONS

• "Dwellings" or "residences" are abstract concepts for most young children. Since they have heard these terms several times in previous exercises, students should begin to use them independently, if they have frequent practice doing so. Dwellings can refer to homes for animals, as well as people; residences refers only to people. Use the terms "dwellings" or "residences" often in these activities and in other contexts and encourage students to do so. Acknowledge students' unprompted use of these terms.

• To reinforce students' responses, you may draw a compare or contrast diagram to record their answers. For a blank compare or contrast diagram see Transparency Master 10 on page 334.

• Model and encourage students to express the following process for comparing buildings:

1. Recall the important characteristics of the building.

2. Find the important characteristics in the pictures.

© 2000 CRITICAL THINKING BOOKS & SOFTWARE • WWW.CRITICALTHINKING.COM • 800-458-4849

BEGINNING BUILDING THINKING SKILLS LESSON PLANS — VERBAL SIMILARITIES AND DIFFERENCES

3. List the important similar characteristics of the two buildings.

4. Check to be sure that I don't leave out anything important or interesting about the two buildings.

**MODEL LESSON**

**LESSON**

**Introduction**

Q: We have practiced selecting a building that is similar to a particular one.

**Explaining the Objective to Students**

Q: In this lesson, we will explain how buildings are alike.

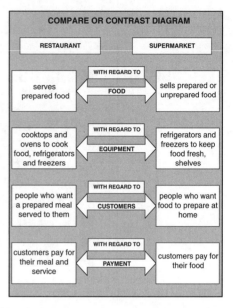

**Class Activity**

- Display the following pictures:

  **F-12 Example:** *restaurant* and *supermarket*

  Q: How are these buildings alike?

  A: Both are places people go to get food. People who work there help customers buy the food they want. Customers must pay before taking food out. People can buy prepared food in both stores. Both contain refrigerators, freezers, and clean shelves to keep food fresh and safe to eat.

  Q: What characteristics did you pay attention to when explaining how these buildings are alike?

  A: How they are used, who works there, their equipment.

**Guided Practice**

- Display the following pictures:

  **F-12 Exercise:** *barn* and *garage*

  Q: How are these buildings alike?

  A: Both buildings have large doors for vehicles. Both may be heated or unheated. Tools are stored there.

  Q: What characteristics did you pay attention to when explaining how these buildings are alike?

  A: Use. Both are buildings used to store vehicles and other equipment.

**Optional Independent Practice**

- Display the following pictures.

  **F-12 Practice:** *fire station* and *gas station*

  Q: How are these buildings alike?

  A: Both are buildings that contain equipment needed to repair vehicles.

  Q: What characteristics did you pay attention to when explaining how these buildings are alike?

  A: Use and equipment. Both buildings shelter workers and their equipment used to keep vehicles running.

### Thinking About Thinking

Q: What kind of characteristics did you discuss to explain how buildings are alike?

A: Size, purpose, who lives or works there, color, design, its materials, its usual location (rural, downtown, suburbs).

### Personal Application

Q: When is it important to explain how two buildings are alike?

A: To give or understand directions. To understand why their construction, location, or use may be similar. To explain a particular building to someone that is unfamiliar with it, a friend, or a younger child.

**LANGUAGE ARTS EXTENSION**

## LANGUAGE INTEGRATION ACTIVITIES

- Drawing: Select a picture of a building or allow students to find or draw a picture of building. Ask students to create a riddle that they will tell or write for a partner.

- Telling: Ask students to create a riddle about a building to tell or write for a partner.

- Ask students within each cooperative learning group to play "Twenty Questions" about a building.

- First/Second Grade Language Activity: For each item, list students' responses and ask students to read the list aloud or write sentences to create a short description that can be added to students' drawings.

- Create a bulletin board display of different kinds of buildings. Discuss how each is used and other special characteristics.

## FOLLOW-UP ACTIVITIES AT HOME

- Ask parents to describe the buildings they see or use. They should then ask the child to describe these buildings to a family member or friend.

- On family trips around the local community and when visiting other cities, parents should ask their child to identify types of buildings and to name the goods or services that are provided there.

## PICTURE BOOK EXTENSION

- Language experiences with picture books extend this lesson. After discussing any of the picture books ask the following questions:

  Q: Are there any new ideas about (<u>barns, fire stations, garages, gas stations, restaurants, or supermarkets</u>) that we learned from this story?

  Q: What ideas or details about (<u>barns, fire stations, garages, gas stations, restaurants, or supermarkets</u>) did you get from the pictures?

  Q: Is this information true of most (<u>barns, fire stations, garages, gas stations, restaurants, or supermarkets</u>)?

- After discussing each story, ask students to add new information about the characteristics of the building described in the story to the lists, posters, or graphic organizers you may have used when discussing the pictures.

BEGINNING BUILDING THINKING SKILLS LESSON PLANS                    VERBAL SIMILARITIES AND DIFFERENCES

**SUPPLEMENTAL PICTURE BOOKS**
- These books feature the buildings discussed in this lesson. Descriptions of these and additional books on topics in this lesson are provided in the extended bibliography at the end of this manual.

**Barn**
> *Farm Animals,* New True series, E. Posell
> *If It Weren't for Farmers,* Allan Fowler
> *The Red Barn,* Eve Bunting
> *The Big Red Barn,* Margaret Wise Brown

**Fire Station**
> *Fire Fighters,* R. Broekel
> *The Fire Station,* Robert Munsch and Michael Martchenko

**Garage**
> *Play Garage*

**Gas Station**
> *Jack Tractor: Five Stories from Smallbill's Garage,* Karen Ludlow and Willy Imax

**Restaurant**
> *The Frog Goes to Dinner,* Mercer Mayer
> *The Paper Crane,* Molly Bang

**Supermarket**
> *A Busy Day at Mr. Kang's Grocery Store,* Our Neighborhood series, Alice Flanagan
> *Market,* Ted Lewin
> *The Shopping Basket,* John Burningham

**EXERCISE F-13**

# SIMILARITIES AND DIFFERENCES—JOBS

---
**ANSWERS F-13**

**F-13 Example:** *doctor* and *nurse*
ALIKE: Both provide a health service to our community. They help us keep our bodies healthy. They go to school for a long time to learn how all the parts of our bodies work, what healthy bodies need, and how to treat injuries or illnesses. They use special tools or medicines. Both wear special clothes, work in offices, and can be male or female.
DIFFERENT: Doctors decide the medicines or treatment each patient should have. Nurses follow the doctors' instructions.
**F-13 Exercise:** *barber* and *dentist*
ALIKE: Both must have special training, use special tools or supplies, and wear special clothes. Both help improve our appearance and cleanliness.
DIFFERENT: The barber uses scissors and clippers on the hair; the dentist uses special tools for working on the teeth. A dentist is called a "doctor" and goes to college for a long time to learn how treating teeth affects our whole body.
**F-13 Practice:** *grocer* and *cook*
ALIKE: Both buy and sell food. Both keep food safe and fresh.
---

206          © 2000 CRITICAL THINKING BOOKS & SOFTWARE • WWW.CRITICALTHINKING.COM • 800-458-4849

**BEGINNING BUILDING THINKING SKILLS LESSON PLANS**          **VERBAL SIMILARITIES AND DIFFERENCES**

> DIFFERENT: The grocer sells fresh, uncooked, canned, and frozen foods to customers who cook or warm it up at home. The cook prepares food and places it on dishes for people eating it in restaurants, hospitals, trains, or airplanes. The grocer buys food from farmers. The cook buys food from the grocer.

**LESSON PREPARATION**

## OBJECTIVE AND MATERIALS
OBJECTIVE: Students will compare and contrast two occupations.
MATERIALS: The following pictures are used in this lesson: *barber (23), cook (11), dentist (20), doctor (19), grocer (22), nurse (14)* • transparency of TM 11 on page 335

## CURRICULUM APPLICATIONS
<u>Health</u>: Identify people who produce and distribute food.
<u>Social Studies</u>: Define consumer as a user of goods and services; identify how a family depends upon products and services to meet its needs; cite examples of community needs and services; identify jobs within the community and understand how community helpers are an example of interdependence.

## TEACHING SUGGESTIONS
* Emphasize the difference between "comparing" (describing how two things are alike) and "contrasting" (explaining how two things are different). Correct mistaken usage of the terms and acknowledge students' correct use of these terms.

* Students may not commonly use the term "occupation." Discuss with students the common synonyms for the word *job*—livelihood, career, work, etc.

* To help young children express contrast, emphasize the use of the conjunction "but." Example: a grocer sells food, <u>but</u> a cook prepares food for customers. Explain that "but" is a signal word to alert the reader or listener that what comes after it will be different than what comes before it. Encourage students to use this sentence pattern and acknowledge students' unprompted statements expressing contrast using this syntax.

* Model and encourage students to express the following process for comparing and contrasting two jobs:
  1. Recall the important characteristics of the job (their goods or services, work location, training, how they spend their time, tools they use, and tasks that a person having this job would do.)
  2. Find the important characteristics in the pictures.
  3. Identify the differences in the pictures.
  4. List the important differences.
  5. Decide what the similarities and difference tell us about the two
  6. Check to be sure that I don't leave out anything important or interesting about the two jobs.

© 2000 CRITICAL THINKING BOOKS & SOFTWARE • WWW.CRITICALTHINKING.COM • 800-458-4849          207

BEGINNING BUILDING THINKING SKILLS LESSON PLANS                    VERBAL SIMILARITIES AND DIFFERENCES

**MODEL LESSON** | **LESSON**

## Introduction

Q: We have described how jobs are alike. When we discuss how things are alike, we are comparing them. Sometimes we want to know how they are different in order to understand something important about them. When we describe how they are different, we contrast them.

## Explaining the Objective to Students

Q: In this lesson, we will explain how two jobs are alike and how they are different.

## Class Activity

• Display the following pictures:

**F-13 Example:** *doctor* and *nurse*

Q: How are these two jobs alike?

  A: Both provide a health service to our community; they help us keep our bodies healthy. They go to school for a long time to learn how all the parts of our bodies work, what healthy bodies need, and how to treat injuries or illnesses. They use special tools or medicines. Both wear special clothes, work in offices, and can be male or female.

Q: How are these two jobs different?

  A: Doctors decide what medicines or treatment to give and the nurse follows the doctor's instructions. The doctor goes to college for a longer time.

Q: What characteristics did you describe to compare and contrast a doctor and a nurse?

  A: What they do, where they work, special tools used, special training required

• To reinforce students' responses, you may draw a compare and contrast diagram to record their answers. For a blank compare and contrast graphic organizer, see TM 11 on page 335.

## Guided Practice

• Display the following pictures:

**F-13 Exercise:** *barber* and *dentist*

Q: How are these two jobs alike?

  A: Both must have special training, use special tools or supplies, and wear special clothes. Both help improve our appearance and cleanliness. Both use mirrors and water to perform their jobs.

Q: How are these two jobs different?

  A: The barber uses scissors and clippers on the hair, the dentist uses special tools for working on the teeth. A dentist is called a "doctor" and

208        © 2000 CRITICAL THINKING BOOKS & SOFTWARE • WWW.CRITICALTHINKING.COM • 800-458-4849

BEGINNING BUILDING THINKING SKILLS LESSON PLANS                    VERBAL SIMILARITIES AND DIFFERENCES

goes to college for a long time to learn how treating teeth affects our whole body.

### Optional Independent Practice
- Display the following pictures:

**F-13 Practice:** *grocer* and *cook*

Q: How are these two jobs alike?
   A: Both buy and sell food. Both keep food safe and fresh.

Q: How are these two jobs different?
   A: The grocer sells fresh, canned, and frozen foods to customers who cook or warm it up at home. The cook prepares food and places it on dishes for people eating it in restaurants, hospitals, trains, or air-planes. The grocer buys food from farmers. The cook buys food from the grocer.

### Thinking About Thinking

Q: What kind of characteristics did you discuss to describe how jobs are alike and different?
   A: The goods or services provided, what consumer seeks these goods or services, work location, training, how they spend their time, and tools they use. Emphasize the actions shown in the pictures and other tasks that a person having this job would do.

Q: What characteristics do you discuss to describe a consumer?
   A: Students may name goods or services, wants or needs, providers, how secured, or how often goods and services are needed.

### Personal Application

Q: When is it important to understand how jobs are alike?
   A: To suggest or recognize jobs that are similar to ones you already understand; to explain what friends or family members do for a living; to describe commercials; to describe services to a newcomer, thinking about the kind of job one might do as an adult; to explain a job to someone who is unfamiliar with it.

## LANGUAGE ARTS EXTENSION

### LANGUAGE INTEGRATION ACTIVITIES
- Drawing: Each student may draw a barber, a cook, a dentist, a doctor, a grocer, or a nurse. Ask students to write or tell a description of the job. Students' drawings may be used to create a class "big book." See page xxvii for directions.

- Telling: Students may create a riddle about jobs that they tell or write for a partner.

- Listening: Play Listening Tic Tac Toe with jobs. For directions, see page xxviii; for the playing grid, photocopy TM 12 on page 336. Use occupations that have been introduced in previous lessons or the entire list of jobs on page 340.

© 2000 CRITICAL THINKING BOOKS & SOFTWARE • WWW.CRITICALTHINKING.COM • 800-458-4849          209

**BEGINNING BUILDING THINKING SKILLS LESSON PLANS**          **VERBAL SIMILARITIES AND DIFFERENCES**

**FOLLOW-UP ACTIVITIES AT HOME**

- Ask parents to describe their jobs. They should then ask the child to describe parents' jobs to another family member or friend.

**PICTURE BOOK EXTENSION**

- Language experiences with picture books extend this lesson. After discussing any of the picture books ask the following questions:

  Q: Are there any new ideas about (barbers, cooks, dentists, doctors, grocers, or nurses) that we learned from this story?

  Q: What ideas or details about (barbers, cooks, dentists, doctors, grocers, or nurses) did you get from the pictures?

  Q: Is this information true of most (barbers, cooks, dentists, doctors, grocers, or nurses)?

- After discussing each story, ask students to add new information about the characteristics of the job described in the story to the lists, posters, or graphic organizers that you may have used when discussing the pictures.

**SUPPLEMENTAL PICTURE BOOKS**

- These books feature the workers discussed in this lesson. Descriptions of these and additional books on topics in this lesson are provided in the extended bibliography at the end of this manual.

**Barber**
> *Uncle Jed's Barbershop,* Margaret Mitchell

**Grocer**
> *A Busy Day at Mr. Kang's Grocery Store,* Alice Flanagan
> *Eats,* Arnold Adoff
> *The Potato Man*, Megan McDonald

**Dentist**
> *Doctor DeSoto,* William Steig
> *Going to the Dentist: Mister Rogers Neighborhood Series,* Fred Rogers
> *My Dentist,* Rockwell Harlow

**Doctor**
> *Going To the Doctor,* T. Barry Brazelton
> *Going to the Doctor: Mister Rogers Neighborhood Series,* Fred Rogers

**Nurse**
> *Nurses,* Robert James

**EXERCISE F-14**

## SIMILARITIES AND DIFFERENCES—FOOD

> **ANSWERS F-14**
>
> **F-14 Example:** *apple* and *tomato*
> ALIKE: Juice can be made from them. They have seeds. They are both the fruit part of the plant.
> DIFFERENT: Apples grow on trees, but tomatoes grow on vines. Apples can be eaten as snacks, baked in pies for dessert, or used to make stuffing for roast chicken or turkey. Tomatoes are usually eaten in salads,

210          © 2000 CRITICAL THINKING BOOKS & SOFTWARE • WWW.CRITICALTHINKING.COM • 800-458-4849

stuffed with meat and baked, or used to make spaghetti sauce for lunch and/or dinner. Apples can be sweet or tart, but tomatoes usually need some kind of seasoning, such as salt, to make them taste better. We call an apple a fruit and a tomato a vegetable.

**F-14 Exercise:** *lettuce* and *cabbage*
ALIKE: Both are round plants with leaves that can be eaten; they can be used to make salads. They are leafy vegetables and can be eaten without cooking.
DIFFERENT: Cabbage is usually eaten raw in salads or boiled in soups. A cabbage leaf is a little thicker and stiffer than lettuce. Cabbage can be green, white, or purple; lettuce is green. Lettuce is usually eaten raw in salads, sandwiches or hamburgers. Lettuce is sometimes "wilted" but rarely cooked.

**F-14 Practice:** *milk* and *butter*
ALIKE: Both are food products that come from cows.
DIFFERENT: Butter is made from milk by churning. Milk is a liquid, but butter is a solid when cooled. Milk is white and butter is yellow.

## LESSON PREPARATION

### OBJECTIVE AND MATERIALS
OBJECTIVE: Students will compare and contrast foods.
MATERIALS: The following pictures are used in this lesson: *apple (92), cabbage (90), lettuce (91), tomatoes (95), milk (79), butter (74)* • transparency of TM 11 on page 335

### CURRICULUM APPLICATIONS
Health: Recognize food that provides good nutrition for proper growth and functions of the body.
Science: Identify the parts of a plant: root, stem, and leaf; recognize that there are many kinds of plants; identify living things as plants or animals; recognize the major physical differences between plants and animals; investigate the importance of seeds; give three ways plants are important to people.

### TEACHING SUGGESTIONS
• Emphasize the difference between "comparing" (describing how two things are alike) and "contrasting" (explaining how two things are different). Correct mistaken usage of the terms and acknowledge students' correct use of these terms.

• To help young children express contrast, emphasize the use of "but" as a conjunction. Example: apples grow on trees, <u>but</u> tomatoes grow on vines. Explain that "but" is a signal word to alert the reader or listener that what comes after it will be different than what comes before it. Encourage students to use this sentence pattern and acknowledge students' unprompted statements expressing contrast using this syntax.

• Model and encourage students to express the following process for comparing and contrasting food:
  1. Recall the important characteristics of the food.
  2. Find the important characteristics in the pictures.

BEGINNING BUILDING THINKING SKILLS LESSON PLANS        VERBAL SIMILARITIES AND DIFFERENCES

    3. Identify the differences in the pictures.

    4. Decide what the similarities and difference tell us about the two foods.

    5. Check to be sure that I don't leave out anything important or interesting about the two foods.

    6. I will check to be sure that I don't leave out anything important or interesting about the two foods.

- Provide pictures of ethnic foods from magazines or cookbooks or secure samples of ethnic foods using the type of food mentioned in the lesson. Assist students in describing and pronouncing the names of ethnic foods.

- For second-grade use, discuss basic nutrients the food contains: fats, protein, carbohydrates, vitamins, minerals and water.

**MODEL LESSON** | **LESSON**

### Introduction

Q: We have described how foods are alike; we compared them. Sometimes we want to know how they are different in order to understand something important about them. When we describe how foods are different, we contrast them.

### Explaining the Objective to the Students

Q: In this lesson, we will compare and contrast different foods.

### Class Activity

- Display the following pictures:
  **F-14 Example:** *apple, tomato*
  Q: How are these two foods alike?
    A: Juice can be made from them. They have seeds. They are both the fruit part of the plant.

  Q: How are these two food different?
    A: Apples grow on trees, but tomatoes grow on vines. Apples can be eaten as snacks, baked in pies for dessert or used to make stuffing for roast chicken or turkey. Tomatoes are usually eaten in salads, stuffed with meat and baked, or used to make spaghetti sauce for lunch and/or dinner. Apples can be sweet or tart, but tomatoes usually need some kind of seasoning, such as salt, to make them taste better. We call an apple a fruit and a tomato a vegetable.

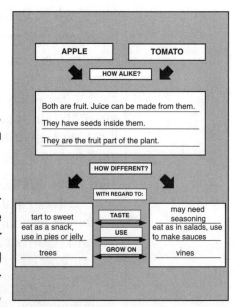

- To reinforce students' responses, you may draw a compare and contrast diagram to record their answers. For a blank compare-and-contrast graphic organizer, see Transparency Master 11 on page 335.

212   © 2000 CRITICAL THINKING BOOKS & SOFTWARE • WWW.CRITICALTHINKING.COM • 800-458-4849

BEGINNING BUILDING THINKING SKILLS LESSON PLANS                    VERBAL SIMILARITIES AND DIFFERENCES

### Guided Practice
- Display the following pictures:

  **F-14 Exercise:** *cabbage, lettuce*

  Q: How are these two foods alike?

    A: Both are round plants with leaves that can be eaten; they can be used to make salads. They are leafy vegetables and can be eaten without cooking.

  Q: How are these two foods different?

    A: Cabbage is usually eaten boiled, in salads, or soups. A cabbage leaf is a little thicker and stiffer than lettuce. Cabbage can be green, white, or purple; lettuce is green. Lettuce is usually eaten in salads, sandwiches or hamburgers. Lettuce is sometimes "wilted" but rarely cooked.

### Optional Independent Practice
- Display the following pictures:

  **F-14 Practice:** *milk, butter*

  Q: How are these two foods alike?

    A: Both are dairy products from cows, they are good sources of calcium, contain fat, and must be refrigerated.

  Q: How are these two foods different?

    A: Butter is made by stirring or churning milk. Butter becomes a solid; milk remains a liquid. Butter is spread or melted for flavor. Milk is a beverage.

### Thinking About Thinking

Q: What kind of characteristics did you discuss to describe food?

  A: If the food is a plant product, describe the kind of plant that produces it—tree, vine, or small bush. Identify the part of the plant that we eat—seed, fruit, leaf, stem, or root. Describe the food's color, shape, and size. If it is an animal product, describe the kind of animal that produces it and how it is prepared. For any food products, students describe how food is cooked, seasoned, and served at specific meals.

### Personal Application

Q: When is it important to compare and contrast foods skillfully?

  A: To understand the advertisements and signs in grocery stores and to select foods from menus; to explain a particular food to someone that is unfamiliar with it, to a friend, or to a younger child; to identify food that you like.

**LANGUAGE ARTS EXTENSION**

### LANGUAGE INTEGRATION ACTIVITIES
- Drawing: Select a picture of a food or allow students to find or draw a picture of food.

- Students may create a riddle about food that they will tell or write for a partner.

© 2000 CRITICAL THINKING BOOKS & SOFTWARE • WWW.CRITICALTHINKING.COM • 800-458-4849

BEGINNING BUILDING THINKING SKILLS LESSON PLANS                    VERBAL SIMILARITIES AND DIFFERENCES

- Telling: Ask students within each cooperative learning group to play "Twenty Questions" about a food.

- Listening: Play Listening Tic Tac Toe with food. For directions, see page xxviii; for the playing grid, photocopy page 336. Use foods that have been introduced in previous lessons or the entire list of food on page 341.

- First/Second Grade Language Activity: For each item, list students' responses and ask students to read the list aloud or write sentences to create a short description that can be added to students' drawings, if desired.

## FOLLOW-UP ACTIVITIES AT HOME

- Ask parents to describe the food that the family eats or has just purchased. They should then ask the child to describe the food to another family member or friend.

## PICTURE BOOK EXTENSION

- Language experiences with picture books extend this lesson and demonstrate how foods across cultures meet family needs. After discussing any of the picture books ask the following questions:

- While discussing picture books ask the following questions.
  Q: Are there any new ideas about (apple, butter, cabbage, lettuce, milk, tomato) that we learned from this story?
  Q: What ideas about (apple, butter, cabbage, lettuce, milk, tomato) did you get from the pictures?
  Q: Is this information true of most (apple, butter, cabbage, lettuce, milk, tomato)?

- After discussing each story, ask students to add new information about the characteristics of the family member described in the story to the lists, posters, or graphic organizers that you may have used when discussing the pictures.

## SUPPLEMENTAL PICTURE BOOKS

- These books feature the food discussed in this lesson. Descriptions of these and additional books on topics in this lesson are provided in the extended bibliography at the end of this manual.

### Apples
*If It Weren't for Farmers,* Allan Fowler
*Apples of Your Eye,* Allan Fowler
*Apples,* Ann Burckhardt
*Johnny Appleseed,* Steven Kellogg
*The Life and Time of the Apple,* Charles Micucci

### Butter
*Butter,* Wake

### Cabbage or Lettuce
*Peter Rabbit,* Beatrix Potter
*Vegetables, Vegetables!,* Fay Robinson

214          © 2000 CRITICAL THINKING BOOKS & SOFTWARE • WWW.CRITICALTHINKING.COM • 800-458-4849

BEGINNING BUILDING THINKING SKILLS LESSON PLANS

VERBAL SIMILARITIES AND DIFFERENCES

**Milk**

*In the Night Kitchen*, Maurice Sendak
*Jeremy Kooloo,* Tim Mahurin
*Milk*, Donald Carrick
*No Milk*, Jennifer A. Ericsson

**Tomato**

*The Pea Patch Jig,* Thatcher Hurd
*Tomato,* Barrie Watts
*Vegetables, Vegetables!,* Fay Robinson

**EXERCISE F-15**

# SIMILARITIES AND DIFFERENCES—VEHICLES

**ANSWERS F-15**

**F-15 Example:** *city bus* and *school bus*
ALIKE: Both are vehicles used to transport many people from one place to another. Usually large, they come in different sizes. They have a similar shape.
DIFFERENT: A school bus is used to take children to school or on field trips to different places. A city bus is used to transport people to different places around the city. Children do not pay as they enter a school bus, but when you enter a city bus you have to pay before you ride. When you ride a school bus, you have to sit at all times. On a city bus, you can remain standing when there are no seats available. School buses are usually yellow.

**F-15 Exercise:** *airplane* and *train*
ALIKE: Both are vehicles used to transport people from one place to another over long distances. People pay to ride. They usually follow schedules and make regular stops. Special planes or trains carry only freight.
DIFFERENT: Trains are land vehicles and must stay on railroad tracks. They are long and rectangular in shape. People on trains can walk to different rooms to eat, sleep or just to sit, while on an airplane you must stay in your seat. Airplanes are air vehicles. They travel faster because they have huge engines and do not have to follow roads or tracks. They have wings to provide lift and a tail to provide lift and to guide the plane.

**F-15 Practice:** *tractor* and *truck*
ALIKE: They are both used on farms and are powered by large engines. They can be used to pull wagons and other equipment.
DIFFERENT: The tractor is used on a farm to pull a plow or other farm equipment. A truck has an open area that is used to carry materials and things.

**LESSON PREPARATION**

**OBJECTIVE AND MATERIALS**

OBJECTIVE: Students will compare and contrast two vehicles.
MATERIALS: The following pictures are used in this lesson: *airplane (27), city bus (28), school bus (32), tractor (34), train (29), pickup truck (26)* • transparency of TM 11 on page 335

© 2000 CRITICAL THINKING BOOKS & SOFTWARE • WWW.CRITICALTHINKING.COM • 800-458-4849

215

BEGINNING BUILDING THINKING SKILLS LESSON PLANS　　　　VERBAL SIMILARITIES AND DIFFERENCES

**CURRICULUM APPLICATIONS**
<u>Social Studies</u>: Identify how a family depends upon transportation to meet its needs; cite examples of community needs and services; understand how community helpers are an example of interdependence.

**TEACHING SUGGESTIONS**
- Emphasize the difference between "comparing" (describing how two things are alike) and "contrasting" (explaining how two things are different). Correct mistaken usages of the terms and acknowledge students' correct use of these terms.

- To help young children express contrast, emphasize the use of "but" as a conjunction. Example: school buses are usually yellow, <u>but</u> city buses can have different colors. Explain that "but" is a signal word to alert the reader or listener that what comes after it will be different than what comes before it. Encourage students to use this sentence pattern and acknowledge students' unprompted statements expressing contrast using this syntax.

- Model and encourage students to express the following process for comparing and contrasting vehicles:
  1. Recall the important characteristics of the vehicle (I will be sure to discuss their size, purpose, where is it is driven, how it looks, what kind of equipment it has, and when it is used.)
  2. Find the important characteristics in the pictures.
  3. Identify the differences in the pictures.
  4. List the important differences.
  5. Decide what the similarities and difference tell us about the two vehicles.
  6. I will check to be sure that I don't leave out anything important or interesting about the two vehicles.

**MODEL LESSON**

**LESSON**

**Introduction**
Q: When we described how vehicles are alike, we compared them. Sometimes we want to know how they are different in order to understand something important about them. When we describe how vehicles are different, we contrast them.

**Explaining the Objective to the Students**
Q: In this lesson, we will compare and contrast two kinds of vehicles.

**Class Activity**
- Display the following pictures:
  **F-15 Example:** *city bus, school bus*

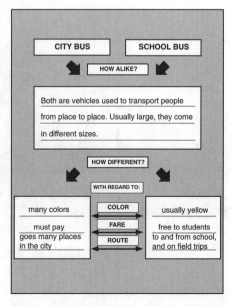

216　© 2000 CRITICAL THINKING BOOKS & SOFTWARE • WWW.CRITICALTHINKING.COM • 800-458-4849

Q: How are these two vehicles alike?

A: Both are vehicles used to transport many people from one place to another. Usually large, they come in different sizes. They have a similar shape.

Q: How are these two vehicles different?

A: A school bus is used to take children to school or on field trips to different places. A city bus is used to transport people to different places around the city. Children do not pay as they enter a school bus; you have to pay to ride a city bus. When you ride a school bus, one has to sit at all times. On a city bus, people can remain standing when there are no seats available. School buses are usually yellow, but other buses come in different colors.

• For a blank compare-and-contrast graphic organizer, see Transparency Master 11 on page 335.

## Guided Practice
• Display the following pictures:
**F-15 Exercise:** *airplane, train.*

Q: How are these two vehicles alike?

A: Both are vehicles used to transport people from one place to another over long distances. People pay to ride. These vehicles usually follow schedules and make regular stops. Special planes or trains carry only freight.

Q: How are these two vehicles different?

A: Trains are land vehicles and must stay on railroad tracks. They are long and rectangular in shape. People on trains can walk to different rooms to eat, sleep or sit. On an airplane, you must stay in your seat. Airplanes are air vehicles. They travel faster because they have huge engines and do not have to follow roads or tracks. They have wings to provide lift and a tail to provide lift and to guide the plane.

## Optional Independent Practice
• Display the following pictures:
**F-15 Practice:** *tractor, pickup truck*

Q: How are these two vehicles alike?

A: They both are used on farms and are powered by large engines. They can be used to pull wagons.

Q: How are these two vehicles different?

A: The tractor is used on a farm to pull a plow or other farm equipment. A truck is used to haul materials and things.

## Thinking About Thinking
Q: What characteristics did you describe to compare and contrast two vehicles?

A: Their size, purpose, where and how they are used, who owns them and uses them, where they are driven, how they are propelled, what kind of equipment they have, and how they look.

**BEGINNING BUILDING THINKING SKILLS LESSON PLANS**　　　　**VERBAL SIMILARITIES AND DIFFERENCES**

## Personal Application

Q: When might you have to compare and contrast two vehicles?

　A: To understand advertisements; to explain a particular vehicle to someone that is unfamiliar with it, such as a friend or a younger child. Parents may compare and contrast to decide whether to buy a truck, a van, or an automobile

**LANGUAGE ARTS EXTENSION**

## LANGUAGE INTEGRATION ACTIVITIES

• Drawing: Select a picture of a vehicle or allow students to find or draw a picture of a vehicle.

• Telling:  Ask students to create a riddle that they will tell or write for a partner.

• Telling: Ask students within each cooperative learning group to play "Twenty Questions" about a vehicle.

• Listening: Play Listening Tic Tac Toe with vehicles. For directions, see page xxviii; for the playing grid, photocopy page 336. Use vehicles that have been introduced in previous lessons or the entire list of vehicles on page 342.

• First/Second Grade Language Activity: For each item, list students' responses and ask students to read the list aloud or write sentences to create a short description that can be added to students' drawings, if desired.

## FOLLOW-UP ACTIVITIES AT HOME

• Ask parents to describe the vehicles they own and to compare them to other vehicles. They should then ask the child to make comparisons of these vehicles to another family member or friend.

## PICTURE BOOK EXTENSION

• Language experiences with picture books extend this lesson and demonstrate how vehicles are used for different community needs. After discussing any of the picture books ask the following questions:

• While discussing picture books ask the following questions.
Q: Are there any new ideas about (<u>vehicles</u>) that we learned from this story?
Q: What ideas about (<u>vehicles</u>) did you get from the pictures?
Q: Is this information true of most (<u>vehicles</u>)?

• After discussing each story, ask students to add new information about the characteristics of the vehicles described in the story to the lists, posters, or graphic organizers that you may have used when discussing the pictures.

## SUPPLEMENTAL PICTURE BOOKS

• These books feature the vehicles discussed in this lesson. Descriptions of these and additional books on topics in this lesson are provided in the extended bibliography at the end of this manual.

218　　　　© 2000 CRITICAL THINKING BOOKS & SOFTWARE • WWW.CRITICALTHINKING.COM • 800-458-4849

**Airplane**

*Airplanes,* Dorling Kindersley
*Airport,* Byron Barton
*Bored—Nothing to Do,* Peter Spier

**Bus**

*Is There Room on the Bus,* Helen Piers and Hannah Giffard
*The Wheels on the Bus,* Paul Zelinsky
*Where's That Bus,* Eileen Brown

**School Bus**

*School Bus,* Donald Crews
*This is the Way We Go to School,* Edith Baer

**Tractor**

*If It Weren't for Farmers,* Allan Fowler
*Katy and the Big Snow,* Virginia Lee Burton
*Tractors,* Gil Chandler
*Tractors,* Peter Brady

**Train**

*Freight Train,* Easy Readers series, Peter Brady
*Freight Train,* Donald Crews
*The Little Engine That Could,* Watty Piper
*Trains,* Eye Opener series

**Truck**

*All Aboard Trucks,* Lynn Conrad
*Pick-Up Trucks,* James Koons
*The Little Black Truck,* Liba Moore Gray
*Truck,* Donald Crews

## EXERCISE F-16

# SIMILARITIES AND DIFFERENCES—ANIMALS

**ANSWERS F-16**

**F-16 Example:** *chicken* and *duck*

ALIKE: Since both are birds, babies hatch from eggs. They are warm-blooded and have backbones (vertebrates). They can be pets or raised on farms for food. They are about the same size and can come in many different colors They eat small plants and insects.

DIFFERENT: Ducks live near the water, and chickens do not. Chickens have beaks, and ducks have bills. Ducks can fly great distances while chickens cannot. Ducks are good swimmers, and chickens do not swim.

**F-16 Exercise:** *horse* and *camel*

ALIKE: Both are large animals. They are warm-blooded and have backbones. They give birth to live babies. They have four legs and can run long distances. They eat plants. They are used for transportation; people can ride them.

DIFFERENT: A horse has a long tail, and it can run very fast. A camel has a short tail and does not run as fast. A camel has a long neck, long legs, and one or two humps on its back. Camels live in the desert and can go

BEGINNING BUILDING THINKING SKILLS LESSON PLANS                    VERBAL SIMILARITIES AND DIFFERENCES

for a long time without water. Horses cannot travel long distances without rest and water.
**F-16 Practice:** *spider* and *lizard*
ALIKE: They are both cold-blooded and lay eggs. Both scamper quickly and hide.
DIFFERENT: A lizard is a reptile with four legs and a tail. A spider is an arachnid with eight legs. A spider catches its food in a web; a lizard captures its food.

**LESSON PREPARATION**

## OBJECTIVE AND MATERIALS
OBJECTIVE: Students will compare and contrast two animals.
MATERIALS: The following pictures are used in this lesson: *camel (58), chicken (65), duck (70), horse (64), lizard (68), spider (60)* • transparency of TM 11

## CURRICULUM APPLICATIONS
Science: Identify living things as plants or animals, recognize that plants and animals reproduce their own kind; recognize the major physical differences between plants and animals; state what animals need to live and grow; recognize examples of common animals as being fish, birds, or mammals.

## TEACHING SUGGESTIONS
• Emphasize the difference between "comparing" (describing how two things are alike) and "contrasting" (explaining how two things are different). Correct mistaken usages of the terms and acknowledge students' correct use of these terms.

• To help young children express contrast, emphasize the use of "but" as a conjunction. Example: chickens have beaks, but ducks have bills. Explain that "but" is a signal word to alert the reader or listener that what comes after it will be different than what comes before it. Encourage students to use this sentence pattern and acknowledge students' unprompted statements expressing contrast using this syntax.

• For young children "cold-blooded" or "warm-blooded" may be new terms. Explain the effect of this difference on the survival needs of animals. The terms "backbone" or "vertebra" may be new concepts. Discuss with students the significance and function of a backbone.

• Model and encourage students to express the following process for comparing and contrasting animals:
  1. Recall the important characteristics of the animal (their body structure, warm- or cold- blooded, whether it has a backbone, whether it hatches or gives live birth, where it lives, how it moves, what it eats.).
  2. Find the important characteristics in the pictures.
  3. Identify the differences in the pictures.
  4. List the important differences.
  5. Decide what the similarities and difference tell us about the two animals.

220          © 2000 CRITICAL THINKING BOOKS & SOFTWARE • WWW.CRITICALTHINKING.COM • 800-458-4849

6. Check to be sure that I don't leave out anything important or interesting about the two animals.

**MODEL LESSON**

**LESSON**

**Introduction**

Q: When we describe how animals are alike, we compare them. Sometimes we want to know how they are different in order to understand something important about them. When we describe how animals are different, we contrast them.

**Explaining the Objective to the Students**

Q: In this lesson, we will compare and contrast animals.

**Class Activity**

- Display the following pictures:

**F-16 Example:** *chicken, duck*

Q: How are these two animals alike?

A: Since both are birds, babies hatch from eggs. They are warm-blooded and have backbones (vertebrates). They can be pets, or raised on farms for food. They are about the same size and can come in many different colors They eat small plants and insects.

Q: How are these two animals different?

A: Ducks lives near the water, but chickens do not. Chickens have beaks, but ducks have bills. Ducks can fly great distances while chickens cannot. Ducks are good swimmers and chickens do not swim.

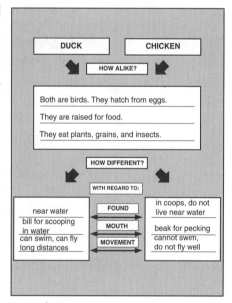

- For a blank compare-and-contrast graphic organizer, see Transparency Master 11 on page 335

**Guided Practice**

- Display the following pictures:

**F-16 Exercise:** *horse, camel*

Q: How are these two animals alike?

A: Both are large animals; they are warm-blooded; they have backbones; they give birth to live babies; they have four legs and can run long distances; they eat plants; they are used for transportation of people and things.

Q: How are these two animals different?

A: A horse has a long tail and it can run very fast while a camel has a short tail and does not run as fast. A camel has a long neck, long legs and either one or two humps on its back. Camels live in the desert and can go for a long time without water. Horses cannot travel long distances without rest and water.

**Optional Independent Practice**
* Display the following pictures:
  **F-16 Practice:** *spider, lizard*
  Q: How are these two animals alike?
    A: They are both cold-blooded. Their babies hatch from tiny eggs and look like the adults. Both move quickly and hide. Both are usually brown, gray, or black, but some have brightly colored markings. People are often afraid of both spiders and lizards.

  Q: How are these two animals different?
    A: A lizard is a reptile with four legs and a tail. A spider is an arachnid with eight legs. A lizard captures its food; a spider uses a web to catch its food. A lizard has a backbone; a spider does not. A spider's body looks like several parts which are connected. Lizards live on the ground or in trees. Spiders live in webs of a thin thread that they make from their bodies.

**Thinking About Thinking**
  Q: What kind of characteristics did you discuss to compare and contrast animals?
    A: Body structure, warm- or cold- blooded, whether it has a backbone, whether it hatches or gives live birth, where it lives, how it moves, what it eats.

**Personal Application**
  Q: When is it important to understand how animals are alike?
    A: To understand the needs of animals that we find at the zoo or the pet store. To care for pets properly.

**LANGUAGE ARTS EXTENSION**

**LANGUAGE INTEGRATION ACTIVITIES**
* Drawing: Each student may draw a picture of a camel, a chicken, a duck, a horse, a lizard, or a spider. Ask students to write or tell a description of the animal. Students' drawings may be used to create a "big book." See page xxvii for directions.
* *What Animal Am I? An Animal Guessing Game,* Iza Trapani. This book models animal riddles with pictures. Select a picture of an animal or allow students to find or draw a picture of food. Ask students to create a riddle that they will tell or write for a partner.
* Drama: Ask students to use animal puppets to act out "Brown bear, brown bear, what do I see?" for various animals discussed in the lesson.
* Telling: Ask students within each cooperative learning group to play "Twenty Questions" about an animal.
* Listening: Play Listening Tic Tac Toe with animals. For directions, see page xxviii; for the playing grid photocopy page 336. Use animals that

have been introduced in previous lessons or the entire list of animals on page 343.

- First/Second Grade Language Activity: For each item, list students' responses and ask students to read the list aloud or write sentences to create a short description that can be added to students' drawings, if desired.

- Create a bulletin board display of different kinds of animals. Discuss how each animal reproduces, whether it is warm- or cold-blooded, and other special characteristics:
  1. Birds: egg-laying, warm-blooded vertebrates with wings
  2. Fish: egg-laying, cold-blooded vertebrates with gills
  3. Reptiles: egg-laying, cold-blooded vertebrates with dry skin
  4. Amphibians: egg-laying, cold-blooded vertebrates with moist skin
  5. Mammals: baby grows inside mother's body; warm-blooded vertebrates with hair

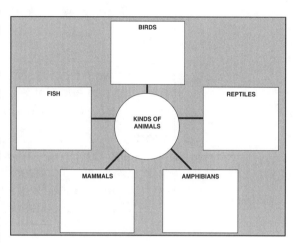

## FOLLOW-UP ACTIVITIES AT HOME
- Ask parents to compare and contrast animals they have seen. They should then ask the child to describe these animal comparisons to another family member or friend.

## PICTURE BOOK EXTENSION
- Language experiences with picture books extend this lesson and demonstrate how family members across cultures meet family needs. After discussing any of the picture books ask the following questions:

- While discussing picture books ask the following questions.
  Q: Are there any new ideas about (camels, chickens, ducks, horses, sharks, or whales) that we learned from this story?
  Q: What ideas about (camels, chickens, ducks, horses, sharks, or whales) did you get from the pictures?
  Q: Is this information true of most (camels, chickens, ducks, horses, sharks, or whales)?

## SUPPLEMENTAL PICTURE BOOKS
- These books feature the animals discussed in this lesson. Descriptions of these and additional books on topics in this lesson are provided in the extended bibliography at the end of this manual.

**BEGINNING BUILDING THINKING SKILLS LESSON PLANS**　　　**VERBAL SIMILARITIES AND DIFFERENCES**

**Camel**

*Pamela Camel,* Bill Peet

**Chicken**

*Chickens* , Ann Burckhardt
*If It Weren't For Farmers,* Rookie Read About Science series
*The Chicken or the Egg,* Rookie Read About Science series
*The Little Red Hen,* Paul Gladone
*The Rooster's Gift,* Pam Conrad

**Ducks**

*Birds We Know,* M. Friskey
*Make Way for Ducklings,* Robert McClosky
*Quack and Honk,* Rookie Read About Science series

**Horse**

*Horses,* K. Jacobsen
*Horses, Horses, Horses,* Allan Fowler
*Horses and Ponies*, (Usborne/EDC, Tulsa, OK).
*The Black Stallion Picture Book*, Walter Farley

**Shark**

*The Best Way to See a Shark,* Rookie Read About Science series
*Clark, the Toothless Shark,* Corinne Mellor
*Sharks,* June Behrens
*Sharks,* Jane Resnick
*Sharks: The Super Fish,* Helen Roney Statler

**EXERCISE
F-17**

# SIMILARITIES AND DIFFERENCES—BUILDINGS

**ANSWERS F-17**

**F-17 Example:** *house* and *mobile home*
ALIKE: Both are buildings people live or work in; they come in different sizes; one or two families can live in them.
DIFFERENT: A house is designed to stay in one place, but a mobile home can be moved to a different location at any time. Houses are made of wood or concrete and sit on a concrete foundation, while a mobile home is made of aluminum or metal and sits on a steel frame. Some mobile homes have wheels and can be pulled by a car or truck and taken while on vacation.

**F-17 Exercise:** *gas station* and *restaurant*
ALIKE: Both are places where people go to buy something they need; someone owns the business. People work there. People do not live in these places, they are used for business.
DIFFERENT: A gas station provides gasoline for a vehicle, while a restaurant provides a place for people to eat. At some gas stations you can buy snacks to eat, but at a restaurant you cannot buy gasoline. In restaurants many people can sit and dine. Gas stations are made to serve several cars at one time. Some gas stations have mechanics that fix cars.

**F-17 Practice:** *farm* and *playground*
ALIKE: Both are usually large open spaces. Equipment that people use

**224**　　　© 2000 CRITICAL THINKING BOOKS & SOFTWARE • WWW.CRITICALTHINKING.COM • 800-458-4849

BEGINNING BUILDING THINKING SKILLS LESSON PLANS                    VERBAL SIMILARITIES AND DIFFERENCES

> to work or play can be found on them. While some farmers live on their farms, both are usually not residences.
> DIFFERENT: People can live on a farm but not on a playground. A farm is a place where food is grown and animals are raised; people work there. A playground is a place people go to for fun, and it is used for recreation, mostly by children. The equipment on a farm is used to do a job, but playground equipment is used as rides or just for enjoyment. The animals that live on a farm belong to the farmer and are usually raised for food and sold at some time. The animals that are found at a playground may not belong to anyone and may not be safe to pet.

**LESSON PREPARATION**

## OBJECTIVE AND MATERIALS

OBJECTIVE: Students will compare and contrast two buildings.
MATERIALS: The following pictures are used in this lesson: *farm (47), gas station (41), house (53), mobile home (44), playground (52), restaurant (48)*

## CURRICULUM APPLICATIONS

Social Studies: Identify how a family depends upon the products and services produced or housed in buildings; cite the role buildings play in providing community needs and services.

## TEACHING SUGGESTIONS

• Emphasize the difference between "comparing" (describing how two things are alike) and "contrasting" (explaining how two things are different). Correct mistaken usages of the terms and acknowledge students' correct use of these terms.

• To help young children express contrast, emphasize the use of "but" as a conjunction. Example: A house cannot be moved easily, but a mobile home can. Explain that "but" is a signal word to alert the reader or listener that what comes after it will be different than what comes before it. Encourage students to use this sentence pattern and acknowledge students' unprompted statements expressing contrast using this syntax.

• Model and encourage students to express the following process for comparing and contrasting buildings:
  1. Recall the important characteristics of the buildings (their size, purpose, who lives or works there, materials, color, design).
  2. Find the important characteristics in the pictures.
  3. Identify the differences in the pictures.
  4. List the important differences.
  5. Decide what the similarities and difference tell us about the two.
  6. Check to be sure that I don't leave out anything important or interesting about the two buildings.

**MODEL LESSON**

## LESSON

### Introduction

Q: We have described how buildings are alike; we compared them.

© 2000 CRITICAL THINKING BOOKS & SOFTWARE • WWW.CRITICALTHINKING.COM • 800-458-4849          225

Sometimes we want to know how they are different in order to understand something important about them. When we describe how buildings are different, we contrast them.

**Explaining the Objective to the Students**
Q: In this lesson, we will compare and contrast buildings

**Class Activity**
- Display the following pictures:
  **F-17 Example:** *house, mobile home*
  Q: How are these two buildings alike?
    A: Both are buildings; people live or work in them; they come in different sizes; one or two families can live in them.

  Q: How are these two buildings different?
    A: A house is designed to stay in one place, but a mobile home can be moved to a different location. Houses are made of wood or concrete and sit on a concrete foundation, but a mobile home is made of aluminum or metal and sits on a steel frame. Some mobile homes have wheels and can be pulled by a car or truck and taken on vacation.

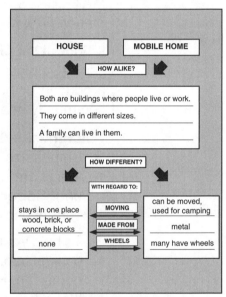

- For a blank compare-and-contrast graphic organizer, see Transparency Master 11 on page 335.

**Guided Practice**
- Display the following pictures:
  **F-17 Exercise:** *gas station, restaurant*
  Q: How are these buildings alike?
    A: Both are places where people go to buy something they need; someone owns the business. People work there. People do not live in these places, they are used for business.

  Q: How are these buildings different?
    A: A gas station provides gasoline for car, while a restaurant provides a place for people to eat. At some gas stations you can buy snacks to eat, but at a restaurant you cannot buy gasoline. In restaurants many people can sit and dine. Gas stations are made to serve several cars at one time. Some gas stations have mechanics that fix cars.

**Optional Independent Practice**
- Display the following pictures:
  **F-17 Practice:** *farm, playground*
  Q: How are these buildings alike?

BEGINNING BUILDING THINKING SKILLS LESSON PLANS                    VERBAL SIMILARITIES AND DIFFERENCES

A: Both are usually large open spaces. Equipment that people use to work or play can be found on them. While some farmers live on their farms, both are usually not residences.

Q: How are these buildings different?

A: People can live on a farm but not on a playground. A farm is a place where food is grown and animals are raised; people work there. A playground is a place people go to for fun, and it is used mostly by children. The equipment on a farm is used to do a job, but playground equipment is used as rides or just for enjoyment. The animals that live on a farm belong to the farmer and are usually raised for food and sold at some time. The animals that are found at a playground may not belong to anyone and may not be safe to pet.

### Thinking About Thinking

Q: What kind of characteristics did you discuss to compare and contrast buildings?

A: Size, purpose, who lives or works there, color, design, its materials, its usual location, who owns the building.

### Personal Application

Q: When is it important to compare and contrast buildings skillfully?

A: To give or understand directions. To understand why their construction, location, or use may be similar. To explain a particular building to someone that is unfamiliar with it, a friend, or a younger child.

**LANGUAGE ARTS EXTENSION**

## LANGUAGE INTEGRATION ACTIVITIES

• Drawing: Select a picture of a building or allow students to find or draw a picture of building.

• Telling: Ask students to create a riddle about a building.

• Telling: Ask students within each cooperative learning group to play "Twenty Questions" about a building.

• Listening: Play Listening Tic Tac Toe with buildings. Use buildings that have been introduced in previous lessons or the entire list of buildings on page 344.

• First/Second Grade Language Activity: For each item, list students' responses and ask students to read the list aloud or write sentences to create a short description that can be added to students' drawings, if desired.

• Create a bulletin board display of different kinds of buildings by class. Discuss how each is used and other special characteristics.

## FOLLOW-UP ACTIVITIES AT HOME

• Ask parents to describe the buildings they see or use. They should then ask the child to describe these buildings to another family member or friend.

• On family trips around the local community and when visiting other cities,

© 2000 CRITICAL THINKING BOOKS & SOFTWARE • WWW.CRITICALTHINKING.COM • 800-458-4849          227

parents should ask their child to identify types of buildings and to name the goods or services that are provided there.

## PICTURE BOOK EXTENSION

- Language experiences with picture books extend this lesson and demonstrate how the concepts found herein can be applied to different situations. After discussing any of the picture books ask the following questions:

Q: Are there any new ideas about (<u>farm, gas station, house, mobile home, playground, or restaurant</u>) that we learned from this story?

Q: What ideas about (<u>farm, gas station, house, mobile home, playground, or restaurant</u>) did you get from the pictures?

Q: Is this information true of most (<u>farm, gas station, house, mobile home, playground, or restaurant</u>)?

## SUPPLEMENTAL PICTURE BOOKS

- These books feature the buildings discussed in this lesson. Descriptions of these and additional books on topics in this lesson are provided in the extended bibliography at the end of this manual.

**Farm**

*Farm Animals,* E. Posell
*If It Weren't for Farmers,* Allan Fowler
*If You Are Not From the Prairie,* David Bouchard
*Winter on the Farm,* Laura Ingalls Wilder

**Gas Station**

*Jack Tractor: Five Stories from Smallbill's Garage*

**Houses**

*A House is a House for Me,* Mary Anne Hoberman
*Homes,* Nicola Baxter
*Houses and Homes,* Anne Morris
*The Little House,* Virginia Lee Burton

**Mobile Home**

*Someplace Else,* Carol Saul

**Playground**

*Maisy Goes to the Playground,* Lucy Cousins
*Rebel,* Allan Baille
*The Playground,* Kate Duke

**Restaurant**

*The Frog Goes to Dinner,* Mercer Mayer
*The Paper Crane,* Molly Bang

BEGINNING BUILDING THINKING SKILLS LESSON PLANS                    VERBAL SEQUENCES

## Chapter 7 | VERBAL SEQUENCES

EXERCISE
G-1

## RANKING FAMILY MEMBERS

---

**ANSWERS G-1**

**G-1 Example:** youngest to oldest: baby, toddler boy, boy, father, grand-father

**G-1 Exercise:** oldest to youngest: grandmother, mother, girl, toddler girl, baby

---

LESSON
PREPARATION

### OBJECTIVE AND MATERIALS

OBJECTIVE: Students will arrange people in a sequence.

MATERIALS: The following pictures are used in this lesson: *baby (1), boy (5), girl (4), father (7), mother (6), grandmother (8), grandfather (9), toddler boy (3), toddler girl (2)* • transparency of TM 21 on page 345

### CURRICULUM APPLICATIONS

Social Studies: Identify the roles of family members and how the family is an example of interdependence.

### TEACHING SUGGESTIONS

• Model and encourage students to express the following process for arranging people in order:

　　1. Look at the pictures and how the people are alike and how they are different (difference in ages, relationships, birthdays in a calendar year, how often you see that relative).

　　2. Look for a pattern of differences.

　　3. Figure out which person shows the least or most of that characteristic and arrange the other people to show that pattern.

• Young children may not commonly use the terms *gender* to mean male or female or *relative* to mean someone in one's family. Encourage students to use these terms and to find synonyms for them.

MODEL LESSON

### LESSON

**Introduction**

• Ask four students of different height to come to the front of the classroom. Q: We have practiced describing people and explaining how they are alike or different. As you look at these four students, how do you notice that they are different?

　　A: Students may name many differences, one of which will be height.

• Ask a student to arrange the four students in order of height from the tallest to the shortest.

• Ask another student to rearrange the students from smallest to tallest.

• Ask the students' birthdays. Ask a student to rearrange the group according to their ages or when their birthdays occur on the calendar.

© 2000 CRITICAL THINKING BOOKS & SOFTWARE • WWW.CRITICALTHINKING.COM • 800-458-4849          229

BEGINNING BUILDING THINKING SKILLS LESSON PLANS                                    VERBAL SEQUENCES

Q: We have seen three kinds of sequences:
1. height from tall to short
2. height from short to tall
3. age from youngest to oldest

- When we put things in order, we are ranking them.
  Q: What other characteristics might be an order by which we could rank these students?
  A: Students may mention length of hair, location in classroom, etc.

**Explaining the Objective to Students**
Q: In this lesson, we will arrange people in different orders.

**Class Activity**
- Display the following pictures:
  **G-1 Example:** *baby, boy, father, grandfather, toddler boy*
  Q: With your partner think about how these family members are different. Try to find a pattern that is growing larger or smaller and decide how you might arrange these family members in order. In what ways can you put these family members in order?
  A: Sequences may include how often we see them, when their birthdays occur in the calendar year, or how far away they live.

  Q: List the family members in order of age from youngest to oldest.
- Allow time for student work.
  Q: What did we learn about family members by putting them in order?
  A: Students' responses will vary, but generally include remembering which family members are parents to other family members, figuring out how old family members may be.

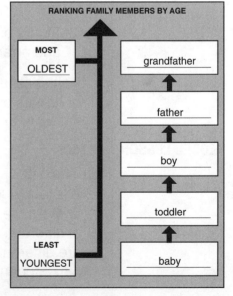

  Q: What clues let you know how to arrange these family members?
  A: Their age, their size, their relationship to other people in the family.

- For a blank transitive order graphic organizer see TM 21 on page 345.

**Guided Practice**
- Display the following pictures:
  **G-1 Exercise:** *baby, girl, grandmother, mother, toddler girl*
  Q: Look at these pictures of family members. Arrange them in order of age from oldest to youngest.

**Thinking About Thinking**
Q: What do you think about to put family members in a particular order?

230                         © 2000 CRITICAL THINKING BOOKS & SOFTWARE • WWW.CRITICALTHINKING.COM • 800-458-4849

A: Ages, relationships, birthdays in a calendar year, how often you see that relative.

**Personal Application**

Q: When is it important to understand how to name family members in order?

A: To remember ages, relationships or birthdays; to describe friends or family members to someone else.

**LANGUAGE ARTS EXTENSION**

## LANGUAGE INTEGRATION ACTIVITIES

• Drawing: Each student has made drawings of his or her family members in the description and similarities and differences lessons. Ask students to arrange their drawings of their family members in order. Students should explain the order and family relationship to a partner.

• Storytelling: Ask students to describe to a partner a special occasion (picnic, birthday party, etc.) that his or her family enjoyed. Ask the storyteller to relate what happened and the order in which the activities happened.

## FOLLOW-UP ACTIVITIES AT HOME

• Students may take home the family tree diagram and ask their parents to help them fill in names to show family relationships. They may draw pictures of family members in the boxes to create a family drawing, or individual drawings may be organized by the family into a poster-size family tree diagram. Use TM 8, the family tree diagram, on page 332.

## PICTURE BOOK EXTENSION

• After discussing any of the picture books ask the following questions:
Q: Are there any new ideas about (family members) that we learned from this story?
Q: What ideas about (family members) did you get from the pictures?
Q: Is this information true of most (family members)?

• After discussing each story , ask students to add new information about the family member described in the story to lists, posters, or graphic organizers that you may have used when discussing the pictures.

## SUPPLEMENTAL PICTURE BOOKS

• These books feature the family members discussed in this lesson. Descriptions of these and additional books on topics in this lesson are provided in the extended bibliography at the end of this manual.

**Families**

*Families*, Nicola Baxter
*I Got a Family,* Melrose Cooper
*Loving,* Ann Morris
*People*, Peter Speir

BEGINNING BUILDING THINKING SKILLS LESSON PLANS                    VERBAL SEQUENCES

**EXERCISE
G-2**

# RANKING JOBS

> **ANSWERS G-2**
> **G-2 Example:** order in which these people help us get food: farmer, grocer, cook
> **G-2 Exercise:** how often a family needs the products or services of these people: teacher (5 times a week), doctor (a few times a year), firefighter or pilot (rarely)

**LESSON
PREPARATION**

## OBJECTIVE AND MATERIALS

OBJECTIVE: Students will arrange occupations in a sequence.
MATERIALS: The following pictures are used in this lesson: *cook (11), doctor (19), farmer (12), firefighter (16), grocer (22), pilot (17), teacher (15)* • transparency of TM 22 on page 346

## CURRICULUM APPLICATIONS

Social Studies: Identify how a family depends upon products and services to meet its needs; cite examples of community needs and services; identify jobs within the community and understand how community helpers are an example of interdependence.

## TEACHING SUGGESTIONS

• Students may not commonly use the term "occupation." Discuss with students the common synonyms for jobs—livelihood, career, work, etc.

• Model and encourage students to express the following process for arranging jobs in order:
  1. Look at the pictures and tell how the jobs are alike and how they are different (difference in the frequency with which families need these goods or services).
  2. Look for a pattern of differences.
  3. Figure out which person shows the least or most of that characteristic
  4. Arrange the other jobs to show that pattern.

**MODEL LESSON**

## LESSON

### Introduction

• Ask students to name three jobs and list them on the chalkboard in the order of the number of times they use the product or service each provides.

### Explaining the Objective to Students

Q: In this lesson, we will arrange jobs in order.

### Class Activity

• Display the following pictures:
  **G-2 Example:** *cook, farmer, grocer*
  Q: With your partner think about how these jobs are different. Try to find a pattern and decide how to arrange these jobs in order.
    A: Order of their jobs in providing food.
  Q: Name the jobs according to the order in which they help us get food.

232          © 2000 CRITICAL THINKING BOOKS & SOFTWARE • WWW.CRITICALTHINKING.COM • 800-458-4849

Which job must come first?
 A: The farmer must first grow the food.

Q: Which job must come last?
 A: The cook prepares the food after he or she purchases it from the grocer.

Q: Arrange the jobs in order.
 A: farmer, grocer, cook

Q: What clues let you know how to arrange these jobs?
 A: I thought about what each of these workers does to provide us with food. Then using what I know about getting food, I decided the order in which each job must occur to provide us with food.

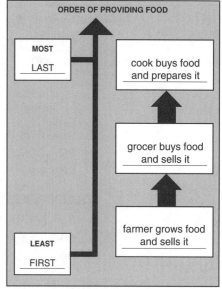

- For a blank transitive order graphic organizer see transparency master TM 22, page 346.

**Guided Practice**
- Display the following pictures:
**G-2 Exercise:** *doctor, firefighter, pilot, teacher*
Q: Name the jobs in the order of how often you or your family need the products or services of each worker.
 A: teacher, doctor, firefighter, pilot

Q: What do we learn about these jobs by putting them in order?
 A: Students realize the significance of these workers in getting what we need. Although we do not see emergency workers often, their help is essential in an emergency.

Q: What clues let you know how to arrange these jobs?
 A: The kind of products or services that the worker provides; how often in a day, a week, or a month we need that product or service.

**Thinking About Thinking**
 Q: What do you think about to put jobs in a particular order?
  A: How often our families need them, how frequently we see people performing these jobs, how close to our homes we can get the goods or services that these jobs provide.

**Personal Application**
 Q: When is it important to understand how to think about jobs in an order?
  A: To understand how much we depend on the goods or services that people offer our families.

BEGINNING BUILDING THINKING SKILLS LESSON PLANS                    VERBAL SEQUENCES

**LANGUAGE ARTS EXTENSION**

## LANGUAGE INTEGRATION ACTIVITIES

- Drawing: Ask students to draw a picture of a farmer, grocer, cook, teacher, doctor, firefighter, or pilot. Ask students to write or tell about that job and how often their families used the products or services of this worker.

- Telling: Each student should select a picture of a worker performing his or her job. Ask students to create a riddle that they will tell or write for a partner called "I am this worker's customer!" From the riddle students must identify the job.

- Telling: Ask students within each cooperative learning group to play "Twenty Questions" about a job.

- Encourage students to identify individual farmers, grocers, cooks, teachers, doctors, firefighters, or pilots from their local community. Identify these workers from various ethnic backgrounds.

## FOLLOW-UP ACTIVITIES AT HOME

- Ask parents to describe the jobs that three friends perform. The parent should ask the child to list the three jobs in the order of how frequently most people need that product or service.

## PICTURE BOOK EXTENSION

- After discussing any of the picture books ask the following questions:
  Q: Are there any new ideas about (jobs) that we learned from this story?
  Q: What ideas about (jobs) did you get from the pictures?
  Q: Is this information true of most (jobs)?

- After discussing each story, ask students to add new information about the jobs described in the story to lists, posters, or graphic organizers that you may have used when discussing the pictures.

## SUPPLEMENTAL PICTURE BOOKS

- These books feature the workers discussed in this lesson. Descriptions of these and additional books on topics in this lesson are provided in the extended bibliography at the end of this manual.

### OCCUPATIONS
*People*, Peter Speir
*Richard Scarry's What Do People Do All Day?*, Richard Scarry
*Who Does This Job?*, Pat Upton

**EXERCISE G-3**

# RANKING FOODS

> **ANSWERS G-3**
> **G-3 Example:** size: rice (smallest), tomato, cabbage (largest)
> **G-3 Exercise:** how often eaten: bread (most often), potatoes, celery (least often)

**LESSON PREPARATION**

## OBJECTIVE AND MATERIALS

OBJECTIVE: Students will arrange foods in sequence.
MATERIALS: The following pictures are used in this lesson: *bread (73), celery*

**BEGINNING BUILDING THINKING SKILLS LESSON PLANS** — **VERBAL SEQUENCES**

*(87), cabbage (90), potato (86), rice (89), tomatoes (95)* • transparency of TM 22 on page 346.

## CURRICULUM APPLICATIONS

<u>Health</u>: Recognize foods that provide good nutrition

<u>Science</u>: Identify the parts of a plant: root, stem, and leaf; identify living things as plants or animals; recognize the major physical differences between plants and animals; give three ways plants are important to people.

## TEACHING SUGGESTIONS

- Model and encourage students to express the following process for arranging foods in order:
  1. Look at the pictures and how the foods are alike and how they are different.
  2. Look for a pattern of differences (difference in size, time that it takes to prepare it, how often the family eats it, kinds of nutrients).
  3. Figure out what food shows the least or most of that characteristic.
  4. Arrange the other foods according to the pattern.

**MODEL LESSON**

## LESSON

### Introduction

Q: What were some of the ways that we ranked jobs?
  A: Order in which they provide service; how often we use their service

Q: If we put food in order, in what ways could we rank them?
  A: Size, when during the day we usually eat them, how they taste, how often we eat them

### Explaining the Objective to Students

Q: In this lesson, we will arrange foods in order.

### Class Activity

- Display the following pictures:

**G-3 Example:** *cabbage, rice, tomato*

Q: With your partner think about how these foods are different. Try to find a pattern and decide how you might arrange these foods in order.
  A: Students usually select size.

Q: What do we learn about these foods by putting them in order?
  A: Students may realize that a single serving of a vegetable may contain:
  - many individual ones, such as rice
  - only one, such as a tomato
  - only a portion of one, such as cabbage.

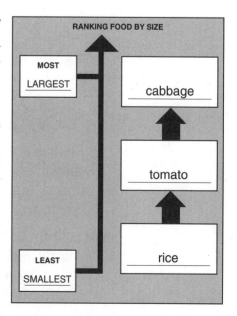

© 2000 CRITICAL THINKING BOOKS & SOFTWARE • www.criticalthinking.com • 800-458-4849

Q: What clues let you know how to arrange these foods?
    A: I think about what the vegetable looks like and how it compares to the other types of vegetables.

- For a blank transitive order graphic organizer see Transparency Master 22 on page 346.

### Guided Practice
- Display the following pictures:
    **G-3 Exercise:** *bread, potatoes, celery*
    Q: List the foods in order of how often students eat each food.
    Q: What do we learn about these foods by putting them in order?
        A: Students realize which food they need on a daily basis and which they eat less often.

### Thinking About Thinking
Q: What do you think about to put foods in a particular order?
    A: How often our families need them, how frequently we need these foods, the time of the day when we eat various foods, what to consider in selecting food.

- This is a rich opportunity to explore how different ethnic groups contribute to the richness of our diet by preparing foods differently. For second grade classes, discuss basic nutrients the food contains: fats, protein, carbohydrates, vitamins, minerals and water.

### Personal Application
Q: When is it important to understand how to arrange foods in order?
    A: How often our families need them, how frequently we need these foods, what to consider in selecting food.

**LANGUAGE ARTS EXTENSION**

## LANGUAGE INTEGRATION ACTIVITIES
- Drawing: Ask student groups to find or draw pictures of four foods. Each group should then sequence their drawings to show how often their families eat the food shown in their drawings. Ask one student from each group to explain the order to the class.

- Telling: Ask students to create a riddle about food that they will tell or write for a partner.

- Telling: Ask students within each cooperative learning group to play "Twenty Questions" about a food.

- First/Second Grade Language Activity: For each item, list students' responses and ask students to read the list aloud or write sentences to create a short description that can be added to students' drawings, if desired.

## FOLLOW-UP ACTIVITIES AT HOME
- Ask parents to describe the food they eat or have just purchased. They should then ask the child to practice description by describing the food to another family member or friend.

BEGINNING BUILDING THINKING SKILLS LESSON PLANS                                          VERBAL SEQUENCES

**PICTURE BOOK EXTENSION**
- After discussing any of the picture books ask the following questions:
  Q: Are there any new ideas about (<u>foods</u>) that we learned from this story?
  Q: What ideas about (<u>foods</u>) did you get from the pictures?
  Q: Is this information true of most (<u>foods</u>)?

- After discussing each story, ask students to add new information about the foods described in the story to lists, posters, or graphic organizers that you may have used when discussing the pictures.

**SUPPLEMENTAL PICTURE BOOKS**
- These books feature the foods discussed in this lesson. Descriptions of these and additional books on topics in this lesson are provided in the extended bibliography at the end of this manual.

**FOOD**

*A Book of Fruit,* Barbara Hirsh Lember
*Eating the Alphabet,* Lois Ehlert
*Foods We Eat,* Lynne Merrison
*Growing Colors*, Bruce McMillan
*Meat,* Elizabeth Clark
*What's on My Plate?,* Ruth Belov Grose

**EXERCISE G-4**

# RANKING VEHICLES

> **ANSWERS G-4**
> **G-4 Example:** by number of passengers that can be transported or by size: motorcycle, car, bus, train
> **G-4 Exercise:** how often used: bicycle or car (most), boat or tractor (least)

**LESSON PREPARATION**

**OBJECTIVE AND MATERIALS**
OBJECTIVE: Students will rank vehicles.
MATERIALS: The following pictures are used in this lesson: *bicycle (30), motorboat (36), city bus (28), car (31), motorcycle (33), tractor (34), train (29)*
• transparency of TM 21 on page 345

**CURRICULUM APPLICATIONS**
<u>Social Studies</u>: Identify how a family depends on transportation to meet its needs; identify some jobs in the home, school, and community; cite examples of community needs and services; understand how community helpers are an example of interdependence.

**TEACHING SUGGESTIONS**
- Students may not commonly use the term "vehicle." Discuss with students that vehicle can refer to any form of transportation.
- Model and encourage students to express the following process for arranging vehicles in order:
  1. Look at the pictures and how the vehicles are alike and how they are different (size, how often we see them or our families use them).

© 2000 CRITICAL THINKING BOOKS & SOFTWARE • WWW.CRITICALTHINKING.COM • 800-458-4849          237

BEGINNING BUILDING THINKING SKILLS LESSON PLANS                    VERBAL SEQUENCES

2. Look for a pattern of differences.

3. Figure out which vehicle shows the least or most of that characteristic

4. Arrange the other vehicles to show that pattern.

**MODEL LESSON**

**LESSON**

**Introduction**

Q: What were some of the ways that we have ranked things?

A: Age, size, etc. If we put vehicles in order, in what ways could we rank them? Students may mention size, how many people they carry, how often students ride on them, etc.

**Explaining the Objective to Students**

Q: In this lesson, we will arrange vehicles in order.

**Class Activity**

- Display the following pictures:

  **G-4 Example:** *bus, car, motorcycle, train*

  Q: With your partner think about how these vehicles are different. Try to find a pattern and decide how you might arrange these vehicles in order.

  Q: How can you put these vehicles in order?

  A: Size, how often students use these vehicles, how many passengers they carry, or how far each vehicle can carry passengers or cargo.

- List the vehicles according to the order the class selects, usually size.

  Q: What do we learn about these vehicles by putting them in order?

  A: Students realize the importance of different vehicles in getting where we need to go.

  Q: What clues let you know how to arrange these vehicles?

  A: I think about the size of those vehicles that I have seen, how many people ride on it or in it, whether or not the vehicle carries cargo.

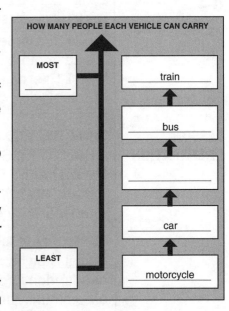

- For a blank transitive order graphic organizer see Transparency Master 21 on page 345.

**Guided Practice**

- Display the following pictures:

  **G-4 Exercise:** *bicycle, boat, car, tractor*

  Q: List the vehicles in order of how often students ride on this vehicle.

  A: Answers will vary

- Allow time for student work.

  Q: What do we learn about these vehicles by putting them in order?

238        © 2000 CRITICAL THINKING BOOKS & SOFTWARE • WWW.CRITICALTHINKING.COM • 800-458-4849

BEGINNING BUILDING THINKING SKILLS LESSON PLANS                    VERBAL SEQUENCES

A: Students realize the importance of different vehicles in getting where we need to go or in securing what we need from faraway places.

Q: What clues let you know how to arrange these vehicles?
A: I think about what the vehicle looks like and if I see one of them once a day or once a week. I think about whether or not I have ever ridden on one.

**Thinking About Thinking**

Q: What did you pay attention to when you decided which vehicle came next?

1. I looked for a difference or differences.

2. I looked for a pattern of differences. Is this a common pattern (difference in size, time, rank, or order)?

3. I figured out what vehicle would be next if the pattern of change continued.

Q: What do you think about to put vehicles in a particular order?
A: Size, how often we see them or our families use them, how fast or how far they can travel, how many passengers each vehicle can carry.

**Personal Application**

Q: When is it important to understand how to arrange vehicles in order?
A: To understand sports events and automobile advertisements; to understand how much we spend on transportation to get what we need and to go where we need to go.

**LANGUAGE ARTS EXTENSION**

**LANGUAGE INTEGRATION ACTIVITIES**

• Drawing: Ask student groups to find or draw pictures of four vehicles. Each group should then sequence their drawings to show how often their families use the vehicles shown. Ask one student from each group to explain the order to the class.

• Telling: Ask students within each cooperative learning group to play "Twenty Questions" about a vehicle.

• First/Second Grade Language Activity: For each item, list students' responses and ask students to read the list aloud or write sentences to create a short description that can be added to students' drawings.

**FOLLOW-UP ACTIVITIES AT HOME**

• Ask parents to describe the vehicles they own or use at work. They should then ask the child to practice description by describing the vehicles to another family member or friend.

**PICTURE BOOK EXTENSION**

• After discussing any of the picture books ask the following questions:
Q: Are there any new ideas about (vehicles) that we learned from this story?
Q: What ideas about (vehicles) did you get from the pictures?
Q: Is this information true of most (vehicles)?

© 2000 CRITICAL THINKING BOOKS & SOFTWARE • WWW.CRITICALTHINKING.COM • 800-458-4849          239

BEGINNING BUILDING THINKING SKILLS LESSON PLANS                    VERBAL SEQUENCES

- After discussing each story, ask students to add new information about the vehicles described in the story to lists, posters, or graphic organizers that you may have used when discussing the pictures.

**SUPPLEMENTAL PICTURE BOOKS**
- These books feature the vehicles discussed in this lesson. Descriptions of these and additional books on topics in this lesson are provided in the extended bibliography at the end of this manual.

**VEHICLES**
> *Machines As Big as Monsters,* Paul Strickland
> *On the Go,* Ann Morris
> *Richard Scarry's What Do People Do All Day?*, Richard Scarry
> *Steven Biesty's Incredible Cross Sections*
> *What's Inside?* Dorling Kindersley
> *Wings, Wheels, and Sails,* Tom Stacy

**EXERCISE G-5**

# RANKING ANIMALS

> **ANSWERS G-5**
> **G-5 Example:** size: chicken, pig, giraffe
> **G-5 Exercise:** size: duck, turkey, ostrich

**LESSON PREPARATION**

**OBJECTIVE AND MATERIALS**
OBJECTIVE: Students will arrange animals in order.
MATERIALS: The following pictures are used in this lesson: *chicken (65), duck (70), giraffe (59), ostrich (62), pig (71), turkey (67)* • transparency of TM 22 on page 346

**CURRICULUM APPLICATIONS**
Science: Identify living things as plants or animals; recognize that plants and animals reproduce their own kind; recognize the major physical differences between plants and animals; state what animals need to live and grow; recognize that needs of different kinds of animals are similar; recognize examples of common animals as being fish, birds, or mammals.

**TEACHING SUGGESTIONS**
- Model and encourage students to express the following process for arranging animals in order:
  1. Look at the pictures and how the animals are alike and how they are different.
  2. Look for a pattern of differences (size, how often we see them, their order in the food chain).
  3. Figure out which animal shows the least or most of that characteristic (size, how often we see them, their order in the food chain).
  4. Arrange the animals in order according to the chosen characteristic.

- Students may generalize that large animals require much food and space to survive.

240          © 2000 CRITICAL THINKING BOOKS & SOFTWARE • WWW.CRITICALTHINKING.COM • 800-458-4849

BEGINNING BUILDING THINKING SKILLS LESSON PLANS                    VERBAL SEQUENCES

**MODEL LESSON** | **LESSON**

### Introduction

Q: What were some of the ways that we have ranked things?
  A: Age, size, etc.

Q: If we put animals in order, in what ways could we rank them?
  A: Size, how long they live, and how fast they can run, swim, or fly.

### Explaining the Objective to Students

Q: In this lesson, we will arrange animals in order of size.

### Class Activity

• Display the following pictures:
  **G-5 Example:** *chicken, giraffe, pig*

Q: With your partner think about how these animals are different. Try to find a pattern and decide how you might arrange these animals in order.

Q: How can you put these animals in order?
  A: Sequences may include size, how dangerous the students think the animals are.

Q: Name the animals according to size from smallest to largest.
  A: Chicken, pig, giraffe

Q: What do we learn about these animals by putting them in order?
  A: Students realize which animals are likely to pose a threat to others, how much food animals may need to survive.

Q: What clues let you know how to arrange these animals?
  A: I think about how large the adult animal is and how it compares to the other animals. I think about how much space it needs to move around.

• For a blank transitive order graphic organizer see TM 22, page 346.

RANKING ANIMALS BY SIZE

MOST
LARGEST

LEAST
SMALLEST

giraffe

pig

chicken

### Guided practice

• Display the following pictures:
  **G-5 Exercise:** *duck, ostrich, turkey*

Q: Name the animals according to size from smallest to largest.
  A: Duck, turkey, ostrich

Q: What do we learn about these animals by putting them in order?
  A: Students realize how much food animals may need to survive.

Q: What clues let you know how to arrange these animals?
  A: I think about how large the adult animal is and how it compares to the other animals. I think about how much space it needs to move around.

© 2000 CRITICAL THINKING BOOKS & SOFTWARE • WWW.CRITICALTHINKING.COM • 800-458-4849                    241

**BEGINNING BUILDING THINKING SKILLS LESSON PLANS**                    **VERBAL SEQUENCES**

### Thinking About Thinking

Q: What did you pay attention to when you decided which animal came next?

1. I looked for a difference or differences.

2. I looked for a pattern of differences. Is this a common pattern (difference in size, time, rank, or order)?

3. I figured out what animal would be next if the pattern of change continued.

Q: What do you think about to put animals in a particular order?

A: Size, how often we see them, their order in the food chain, how much space they need to live comfortably.

### Personal Application

Q: When is it important to understand how to arrange animals in order?

A: To understand how much food or space they need to get food and live comfortably. To understand why many animals cannot be pets and that pets of different sizes need more food and space. To understand the food chain.

**LANGUAGE ARTS EXTENSION**

### LANGUAGE INTEGRATION ACTIVITIES

• Drawing: Select a picture of an animal or allow students to find or draw a picture of an animal. Ask students in groups of four to sequence their drawings to show the size of these animals. Ask one student from each group to explain the order to the class.

• Drama: Ask students to use animal puppets to act out "Brown bear, brown bear, what do I see?" to rank the animals according to size.

### FOLLOW-UP ACTIVITIES AT HOME

• Ask parents to describe the animals they have seen. They should then ask the child to practice description by describing the animals or a family pet to another family member or friend.

### PICTURE BOOK EXTENSION

• After discussing any of the picture books ask the following questions:
Q: Are there any new ideas about (animals) that we learned from this story?
Q: What ideas about (animals) did you get from the pictures?
Q: Is this information true of most (animals)?

• After discussing each story, ask students to add new information about the animals described in the story to lists, posters, or graphic organizers that you may have used when discussing the pictures.

### SUPPLEMENTAL PICTURE BOOKS

• These books feature the animals discussed in this lesson. Descriptions of these and additional books on topics in this lesson are provided in the extended bibliography at the end of this manual.

242          © 2000 CRITICAL THINKING BOOKS & SOFTWARE • WWW.CRITICALTHINKING.COM • 800-458-4849

**BEGINNING BUILDING THINKING SKILLS LESSON PLANS**          **VERBAL SEQUENCES**

### ANIMALS

*Egg! A Dozen Eggs, What Will They Be?* A. J. Wood
*Hoot, Howl, Hiss,* Michelle Koch
*The Big Red Barn,* Margaret Wise Brown
*What Animal Am I? An Animal Guessing Game,* Iza Trapani

**EXERCISE G-6**

# RANKING BUILDINGS

---

**ANSWERS G-6**
**G-6 Example:** size: mobile home, house, apartment building
**G-6 Exercise:** how often used: bank or post office (least), school (5 days a week), house (most—daily)

---

**LESSON PREPARATION**

## OBJECTIVE AND MATERIALS

OBJECTIVE: Students will rank buildings.
MATERIALS: The following pictures are used in this lesson: *apartment building (50), house (53), library (40), mobile home (44), post office (51), school (54)* • transparency of TM 22 on page 346

## TEACHING SUGGESTIONS

• Model and encourage students to express the following process for arranging buildings in order:
  1. Look at the pictures and how the buildings are alike and how they are different (size, how often we see them or our families ride in them or use them).
  2. Look for a pattern of differences.
  3. Figure out which building shows the least or most of that characteristic
  4. Arrange the other buildings to show that pattern.

**MODEL LESSON**

## LESSON

### Introduction

Q: What were some of the ways that we have ranked things?
  A: Age, size, etc.

Q: If we put buildings in order, in what ways could we rank them?
  A: Size, how many we see in our neighborhood.

### Explaining the Objective to Students

Q: In this lesson, we will arrange buildings in order.

### Class Activity

• Display the following pictures:
**G-6 Example:** *apartment building, house, mobile home*
Q: With your partner think about how these buildings are different. Try to find a pattern and decide how you might arrange these buildings in order.
Q: How can you put these buildings in order?
  A: Sequences may include size, use, how often they use or see the buildings.

© 2000 CRITICAL THINKING BOOKS & SOFTWARE • WWW.CRITICALTHINKING.COM • 800-458-4849          243

BEGINNING BUILDING THINKING SKILLS LESSON PLANS                           VERBAL SEQUENCES

Q: Name the buildings according to size from smallest to largest.
A: Mobile home, house, apartment building

Q: What do we learn about these buildings by putting them in order?
A: Students realize that the size of a dwelling space influences what we can do and have in our homes and how close we may be to neighbors.

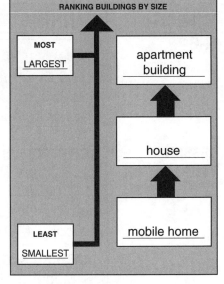

Q: What clues let you know how to arrange these buildings?
A: I think about what each building looks like and how it compares to the other buildings.

- For a blank transitive order graphic organizer see TM 22, page 346.

**Guided Practice**
- Display the following pictures:
  **G-6 Exercise:** *library, house, post office, school*
  Q: Name the buildings in the order of how often students see or enter them.
  A: From most to least: house, school, post office, or library
  From least to most: post office, library, school, house

Q: What do we learn about these buildings by putting them in order?
A: Students realize the importance of various buildings in their lives.

Q: What clues let you know how to arrange these buildings?
A: I think about what each building looks like and how it compares to the other buildings.

**THINKING ABOUT THINKING**
Q: What did you pay attention to when you decided which building came next?
1. I looked for change or difference among the buildings.
2. I looked for a pattern of differences. Is this a common pattern (difference in size, time, rank, or order)?
3. I figured out what building shows the least or most of that characteristic and arranged the other buildings according to the pattern.

Q: What do you think about to put buildings in a particular order?
A: Size, age of the building, how often we visit this building.

**Personal Application**
Q: When is it important to understand how to arrange buildings in order?
A: To understand the significance of the size, age, or number of people who use a building

244    © 2000 CRITICAL THINKING BOOKS & SOFTWARE • WWW.CRITICALTHINKING.COM • 800-458-4849

**BEGINNING BUILDING THINKING SKILLS LESSON PLANS**　　　　　　　　　　　**VERBAL SEQUENCES**

## LANGUAGE ARTS EXTENSION

### LANGUAGE INTEGRATION ACTIVITIES

- Drawing: Ask student groups to find or draw pictures of four buildings. Each group should then sequence their drawings to show how often their families visit these buildings. Ask one student from each group to explain the order to the class.

### FOLLOW-UP ACTIVITIES AT HOME

- Ask parents to describe the buildings they work in. They should then ask the child to practice description by describing the buildings to another family member or friend.

### PICTURE BOOK EXTENSION

- After discussing any of the picture books ask the following questions:
  Q: Are there any new ideas about (buildings) that we learned from this story?
  Q: What ideas about (buildings) did you get from the pictures?
  Q: Is this information true of most (buildings)?

- After discussing each story, ask students to add new information about the buildings described in the story to lists, posters, or graphic organizers that you may have used when discussing the pictures.

### SUPPLEMENTAL PICTURE BOOKS

- These books feature the buildings discussed in this lesson. Descriptions of these and additional books on topics in this lesson are provided in the extended bibliography at the end of this manual.

**Buildings**

*Children Just Like Me,* Barnabas Kindersley
*Richard Scarry's What Do People Do All Day?*, Richard Scarry
*Round Buildings, Square Buildings, Buildings that Wiggle Like a Fish*, Phillip M. Isaacson
*Town and Country,* Alice and Martin Provensen

© 2000 CRITICAL THINKING BOOKS & SOFTWARE • WWW.CRITICALTHINKING.COM • 800-458-4849　　　245

BEGINNING BUILDING THINKING SKILLS LESSON PLANS                    VERBAL CLASSIFICATIONS

## Chapter 8 | VERBAL CLASSIFICATIONS

**EXERCISE H-1**

## HOW ARE THESE FAMILY MEMBERS ALIKE?

> **ANSWERS H-1**
> **H-1 Example:** Young children
> **H-1 Exercise:** Females

**LESSON PREPARATION**

### OBJECTIVE AND MATERIALS

OBJECTIVE: Students will classify family members.
MATERIALS: The following pictures are used in this lesson: *baby (1), girl (4), grandmother (8), mother (6), toddler boy (3), toddler girl (2)* • transparencies of TM 23 on page 347 and TM 25 on page 349

### CURRICULUM APPLICATIONS

Social Studies: Students will identify similarities and differences in family members; identify how a family depends upon one another; identify roles and responsibilities within the family; understand how families are an example of interdependence; identify how human needs are met within the family in different cultures; examine the roles of various family members in celebrating holidays and traditions

### TEACHING SUGGESTIONS

• Classification is different from comparing and contrasting because it involves <u>naming</u> the group or class to which all members belong and <u>naming</u> the key characteristics of that group. When forming definitions, students should become accustomed to naming the category to which a person, an organism, or an object belongs, as well as the distinguishing characteristics that make it different from other things of that type. Rehearse with your students some common categories related to family members: children, adults, parents, males, females, etc.

• Young children may not commonly use the terms *gender* to mean male or female or *relative* to mean someone in one's family. Encourage students to use these terms and to find synonyms for them.

• Model and encourage students to express the following process for classifying family members:
    1. I will think about the important characteristics of the people.
    2. I will find a word that describes all of them
    3. I will identify another person that belongs in the same group.
    4. I will check whether there are other terms that describe other important characteristics of the same people.

© 2000 CRITICAL THINKING BOOKS & SOFTWARE • WWW.CRITICALTHINKING.COM • 800-458-4849          247

BEGINNING BUILDING THINKING SKILLS LESSON PLANS                    VERBAL CLASSIFICATIONS

**MODEL LESSON** | **LESSON**

## Introduction

Q: We have practiced describing how family members are similar.

### Explaining the Objective to Students

Q: In this lesson, we will explain how family members are alike and name the group that is being described.

### Class Activity

• Display the following pictures:
  **H-1 Example:** *baby, toddler boy, toddler girl*
  Q: With your partner, give as many ideas as you can think of to describe how these family members are alike.

• Confirm students' answers with the whole class.
  A: They are all young children, two years old or younger. They can be lifted and carried. They can smile, turn over, move around, and are learning to talk. They have, or are cutting, some teeth. They wear diapers and have to be fed.

Q: What word can we use to describe all these family members?
  A: Young children or preschoolers

Q: Name another family member that belongs to this group.
  A: Any preschool girl, boy, brother, or sister

Q: What did you think about to decide what characteristics all these people have in common?
  A. Their age, their size, their relationship to other people in the family, what they know how to do.

• For a blank class-and-members graphic organizer, see TM 23 on page 347.

| YOUNG CHILDREN |  |
|---|---|
| CLASS | |
| MEMBER | MEMBER |
| *baby* | *toddler boy* |
| MEMBER | MEMBER |
|  | *toddler girl* |

### GUIDED PRACTICE

• Display the following pictures:
  **H-1 Exercise:** *girl, grandmother, mother*
  Q: How are these family members alike?
  A: Girls grow up and can become mothers. Mothers can become grandmothers when their children grow up.

Q: What word can we use to describe all these family members?
  A. Female

Q: Name another family member that belongs to this group.
  A: Toddler girl, aunt, sister

Q: What did you think about to decide what characteristics all these three people have in common?
  A: Their gender (their ages are all different)

248            © 2000 CRITICAL THINKING BOOKS & SOFTWARE • WWW.CRITICALTHINKING.COM • 800-458-4849

## THINKING ABOUT THINKING

Q: What characteristics are used to classify family members?
  A: How they are related, their ages, gender, and roles, feelings about them, interests, experiences that make them special.

## PERSONAL APPLICATION

Q: When is it important to understand how family members are alike?
  A: To explain family relationships to someone else or to understand introductions that involve other people's families.

**LANGUAGE ARTS EXTENSION**

## LANGUAGE INTEGRATION ACTIVITIES

- Creating definitions: Help students state appropriate definitions. DEFINITION OF ANY NOUN = CATEGORY + CHARACTERISTICS THAT DISTINGUISH IT FROM OTHERS IN THAT CATEGORY. Emphasize these elements when explaining terms, objects, or ideas and prompt students to practice using the same model. Create sentence strips of the model and use the same model for writing definitions from social studies, science, or mathematics textbooks or vocabulary lists.

    A (term, object, or idea) is a (category) that (qualifiers).

    A <u>toddler</u> is a <u>young child</u> who is <u>older than a baby</u> and <u>is just learning to walk</u>.

    A <u>grandmother</u> is a <u>woman</u> whose <u>son or daughter has children</u>.

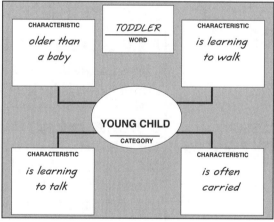

- For a blank definition graphic organizer, see TM 25 on page 349.

- Drawing: Select a picture of a family member or allow students to find or draw a picture of a family member. Ask students to create a riddle that they will tell or write for a partner.

- Telling: Ask students within each cooperative learning group to play "Twenty Questions" about a family member.

- First/Second Grade Language Activity: For each item, list students' responses and ask students to read the list aloud or write sentences to create a short description that can be added to students' drawings.

## FOLLOW-UP ACTIVITIES AT HOME

- Family relationships: Which members of our family are all males? Which are all grandparents? Which are your cousins? Which are children of the same parents?

- Family history: Which family members live in (<u>locality</u>)? Which came from (<u>country</u>)? Which speak (<u>language</u>)? Which know how to (<u>craft, hobby</u>)?

**BEGINNING BUILDING THINKING SKILLS LESSON PLANS**    **VERBAL CLASSIFICATIONS**

- Doing things with family members: Which family members like to (hobby, sport)? Which like (music, food)? Which know how to (craft, hobby)?

### PICTURE BOOK EXTENSION

- After discussing any of the picture books ask the following questions:
  Q: Are there any new ideas about (babies, girls, grandmothers, mothers, or toddlers) that we learned from this story?
  Q: What ideas about (babies, girls, grandmothers, mothers, or toddlers) did you get from the pictures?
  Q: Is this information true of most (babies, girls, grandmothers, mothers, or toddlers)?

### SUPPLEMENTAL PICTURE BOOKS

- These books feature the family members discussed in this lesson. Descriptions of these and additional books on topics in this lesson are provided in the extended bibliography at the end of this manual.

#### Families

*Children Just Like Me,* Barnabas Kindersley
*Families,* Nicola Baxter
*I Got a Family,* Melrose Cooper
*Loving,* Ann Morris
*My First Family Tree Book,* Catherine Bruzzone
*People,* Peter Speir

**EXERCISE H-2**

## HOW ARE THESE JOBS ALIKE?

**ANSWERS H-2**
**H-2 Example:** Producers
**H-2 Exercise:** Health workers

**LESSON PREPARATION**

### OBJECTIVE AND MATERIALS

OBJECTIVE: Students will classify occupations.
MATERIALS: The following pictures are used in this lesson: *artist (21), construction worker (10), doctor (19), dentist (20), farmer (12), nurse (14)* • blank transparencies of TM 23 on page 347 and TM 25 on page 349

### CURRICULUM APPLICATIONS

Social Studies: Identify how a family depends upon products and services to meet its needs; identify some job roles in the home, school, and community; cite examples of community needs and services; identify jobs within the community and understand how community helpers are an example of interdependence.

### TEACHING SUGGESTIONS

- Students should be encouraged to name the category to which a person, an organism, or an object belongs, as well as the distinguishing characteristics that make it different from other things of that type. Rehearse with your students some common categories related to jobs: health workers, emergency workers, merchants, etc.

250    © 2000 CRITICAL THINKING BOOKS & SOFTWARE • WWW.CRITICALTHINKING.COM • 800-458-4849

# BEGINNING BUILDING THINKING SKILLS LESSON PLANS — VERBAL CLASSIFICATIONS

- Model and encourage students to express the following process for classifying jobs:
  1. I will think about the important characteristics of the jobs. (I will be sure to discuss their goods or service, training, how they spend their time, tools, etc.)
  2. I will find a word that describes all of them.
  3. I will identify another job that belongs in the same group.
  4. I will check whether there are other terms that describe other important characteristics of the same jobs.

**MODEL LESSON**

## LESSON

### Introduction
Q: We have practiced describing how family members can be classified.

### Explaining the Objective to Students
Q: In this lesson, we will explain how jobs are alike and name the type of job that is being described.

### Class Activity
- Display the following pictures:
  **H-2 Example:** *artist, construction worker, farmer*
  Q: With your partner describe how these jobs are alike.

- Confirm students' answers with the whole class.
    A: They create a product that people need or value. They use special tools for their jobs. They can be male or female. Sometimes they learn their job in classes; sometimes they learn their work from people who are very good at these jobs.

  Q: What words can we use to describe all these jobs?
    A: Producers or people that make things

  Q: Name another job that belongs to this group.
    A: Carpenter, writer, seamstress, automobile manufacturing worker, appliance manufacturing worker, etc.

  Q: What did you think about to decide how these three jobs are alike?
    A: I remember that they all produce things. They have special tools for their jobs and learn to do them in classes or on the job.

- For a blank class-and-members graphic organizer, see TM 23 on page 347.

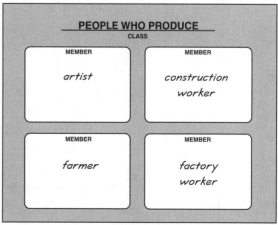

### GUIDED PRACTICE
- Display the following pictures:
  **H-2 Exercise:** *dentist, doctor, nurse*
  Q: How are these jobs alike?

A: The people who do them help us keep our bodies healthy. They go to school for a long time to learn how our bodies work, what healthy bodies need, and how to treat injuries or illnesses. They use special tools or medicines. They keep themselves and their tools very clean to prevent spreading illness. They all wear special clothes and work in offices.

Q: What word can we use to describe all these jobs?
A: Health workers.

Q: Name another job that belongs to this group.
A: Paramedic, physical therapist, chiropractor, dental hygienist

Q: What did you think about to decide what characteristics all these three jobs have in common?
A: I remember what they do to help people stay healthy, where they work, what they wear, what tools they use, and how they learn their jobs.

## THINKING ABOUT THINKING

Q: What characteristics do you discuss to describe someone's job?
A: Do these jobs provide goods or service? Are these jobs producers or consumers? How much training is required, how do they spend their time, what tools do they use?

## PERSONAL APPLICATION

Q: When is it important to understand how jobs are alike?
A: To suggest or recognize jobs that are similar to ones you already understand. To explain a job to someone who is unfamiliar with it.

**LANGUAGE ARTS EXTENSION**

## LANGUAGE INTEGRATION ACTIVITIES

• Drawing: Ask students to draw a picture of any three jobs from the occupations list and label the drawing to describe how the three jobs are alike (health workers, merchants, maintenance workers, agricultural workers, food service workers, etc.). Create a jobs bulletin board display of students' drawings. Use the web graphic organizer shown on page 333 as a model for the bulletin board display and place students' pictures in the "boxes" on the web diagram.

• Telling: Ask students within each cooperative learning group to play "Twenty Questions" about a family member's job.

• Listening: Play Listening Tic Tac Toe with jobs. For directions see page xxviii; for the playing grid photocopy TM 12 on page 336. Use jobs that have been introduced in previous lessons or the list of occupations (TM 16) on page 340.

• Creating definitions: Help students state appropriate definitions.
DEFINITION OF ANY NOUN = CATEGORY + CHARACTERISTICS THAT DISTINGUISH IT FROM OTHERS IN THAT CATEGORY.
Emphasize this model when explaining terms, objects, or ideas and prompt students to practice using it. Create sentence strips of the model and use the same model for writing definitions from social studies, science, or mathematics textbooks or vocabulary lists.

A (term, object, or idea) is a (category) that (qualifiers).

An <u>artist</u> is a <u>producer</u> that <u>creates paintings or sculpture or objects that are beautiful and carefully made</u>.

A <u>nurse</u> is a <u>health worker</u> who <u>carries out the treatment recommended by doctors</u>.

- For a blank definition graphic organizer see TM 25 on page 349.

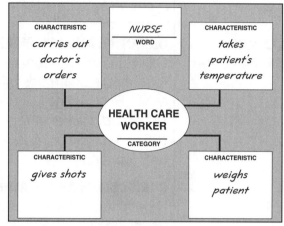

- First/Second Grade Language Activity: For each item, list students' responses and ask students to read the list aloud or write sentences to create a short description that can be added to students' drawings, if desired.

**FOLLOW-UP ACTIVITIES AT HOME**
- Show children how jobs are classified in the classified section of the telephone book. Point out which services the family needs and who provides that service.
- Family history: Which family members work as (<u>health workers</u>, <u>merchants</u>, <u>makers of things</u>)? Which came from (<u>country</u>)? Which speak (<u>language</u>)? Which know how to (<u>craft, hobby</u>)?

**PICTURE BOOK EXTENSION**
- After discussing any of the picture books ask the following questions:
  Q: Are there any new ideas about (<u>artists</u>, <u>construction workers</u>, <u>doctors</u>, <u>dentists</u>, <u>farmers</u>, or <u>nurses</u>) that we learned from this story?
  Q: What ideas about (<u>artists</u>, <u>construction workers</u>, <u>doctors</u>, <u>dentists</u>, <u>farmers</u>, or <u>nurses</u>) did you get from the pictures?
  Q: Is this information true of most (<u>artists</u>, <u>construction workers</u>, <u>doctors</u>, <u>dentists</u>, <u>farmers</u>, or <u>nurses</u>)?

**SUPPLEMENTAL PICTURE BOOKS**
- These books feature the workers discussed in this lesson. Descriptions of these and additional books on topics in this lesson are provided in the extended bibliography at the end of this manual.

**OCCUPATIONS**
*People*, Peter Speir
*Richard Scarry's What Do People Do All Day?*, Richard Scarry
*Who Does This Job?*, Pat Upton

**BEGINNING BUILDING THINKING SKILLS LESSON PLANS**  |  **VERBAL CLASSIFICATIONS**

**EXERCISE H-3**

# HOW ARE THESE FOODS ALIKE? EXPLAIN

> **ANSWERS H-3**
> H-3 **Example**—Fruit
> H-3 **Exercise**—Green vegetables
> H-3 **Practice**—Meat

**LESSON PREPARATION**

**OBJECTIVE AND MATERIALS**
OBJECTIVE: Students will explain how foods are alike and name the type of food that is being described.
MATERIALS: The following pictures are used in this lesson: *apple (92), celery (87), fried chicken (80), ham (76), lettuce (91), orange (93), peach (96), peas (85), steak (81)* • transparencies of TM 23 on page 347 and TM 25 on page 349 (optional)

**CURRICULUM APPLICATIONS**
Health: Recognize food that provides good nutrition for proper growth and functions of the body; identify a variety of foods. For second-grade classes, discuss basic nutrients the food contains: fats, protein, carbohydrates, vitamins, minerals and water.
Science: Identify the parts of a plant: root, stem, and leaf; recognize that there are many kinds of plants; recognize that plants are made of many things; recognize that there are many kinds of animals; identify living things as plants or animals; recognize the major physical differences between plants and animals; identify how plants are important to people; recognize examples of common animals as being fish, birds, or mammals.

**TEACHING SUGGESTIONS**
• Help students review and clarify which types of foods do not have to be cooked to be eaten, which do, and examples of each. By this age, students realize that some foods must be cooked to be digested easily (meat, beans, and some vegetables). Some foods are seldom cooked (fruit, some vegetables such as lettuce). Some foods are commonly cooked or eaten raw (spinach, celery, carrots, etc.).

• Stating Definitions: Help students state appropriate definitions.
DEFINITION OF ANY NOUN = CATEGORY + CHARACTERISTICS THAT DISTINGUISH IT FROM OTHERS IN THAT CATEGORY.
Emphasize these elements when explaining terms, objects, or ideas and prompt students to practice using the same model. Create sentence strips of the model and use the same model for writing definitions of foods.

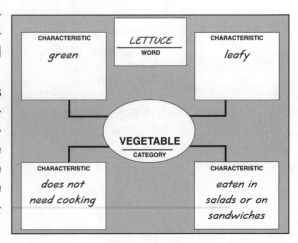

254  © 2000 CRITICAL THINKING BOOKS & SOFTWARE • WWW.CRITICALTHINKING.COM • 800-458-4849

A (term, object, or idea) is a (category) that (qualifiers).

<u>Steak</u> is <u>meat</u> that <u>comes from cows.</u>

<u>Lettuce</u> is a <u>green vegetable</u> that <u>we eat uncooked in salads.</u>

- For a blank definition graphic organizer see TM 25 on page 349.

- Model and encourage students to express the following process for classifying foods:
    1. I will think about the important characteristics of the foods (whether it is a plant or animals product, the part of plants we eat, how different ethnic groups prepare it differently what nutrients the food contains).
    2. I will find a word that describes all of them.
    3. I will identify another food that belongs in the same group.
    4. I will check whether there are other terms that describe other important characteristics of the same foods.

- Second-grade science texts offer the scientific definition of fruit which applies to foods commonly called vegetables (tomatoes, squash, cucumbers, pumpkins, etc.). Clarify students' use of the term *fruit* in appropriate contexts: "vegetable" in cookbooks and grocery stores, "fruit" in scientific discussion of parts of a plant.

**MODEL LESSON**

## LESSON

### Introduction

Q: We have practiced describing how foods are similar.

### Explaining the Objective to Students

Q: In this lesson we will explain how foods are alike and name the type of food that is being described.

### Class Activity

- Display the following pictures:

    **H-3 Example:** *apple, orange, peach*

    Q: With your partner discuss how these foods are alike.
      A: They are all fruit. They taste sweet and can be eaten without cooking. They all grow on trees and contain seeds.

    Q: What word can we use to describe all these foods?
      A: Fruit

    Q: Name another food that belongs to this group.
      A: Banana, pear, pineapple, tangerine, grapefruit, mango, kiwi, strawberry

- For a blank class-and-members graphic organizer, see TM 23 on page 347.

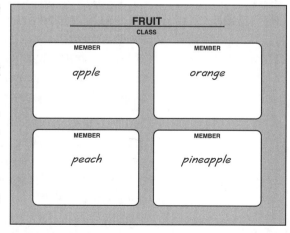

BEGINNING BUILDING THINKING SKILLS LESSON PLANS                    VERBAL CLASSIFICATIONS

### Guided Practice
- Display the following pictures:
  **H-3 Exercise:** *celery, lettuce, peas*

  Q: With your partner discuss how these foods are alike.
  A: They are green and are parts of a plant.

  Q: What words can we use to describe all these foods?
  A: Green vegetables

  Q: Name another food that belongs in that class.
  A: Spinach, green beans, broccoli

### Optional Independent Practice
- Display the following pictures:
  **H-3 Practice:** *chicken, ham, steak*

  Q: With your partner discuss how these foods are alike.
  A: They come from animals and must be cooked to be eaten.

  Q: What words can we use to describe all these foods?
  A: Meat

  Q: Name another food that belongs in that class.
  A: Bacon, hamburger, pork

### Thinking About Thinking
Q: What did you think about to decide what characteristics all these three foods have in common?
A: Whether the food is from a plant or an animal, what part of it we eat, whether or not it has to be cooked, its color

### Personal Application
Q: When is it important to explain how food is alike?
A: Reading the grocery advertisements in the newspaper; finding food in the grocery store, checking whether a coupon applies to a certain food; understanding a doctor's or nurse's directions about what to eat while taking various medicines, choosing the best foods to purchase.

**LANGUAGE ARTS EXTENSION**

### LANGUAGE INTEGRATION ACTIVITIES
- Drawing: Ask students to draw a picture of any three foods from the food list and label the drawing to describe how the three foods are alike (dairy foods, meat, vegetables, bakery products, fruit, etc.). Create a food bulletin board display of students' drawings. Use the web graphic organizer shown on page 333 as a model for the bulletin board display and place students' pictures in the "boxes" on the web diagram.

- Story telling: Select a common story or fairy tale about food, such as *The Little Red Hen.* Ask students to retell the story about another food, such as butter instead of bread. Discuss how the revised story is different from the original. (For example, the steps in making the butter would be different.)

- Listening: Play Listening Tic Tac Toe with food. For directions see page

256          © 2000 CRITICAL THINKING BOOKS & SOFTWARE • WWW.CRITICALTHINKING.COM • 800-458-4849

| | |
|---|---|
| **BEGINNING BUILDING THINKING SKILLS LESSON PLANS** | **VERBAL CLASSIFICATIONS** |

xxviii; for the playing grid photocopy TM 12 page 336. Use foods that have been introduced in previous lessons or the list of food on page 341.

### FOLLOW-UP ACTIVITIES AT HOME
- Ask parents to identify a food that their family likes (such as ice cream). Ask the child what type of food it is (dairy) and have him or her describe other food of that kind (yogurt, butter, cheese, etc.).

### PICTURE BOOK EXTENSION
- After discussing any of the picture books ask the following questions:
  Q: Are there any new ideas about (<u>vegetables, fruit, or meat</u>) that we learned from this story?
  Q: What ideas or details about (<u>vegetables, fruit, or meat</u>) did you get from the pictures?
  Q: Is this information true of most (<u>vegetables, fruit, or meat</u>)?

- After discussing each story, ask students to add new information about the characteristics of the food described in the story to the lists, posters, or graphic organizers that you may have used when discussing the pictures.

### SUPPLEMENTAL PICTURE BOOKS
- These books feature the food discussed in this lesson. Descriptions of these and additional books on topics in this lesson are provided in the extended bibliography at the end of this manual.
  *A Book of Fruit,* Barbara Hirsh Lember
  *Foods We Eat,* Lynne Merrison
  *Growing Colors,* Bruce McMillan
  *Meat,* Elizabeth Clark
  *Vegetables, Vegetables!* Fay Robinson
  *We Love Fruit,* Fay Robinson

**EXERCISE H-4**

## HOW ARE THESE VEHICLES ALIKE?—EXPLAIN

> **ANSWERS H-4**
> **H-4 Example**—Emergency vehicles
> **H-4 Exercise**—Recreational vehicles
> **H-4 Practice**—Public transportation

**LESSON PREPARATION**

### OBJECTIVE AND MATERIALS
OBJECTIVE: Students will explain how vehicles are alike and name the type of vehicle that is being described.
MATERIALS: The following pictures are used in this lesson: *airplane (27), ambulance (24), bicycle (30), motorboat (36), city bus (28), car (31), fire truck (37), motorcycle (33), police car (25), train (29)* • transparencies of TM 23 on page 347 and TM 25 on page 349

### CURRICULUM APPLICATIONS
<u>Social Studies</u>: Identify how a family depends upon transportation to meet its needs; identify some jobs in the home, school, and community; cite examples of community needs and services; understand how community helpers are an example of interdependence.

© 2000 CRITICAL THINKING BOOKS & SOFTWARE • WWW.CRITICALTHINKING.COM • 800-458-4849          257

BEGINNING BUILDING THINKING SKILLS LESSON PLANS                    VERBAL CLASSIFICATIONS

## TEACHING SUGGESTIONS

- "Vehicles" or "public transportation" are abstract concepts for most young children. Since they have heard these terms several times in previous exercises, students should begin to use them independently, if they have frequent practice doing so. Use the terms "vehicles" or "public transportation" often in these activities and in other contexts and encourage students to do so. Acknowledge students' unprompted use of these terms.

- Many young children, especially in rural areas, may not understand mass transportation. Supplement the discussion with children's books or films that show how people who live in large cities use public transportation.

- While most young children realize that gasoline is necessary for the functioning of an automobile, the general concepts of engines and fuel may not be clear to them. Use books or films to show how engines work and why fuel is important.

- Stating definitions: Reinforce the pattern for stating definitions demonstrated in previous classification activities. Emphasize these elements when explaining terms, objects, or ideas and prompt students to practice using the same model. Create sentence strips of the model and use the same model for writing definitions of vehicles.
DEFINITION OF ANY NOUN = CATEGORY + CHARACTERISTICS THAT DISTINGUISH IT FROM OTHERS IN THAT CATEGORY.
   A (person, object, or idea) is a (category) that (qualifiers).

   A <u>bicycle</u> is a <u>vehicle</u> that <u>has two wheels, handlebars, and is moved by pedaling.</u>

| | BICYCLE WORD | |
|---|---|---|
| CHARACTERISTIC *is moved by pedaling* | | CHARACTERISTIC *has handlebars for steering* |
| | **VEHICLE** CATEGORY | |
| CHARACTERISTIC *has two wheels* | | CHARACTERISTIC *has a seat for the rider* |

- For a blank definition graphic organizer, see TM 25 on page 349.

- Model and encourage students to express the following process for classifying vehicles:
   1. I will think about the important characteristics of the vehicles (size, how it is used, how many people it can carry, where it is driven).

   2. I will find a word that describes all of them.

   3. I will identify another vehicle that belongs in the same group.

   4. I will check whether there are other terms that describe other important characteristics of the same vehicles.

**MODEL LESSON**

## LESSON

### Introduction

   Q: We have practiced describing how vehicles are similar.

258                    © 2000 CRITICAL THINKING BOOKS & SOFTWARE • WWW.CRITICALTHINKING.COM • 800-458-4849

### Explaining the Objective to Students
Q: In this lesson, we will explain how vehicles are alike and name the type of vehicle that is being described.

### Class Activity
- Display the following pictures:

  **H-4 Example:** *ambulance, fire truck, police car*

  Q: With your partner discuss how these vehicles are alike.
  - A: They all bring rescuers in a hurry to help people who are in danger. They have lights and sirens to warn other people to get out of the way so that they can quickly get to those who need help. They have powerful engines that help the vehicle move fast. They have special radios to communicate with their headquarters and special equipment that they may need at an emergency.

  Q: What words can we use to describe all these vehicles?
  - A: Emergency vehicles

  Q: Name another vehicle that belongs to this group.
  - A: Coast guard boat, rescue helicopter

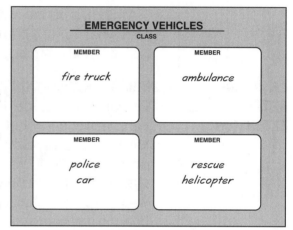

- For a blank class-and-members graphic organizer, see TM 23 on page 347.

### Guided Practice
- Display the following pictures:

  **H-4 Exercise:** *bicycle, boat, motorcycle*

  Q: With your partner discuss how these vehicles are alike.
  - A: While they all can be used for business, they are used by more people for recreation. One person can operate them alone. Families can sometimes afford to have one. They can carry at least one passenger.

  Q: What words can we use to describe all these foods?
  - A: Recreational vehicles

  Q: Name another vehicle that belongs to this group.
  - A: Moped, skateboard, trail bike

### Optional Independent Practice
- Display the following pictures:

  **H-4 Practice:** *airplane, bus, train*

  Q: With your partner discuss how these vehicles are alike.
  - A: They are all huge vehicles that carry large numbers of people or cargo. They normally travel long distances on regular schedules. It takes many transportation workers to operate and schedule them. They have huge engines to make such large vehicles go.

Q: What words can we use to describe all these vehicles?
  A: Public transportation

Q: Name another vehicle that belongs to this group.
  A: Subway train or monorail, passenger ship

**Thinking About Thinking**

Q: What did you think about to decide what characteristics all these three vehicles have in common?
  A: Why people ride them, how many people may own one, their size, why people use them, their capacity to carry cargo or passengers, how many people work on them, and where they are driven.

**Personal application**

Q: What will you pay attention to whenever you classify vehicles?
  A: Size, purpose, where they are driven, who uses them, how they look, what kind of equipment they have, when they are used, how they move, how many people must operate them.

**LANGUAGE ARTS EXTENSION**

**LANGUAGE INTEGRATION ACTIVITIES**

• Drawing: Ask students to draw a picture of any three vehicles from the vehicles list and label the drawing to describe how the three vehicles are alike (public or individual transportation; driven on land, sea, or air; construction vehicles; recreation vehicles; emergency vehicles; etc.). Create a vehicles bulletin board display of students' drawings. Use the web graphic organizer shown on page 333 as a model for the bulletin board display and place students' pictures in the "boxes" on the diagram.

• Drawing: On large newsprint, ask students to draw a concept map with four branches with large boxes at each end. Students should decide the class of vehicles they want to draw (public or individual transportation; use; driven on land, sea, or air; construction vehicles; recreation vehicles; emergency vehicles; etc.) and write that label in the middle of the diagram. Students will then draw a vehicle that belongs to that class in each of the four boxes.

• Story telling: Select a common story or fairy tale about vehicles, such as *Little Toot.* Ask students to retell the story about another member of that class of vehicles, such as a tractor. How is the revised story different from the original? (The tractor would face land obstacles, rather than a stormy sea or thick fog.)

• Listening: Play Listening Tic Tac Toe with vehicles. For directions see page xxviii; for the playing grid photocopy TM 12 on page 336. Use vehicles that have been introduced in previous lessons or the list of vehicles on page 342 (TM 18).

**FOLLOW-UP ACTIVITIES AT HOME**

• Have parents name a kind of vehicle (such as a station wagon) and then ask the child to tell what type of vehicle it is (car) and to name different vehicles of that kind (racing cars, jeeps, convertibles, etc.).

BEGINNING BUILDING THINKING SKILLS LESSON PLANS                    VERBAL CLASSIFICATIONS

**PICTURE BOOK EXTENSION**
- After discussing any of the picture books ask the following questions:
  Q: Are there any new ideas about (emergency vehicles, public transportation, or recreational vehicles) that we learned from this story?
  Q: What ideas or details about (emergency vehicles, public transportation, or recreational vehicles) did you get from the pictures?
  Q: Is this information true of most (emergency vehicles, public transportation, or recreational vehicles)?
    A: After discussing each story, ask students to add new information about the characteristics of the vehicles described in the story to the lists, posters, or graphic organizers that you may have used when discussing the pictures.

**SUPPLEMENTAL PICTURE BOOKS**
- These books feature the vehicles discussed in this lesson. Descriptions of these and additional books on topics in this lesson are provided in the extended bibliography at the end of this manual.
  *I Promise I'll Find You,* Heather Patricia Ward
  *Machines As Big as Monsters,* Paul Strickland
  *On the Go,* Ann Morris
  *Richard Scarry's What Do People Do All Day?,* Richard Scarry
  *Steven Biesty's Incredible Cross Sections,* Steven Biesty
  *What's Inside?* Dorling Kindersley
  *Wings, Wheels, and Sails,* Tom Stacy

**EXERCISE H-5**

# HOW ARE THESE ANIMALS ALIKE?

**ANSWERS H-5**
**H-5 Example** Four-legged hoofed mammals
**H-5 Exercise** Reptiles
**H-5 Practice** Farm animals

**LESSON PREPARATION**

**OBJECTIVE AND MATERIALS**
OBJECTIVE: Students will explain how animals are alike and name the type of animal that is being described.
MATERIALS: The following pictures are used in this lesson: *camel (58), cow (72), duck (70), giraffe (59), lizard (68), pig (71), snake (69), turtle (61)* • transparencies of TM 23 on page 347 and TM 25 on page 349

**CURRICULUM APPLICATIONS**
Science: Recognize that there are many kinds of animals; identify living things as plants or animals; recognize that plants and animals reproduce their own kind; recognize that needs of different kinds of animals are similar, e.g., between plants and animals; state what animals need to live and grow; recognize examples of common animals as being fish, birds, or mammals.

**TEACHING SUGGESTIONS**
- "Mammals" or "reptiles" are abstract concepts for most young children. Since they have heard these terms several times in previous exercises,

© 2000 CRITICAL THINKING BOOKS & SOFTWARE • WWW.CRITICALTHINKING.COM • 800-458-4849          261

students should begin to use them independently, if they have frequent practice doing so. Use the terms "mammals" or "reptiles" often in these activities and in other contexts and encourage students to do so. Acknowledge students' unprompted use of these terms. Students may be reminded that using the term "reptile" means that the animal has a backbone, is cold-blooded, and lays eggs.

- Students should be encourage to state the category to which an animal belongs, as well as the distinguishing characteristics that make it different from other animals. Rehearse with your students some common categories related to animals: birds, mammals, reptiles, insects, fish, farm animals, hoofed animals, amphibians, etc.

- Stating definitions: Reinforce the pattern for stating definitions demonstrated in previous classification activities. Emphasize these elements when explaining terms, objects, or ideas and prompt students to practice using the same model. Create sentence strips of the model and use the same model for writing definitions of animals.
DEFINITION OF ANY NOUN = CATEGORY + CHARACTERISTICS THAT DISTINGUISH IT FROM OTHERS IN THAT CATEGORY.
   A (person, object, or idea) is a (category) that (qualifiers).

   A <u>pig</u> is a <u>farm animal</u> that is <u>raised for meat (pork, ham, and bacon)</u>.

   A <u>turtle</u> is a <u>reptile</u> that <u>has a hard shell into which it can put its head, legs, and tail.</u>

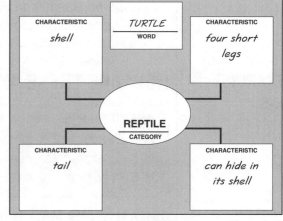

- For a blank definition graphic organizer see TM 25 on page 349.

- Model and encourage students to express the following process for classifying animals:
   1. I will think about the important characteristics of the animals (kind of animal, whether the animal is warm- or cold-blooded, whether it hatches or gives live birth, where it lives, how it moves, what it eats, etc.)
   2. I will find a word that describes all of them.
   3. I will identify another animal that belongs in the same group.
   4. I will check whether there are other terms that describe other important characteristics of the same animals.

**MODEL LESSON** | **LESSON**

**Introduction**

Q: We have practiced describing how animals are similar.

BEGINNING BUILDING THINKING SKILLS LESSON PLANS                    VERBAL CLASSIFICATIONS

**Explaining the Objective to Students**

Q: In this lesson, we will explain how animals are alike and name the type of animal that is being described.

**Class Activity**

- Display the following pictures:
  **H-5 Example:** *camel, horse, giraffe*
  Q: With your partner discuss how these animals are alike.
    A: They are all mammals that have four long, thin legs that are the same length. They can run really fast. They have hooves. They have heads, necks, bodies, and legs in about the same positions. They eat grass or leaves.

  Q: What words can we use to describe all these animals?
    A: Four-legged hoofed mammals

  Q: Name another animal that belongs to this group.
    A: Zebra, elk, cow, moose, antelope

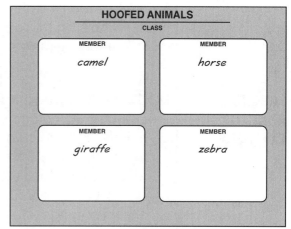

- For a blank class-and-members graphic organizer, see TM 23 on page 347.

**Guided Practice**

- Display the following pictures:
  **H-5 Exercise:** *lizard, snake, turtle*
  Q: With your partner discuss how these animals are alike.
    A: They have a backbone, are cold-blooded, and lay eggs. Most of them live on land (a few species of them can live in water or in a moist place). They eat insects or small animals. They move by crawling or slithering.

  Q: What words can we use to describe all these animals?
    A: Reptiles

  Q: Name another animal that belongs to this group.
    A: Alligator, crocodile, iguana

**Optional Independent Practice**

- Display the following pictures:
  **H-5 Practice:** *cow, duck, pig*
  Q: With your partner discuss how these animals are alike.
    A: They are all farm animals that are raised for food. A farmer supplies them with food and shelter and takes care of them.

  Q: What words can we use to describe all these animals?
    A: Farm animals raised for food

**BEGINNING BUILDING THINKING SKILLS LESSON PLANS**                    **VERBAL CLASSIFICATIONS**

Q: Name another animal that belongs to this group.
   A: Sheep, chicken, turkey

**Thinking About Thinking**

Q: What did you think about to decide what characteristics these three animals have in common?
   A: Whether they are warm- or cold-blooded, whether they have a backbone, whether they hatch or give live birth, where they live, how they move, what they eat, where they are found, how their shelter needs are met, what they are used for, their shape, etc.

**Personal Application**

Q: When is it important to explain how animals are alike?
   A: To recognize the needs of different kind of pets or zoo animals; to know what to pay attention to in books, movies, or television shows about animals: to recognize examples of common animals as being fish, birds, reptiles, or mammals

**LANGUAGE ARTS EXTENSION**

## LANGUAGE INTEGRATION ACTIVITIES

- Drawing: Ask students to draw a picture of any three animals from the animals list (TM 19 on page 343) and label the drawing to describe how the three animals are alike (type of animals, what the animals eat, what food products they supply, where they live, baby animals, etc.). Create an animal bulletin board display of students' drawings. Use the web organizer shown on page 333 as a model for the bulletin board display and place students' pictures in the "boxes" on the web diagram.

- Story telling: Select a common story or fairy tale about animals, such as *Are You My Mother?* Ask students to retell the story about another animal, such as a duck and a duckling, instead of a mother bird and a baby bird. What interesting animals might the duckling meet? How is the revised story different from the original? (Since the duckling's home is in the water, he will ask different animals or things whether they are his mother. He must get home another way.)

- Listening: Play Listening Tic Tac Toe with animals. For directions see page xxviii; for the playing grid photocopy TM 12 on page 336. Use animals that have been introduced in previous lessons or the list of animals on page 343.

## FOLLOW-UP ACTIVITIES AT HOME

- Ask parents to name a kind of animal (such as a tiger) and have the child tell what type of animal it is (cat) and then name different animals of that kind (house cat, lion, etc.)

## PICTURE BOOK EXTENSION

- After discussing any of the picture books ask the following questions:
  Q: Are there any new ideas about (<u>reptiles, farm animals, or hoofed animals</u>) that we learned from this story?

264          © 2000 CRITICAL THINKING BOOKS & SOFTWARE • WWW.CRITICALTHINKING.COM • 800-458-4849

BEGINNING BUILDING THINKING SKILLS LESSON PLANS                    VERBAL CLASSIFICATIONS

Q: What ideas or details about (reptiles, farm animals, or hoofed animals) did you get from the pictures?

Q: Is this information true of most (reptiles, farm animals, or hoofed animals)?

• After discussing each story, ask students to add new information about the characteristics of the animal described in the story to the lists, posters, or graphic organizers that you may have used when discussing the pictures.

## SUPPLEMENTAL PICTURE BOOKS

• These books feature the animals discussed in this lesson. Descriptions of these and additional books on topics in this lesson are provided in the extended bibliography at the end of this manual.

*Early Morning in the Barn,* Nancy Tafuri
*Hoot, Howl, Hiss,* Michelle Koch
*The Big Red Barn,* Margaret Wise Brown
*What Animal Am I? An Animal Guessing Game,* Iza Trapani

**EXERCISE H-6**

# HOW ARE THESE BUILDINGS ALIKE?

> **ANSWERS H-6**
> **H-6 Example:** Emergency buildings
> **H-6 Exercise:** Vehicle storage buildings

**LESSON PREPARATION**

## OBJECTIVE AND MATERIALS

OBJECTIVE: Students will explain how buildings are alike and name the type of building that is being described.

MATERIALS: The following pictures are used in this lesson: *barn (47), fire station (45), garage (53), hospital (39), police station (46)* • transparencies of TM 23 on page 347 and TM 25 on page 349

## CURRICULUM APPLICATIONS

Social Studies: Identify how a family and community use buildings to meet their needs; cite examples of community needs and services; identify public buildings within the community that meet special needs, such as a hospital

## TEACHING SUGGESTIONS

• "Dwellings" or "residences" are abstract concepts for most young children. Since they have heard these terms several times in previous exercises, students should begin to use them independently, if they have frequent practice doing so. Dwellings can refer to homes for animals, as well as people; residences refers only to people. Use the terms "dwellings" or "residences" often in these activities and in other contexts and encourage students to do so. Acknowledge students' unprompted use of these terms.

• Stating definitions: Reinforce the pattern for stating definitions demonstrated in previous classification activities. Emphasize these elements when explaining terms, objects, or ideas and prompt students to practice using the same model. Create sentence strips of the model and use the same model for writing definitions of buildings.

© 2000 CRITICAL THINKING BOOKS & SOFTWARE • WWW.CRITICALTHINKING.COM • 800-458-4849          265

**DEFINITION OF ANY NOUN = CATEGORY + CHARACTERISTICS THAT DISTINGUISH IT FROM OTHERS IN THAT CATEGORY.**

A (person, object, or idea) is a (category) that (qualifiers).

A <u>hospital</u> is a <u>large building</u> where <u>doctors and nurses have equipment and medicine to help sick or wounded people.</u>

A <u>garage</u> is a <u>storage building</u> where <u>people keep their cars and the things they need to keep the car running.</u>

| CHARACTERISTIC | *GARAGE* | CHARACTERISTIC |
| --- | --- | --- |
| cars park inside | WORD | cars fixed inside |

**BUILDING**
CATEGORY

| CHARACTERISTIC | CHARACTERISTIC |
| --- | --- |
| tools may be stored | cars polished inside |

- For a blank definition graphic organizer, see TM 25 on page 349.

- Model and encourage students to express the following process for classifying:

  1. I will think about the important characteristics of the buildings. (I will be sure to discuss their size, purpose, who lives or works there, materials, color, design, etc.).

  2. I will find a word that describes all of them.

  3. I will identify another building that belongs in the same group.

  4. I will check whether there are other terms that describe other important characteristics of the same buildings.

**MODEL LESSON**

## LESSON

### Introduction

Q: We have practiced describing how buildings are similar.

### Explaining the Objective to Students

Q: In this lesson, we will explain how buildings are alike and name the type of buildings that is being described.

### Class Activity

- Display the following pictures:

  **H-6 Example:** *fire station, hospital, police station*

  Q: With your partner discuss how these buildings are alike.
  - A: They all are the headquarters of workers who help people in emergencies. These buildings house the equipment that these emergency workers need to use. They can communicate with rescuers rushing to help people who are in danger.

  Q: What words can we use to describe all these buildings?
  - A: Emergency services buildings

  Q: Name another building that belongs to this group.
  - A: Community storm shelter

- For a blank class-and-members graphic organizer, see TM 23 on page 347.

BEGINNING BUILDING THINKING SKILLS LESSON PLANS · VERBAL CLASSIFICATIONS

### Guided Practice
• Display the following pictures:
**H-6 Exercise:** *barn, fire station, garage*

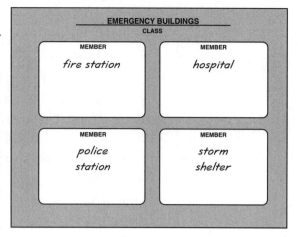

Q: With your partner discuss how these buildings are alike.
  A: They are all used to store vehicles. They must have a large space in which to move the vehicles and large doors that can be closed to protect them. The large spaces are often not heated.

Q: What words can we use to describe all these buildings?
  A: Vehicle storage buildings

Q: Name another building that belongs to this group.
  A: Hangar, boathouse, shed

### Optional Independent Practice
Display the following pictures:
**H-6 Practice:** *library, post office, school*

Q: With your partner discuss how these buildings are alike.
  A: They are all government buildings where people get information.

Q: What words can we use to describe all these buildings?
  A: Government service buildings

Q: Name another building that belongs to this group.
  A: Police station, fire station, community hospital

### Thinking About Thinking
Q: What will you pay attention to whenever you classify buildings?
  A: Size, purpose, who lives or works there, color, design, materials, usual location (rural, downtown, suburbs), and equipment it houses.

### Personal Application
Q: When is it important to classify buildings skillfully?
  A: To understand why their construction, location, or use may be similar. To explain a particular building to someone who is unfamiliar with it, a friend, or a younger child, describing deliveries, describing traffic, giving or understanding directions, understanding why the construction, location, or use of buildings may be similar, explaining a particular building to someone who is unfamiliar with it, a friend or a younger child.

**LANGUAGE ARTS EXTENSION**

### LANGUAGE INTEGRATION ACTIVITIES
• Drawing: Ask students to draw a picture of any three buildings from the vehicles list and label the drawing to describe how the three buildings are

BEGINNING BUILDING THINKING SKILLS LESSON PLANS                                    VERBAL CLASSIFICATIONS

alike (dwellings, stores, government buildings, churches, etc.). Create a building bulletin board display of students' drawings. Use the web graphic organizer shown on page 333 as a model for the bulletin board display and place students' pictures in the "boxes" on the web diagram.

- Drawing: On large newsprint, ask students to draw a concept map with four branches with large boxes at each end. Students should decide the class of buildings they want to draw (dwelling, stores, government buildings, churches, etc.) and write that label in the middle of the diagram. Students will then draw a building that belongs to that class in each of the four boxes.

- Story telling: Select a common story or fairy tale about buildings, such as *The Little House.* Ask students to retell the story about another building, such as an apartment house. How is the revised story different from the original? (Although the little house can be moved to begin life again, an apartment building is too large to move. It might be renovated or used for another purpose.)

- Listening: Play Listening Tic Tac Toe with buildings. For directions see page xxviii; for the playing grid photocopy TM 12 on page 336. Use buildings that have been introduced in previous lessons or the building list on page 344 (TM 20).

## FOLLOW-UP ACTIVITIES AT HOME
- Have parents name a kind of building (such as a supermarket) and then ask the child what type of building it is (store) and to name different buildings of that kind (dress shop, bookstore, etc.).

- On family trips around the local community and when visiting other cities, parents should ask their child to identify types of buildings and to name the goods or services that are provided there.

## PICTURE BOOK EXTENSION
- After discussing any of the picture books ask the following questions:
  Q: Are there any new ideas about (<u>barns, fire stations, garages, hospitals, or police stations</u>) that we learned from this story?
  Q: What ideas or details about (<u>barns, fire stations, garages, or police stations</u>) did you get from the pictures?
  Q: Is this information true of most (<u>barns, fire stations, garages, hospitals, or police stations</u>)?

- After discussing each story, ask students to add new information about the characteristics of the buildings described in the story to the lists, posters, or graphic organizers that you may have used when discussing the pictures.

## SUPPLEMENTAL PICTURE BOOKS
- These books feature the buildings discussed in this lesson. Descriptions of these and additional books on topics in this lesson are provided in the extended bibliography at the end of this manual.
  *City Sounds,* Rebecca Emberley

268            © 2000 CRITICAL THINKING BOOKS & SOFTWARE • WWW.CRITICALTHINKING.COM • 800-458-4849

**BEGINNING BUILDING THINKING SKILLS LESSON PLANS**  **VERBAL CLASSIFICATIONS**

*Dig, Drill, Dump, Fill,* Tana Hoban
*Round Buildings, Square Buildings, Buildings that Wiggle Like a Fish,*
   Phillip M. Isaacson
*Town and Country,* Alice and Martin Provensen

**EXERCISE H-7**

# EXPLAIN THE EXCEPTION—FAMILY MEMBERS

**ANSWERS H-7**
**H-7 Example**—A boy is a child who needs the care of parents.
**H-7 Exercise**—Grandmother is the exception to the group "children." Grandmother is an older woman whose children are grown and have children of their own. Students may recognize an alternative answer. Toddler boy is the exception to the group "female." The toddler boy is a young male child.

**LESSON PREPARATION**

### OBJECTIVE AND MATERIALS
OBJECTIVE: Students will sort jobs into classes.
MATERIALS: The following pictures are used in this lesson: *boy (5), father (7), girl (4), grandmother (8), mother (6), toddler boy (3), toddler girl (2)* • transparencies of TM 23 on page 347 and TM 25 on page 349

### CURRICULUM APPLICATIONS
Social Studies. Students will identify similarities and differences in family members; identify how a family depends upon each other and upon products and services to meet its needs; identify roles and responsibilities within the family; understand how families are an example of interdependence.

### TEACHING SUGGESTIONS
• "Exception" is an abstract concept for most young children. Since they usually think in terms of their concrete observations, identifying a property that is not true of a person, animal, or thing may be puzzling. Students describe exceptions and are comfortable with thinking about exceptions if they have frequent practice doing so. Use the term "exception" often in these activities and in other contexts and encourage students to do so. Acknowledge instances when students use the term independently.

• Young children may not commonly use the terms *gender* to mean male or female or *relative* to mean someone in one's family. Encourage students to use these terms and to find synonyms for them.

• Stating definitions: Reinforce the pattern for stating definitions demonstrated in previous classification activities. Emphasize these elements when explaining terms, objects, or ideas and prompt students to practice using the same model. Create sentence strips of the model and use the same model for writing definitions of family members.
DEFINITION OF ANY NOUN = CATEGORY + CHARACTERISTICS THAT DISTINGUISH IT FROM OTHERS IN THAT CATEGORY.
   A (person, object, or idea) is a (category) that (qualifiers).

   A <u>grandmother</u> is an<u> older woman</u> whose <u>children are grown and have children of their own.</u>

© 2000 CRITICAL THINKING BOOKS & SOFTWARE • WWW.CRITICALTHINKING.COM • 800-458-4849          269

BEGINNING BUILDING THINKING SKILLS LESSON PLANS    VERBAL CLASSIFICATIONS

- Model and encourage students to express the following process for classifying family members:
  1. I will think about the important characteristics of family members in the pictures (age, gender, relationship to other family members, etc.)
  2. I will find a class that fits three of them.
  3. I will explain how the exception is different from that class.
- For a blank definition graphic organizer, see TM 25 on page 349.

**MODEL LESSON**

**LESSON**

**Introduction**

Q. We have named types of family members.

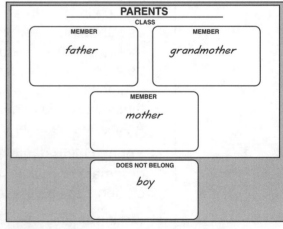

**Explaining the Objective to Students**

Q. In this lesson, we will identify a family member who doesn't fit in the same class as the others.

**Class Activity**

- Display the following pictures:
  **H-7 Example** <u>boy</u>, father, grandmother, mother
  Q. Discuss with your partner how three of the family members are alike and find the exception.

- After students have discussed the exception with their partners, confirm answers with the whole class.
  A. The grandmother, the father, and the mother are all adults who have children. They know how to take care of their children. They love their children and help their children get what they need.

Q. How can we describe this class of family members?
A. People who have children are parents.

Q. Which one doesn't fit that class?
A. A boy is a child who needs the care of parents.

Q. Why is the boy an exception to this group?
A. A boy is too young to be a parent.

270    © 2000 CRITICAL THINKING BOOKS & SOFTWARE • WWW.CRITICALTHINKING.COM • 800-458-4849

BEGINNING BUILDING THINKING SKILLS LESSON PLANS                    VERBAL CLASSIFICATIONS

- For a blank class/members/exception graphic organizer, see TM 23 on page 347.

**Guided Practice**

- Use the same process with the following items.
  **H-7 Exercise** *girl, girl, <u>grandmother</u>, toddler boy, toddler girl*
  Q. Discuss with your partner how three of the family members are alike and find the exception.

- After students have discussed the exception with their partners, confirm answers with the whole class.
  - A. The girl, the toddler boy and the toddler girl are all children. They still have to learn how to take care of themselves. They are cared for by their parents and grandparents. The grandmother, the girl, and the toddler girl are all females. They can or will have babies during their lives.

  Q. How can we describe this class of family members?
  - A. Three are children, or three are female.

  Q. Which one doesn't fit that class?
  - A. A grandmother or a toddler boy.

  Q. Why is the grandmother or the toddler boy an exception to the group?
  - A. Grandmother is an older woman whose children are grown and have children of their own. Grandmother is the exception to the group "children." The toddler boy is a young male child who can walk, feed himself, and knows his surroundings, but can't do very much alone. Toddler boy is the exception to the group "female."

**Thinking About Thinking**

Q. What did you think about to classify family members?
- A. How the members of the group are related, their ages, gender, and roles, feelings about them, interests, experiences that make them special.

**Personal Application**

Q. When is it important to explain which family member is different from others?
- A. To understand stories about one's own family, the families of others, or families in works of literature; to describe events that happen in the family.

**LANGUAGE ARTS EXTENSION**

**LANGUAGE INTEGRATION ACTIVITIES**

- Drawing: On large newsprint ask students to add their drawing of a boy or a grandmother to their family tree. For a family tree diagram see TM 8 on page 332.

- Story telling: Select a common story or fairy tale about family members, such as *Are You My Mother?* Ask students to retell the story about another family member, such as a brother, instead of a mother. How is the revised story different from the original? (What questions might the baby bird ask? What animals or things might the baby bird mistake as "brothers"?)

© 2000 CRITICAL THINKING BOOKS & SOFTWARE • WWW.CRITICALTHINKING.COM • 800-458-4849          271

BEGINNING BUILDING THINKING SKILLS LESSON PLANS                    VERBAL CLASSIFICATIONS

**FOLLOW-UP ACTIVITIES AT HOME**
- Ask parents to identify a family member (such as a grandmother) and ask the child to identify grandmothers in the families of friends.

**PICTURE BOOK EXTENSION**
- After discussing any of the picture books ask the following questions:

Q. Are there any new ideas about (boys, toddlers, or grandmothers) that we learned from this story?

Q. What ideas or details about (boys, toddlers, or grandmothers) did you get from the pictures?

Q. Is this information true of most (boys, toddlers, or grandmothers)?

- After discussing each story, ask students to add new information about the family member described in the story to lists, posters, or graphic organizers that you may have used when discussing the pictures.

**SUPPLEMENTAL PICTURE BOOKS**
- These books feature the family members discussed in this lesson. Descriptions of these and additional books on topics in this lesson are provided in the extended bibliography at the end of this manual.

**Boy**

*All the Places to Love,* Patricia MacLachlan
*Island Boy,* Barbara Cooney
*Owl Moon,* Jane Yolen

**Grandmother**

*A Song for Lena,* Hilary Horder Hippely
*Grandma According to Me*, Karen Magnuson Bell
*Something Special for Me,* Vera Williams

**Toddler**

*Glorious Angels,* Walter Dean Myers
*I Can,* Helen Oxenbury
*When I Was Young: A Four Year Old's Memoir of Her Youth,* Jamie Lee Curtis

**EXERCISE H-8**

# EXPLAIN THE EXCEPTION—JOBS

> **ANSWERS H-8**
>
> **H-8 Example**—The artist creates works of art that people buy, but does not provide a service to people directly. These works may include drawings, paintings, photographs, sculptures, quilts, murals, etc.
>
> **H-8 Exercise**—The pilot provides air transportation for large numbers of people. A pilot rarely performs emergency service. The emergency workers do not fly airplanes as part of their jobs.

**LESSON PREPARATION**

**OBJECTIVE AND MATERIALS**

OBJECTIVE: Students will sort jobs into the classes in which they belong.

MATERIALS: The following pictures are used in this lesson: *artist (21), barber (23), doctor (19), firefighter (16), mail carrier (13), pilot (17), police officer (18), teacher (15)* • transparencies of TM 23 on page 347 and TM 25 on page 349

272                    © 2000 CRITICAL THINKING BOOKS & SOFTWARE • WWW.CRITICALTHINKING.COM • 800-458-4849

**CURRICULUM APPLICATIONS**

Social Studies. Identify similarities and differences of jobs; identify how a family depends upon products and services to meet its needs; cite examples of community needs and services; identify jobs within the community and understand how community helpers are an example of interdependence.

**TEACHING SUGGESTIONS**

- "Goods" or "services" are abstract concepts for most young children. Since they have heard these terms several times in previous exercises, students should begin to use them independently. Use the terms "goods and services" often in these activities and in other contexts and encourage students to do so. Acknowledge instances when students use these terms independently.

- Stating definitions: Emphasize this model when explaining terms, objects, or ideas and prompt students to practice it. Create sentence strips of the model and use the same model for writing definitions of jobs.
DEFINITION OF ANY NOUN = CATEGORY + CHARACTERISTICS THAT DISTINGUISH IT FROM OTHERS IN THAT CATEGORY.
   A (person, object, or idea) is a (category) that (qualifiers).
   An <u>artist</u> is the <u>creator</u> of <u>works of art (drawings, paintings, photographs, sculptures, quilts, murals, etc.) that people buy.</u>

- For a blank definition graphic organizer see TM 25 on page 349.

- Model and encourage students to express the following process for classifying jobs:
   1. I will think about the important characteristics of the jobs in the pictures (their goods or service, training, how they spend their time, tools, etc.).
   2. I will find a class that fits three of them.
   3. I will explain how the exception is different from that class.

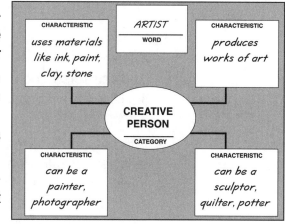

**MODEL LESSON**

**LESSON**

**Introduction**
   Q. We have named types of jobs.

**Explaining the Objective to Students**
   Q. In this lesson, we will identify a job that doesn't fit in the same class as the others.

**Class Activity**
- Display the following pictures:
   **H-8 Example** <u>artist</u>, barber, mail carrier, teacher

Q. Discuss with your partner how three of the jobs are alike and find the exception.

- After students have discussed the exception with their partners, confirm answers with the whole class.

Q. How are three of the jobs alike?
  A. A barber helps people by cutting their hair. A mail carrier helps people by delivering their mail. A teacher helps people by teaching them what they need to know. Each job helps other people by doing something they need.

Q. How can we describe this class of jobs?
  A. Workers who provide services.

Q. Which one doesn't fit that class?
  A. An artist

Q. Why is the artist an exception to this group?
  A. The artist creates a work of art (drawing, painting, photograph, sculpture, quilt, mural, etc.) that people buy, but does not help people directly.

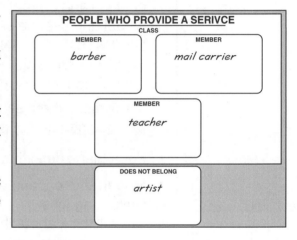

- For a blank exception graphic organizer, see TM 24 on page 348.

**Guided Practice**

- Display the following pictures:
  **H-8 Exercise** *doctor, fire fighter, pilot, police officer*
  Q. Discuss with your partner how three of the jobs are alike and find the exception.

- After students have discussed the exception with their partners, confirm answers with the whole class.

Q. How are three of the jobs alike?
  A: They offer a service to the community. They help people who are having very dangerous problems. They find out what is wrong in order to prevent harm. They wear special clothes and use special tools.

Q. How can we describe this class of jobs?
  A. These workers provide emergency services.

Q. Which one doesn't fit that class?
  A. A pilot

Q. Why is the pilot an exception to this group?
  A. The pilot drives transportation that large numbers of people ride. A pilot rarely performs emergency service. The emergency workers do not fly airplanes as part of their jobs.

### Thinking About Thinking
Q. What did you think about to classify jobs?
A. Their goods or service, training, how they spend their time, how people depend on them, their tools or equipment, etc.

### Personal Application
Q. When is it important to explain which job is different from others?
A. To recognize new jobs that are different from ones you already understand. To prevent being confused about what people do at work.

**LANGUAGE ARTS EXTENSION**

### LANGUAGE INTEGRATION ACTIVITIES
- Drawing: On large newsprint ask students to draw a class and members graphic. Students should decide the class of jobs they want to draw (whether the job is a health worker, an emergency worker, a driver, what goods the jobs produce or service they provide, where workers work, etc.) and write that label at the top of the diagram. Students will then draw a job that belongs to that class in each of the four boxes. For a blank class and members graphic see TM 23 on page 347.

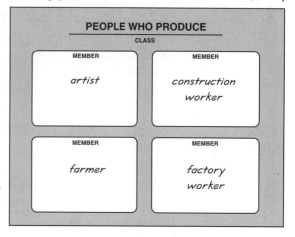

- Story telling: Select a common story or fairy tale about jobs, such as *The Shoemaker and the Elves.* Ask students to retell the story about another job, such as a *construction worker*, instead of a *shoemaker.* How might the elves help the construction worker? What might the construction worker make for the elves in return? How is the revised story different from the original?

- Listening: Play Listening Tic Tac Toe with jobs. For directions, see page xxviii; for the playing grid photocopy TM 12 on page 336. Use jobs that have been introduced in previous lessons or the list of occupations on page 340 (TM 16).

### FOLLOW-UP ACTIVITIES AT HOME
- Ask parents to identify a job their children know (such as a bus driver) and to describe other jobs of that kind (truck driver, pilot, train engineer, etc.).

### PICTURE BOOK EXTENSION
- After discussing any of the picture books ask the following questions:
Q: Are there any new ideas about (artists or pilots) that we learned from this story?
Q. What ideas or details about (artists or pilots) did you get from the pictures?
Q. Is this information true of most (artists or pilots)?

BEGINNING BUILDING THINKING SKILLS LESSON PLANS                                    VERBAL CLASSIFICATIONS

- After discussing each story, ask students to add new information about the job described in the story to lists, posters, or graphic organizers that you may have used when discussing the pictures.

### SUPPLEMENTAL PICTURE BOOKS
- These books feature the occupations discussed in this lesson. Descriptions of these and additional books on topics in this lesson are provided in the extended bibliography at the end of this manual.

### Artist
*Getting to Know the World's Artists,* Mike Venezia
*Miss Rumphius,* Barbara Cooney
*Sketching the Outdoors in Summer,* Jim Arnosky

### Pilot
*I Am A Pilot,* Cynthia Benjamin
*Nobody Owns the Sky,* Reeve Lindbergh

**EXERCISE H-9**

# EXPLAIN THE EXCEPTION—FOODS

> **ANSWERS H-9**
> **H-9 Example**—Eggs (Other foods are dairy products)
> **H-9 Exercise**—Potato (Other foods are green vegetables)

**LESSON PREPARATION**

## OBJECTIVE AND MATERIALS
OBJECTIVE: Students will identify which food is not in the same class as the others.
MATERIALS: The following pictures are used in this lesson: *butter (74), cabbage (90), celery (87), cheese (75), eggs (78), lettuce (91), milk (79), potato (86)* • transparencies of TM 23 on page 347 and TM 25 on page 349

## CURRICULUM APPLICATIONS
Health: Recognize food that provides good nutrition for proper growth and functions of the body; identify a variety of foods. For second-grade classes, discuss basic nutrients the food contains: fats, protein, carbohydrates, vitamins, minerals and water.
Science: Identify the parts of a plant: root, stem, and leaf; recognize that there are many kinds of plants; recognize that there are many kinds of animals; identify living things as plants or animals; recognize the major physical differences between plants and animals; identify how plants are important to people; recognize examples of common animals as being fish, birds, or mammals.

## TEACHING SUGGESTIONS
- If the food is a plant product, describe the kind of plant that produces it—tree, vine, or small bush. Identify the part of the plant that we eat—seed, fruit, leaf, stem, or root. Describe the food's color, shape, and size. If it is an animal product, describe the kind of animal that produces it and how it is prepared.

276        © 2000 CRITICAL THINKING BOOKS & SOFTWARE • WWW.CRITICALTHINKING.COM • 800-458-4849

- For all food products, describe how it is cooked, seasoned, and served at specific meals. This discussion is a rich opportunity to explore how different ethnic groups contribute to the richness of our diet by preparing foods differently.

- Stating definitions: Emphasize this model when explaining terms, objects, or ideas and prompt students to practice using the same model. Create sentence strips of the model and use the same model for writing definitions of food.
  DEFINITION OF ANY NOUN = CATEGORY + CHARACTERISTICS THAT DISTINGUISH IT FROM OTHERS IN THAT CATEGORY.
    A (person, object, or idea) is a (category) that (qualifiers).
    A <u>tomato</u> is a <u>red fruit that grows on vines and is usually used in vegetable salads and red sauces.</u>

- Model and encourage students to express the following process for classifying foods
  1. I will think about the important characteristics of the foods in the pictures (whether the food is from a plant or an animal, what part of it we eat, whether or not it has to be cooked, its color. etc.)
  2. I will find a class that fits three of them.
  3. I will explain how the exception is different from that class.

- Second-grade science texts offer the scientific definition of fruit which applies to foods commonly called vegetables (tomatoes, squash, cucumbers, pumpkins, etc.). Clarify students' use of the term *fruit* in appropriate contexts: "vegetable" in cookbooks and grocery stores, "fruit" in scientific discussion of parts of a plant.

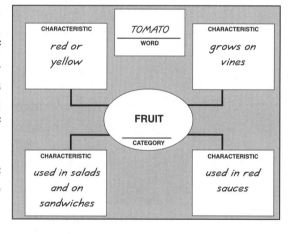

- For a blank definition graphic organizer, see TM 25 on page 349.

**MODEL LESSON** | **LESSON**

### Introduction
Q: We have named types of food, the class in which a food fits, such as meat or vegetable.

### Explaining the Objective to Students
Q: In this lesson, we will identify a food that is not like the others, the food that doesn't fit in the same class as the others.

### Class Activity
- Display the following pictures:
  **H-9 Example** *butter, cheese, milk, <u>eggs</u>*

Q: Discuss with your partner how three of the four foods are alike and find the exception.

- After students have discussed the exception with their partners, confirm answers with the whole class.

   Q: What class fits three of these foods?
   A: Milk or dairy products. Butter and cheese are made from milk.

   Q: Which one doesn't fit that class?
   A: Eggs

   Q: Why are eggs an exception to this group?
   A: Eggs are not a milk product; they are obtained from chickens.

- For a blank class exception graphic organizer, see TM 24 on page 348.

### Guided Practice

- If students need additional practice, display the pictures:
  **H-9 Exercise** *cabbage, celery, lettuce, <u>potato</u>*

   Q: What class fits three of these foods?
   A: Green leafy vegetables

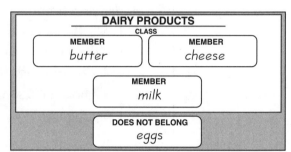

   Q: Which one doesn't fit that class?
   A: A potato

   Q: Why is the potato an exception to this group?
   A: Potatoes grow underground. They are usually white and round in shape, not green or leafy. The potato is the root part of the plant. It must be cooked. The green vegetables can be eaten raw.

### Thinking About Thinking

Q: What did you think about to classify the foods?
A: Whether the food is from a plant or an animal, what part of it we eat, whether or not it has to be cooked, how it looks, how it is grown.

### Personal Application

Q: When is it important to explain which food is different from others?
A: Reading the grocery advertisements in the newspaper; finding food in the grocery store; checking whether a coupon applies to a certain food; understanding a doctor's or nurse's directions about what to eat while taking various medicines; choosing the best foods to purchase and eat.

**LANGUAGE ARTS EXTENSION**

### LANGUAGE INTEGRATION ACTIVITIES

- Drawing: On large newsprint, ask students to draw a class and members graphic. Students should decide the class of foods they want to draw (type of food, how it is prepared, favorite food, food served at special holiday meals, etc.) and write that label at the top of the diagram. Students will then

BEGINNING BUILDING THINKING SKILLS LESSON PLANS

VERBAL CLASSIFICATIONS

draw a food that belongs to that class in each of the four boxes. For a blank class and members graphic see TM 23 on page 347.

- Story telling: Select a common story or fairy tale about food, such as *The Little Red Hen.* Ask students to retell the story about another food, such as butter instead of bread. How is the revised story different from the original? (The steps in making the butter would be different.)

- Listening: Play Listening Tic Tac Toe with food. For directions see page xxviii; for the playing grid photocopy TM 12 on page 336. Use foods that have been introduced in previous lessons or the list of food on page 341 (TM 17).

### FOLLOW-UP ACTIVITIES AT HOME

- Have parents name a kind of food (such as fruit, meat, bread) and ask their children to name other foods of that kind.

### PICTURE BOOK EXTENSION

- After discussing any of the picture books ask the following questions:
  Q: Are there any new ideas about (eggs or potatoes) that we learned from this story?
  Q: What ideas or details about (eggs or potatoes) did you get from the pictures?
  Q: Is this information true of most (eggs or potatoes)?

- After discussing each story, ask students to add new information about the family member described in the story to lists, posters, or graphic organizers that you may have used when discussing the pictures.

### SUPPLEMENTAL PICTURE BOOKS

- These books feature the food discussed in this lesson. Descriptions of these and additional books on topics in this lesson are provided in the extended bibliography at the end of this manual.

**Potato**

*Jamie O'Rourke and the Big Potato: An Irish Folktale,* Tomie DePaola
*Potatoes,* Ann Burckhardt
*The Amazing Potato,* Milton Meltzer
*Vegetables, Vegetables!,* Fay Robinson

**Eggs**

*Down the Road,* Alice Schertle
*Green Eggs and Ham,* Dr. Seuss
*If It Weren't for Farmers,* Allan Fowler

## EXERCISE H-10

## EXPLAIN THE EXCEPTION—VEHICLES

> **ANSWERS H-10**
> **H-10 Example:** Fire truck. A fire truck is an emergency vehicle, not public transportation.
> **H-10 Exercise:** Tractor. A tractor is used for farmwork, not recreation.

© 2000 CRITICAL THINKING BOOKS & SOFTWARE • WWW.CRITICALTHINKING.COM • 800-458-4849

BEGINNING BUILDING THINKING SKILLS LESSON PLANS      VERBAL CLASSIFICATIONS

**LESSON PREPARATION**

**OBJECTIVE AND MATERIALS**

OBJECTIVE: Students will identify which vehicle is not in the same class as the others.

MATERIALS: The following pictures are used in this lesson: *airplane (27), bicycle (30), boat (36), fire truck (37), motorcycle (33), school bus (32), tractor (34), train (29)* • transparencies of TM 24 on page 348 and TM 25 on page 349

**CURRICULUM APPLICATIONS**

<u>Social Studies</u>: Students will identify how a family depends upon transportation to meet its needs; identify some jobs in the home, school, and community; cite examples of community needs and services; understand how community helpers are an example of interdependence.

**TEACHING SUGGESTIONS**

- "Vehicles" or "public transportation" are abstract concepts for most young children. Since they have heard these terms several times in previous exercises, students should begin to use them independently, if they have frequent practice doing so. Use the terms "vehicles" or "public transportation" often in these activities and in other contexts and encourage students to do so. Acknowledge instances when students use these terms independently.

- Stating definitions: Reinforce the pattern for stating definitions demonstrated in previous classification activities. Emphasize these elements when explaining terms, objects, or ideas and prompt students to practice using the same model. Create sentence strips of the model and use the same model for writing definitions of vehicles.
DEFINITION OF ANY NOUN = CATEGORY + CHARACTERISTICS THAT DISTINGUISH IT FROM OTHERS IN THAT CATEGORY.

    A (person, object, or idea) is a (category) that (qualifiers).

    A <u>bicycle</u> is a <u>vehicle</u> that <u>has two wheels, handlebars, and is moved by pedaling.</u>

- Model and encourage students to express the following process for classifying animals:
    1. I will think about the important characteristics of the vehicles in the pictures (size, purpose, where they are driven, how they look, what kind of equipment they have, and when they are used, etc.)
    2. I will find a class that fits three of them.
    3. I will explain how the exception is different from that class.

- For a blank definition graphic organizer see TM 25 on page 349.

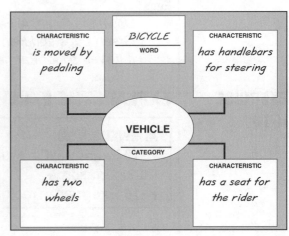

280    © 2000 CRITICAL THINKING BOOKS & SOFTWARE • WWW.CRITICALTHINKING.COM • 800-458-4849

BEGINNING BUILDING THINKING SKILLS LESSON PLANS — VERBAL CLASSIFICATIONS

**MODEL LESSON** | **LESSON**

### Introduction
Q: We have named types of vehicles.

### Explaining the Objective to the Students
Q: In this lesson, we will identify a vehicle that doesn't fit in the same class as the others.

### Class Activity
- Display the following pictures:
  **H-10 Example**: *airplane, <u>fire truck</u>, school bus, train*
  Q: Discuss with your partner how three of the vehicles are alike and find the exception.

- After students have discussed the exception with their partners, confirm answers with the whole class.
  Q: How are three of the vehicles alike?
    A: An airplane, a school bus, and a train are powered by motors and carry many passengers.

  Q: How can we describe this class of vehicle?
    A: Passenger vehicles

  Q: Which one doesn't fit that class?
    A: A fire truck

  Q: Why is the fire truck an exception to this group?
  Q: Although the fire truck does carry firefighters, it is an emergency vehicle, not public transportation.

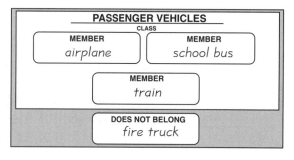

- For a blank class exception graphic organizer, see TM 24 on page 348.

### Guided Practice
- Display the following pictures
  **H-10 Exercise** *bicycle, boat, motorcycle, <u>tractor</u>.*
  Q: Discuss with your partner how three of the vehicles are alike and find the exception.

- After students have discussed the exception with their partners, confirm answers with the whole class.
  Q: How are three of the vehicles alike?
    A: A bicycle, a boat, and a motorcycle are used for fun and carry one or two passengers.

  Q: How can we describe this class of vehicles?
    A: Recreational vehicles

  Q: Which one doesn't fit that class?
    A: A tractor

Q: Why is the tractor an exception to this group?
> A: Although a tractor can be used to pull a hay wagon for a hay ride, its primary purpose is farm work, not recreation.

### Thinking About Thinking

Q: What did you think about to decide what characteristics these three vehicles have in common?
> A: Size, purpose, where they are driven, how they look, what kind of equipment they have, and when they are used.

### Personal Application

Q: When is it important to explain which vehicle is different from others?
> A: Describing deliveries, describing traffic, giving directions when using public transportation

## LANGUAGE INTEGRATION ACTIVITIES

- Drawing: On large newsprint ask students to draw a class and members graphic. Students should decide the class of vehicles they want to draw (public or individual transportation, use, driven on land, sea, or air, construction vehicles, recreation vehicles, emergency vehicles, etc.) and write that label at the top of the diagram. Students will then draw a vehicle that belongs to that class in each of the four boxes. For a blank class and members graphic see TM 23 on page 347.

- Story telling: Select a common story or fairy tale about vehicles, such as *Little Toot.* Ask students to retell the story about another member of that class of vehicles, such as a tractor. How is the revised story different from the original? (The tractor would face different obstacles than a stormy sea or thick fog.)

- Listening: Play Listening Tic Tac Toe with vehicles. For directions see page xxviii; for the playing grid photocopy TM 12 on page 336. Use vehicles that have been introduced in previous lessons or the list of vehicles on page 342 (TM 18).

## FOLLOW-UP ACTIVITIES AT HOME

- Have parents name a kind of vehicle and ask their children to name different vehicles of that kind. Example: car (station wagon, racing car, jeep, convertible, etc.)

## PICTURE BOOK EXTENSION

- After discussing any of the picture books ask the following questions:
  Q: Are there any new ideas about (<u>fire trucks or tractors</u>) that we learned from this story?
  Q: What ideas or details about (<u>fire trucks or tractors</u>) did you get from the pictures?
  Q: Is this information true of most (<u>fire trucks or tractors</u>)?

- After discussing each story, ask students to add new information about the characteristics of the vehicles described in the story to the lists, posters, or graphic organizers you may have used when discussing the pictures.

BEGINNING BUILDING THINKING SKILLS LESSON PLANS                    VERBAL CLASSIFICATIONS

## SUPPLEMENTAL PICTURE BOOKS

- These books feature the vehicles discussed in this lesson. Descriptions of these and additional books on topics in this lesson are provided in the extended bibliography at the end of this manual.

**Fire Truck**

*Emergency Vehicles,* Dayna Wolhart
*Fire Fighters,* R. Broekel
*Fire Trucks,* Peter Brady

**Tractor**

*If It Weren't for Farmers,* Allan Fowler
*Katy and the Big Snow,* Virginia Lee Burton
*Tractors,* Gil Chandler
*Tractors,* Peter Brady

**EXERCISE H-11**

# EXPLAIN THE EXCEPTION—ANIMALS

> **ANSWERS H-11**
> **H-11 Example:** Chicken. It is a bird, not a mammal. It lays eggs and has feathers instead of fur. It lives in small pens on farms, not in large open spaces.
> **H-11 Exercise:** Owl. An owl is a bird, not a mammal. It lays eggs and has feathers instead of fur. It lives in trees and flies.

**LESSON PREPARATION**

## OBJECTIVE AND MATERIALS

OBJECTIVE: Students will sort animals into the classes.
MATERIALS: The following pictures are used in this lesson: *chicken (65), cows (72), giraffe (59), horse (64), owl (66), zebra (63)* • transparencies of TM 24 on page 348 and TM 25 on page 349

## CURRICULUM APPLICATIONS

<u>Science</u>: Recognize that there are many kinds of animals; identify living things as plants or animals; recognize that plants and animals reproduce their own kind; recognize that needs of different kinds of animals are similar, e.g. mother, father, food water, place to live; recognize the major physical differences between plants and animals; state what animals need to live and grow; recognize that needs of different kinds of animals are similar; recognize examples of common animals as being fish, birds, or mammals.

## TEACHING SUGGESTIONS

- "Mammals" or "reptiles" are abstract concepts for most young children. Since they have heard these terms several times in previous exercises, students should begin to use them independently, if they have frequent practice doing so. Use the terms "mammals" or "reptiles" often in these activities and in other contexts and encourage students to do so. Acknowledge instances when students use these terms independently.

- Stating definitions: Reinforce the pattern for stating definitions demonstrated in previous classification activities. Emphasize these elements when explaining terms, objects, or ideas and prompt students to practice

© 2000 CRITICAL THINKING BOOKS & SOFTWARE • WWW.CRITICALTHINKING.COM • 800-458-4849                    283

| BEGINNING BUILDING THINKING SKILLS LESSON PLANS | VERBAL CLASSIFICATIONS |

using the same model. Create sentence strips of the model and use the same model for writing definitions of animals.

DEFINITION OF ANY NOUN = CATEGORY + CHARACTERISTICS THAT DISTINGUISH IT FROM OTHERS IN THAT CATEGORY.

A (person, object, or idea) is a (category) that (qualifiers).

An <u>owl</u> is a <u>large bird</u> that <u>has large, round eyes, lives in trees, and flies at night</u>.

| CHARACTERISTIC | OWL | CHARACTERISTIC |
|----------------|-----|----------------|
| large | WORD | lives in trees |
| | **BIRD** | |
| | CATEGORY | |
| CHARACTERISTIC | | CHARACTERISTIC |
| has large round eyes | | flies at night |

- For a blank definition graphic organizer see TM 25 on page 349.

- Model and encourage students to express the following process for classifying animals:

  1. I will think about the important characteristics of the animals in the pictures (kind of animal, whether the animal is warm- or cold-blooded, whether it hatches or gives live birth, where it lives, how it moves, what it eats, etc.)

  2. I will find a class that fits three of them.

  3. I will explain how the exception is different from that class.

**MODEL LESSON**

## LESSON

### Introduction

Q: We have named types of animals.

### Explaining the Objective to the Students

Q: In this lesson, we will identify an animal that doesn't fit in the same class as the others.

### Class Activity

- Display the following pictures:

  **H-11 Example** *chicken, turkey, <u>pig,</u> duck*

  Q: Discuss with your partner how three of the animals are alike and find the exception.

- After students have discussed the exception with their partners, confirm answers with the whole class.

  Q: How are three of the animals alike?
    A: A chicken, a turkey, and a duck lay eggs. They have feathers. They all live on the land and can fly to move.

  Q: How can we describe this class of animals?
    A: Birds

  Q: Which one doesn't fit that class?
    A: A pig

284  © 2000 CRITICAL THINKING BOOKS & SOFTWARE • WWW.CRITICALTHINKING.COM • 800-458-4849

Q: Why is the pig an exception to this group?
 A: A pig is a mammal. It gives birth to live babies and has fur instead of feathers. It lives on land and cannot fly.

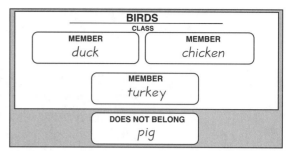

- For a blank class exception graphic organizer, see TM 24 on page 348.

**Guided Practice**
- Display the following pictures:
**H-11 Exercise** <u>owl</u>, cow, horse, zebra
Q: Discuss with your partner how three of the animals are alike and find the exception.

- After students have discussed the exception with their partners, confirm answers with the whole class.
Q: How are three of the animals alike?
 A: A cow, a horse, and a zebra do not lay eggs. They give birth to babies that look like the adult. They have fur. They all live on the land and walk on hooves.

Q: How can we describe this class of animals?
 A: Mammals

Q: Which one doesn't fit that class?
 A: An owl

Q: Why is the owl an exception to this group?
 A: An owl is a bird, not a mammal. It lays eggs and has feathers instead of fur. It lives in trees, not in large open spaces.

**Thinking About Thinking**
Q: What will you pay attention to whenever you classify animals?
 A: Body structure, whether the animal is warm- or cold-blooded, whether it has a backbone, whether it hatches eggs or gives live birth, where it lives, how it moves, what it eats.

**Personal Application**
Q: When is it important to explain which animal is different from others?
 A: To recognize why the needs of different kinds of pets or zoo animals may be different; to know what to pay attention to in books, movies, or television shows about animals.

**LANGUAGE ARTS EXTENSION**

**LANGUAGE INTEGRATION ACTIVITIES**
- Drawing: On large newsprint ask students to draw a class and members graphic. Students should decide the class of animals they want to draw (type of animals, what the animals eat, what food products they supply, where they live, baby animals, etc.) and write that label at the top of the

**BEGINNING BUILDING THINKING SKILLS LESSON PLANS**    **VERBAL CLASSIFICATIONS**

diagram. Students will then draw an animal that belongs to that class in each of the four boxes. For a blank class and members graphic see TM 23 on page 347.

- Story telling: Select a common story or fairy tale about animals, such as *Are You My Mother?* Ask students to retell the story about another animal, such as a duck and a duckling, instead of a mother bird and a baby bird. What interesting animals might the duckling meet? How is the revised story different from the original? (Since the duckling's home is in the water, he will meet different animals and must get home another way.)

- Listening: Play Listening Tic Tac Toe with animals. For directions see page xxviii; for the playing grid photocopy TM 12 on page 336. Use animals that have been introduced in previous lessons or the list of animals on page 343 (TM 19).

## FOLLOW-UP ACTIVITIES AT HOME
- Have parents name a kind of animal and then ask their children to name animals of that kind. Example: cat (tiger, house cat, lion, etc.)

## PICTURE BOOK EXTENSION
- After discussing any of the picture books ask the following questions:
  Q: Are there any new ideas about (<u>owls or chickens</u>) that we learned from this story?
  Q: What ideas or details about (<u>owls or chickens</u>) did you get from the pictures?
  Q: Is this information true of most (<u>owls or chickens</u>)?

- After discussing each story, ask students to add new information about the characteristics of the animals described in the story to the lists, posters, or graphic organizers that you may have used when discussing the pictures.

## SUPPLEMENTAL PICTURE BOOKS
- These books feature the animals discussed in this lesson. Descriptions of these and additional books on topics in this lesson are provided in the extended bibliography at the end of this manual.

**Chicken**
> *Chickens*, Ann Burckhardt
> *Farm Animals*, K. Jacobsen
> *If It Weren't For Farmers*, Rookie Read About Science series
> *The Chicken or the Egg,* Rookie Read About Science series
> *The Rooster's Gift,* Pam Conrad

**Owl**
> *Animal Lore and Legend: Owl,* Vee Browne
> *Birds We Know,* M. Friskey
> *Owl Babies,* Martin Waddell
> *Owl Lake,* Keizaburo Tejima
> *Owl Moon,* Jane Yolen

286    © 2000 CRITICAL THINKING BOOKS & SOFTWARE • WWW.CRITICALTHINKING.COM • 800-458-4849

BEGINNING BUILDING THINKING SKILLS LESSON PLANS                    VERBAL CLASSIFICATIONS

**EXERCISE H-12**

# EXPLAIN THE EXCEPTION—BUILDINGS

**ANSWERS H-12**
H-12 Example—School. The other buildings are residences.
H-12 Exercise—Library. The library does not sell or prepare food. A library helps people get information and lends books.

**LESSON PREPARATION**

**OBJECTIVE AND MATERIALS**
OBJECTIVE: Students will identify which building is not in the same class as the others.
MATERIALS: The following pictures are used in this lesson: *apartment building (50), farm (47), house (53), library (40), mobile home (44), restaurant (48), school (54), supermarket (49)* • transparencies of TM 24 on page 348 and TM 25 on page 349

**TEACHING SUGGESTIONS**

- "Dwellings" or "residences" are abstract concepts for most young children. Since they have heard these terms several times in previous exercises, students should begin to use them independently, if they have frequent practice doing so. Dwellings can refer to homes from animals as well as people; residences refers only to people. Use the terms "dwellings" or "residences" often in these activities and in other contexts and encourage students to do so. Acknowledge instances when students use these terms independently.

- Stating definitions: Reinforce the pattern for stating definitions demonstrated in previous classification activities. Emphasize these elements when explaining terms, objects, or ideas and prompt students to practice using the same model. Create sentence strips of the model and use the same model for writing definitions of buildings.
DEFINITION OF ANY NOUN = CATEGORY + CHARACTERISTICS THAT DISTINGUISH IT FROM OTHERS IN THAT CATEGORY.

A (person, object, or idea) is a (category) that (qualifiers).

A <u>library</u> is a <u>government building</u> where <u>people borrow books and get information.</u>

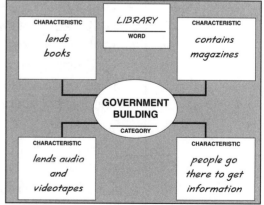

- For a blank definition graphic organizer, see TM 25 on page 349.

- Model and encourage students to express the following process for classifying buildings:
  1. I will think about the important characteristics of the buildings in the pictures (etc.)
  2. I will find a class that fits three of them.
  3. I will explain how the exception is different from that class.

© 2000 CRITICAL THINKING BOOKS & SOFTWARE • WWW.CRITICALTHINKING.COM • 800-458-4849        287

BEGINNING BUILDING THINKING SKILLS LESSON PLANS                    VERBAL CLASSIFICATIONS

**MODEL LESSON** | **LESSON**

**Introduction**
  Q: We have named types of buildings.

**Explaining the Objective to Students**
  Q: In this lesson, we will identify a building that doesn't fit in the same class as the others.

**Class Activity**
• Display the following pictures:
  **H-12 Example** *apartment building, house, <u>school</u>, mobile home*
  Q: Discuss with your partner how three of the buildings are alike and find the exception.

• After students have discussed the exception with their partners, confirm answers with the whole class.
  Q: How are three of the buildings alike?
    A: People live in apartment buildings, houses, and mobile homes. Families eat there, sleep there, play there, invite their friends to visit there, and store their belongings there.

  Q: How can we describe this class of building?
    A: Dwellings or residences

  Q: Which one doesn't fit that class?
    A: A school

  Q: Why is the school an exception to this group?
    A: People don't live in a school. Note: Young students at residential schools may find this distinction confusing. They should recognize that school is not their permanent home.

• For a blank class exception graphic organizer, see TM 24 on page 348.

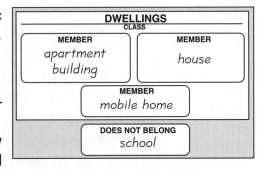

**Guided Practice**
• Display the following pictures:
  **H-12 Exercise** *farm, <u>library</u>, restaurant, supermarket*
  Q: Discuss with your partner how three of the buildings are alike and find the exception.

• After students have discussed the exception with their partners, confirm answers with the whole class.
  Q: How are three of the buildings alike?
    A: A farm, a restaurant, and a supermarket are all businesses that help us get food.

  Q: How can we describe this class of buildings?
    A: Buildings involved in food production, preparation, or distribution

  Q: Which one doesn't fit that class?
    A: A library

Q: Why is the library an exception to this group?
A: The library does not sell or prepare food. A library is a large building where people go to read or borrow books. Books, magazines, videotapes, and audiotapes are stored on library shelves. Most libraries are owned by the government of the town or county. You usually don't pay to use a library.

**Thinking About Thinking**

Q: What did you think about to decide what characteristics these three buildings have in common?
A: Its size, purpose, who lives or works there, its design (materials, color, or shape, its usual location (rural, downtown, suburbs), etc.

**Personal Application**

Q: When is it important to explain which building is different from others?
A: Describing deliveries, describing traffic, giving or understanding directions, understanding why the construction, location, or use of buildings may be similar, explaining a particular building to someone that is unfamiliar with it, a friend, or a younger child.

**LANGUAGE ARTS EXTENSION**

**LANGUAGE INTEGRATION ACTIVITIES**

- Drawing: On large newsprint ask students to draw a class and members graphic. Students should decide the class of buildings they want to draw (dwellings, stores, government buildings, churches, etc.) and write that label at the top of the diagram. Students will then draw a building that belongs to that class in each of the four boxes. For a blank class and members graphic see TM 23 on page 347.

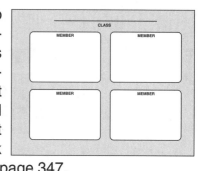

- Story telling: Select a common story or fairy tale about buildings, such as *The Little House.* Ask students to retell the story about another building, such as an apartment house. How is the revised story different from the original? (Although the little house could be moved, an apartment building is too large to move. It might be renovated, be used for another purpose or be transformed from a large building that served another purpose.)

- Listening: Play Listening Tic Tac Toe with buildings. For directions see page xxviii; for the playing grid photocopy TM 12 on page 336. Use buildings that have been introduced in previous lessons or the building list on page 344 (TM 20).

**FOLLOW-UP ACTIVITIES AT HOME**

- Have parents name a kind of building and ask their children to name other buildings of that kind. Example: store (supermarket, dress shop, bookstore, etc.)

**PICTURE BOOK EXTENSION**

- After discussing any of the picture books ask the following questions:

Q: Are there any new ideas about (<u>schools or libraries</u>) that we learned from this story?

Q: What ideas or details about (<u>schools or libraries</u>) did you get from the pictures?

Q: Is this information true of most (<u>schools or libraries</u>)?

- After discussing each story, ask students to add new information about the characteristics of the buildings described in the story to the lists, posters, or graphic organizers you may have used when discussing the pictures.

**SUPPLEMENTAL PICTURE BOOKS**

- These books feature the buildings discussed in this lesson. Descriptions of these and additional books on topics in this lesson are provided in the extended bibliography at the end of this manual.

**School**
*Mitch and Amy,* Beverly Cleary
*My Teacher's Secret Life,* Stephen Krensky
*School,* Emily Arnold McCully
*Will I Have a Friend?,* Miriam Hoban

**Library**
*Check It Out: The Book About Libraries,* Gail Gibbons
*The Library,* Sarah Stewart

**EXERCISE H-13**

## SORTING INTO CLASSES—JOBS

**ANSWERS H-13**
**H-13 Exercise:** See diagram below.

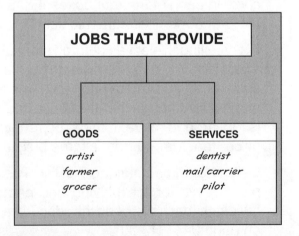

**LESSON PREPARATION**

**OBJECTIVE AND MATERIALS**

OBJECTIVE: Students will sort jobs into the classes in which they belong.
MATERIALS: One large piece of newsprint for each group of four students. Pictures of workers, index cards labeled with the names of various jobs. The following pictures are used in this lesson: *artist (21), dentist (20), farmer (12), grocer (22), mail carrier (13), pilot (17)* • transparencies of TM 13 on page 337 and TM 15 on page 339

BEGINNING BUILDING THINKING SKILLS LESSON PLANS                    VERBAL CLASSIFICATIONS

## CURRICULUM APPLICATIONS

<u>Social Studies</u>: Identify similarities and differences in jobs; identify how a family depends upon products and services to meet its needs; cite examples of community needs and services; identify jobs within the community and understand how community helpers are an example of interdependence.

## TEACHING SUGGESTIONS

* Since there may be more than one characteristic by which one may classify these jobs, students' suggestions for alternative ways of classifying the jobs should be honored. If another system for sorting the jobs is suggested, such as special clothes or indoor/outdoor jobs, encourage students to explain the sorting process for the other characteristic as well.

* Model and encourage students to express the following process for classifying jobs:

    1. I will think about the important characteristics of the jobs. (where they work, whether they provide goods or services, training, how they spend their time, tools, etc.)

    2. I will find a word that describes all of them.

    3. I will identify another group of jobs.

    4. I will find a word that describes all of them.

    5. I will look for other groups of jobs until I have classified all the jobs.

**MODEL LESSON**

## LESSON

Q: We have named types of jobs. Some workers produce things that people buy (food, clothing, toys, machines, etc.); they sell or make goods. Some workers earn money by doing something for other people (treat injuries, cut their hair, drive trucks, program computers, etc.) These workers provide services.

### Explaining the Objective to Students

Q: In this lesson, we will sort jobs into classes.

### Class Activity

* Display the following pictures:

    **H-13 Example:** *artist, dentist, farmer, grocer, mail carrier, pilot*

    Q: What are some classes for the jobs shown by these pictures?

    A: Usually students will suggest sorting the jobs by general type: goods or services.

* Write the categories on the chalkboard above the pictures. Ask different students to place each of the pictures under the category in which it fits.

* Ask students to add other jobs to each category.

* For a blank two-branching diagram see TM 13 on page 337.

### Thinking About Thinking

Q: What will you think about any time you classify jobs?

A: Their goods or services; training; how workers spend their time; tools, equipment or special clothes that workers wear; whether

© 2000 CRITICAL THINKING BOOKS & SOFTWARE • WWW.CRITICALTHINKING.COM • 800-458-4849          291

workers own their business or work for a company or government, etc.

**Personal Application**

Q: When is it important to understand how jobs are alike?
   A: To suggest or recognize jobs that are similar to ones you already understand. To explain a job to someone that is unfamiliar with it.

**LANGUAGE ARTS EXTENSION**

**LANGUAGE INTEGRATION ACTIVITIES**

- Drawing: On large newsprint ask students to draw a branching diagram. Students should decide how to sort jobs (type of jobs, what the jobs produce or provide, where workers work, etc.) and write that label at the top of the diagram. Students will then label each category and write or draw a job that belongs to that class. See a sample diagram at right. For a blank four-branching diagram, see TM 15 on page 339.

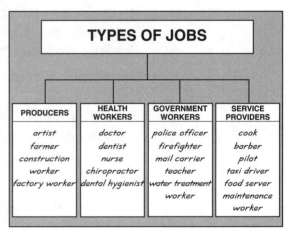

- Story telling: Select a common story or fairy tale about jobs, such as *The Shoemaker and the Elves.* Ask students to retell the story about another job, such as a *construction worker*, instead of a *shoemaker*. How might the elves help the construction worker? What might the construction worker make for the elves in return? How is the revised story different from the original?

- Listening: Play Listening Tic Tac Toe with jobs. For directions see page xxviii; for the playing grid photocopy TM 12 on page 336. Use jobs that have been introduced in previous lessons or the jobs list on page 340 (TM 16).

**FOLLOW-UP ACTIVITIES AT HOME**

- Ask parents to identify a job that their children know (such as a bus driver) and to describe other jobs of that kind (truck driver, pilot, taxi driver).

**PICTURE BOOK EXTENSION**

- Language experiences with any of the following books extend this lesson and demonstrate how similar jobs are carried out across cultures. Additional books on topics in this lesson are described in the bibliography.
  Q: Are there any new ideas about jobs that we learned from this story?
  Q: What ideas or details about jobs did you get from the pictures?
  Q: Is this information true of most jobs?

- After discussing each story, ask students to add new information about the characteristics of the jobs described in the story to the lists, posters, or graphic organizers that you may have used when discussing the pictures.

BEGINNING BUILDING THINKING SKILLS LESSON PLANS                                          VERBAL CLASSIFICATIONS

**SUPPLEMENTAL PICTURE BOOKS**
*People*, Peter Speir
*Richard Scarry's What Do People Do All Day?*, Richard Scarry
*Who Does This Job?*, Pat Upton

**EXERCISE H-14**

## SORTING INTO CLASSES—FOODS

**ANSWERS H-14**
**H-14 Example:** See diagram below.

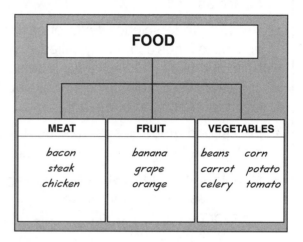

**LESSON PREPARATION**

**OBJECTIVE AND MATERIALS**
OBJECTIVE: Students will sort foods into the classes.
MATERIALS: The following pictures are used in this lesson: *bacon (77), green beans (84), carrots (82), celery (87), fried chicken (80), corn (88), grapes (94), orange (93), potato (86), steak (81), tomatoes (95)* • transparencies of TM 14 on page 338 and TM 15 on page 339

**CURRICULUM APPLICATIONS**
<u>Health</u>: Recognize food that provides good nutrition for proper growth and functions of the body; identify a variety of foods
<u>Science</u>: Identify the parts of a plant: root, stem, and leaf; recognize that there are many kinds of plants; identify living things as plants or animals; recognize the major physical differences between plants and animals; identify how plants are important to people; recognize examples of common animals as being fish, birds, or mammals.

**TEACHING SUGGESTIONS**
- COOPERATIVE GROUP VERSION: Each group of four students will use one large piece of newsprint, pictures of foods, or index cards labeled with the names of various foods. Since sorting the pictures is more easily handled on a flat surface, groups of four to six students may stand around a table as members of the group put the pictures in the correct categories. Draw a large branching diagram as a background for sorting. For a model branching diagram see the answer at the beginning of this lesson.

- Ask each group of students to agree on a category for sorting the foods.

One student should label the categories on the diagram. Each member of the group should tape a picture in the correct part of the diagram. Display each diagram that was sorted by a different characteristic and ask students to explain why they sorted the food this way.

- Since there may be more than one characteristic by which one may classify foods, students' suggestions for alternative ways of classifying the foods should be honored. If another system for sorting the food is suggested, such as preparation (cooked or uncooked), by food groups or nutrients, ask students to explain the sorting process for another characteristic as well.

- Second-grade science texts offer the scientific definition of fruit which applies to foods commonly called vegetables (tomatoes, squash, cucumbers, pumpkins, etc.). Clarify students' use of the term *fruit* in appropriate contexts: "vegetable" in cookbooks and grocery stores, "fruit" in scientific discussion of parts of a plant.

- For second-grade classes, discuss basic nutrients the food contains: fats, protein, carbohydrates, vitamins, minerals and water.

- Model and encourage students to express the following process for classifying foods
    1. I will think about the important characteristics the foods have, whether the food is a plant or an animal, what part of it we eat, where it is found
    2. I will find a word that describes all of them and group them under that category.

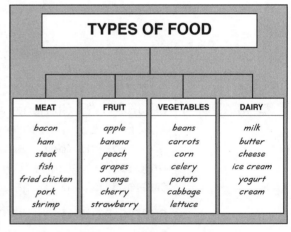

   3. I will identify another category in which other foods belong.
   4. I will group all of the foods that fit that category.
   5. I repeat the grouping until all the foods are classified.

**MODEL LESSON**

## LESSON

### Introduction
Q: We have named types of food. The name for a type of food is called the class in which that food fits, such as fruit and vegetables.

### Explaining the Objective to Students
Q: In this lesson, we will sort foods into classes.

### Class Activity
- Display the following pictures:
  **H-14** *bacon, beans, carrot, celery, fried chicken, corn, grape, orange, peach, potato, steak, tomato*

Q: What are some classes that fit the food shown on these cards?
   A: Usually students will suggest sorting the foods by general types: plant products (fruit and vegetables) and meat.

- Write the categories on the board above the chalkboard tray and ask different students to place each of the pictures under the category in which it fits.

### Thinking About Thinking
Q: What did you think about to classify the foods the way we did?
   A: Whether the food was a fruit, vegetable, or meat.

### Personal Application
Q: When is it important to understand how a food may be different from others?
   A: Reading the grocery ads in the newspaper; finding food in the grocery store. Checking whether a coupon applies to a certain food; understanding a doctor's or nurse's directions about what to eat while taking various medicines, considering similar food that one doesn't usually eat.

**LANGUAGE ARTS EXTENSION**

## LANGUAGE INTEGRATION ACTIVITIES
- Drawing: On large newsprint ask students to draw a branching diagram. Students should decide how to sort foods (vegetables, fruit, dairy products, bread, etc.) and write that label at the top of the diagram. Students will then label each category and write or draw a food that belongs to that class.

- For a blank branching diagram, see TM 15 on page 339.

- Story telling: Select a common story or fairy tale about food, such as *The Little Red Hen.* Ask students to retell the story about another food, such as butter instead of bread. How is the revised story different from the original? (The steps in making the butter would be different.)

- Listening: Play Listening Tic Tac Toe with food. For directions see page xxviii; for the playing grid photocopy TM 12 on page 336. Use food that has been introduced in previous lessons or the food list on page 341 (TM 17).

## FOLLOW-UP ACTIVITIES AT HOME
- Ask parents to identify a food the family enjoys and ask the children to describe many ways that food may be prepared. Identify similar foods that the family does not usually select and discuss how that food is usually cooked.

## PICTURE BOOK EXTENSION
- Language experiences with any of the following books extend this lesson and demonstrate how foods are obtained and prepared across cultures. Additional books on topics in this lesson are described in the bibliography.
   Q: Are there any new ideas about (<u>vegetables, fruit, or meat</u>) that we learned from this story?
   Q: What ideas or details about (<u>vegetables, fruit, or meat</u>) did you get from the pictures?
   Q: Is this information true of most (<u>vegetables, fruit, or meat</u>)?

| BEGINNING BUILDING THINKING SKILLS LESSON PLANS | VERBAL CLASSIFICATIONS |

- After discussing each story, ask students to add new information about the characteristics of the animals and foods described in the story to the lists, posters, or graphic organizers that you may have used when discussing the pictures.

**SUPPLEMENTAL PICTURE BOOKS**
*A Book of Fruit,* Barbara Hirsh Lember
*Foods We Eat,* Lynne Merrison
*Growing Colors,* Bruce McMillan
*Meat,* Elizabeth Clark
*Vegetables, Vegetables!,* Fay Robinson
*We Love Fruit,* Fay Robinson
*What's on My Plate?* Ruth Belov Grose

**EXERCISE H-15**

## SORTING INTO CLASSES—VEHICLES

**ANSWERS H-15**
**H-15 Example:** See diagram below.

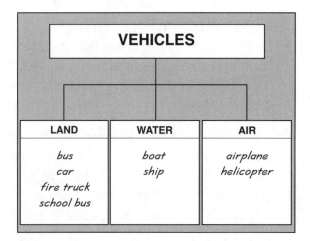

**LESSON PREPARATION**

**OBJECTIVE AND MATERIALS**
OBJECTIVE: Students will sort vehicles into the classes.
MATERIALS: One large piece of newsprint for each group of four students. Pictures, index cards labeled with the names of various vehicles. The following pictures are used in this lesson: *airplane (27), motorboat (36), city bus (28), car (31), fire truck (37), helicopter (38), school bus (32), ship (35), train (29)* • transparencies of TM 14 on page 338 and TM 15 on page 339

**CURRICULUM APPLICATIONS**
Social Studies: Identify how a family depends upon transportation to meet its needs; identify some jobs in the home, school, and community; cite examples of community needs and services; understand how community helpers are an example of interdependence.

**TEACHING SUGGESTIONS**
- COOPERATIVE GROUP VERSION: Each group of four students will use one large piece of newsprint, pictures of vehicles, or index cards labeled

with the names of various vehicles. Since sorting the pictures is more easily handled on a flat surface, groups of four to six students may stand around a table as members of the group put the pictures in the correct categories. Draw a large branching diagram as a background for sorting. For a model branching diagram see the answer at the beginning of this lesson.

- Ask each group of students to agree on a category for sorting the vehicles. One student should label the categories on the diagram. Each member of the group should tape a picture in the correct part of the diagram. Display each diagram that is sorted by a different characteristic and ask students to explain why they sorted the food this way.

- Since there may be more than one way to classify these vehicles, students' suggestions for alternative ways of classifying them should be honored. If another system for sorting the vehicles is suggested, such as air/land/water or motorized/non-motorized, encourage students to explain the sorting process for other characteristics as well.

- Model and encourage students to express the following process for classifying vehicles:

1. I will think about the important characteristics of the vehicles. (I will be sure to discuss their size, purpose, where its driven, how it looks, what kind of equipment it has, and when it is used, etc.)

| **TYPES OF VEHICLES** | | | |
|---|---|---|---|
| **PUBLIC VEHICLES** | **RECREATION VEHICLES** | **EMERGENCY VEHICLES** | **CARGO VEHICLES** |
| city bus | bicycle | ambulance | truck |
| school bus | motorcycle | fire truck | freight train |
| train | motorboat | police car | airplane |
| airplane | moped | helicopter | ship |
| taxi | skateboard | tractor | van |
| ferry | sailboat | rescue boat | tanker |

2. I will find a word that describes all of them.

3. I will identify another group of vehicles.

4. I will find a word that describes this group.

5. I will look for other groups of vehicles until I have classified all the vehicles.

**MODEL LESSON**

## LESSON

### Introduction

Q: We have named types of vehicle. The name for a type of vehicle is called the class in which that vehicle fits, such as trucks.

### Explaining the Objective to Students

Q: In this lesson, we will sort vehicles into the classes in which they belong.

### Class Activity

- Place the following pictures on the tray of the chalkboard.
  **H-15:** *airplane, boat, bus, car, fire truck, helicopter, school bus, ship, train*
  Q: What are some classes for the vehicles shown on these cards?

© 2000 CRITICAL THINKING BOOKS & SOFTWARE • WWW.CRITICALTHINKING.COM • 800-458-4849        297

A: Usually students will suggest sorting the vehicles by general type: land, sea, and air.

- Write the categories on the board above the chalkboard tray and ask different students to place each of the pictures under the category in which it fits.

### Thinking About Thinking

Q: What did you think about to classify the vehicles the way we did?
   A: Each vehicle's size, purpose, where its driven, how it looks, what kind of equipment it has, and when it is used.

### Personal Application

Q: When is it important to describe vehicles accurately?
   A: Describing deliveries, describing traffic, giving directions

**LANGUAGE ARTS EXTENSION**

### LANGUAGE INTEGRATION ACTIVITIES

- Drawing: On large newsprint ask students to draw a class and members diagram. Students should decide the class of vehicles they want to draw (type of vehicles, public or individual transportation, use, land, sea, or air, etc.) and write that label at the top of the diagram. Students will then draw a vehicle that belongs to that class in each of the four boxes. For a blank class-and-members graphic, see TM 23 on page 347.

- Story telling: Select a common story or fairy tale about vehicles, such as *Little Toot.* Ask students to retell the story about another vehicle, such as a tractor. How is the revised story different from the original? (The tractor would face different land obstacles instead of stormy seas or fog.)

- Listening: Play Listening Tic Tac Toe with vehicles. For directions see page xxviii; for the playing grid photocopy TM 12 on page 336. Use vehicles that have been introduced in previous lessons or the vehicle list on page 342 (TM 18).

### FOLLOW-UP ACTIVITIES AT HOME

- Have parents name a kind of vehicle and ask their children to name different vehicles of that kind. Example: cars (station wagons, racing cars, jeeps, convertibles, etc.)

### PICTURE BOOK EXTENSION

- Language experiences with any of the following books extend this lesson and demonstrate how foods are obtained and prepared across cultures. Additional books on topics in this lesson are described in the bibliography.
   Q: Are there any new ideas about vehicles that we learned from this story?
   Q: What ideas or details about vehicles did you get from the pictures?
   Q: Is this information true of most vehicles?

- After discussing each story, ask students to add new information about the characteristics of the vehicles described in the story to the lists, posters, or graphic organizers that you may have used when discussing the pictures.

BEGINNING BUILDING THINKING SKILLS LESSON PLANS • VERBAL CLASSIFICATIONS

**SUPPLEMENTAL PICTURE BOOKS**
*Machines As Big as Monsters,* Paul Strickland
*On the Go,* Ann Morris
*Promise I'll Find You,* Heather Patricia Ward
*Richard Scarry's What Do People Do All Day?,* Richard Scarry
*Steven Biesty's Incredible Cross Sections,* Steven Biesty
*What's Inside?,* Dorling Kindersley
*Wings, Wheels, and Sails,* Tom Stacy

**EXERCISE H-16**

# SORTING INTO CLASSES—ANIMALS

**ANSWERS H-16**
H-16 Example: See diagram below.

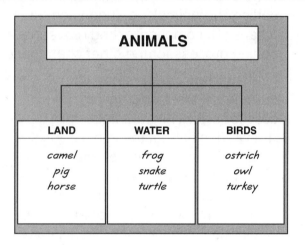

**LESSON PREPARATION**

**OBJECTIVE AND MATERIALS**
OBJECTIVE: Students will sort animals into classes.
MATERIALS: One large piece of newsprint for each group of four students. Pictures or index cards labeled with the names of various animals. The following pictures are used in this lesson: *camel (58), pig (71), frog (55), horse (64), owl (66), snake (69), turkey (67), turtle (61)* • transparencies of TM 14 on page 338 and TM 15 on page 339

**CURRICULUM APPLICATIONS**
<u>Science</u>. Students will recognize that there are many kinds of animals; identify living things as plants or animals; recognize that plants and animals reproduce their own kind; recognize that needs of different kinds of animals are similar, e.g., mother, father, food water, place to live; recognize the major physical differences between plants and animals; state what animals need to live and grow; recognize that needs of different kinds of animals are similar; recognize examples of common animals as being fish, birds, or mammals.

**TEACHING SUGGESTIONS**
• COOPERATIVE GROUP VERSION: Each group of four students will use one large piece of newsprint and pictures of animals, or index cards labeled with the names of various animals. Since sorting the pictures is more easily handled on a flat surface, groups of four to six students may

stand around a table as members of the group put the pictures in the correct categories. Draw a large branching diagram as a background for sorting. For a model branching diagram see the answer at the beginning of this lesson.

- Ask each group of students to decide on a category for sorting the animals. One student should label the categories on the diagram. Each member of the group should tape a picture in the correct part of the diagram. Display each diagram that sorted by a different characteristic and ask students to explain why they sorted the food this way.

- Usually students will sort the animals by general type: mammals, birds, reptiles, etc. Since there may be more than one characteristic by which one may classify these animals, students' suggestions for alternative ways of classifying the animals should be honored. If another system for sorting the animals is suggested, such as classifying them by habitat, means of locomotion, or body covering, encourage students to explain the sorting process for the other characteristic as well.

- Model and encourage students to express the following process for classifying animals:

  1. I will think about the important characteristics of the animals. (I will be sure to discuss their size, whether they are warm or cold blooded, where they live, how they reproduce, etc.)

  2. I will find a word that describes all of them.

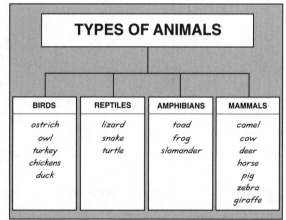

  3. I will identify another animal that belongs in the same group.

  4. I will check whether there are other terms that describe other important characteristics of the same animals.

**MODEL LESSON**

## LESSON

### Introduction
Q: We have named types of animals. The name for a type of animals is called the class in which that animal fits, such as birds.

### Explaining the Objective to Students
Q: In this lesson, we will sort animals into the classes in which they belong.

### Class Activity
- Display the following pictures:
  **H-16:** *camel, pig, frog, horse, ostrich, owl, snake, turkey, turtle*
  Q: What are some classes for the animals shown in these pictures?
   A: Usually students will suggest sorting the vehicles by general type: birds, reptiles, mammals.

- Write the categories on the board above the chalkboard tray and ask different students to place each of the pictures under the category in which it fits.

### Thinking About Thinking

Q: What will you pay attention to whenever you classify animals?

A: Body structure, whether the animal is warm- or cold-blooded, whether it has a backbone, whether it hatches eggs or gives live birth, where it lives, how it moves, what it eats.

### Personal Application

Q: When is it important to classify animals accurately?

A: To recognize that there are many kinds of animals. To recognize examples of common animals as being fish, birds, or mammals.

**LANGUAGE ARTS EXTENSION**

## LANGUAGE INTEGRATION ACTIVITIES

- Drawing: On large newsprint ask students to draw a class and members diagram. Students should decide the class of animals they want to draw (type of animals, what the animals eat, what food products they supply, where they live, baby animals, etc.) and write that label at the top of the diagram. Students will then draw an animal that belongs to that class in each of the four boxes. For a blank class-and-members graphic, see TM 23 on page 347.

- Story telling: Select a common story or fairy tale about animals, such as *Are You My Mother?* Ask students to retell the story about another member of that class of animals, such as a duck and a duckling, instead of a mother bird and a baby bird. What interesting animals might the cub meet? How is the revised story different from the original? (Since the duckling's home is in the water, he must get home another way.)

- Listening: Play Listening Tic Tac Toe with animals. For directions see page xxviii; for the playing grid photocopy TM 12 on page 336. Use animals that have been introduced in previous lessons or the animal list on page 343 (TM 19).

## FOLLOW-UP ACTIVITIES AT HOME

- Have parents name a kind of animal and ask their children to name animals of that kind. Example: cat (tiger, house cat, lion, etc.)

## PICTURE BOOK EXTENSION

- Language experiences with any of the following books extend this lesson and demonstrate the characteristics and needs of different animals. Additional books on topics in this lesson are described in the bibliography.

  Q: Are there any new ideas about (<u>fish, birds, or mammals</u>) that we learned from this story?

  Q: What ideas or details about (<u>fish, birds, or mammals</u>) did you get from the pictures?

  Q: Is this information true of most (<u>fish, birds, or mammals</u>)?

- After discussing each story, ask students to add new information about the

BEGINNING BUILDING THINKING SKILLS LESSON PLANS — VERBAL CLASSIFICATIONS

characteristics of the animals described in the story to the lists, posters, or graphic organizers that you may have used when discussing the pictures.

**SUPPLEMENTAL PICTURE BOOKS**
*Egg! A Dozen Eggs, What Will They Be?* A: J. Wood
*Hoot, Howl, Hiss,* Michelle Koch
*The Big Red Barn,* Margaret Wise Brown
*What Animal Am I? An Animal Guessing Game,* Iza Trapani

**EXERCISE H-17**

## SORTING INTO CLASSES—BUILDINGS

**ANSWERS H-17**
**H-17 Example:** See diagram below.

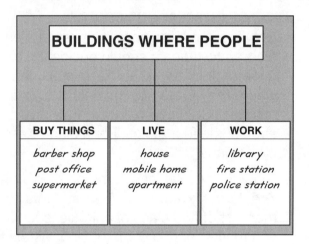

**LESSON PREPARATION**

**OBJECTIVE AND MATERIALS**
OBJECTIVE: Students will sort buildings into classes.
MATERIALS: One large piece of newsprint for each group of four students. Pictures of buildings or index cards labeled with the names of various buildings. The following pictures are used in this lesson: *library (40), barber shop (43), fire station (45), house (53), mobile home (44), police station (46), post office (51), supermarket (49)* • transparencies of TM 14 on page 338 and TM 15 on page 339

**CURRICULUM APPLICATIONS**
<u>Social Studies</u>: Identify how a family depends upon the products and services produced or housed in buildings; cite the role buildings play in providing community needs and services.

**TEACHING SUGGESTIONS**
• COOPERATIVE GROUP VERSION: Each group of four students will use one large piece of newsprint and pictures of buildings, or index cards labeled with the names of various buildings. Since sorting the pictures is more easily handled on a flat surface, groups of four to six students may stand around a table as members of the group put the pictures in the correct categories. Draw a large branching diagram as a background for

sorting. For a model branching diagram see the answers at the beginning of this lesson.

- Ask each group of students to agree on a category for sorting the buildings. One student should label the categories on the diagram. Each member of the group should tape a picture in the correct part of the diagram. Display each diagram that sorted by a different characteristic and ask students to explain why they sorted the food this way.

- Each group must agree on a categories for the first round of sorting. Usually students will sort the buildings by general type: residences, stores, public services buildings. Since there may be more than one characteristic by which one may classify buildings, students' suggestions for alternative ways of classifying them should be honored. If another system for sorting the buildings is suggested, such as size or location (rural, suburban, downtown), repeat the sorting process for the other characteristic as well.

- Model and encourage students to express the following process for classifying buildings:
    1. I will think about the important characteristics of the buildings. (I will be sure to discuss their size, purpose, construction, location and when it is used, etc.)
    2. I will find a word that describes all of them.
    3. I will identify another group of buildings.
    4. I will find a word that describes this group.
    5. I will look for other groups of buildings until I have classified all the buildings.

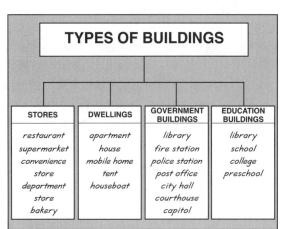

## MODEL LESSON

### LESSON

**Introduction**

Q: We have named types of buildings. The name for a type of building is called the class in which that building fits, such as residence.

**Explaining the Objective to Students**

Q: In this lesson, we will sort buildings into the classes in which they belong.

**Class Activity**

- Display the following pictures:
  **H-17:** *library, barber shop, fire station, house, mobile home, police station, post office, supermarket*
  Q: What are some classes for the buildings shown on these cards?

BEGINNING BUILDING THINKING SKILLS LESSON PLANS                    VERBAL CLASSIFICATIONS

> A: Usually students will suggest sorting the buildings by general type: residence, store, workplace.

- Write the categories over spaces on the chalkboard tray and ask different students to place each of the pictures under the category in which it fits.

### Thinking About Thinking

> Q: What did you think about to classify the buildings the way we did?
> A: The size of the building, its purpose, who lives or works there, color, design its materials, its usual location (rural, downtown, suburbs).

### Personal Application

> Q: When is it important to classify buildings skillfully?
> A: To give or understand directions. To understand why their construction, location, or use may be similar. To explain a particular building to someone that is unfamiliar with it, a friend, or a younger child.

## LANGUAGE ARTS EXTENSION

### LANGUAGE INTEGRATION ACTIVITIES

- Drawing: On large newsprint ask students to draw a branching diagram. Students should decide how to sort buildings (dwellings, stores, government buildings, churches, etc.) and write that label at the top of the diagram. Students will then label each category and write or draw a building that belongs to that class. For a blank branching diagram, see TM 23 on page 347.

- Story telling: Select a common story or fairy tale about buildings, such as *The Little House.* Ask students to retell the story about another member of that class of buildings, such as an apartment house. How is the revised story different from the original? (Although the little house could be moved to begin life again, an apartment building is too large to move. It might be renovated or used for another purpose.)

- Listening: Play Listening Tic Tac Toe with buildings. For directions see page xxviii; for the playing grid photocopy TM 12 on page 336. Use buildings that have been introduced in previous lessons or the building list on page 344 (TM 20).

### FOLLOW-UP ACTIVITIES AT HOME

- Have parents name a kind of building and ask their children to name buildings of that kind. Example: store (supermarket, dress shop, bookstore, etc.)

### PICTURE BOOK EXTENSION

- Language experiences with any of the following books extend this lesson and demonstrate how buildings differ across cultures. Additional books on topics in this lesson are described in the bibliography.

> Q: Are there any new ideas about (<u>buildings</u>) that we learned from this story?

> Q: What ideas or details about (<u>buildings</u>) did you get from the pictures?

> Q: Is this information true of most (<u>buildings</u>)?

304          © 2000 CRITICAL THINKING BOOKS & SOFTWARE • WWW.CRITICALTHINKING.COM • 800-458-4849

BEGINNING BUILDING THINKING SKILLS LESSON PLANS                    VERBAL CLASSIFICATIONS

- After discussing each story, ask students to add new information about the characteristics of the buildings described in the story to the lists, posters, or graphic organizers that you may have used when discussing the pictures.

## SUPPLEMENTAL PICTURE BOOKS

**Buildings**

*Children Just Like Me,* Barnabas Kindersley
*City Sounds,* Rebecca Emberley
*Dig, Drill, Dump, Fill,* Tana Hoban
*Round Buildings, Square Buildings, Buildings that Wiggle Like a Fish*,
    Phillip M. Isaacson
*Taxi: A Book of City Words,* Betsy and Guilio Maestro
*Town and Country,* Alice and Martin Provensen

BEGINNING BUILDING THINKING SKILLS LESSON PLANS                    DESCRIBING ANALOGIES

## Chapter 9

# DESCRIBING ANALOGIES

### EXERCISE I-1

## ANALOGIES REGARDING FOOD—SELECT

**ANSWERS I-1**
**I-1 Example:** apple
**I-1 Exercise:** milk
**I-1 Practice:** ham

### LESSON PREPARATION

**OBJECTIVE AND MATERIALS**

OBJECTIVE: Students will select the food that correctly completes an analogy.
MATERIALS: The following pictures are used in this lesson: *apple (92), bacon (77), bread (73), cabbage (90), corn (88), chicken (65), cows (72), eggs (78), ham (76), pig (71), horse (64), milk (79), onion (83), steak (81)*

**CURRICULUM APPLICATIONS**

Health: Recognize food that provides good nutrition for proper growth and functions of the body; identify a variety of foods.
Science: Identify the parts of a plant: root, stem, and leaf; identify living things as plants or animals; recognize the major physical differences between plants and animals; identify how plants are important to people; recognize examples of common animals as being fish, birds, or mammals.

**TEACHING SUGGESTIONS**

- Second-grade science texts offer the scientific definition of fruit which applies to foods commonly called vegetables (tomatoes, squash, cucumbers, pumpkins, etc.). Clarify students' use of the term fruit in appropriate contexts: "vegetable" in cookbooks and grocery stores, "fruit" in scientific discussion of parts of a plant.

- If the food is a plant product, describe the kind of plant that produces it — tree, vine, or small bush. Identify the part of the plant that we eat—seed, fruit, leaf, stem, or root. Describe the food's color, shape, and size. If it is an animal product, describe the kind of animal that produces it and how it is prepared. For any food products, students describe how food is cooked, seasoned, and served at specific meals. Provide pictures of ethnic foods from magazines or cookbooks or secure samples of ethnic foods using the type of food mentioned in the lesson. Assist students in describing and pronouncing the names of ethnic foods.

- For second-grade use, discuss basic nutrients the food contains: fats, protein, carbohydrates, vitamins, minerals, and water.

- Model and encourage students to express the following process for explaining an analogy:
  1. I will think how the first pair of pictures are related.
  2. I will look at the three possible answers and decide which one is related to picture three in the same way that the first pair is related.
  3. I will describe that relationship as an analogy.

© 2000 CRITICAL THINKING BOOKS & SOFTWARE • WWW.CRITICALTHINKING.COM • 800-458-4849          307

BEGINNING BUILDING THINKING SKILLS LESSON PLANS                    DESCRIBING ANALOGIES

**MODEL LESSON** | **LESSON**

### Introduction

Q: In other lessons, you selected pictures to compare and classify animals or food.

### Explaining the Objective to Students

Q: In this lesson, we will identify some connections between animals and food. When pairs of things are connected in the same way, that connection is called an analogy.

### Class activity

• Display the following pictures, grouping the first three together at some distance to the left of the other three pictures.
  **I-1 Example:** *chicken/ corn, horse, <u>apple</u>, bacon, onions*
  Q: How is the first pair of pictures related?
  A: A chicken eats corn.

Q: To make an analogy, we must now find a picture that shows the same relationship. Which food does a horse eat?
  A: A horse eats apples.

• Move the picture of the apple next to the picture of the horse.
  Q: How do we say this analogy?
  A: A chicken eats corn, like a horse eats apples.

Q: What clues helped you decide how the pairs of words were related?
  A: I looked for a connection between chicken and corn. A chicken eats corn, so I looked for a food that a horse eats—apples. A horse doesn't eat bacon or onions.

### Guided Practice

Q: Use the same process with the following items.
  **I-1 Exercise** *chicken/ eggs, cow, bacon, corn, <u>milk</u>*
  Q: How is the first pair of pictures related?
  A: A chicken makes eggs.

Q: To make an analogy we must now find a picture that shows the same relationship. What does a cow make?
  A: A cow makes milk.

• Move the picture of the milk next to the picture of the cow.
  Q: How do we say this analogy?
  A: A chicken makes eggs, like a cow makes milk.

Q: What clues helped you decide how the pairs of words were related?
  A: I looked for a connection between a chicken and eggs. A chicken produces eggs within its body, so I looked for the food that a cow produces within its body—milk. A cow does not produce corn or bacon. Another analogy could be: We eat the eggs that the chicken produces and drink the milk that the cow produces.

**308**          © 2000 CRITICAL THINKING BOOKS & SOFTWARE • WWW.CRITICALTHINKING.COM • 800-458-4849

BEGINNING BUILDING THINKING SKILLS LESSON PLANS                                           DESCRIBING ANALOGIES

**Optional Independent Practice**
- If students need additional practice, display these cards and ask students to describe the relationship among the items.
  **I-1 Practice** *steak/cow, ham, chicken, pig*
  Q: How are the first pair of pictures related?
    A: A steak is meat from a cow.

  Q: To make an analogy, we must now find a picture that shows the same relationship. Ham is meat from what animal?
    A: A pig

- Move the picture of the ham next to the picture of the pig.
  Q: How do we say this analogy?
    A: A steak is the meat of a cow, like a ham is the meat of a pig.

  Q: What clues helped you decide how the pairs of words were related?
    A: I looked for a connection between steak and cow. A steak is meat of a cow. Ham is the meat of which animal? Chicken meat is not ham, but ham is the meat of a pig.

**Thinking About Thinking**
  Q: What kind of relationships did you find among the words relating to food and animals?
    A: The food produced by an animal or the food eaten an animal.

**Personal Application**
  Q: When is it important to understand the relationship between food and plants or animals?
    A: To recognize which foods are animal products, having the nutrients that animal products provide, and which are plant products, having the nutrients that plant products provide; to be sure that our diet contains a variety of foods; to understand the source of our food.

**LANGUAGE ARTS EXTENSION**

**LANGUAGE INTEGRATION ACTIVITIES**
- Drawing: Ask students to draw two animals in similar situations (what they eat, where they live, with baby animals, etc.) Ask them to discuss with a partner each part of the picture that shows an analogy between the animals.

- Ask students to draw two similar foods (type of food, where we get it, how it is prepared, when we eat it, etc.) Ask students to discuss with a partner each part of the picture that shows an analogy between the foods.

- Story telling: Select a common story or fairy tale about animals, such as *Are You My Mother?* Ask students to retell the story as an analogy, such as a lion and a cub, instead of a mother bird and a baby bird. What interesting animals might the cub meet? How is the analogous story different from the original? (Since the cub's home is not in a nest, he must get home another way.)

© 2000 CRITICAL THINKING BOOKS & SOFTWARE • WWW.CRITICALTHINKING.COM • 800-458-4849          309

BEGINNING BUILDING THINKING SKILLS LESSON PLANS                                    DESCRIBING ANALOGIES

## FOLLOW-UP ACTIVITIES AT HOME
- Have parents identify two animals or pets that their children are familiar with and then ask the child to describe something about the two animals that is analogous (what they eat, what food products they supply, where they live, the names and appearance of baby animals, etc.). Parents should then describe the two animals as an analogy and ask the child to describe another analogy about the two animals. (A calf is a baby cow, like a duckling is a baby duck. A calf lives on a farm, like the duckling lives on a pond.)

- Have parents identify two foods that their children are familiar with and then ask the child to describe something about the foods that is analogous (where the food comes from, how it is prepared, holidays when the family eats it, etc.). Parents should then describe the two foods as an analogy (We broil a steak, like we boil or fry eggs) and ask the child to describe another analogy about the two foods. (We eat steak for dinner, like we eat eggs for breakfast.)

## PICTURE BOOK EXTENSION
- Language experiences with any of the following books extend this lesson and demonstrate how foods are obtained and prepared across cultures. Additional books on topics in this lesson are listed in the bibliography.
  Q: Are there any new ideas about (apples, horses, cows, milk, pigs, or ham) that we learned from this story?
  Q: What ideas or details about (apples, horses, cows, milk, pigs, or ham) did you get from the pictures?
  Q: Is this information true of most (apples, horses, cows, milk, pigs, or ham)?

- After discussing each story, ask students to add new information about the characteristics of the animals and foods described in the story to the lists, posters, or graphic organizers that you may have used when discussing the pictures.

## SUPPLEMENTAL PICTURE BOOKS
### FOOD

**Apples**
> *Apples*, Ann Burckhardt
> *Apples of Your Eye,* Allan Fowler
> *If It Weren't for Farmers,* Allan Fowler
> *Johnny Appleseed,* Steven Kellogg

**Cabbage**
> *Peter Rabbit,* Beatrix Potter
> *Vegetables, Vegetables!,* Fay Robinson

**Eggs**
> *Down the Road*, Alice Schertle
> *Green Eggs and Ham,* Dr. Seuss
> *If It Weren't for Farmers,* Allan Fowler

310                 © 2000 CRITICAL THINKING BOOKS & SOFTWARE • WWW.CRITICALTHINKING.COM • 800-458-4849

**BEGINNING BUILDING THINKING SKILLS LESSON PLANS**        **DESCRIBING ANALOGIES**

**Ham**

*Green Eggs and Ham,* Dr. Seuss
*Meat,* Elizabeth Clark

**Milk**

*Farm Animals,* Kay Jacobsen
*Milk,* Donald Carrick
*No Milk,* Jennifer A. Ericsson

**ANIMALS**

**Chicken**

*Chickens,* Ann Burckhardt
*Farm Animals,* K. Jacobsen
*If It Weren't For Farmers,* Rookie Read About Science series
*The Chicken or the Egg,* Rookie Read About Science series
*The Painter Who Loved Chickens,* Oliver Dunrea
*The Rooster's Gift,* Pam Conrad

**Cow**

*Cows,* Peter Brady
*Farm Animals,* K. Jacobsen
*If It Weren't for Farmers,* Allan Fowler
*Milk,* Donald Carrick
*No Milk,* Jennifer A. Ericsson
*Winter on the Farm,* Laura Ingalls Wilder

**Horses**

*Farm Animals,* E. Posell
*Horses,* K. Jacobsen
*Horses, Horses, Horses,* Allan Fowler
*Horses and Ponies,* Usborne/EDC
*The Black Stallion Picture Book,* Walter Farley
*The Mare on the Hill,* Thomas Locker

**Pig**

*Babe the Gallant Pig,* Dick King-Smith
*Farm Animals,* K. Jacobsen
*Pigs,* Ann Burckhardt
*Pigs,* Robert Munsch
*Smart, Clean Pigs,* Rookie Read About Science series

**EXERCISE I-2**

# ANALOGIES REGARDING COMMUNITY—SELECT

> **ANSWERS I-2**
> **I-2 Example:** Hospital
> **I-2 Exercise:** Restaurant
> **I-2 Practice:** Tractor

**LESSON PREPARATION**

**OBJECTIVE AND MATERIALS**

OBJECTIVE: Students will select a picture that correctly completes an analogy involving occupations, buildings or vehicles that they see commonly in the community.

© 2000 CRITICAL THINKING BOOKS & SOFTWARE • WWW.CRITICALTHINKING.COM • 800-458-4849     311

MATERIALS: The following pictures are used in this lesson: *barber (23), barber shop (43), construction worker (10), cook (11), farm (47), farmer (12), hospital (39), car (31), motorcycle (33), nurse (14), playground (52), police station (46), restaurant (48), school (54), supermarket (49), teacher (15), pickup truck (26), tractor (34)*

## CURRICULUM APPLICATIONS

Social Studies: Identify how a family depends upon the products and services produced or housed in buildings; cite the role buildings, vehicles, and occupations play in providing community needs and services.

## TEACHING SUGGESTIONS

• Model and encourage students to express the following process for explaining an analogy:

1. I will think how the first pair of pictures are related.

2. I will look at the three possible answers and decide which one is related to picture three in the same way that the first pair is related.

3. I will describe that relationship as an analogy.

**MODEL LESSON**

## LESSON

### Introduction

Q: In other lessons, you selected pictures to compare or classify jobs, buildings, and vehicles that we see in our community.

### Explaining the Objective to Students

Q: In this lesson, we will select pictures to show relationships between jobs, buildings, and vehicles.

### Class activity

• Display the following pictures, grouping the first pair at some distance to the left of the other four pictures.

**I-2 Example:** *teacher/school, nurse, hospital, playground, police station*
Q: How are the first pair of pictures related?
  A: A teacher works in a school.

Q: To make an analogy we must now find a picture that shows the same relationship. Where does a nurse work?
  A: A nurse works in a hospital.

• Move the picture of the hospital next to the picture of the nurse.
  Q: How do we say this?
  A: A teacher works in a school, like a nurse works in a hospital.
  Q: What clues helped you decide how the pairs of words were related?
  A: I looked for a connection between teacher and school. A teacher works in a school. So I looked for the place where a nurse works—a hospital. Nurses don't work on a playground or in a police station.

## Guided Practice

- Display the following pictures, grouping the first three at some distance to the left of the other three pictures.

  **I-2 Exercise:** *barber, barber shop, cook, farm, restaurant, supermarket*

  Q: How are the first pair of pictures related?

    A: A barber works in a barber shop.

  Q: Where does a cook work?

    A: A cook works in a restaurant.

- Move the picture of the restaurant next to the picture of the cook.

  Q: How do we say this analogy?

    A: A barber works in a barber shop, like a cook works in a restaurant.

  Q: What clues helped you decide how the pairs of words were related?

    A: I looked for a connection between barber and barber shop. A barber works in a barber shop. So I looked for the place where a cook works—a restaurant. Cooks don't usually work on a farm or in a supermarket.

## Optional Independent Practice

- If students need additional practice, display these cards and ask students to describe the relationship among the items.

  **I-2 Practice** *construction worker/truck, farmer, car, motorcycle, tractor*

  Q: How are the first pair of pictures related?

    A: A construction worker uses a truck to carry the material and equipment that he uses in his work.

  Q: Find a picture that shows the same relationship. What vehicle does a farmer use in his work?

    A: A farmer uses a tractor to haul the material and equipment that he uses in his work.

- Move the picture of the tractor next to the picture of the farmer.

  Q: How do we say this analogy?

    A: A construction worker uses a truck to haul the material and equipment that he uses in his work, like a farmer uses a tractor to haul the material and equipment that he uses in his work.

  Q: What clues helped you decide how the pairs of words were related?

    A: I looked for a connection between construction worker and truck. A construction worker uses a truck to carry what he needs in his work. So I looked for the vehicle the farmer uses in his work—a tractor. Farmers may have cars or motorcycles but don't use them to plow fields or pull heavy equipment.

## Thinking About Thinking

Q: What kinds of relationships did you find in the analogies about jobs, buildings, and vehicles?

  A: Vehicles or buildings that are used by various workers, vehicles that take people to certain buildings.

**Personal Application**

Q: When is it important to understand which buildings or vehicles people use in their work?

   A: To identify jobs and job locations correctly; to find something that you need or someone whose help you need; to follow directions for errands.

## LANGUAGE INTEGRATION ACTIVITIES

**LANGUAGE ARTS EXTENSION**

- Drawing: Ask students to draw two people at different jobs. Ask them to discuss with a partner each part of the picture that shows an analogy between the jobs (what they do, vehicles they use and whether the vehicle travels on land, sea, or in the air, where they work, the clothes they wear, the equipment they use, etc.).

- Story telling: Select a common story or fairy tale about jobs or vehicles, such as *Little Toot.* Ask students to retell the story as an analogy, such as a tractor, instead of a boat. How is the analogous story different from the original? (The little tractor must perform his act of courage and determination on land.)

- Listening: Play Listening Tic Tac Toe with occupations. For directions see page xxviii; for the playing grid, photocopy TM 12 on page 336. Describe an occupation only in terms of a vehicle or building that is used in connection with the job. For example, when the teacher describes a hospital or ambulance, students may cover the words for "doctor" or "nurse."

## FOLLOW-UP ACTIVITY AT HOME

- Have parents identify two jobs that their children see regularly and have the child describe something about the two jobs that is analogous (what they do, vehicles they use, where they work, the clothes they wear, the equipment they use, etc.). Parents should then describe the two jobs as an analogy. (A fire truck is parked in a fire station when it isn't used, like a tractor is parked in a barn when it is not used) and ask the child to describe another analogy about the two jobs (A firefighter drives a fire truck, like a farmer drives a tractor).

## PICTURE BOOK EXTENSION

- Language experiences with any of the following books extend this lesson and demonstrate how jobs are performed across cultures. Additional books on topics in this lesson are listed in the bibliography.

  Q: Are there any new ideas about (<u>nurses, hospitals, cooks, restaurants, farmers, or tractors</u>) that we learned from this story?

  Q: What ideas or details about (<u>nurses, hospitals, cooks, restaurants, farmers, or tractors</u>) did you get from the pictures?

  Q: Is this information true of most (<u>nurses, hospitals, cooks, restaurants, farmers, or tractors</u>)?

- After discussing each story, ask students to add new information about the characteristics of the jobs, vehicles, or buildings described in the story to

BEGINNING BUILDING THINKING SKILLS LESSON PLANS                    DESCRIBING ANALOGIES

the lists, posters, or graphic organizers that you may have used when discussing the pictures.

## SUPPLEMENTAL PICTURE BOOKS

**Farmer**
> *Family Farm,* Thomas Locker
> *Farm Morning,* David McPhail
> *If You Are Not From the Prairie...,* David Bouchard

**Nurse**
> *Nurses,* Robert James

**Hospital**
> *Getting Ready for a Career in Health Care,* Bill Lund
> *Going to the Hospital: Mister Rogers Neighborhood Series,* Fred Rogers

**Tractors**
> *Katy and the Big Snow,* Virginia Lee Burton
> *Tractors,* Gil Chandler
> *Tractors,* Peter Brady

**EXERCISE I-3**

# ANALOGIES REGARDING FOOD—EXPLAIN

---
**ANSWERS I-3**

**I-3 Example:** Rice and corn are both grains, like cabbage and lettuce are both green leafy vegetables. We eat rice and corn as cooked vegetables or as cereal. We eat cabbage and lettuce uncooked as a salad.

**I-3 Exercise:** Bacon is a pig's meat that people cook and eat, just as steak is a cow's meat that people cook and eat.

**I-3 Practice:** We eat potatoes and carrots, the parts of a plant that grow underground, like we eat beans and peas, the seeds that grow in pods on the stems of plants.

---

**LESSON PREPARATION**

## OBJECTIVE AND MATERIALS

OBJECTIVE: Students will explain an analogy involving food.
MATERIALS: The following pictures are used in this lesson: *bacon (77), green beans (84), cabbage (90), carrots (82), corn (88), cows (72), lettuce (91), peas (85), pig (71), potato (86), rice (89), steak (81)*

## CURRICULUM APPLICATIONS

<u>Health</u>: Recognize food that provides good nutrition for proper growth and functions of the body; identify a variety of foods.
<u>Science</u>: Identify the parts of a plant: root, stem, and leaf; identify living things as plants or animals; recognize the major physical differences between plants and animals; identify how plants are important to people; recognize examples of common animals as being fish, birds, or mammals.

## TEACHING SUGGESTIONS

- Second-grade science texts offer the scientific definition of fruit which applies to foods commonly called vegetables (tomatoes, squash, cucumbers, pumpkins, etc.). Clarify students' use of the term *fruit* in appropriate

© 2000 CRITICAL THINKING BOOKS & SOFTWARE • WWW.CRITICALTHINKING.COM • 800-458-4849      315

BEGINNING BUILDING THINKING SKILLS LESSON PLANS                    DESCRIBING ANALOGIES

contexts: "vegetable" in cookbooks and grocery stores, "fruit" in scientific discussion of parts of a plant.

• If the food is a plant product, describe the kind of plant that produces it — tree, vine, or small bush. Identify the part of the plant that we eat—seed, fruit, leaf, stem, or root. Describe the food's color shape and size. If it is an animal product, describe the kind of animal that produces it and how it is prepared.

• For plant or animal food products, students describe how food is cooked, seasoned, and served at specific meals. This discussion is a rich opportunity to explore how different ethnic groups contribute to the richness of our diet by preparing foods differently.

• For second-grade use, discuss basic nutrients the food contains: fats, protein, carbohydrates, vitamins, minerals and water.

• Model and encourage students to express the following process for explaining an analogy:

  1. I will think how the first pair of pictures are related.

  2. I will look at the three possible answers and decide which one is related to picture three in the same way that the first pair is related.

  3. I will describe that relationship as an analogy.

**MODEL LESSON** | **LESSON**

**Introduction**

    Q: In other lessons you described animals and food.

**Explaining the Objective to Students**

    Q: In this lesson, we will explain relationships between pairs of foods or animals.

**Class activity**

• Display the following pictures, grouping them in pairs with some distance between each pair.

    **I-3 Example:** *rice/corn, cabbage/lettuce*

    Q: How are the first pair of pictures related?

      A: Rice and corn are both grains that we eat. They must be cooked to be eaten and can be made into breakfast cereals.

    Q: How are the second pair of pictures related in a similar way?

      A: Cabbage and lettuce are both green plants that we eat. We can eat their leaves uncooked in salads.

    Q: What clues helped you decide how the pairs of words were related?

      A: I looked for a connection between rice and corn. They are similar parts of a plant. Rice and corn are both the seeds of plants that are eaten. I then thought about the part of the cabbage and lettuce plants that we eat. We can eat the leaves in salads.

    Q: How do we say this analogy?

      A: Rice and corn are both grains, like cabbage and lettuce are both

316                 © 2000 CRITICAL THINKING BOOKS & SOFTWARE • WWW.CRITICALTHINKING.COM • 800-458-4849

**BEGINNING BUILDING THINKING SKILLS LESSON PLANS**                    **DESCRIBING ANALOGIES**

green leafy vegetables. We eat rice and corn as vegetables or as cereal. We eat cabbage and lettuce as a salad.

### Guided Practice

- Display the following pictures, grouping them in pairs with some distance between each pair.

  **I-3 Exercise:** *bacon/pig, steak/cow*

  Q: How are the first pair of pictures related?
    A: Bacon is a kind of pig's meat prepared by a butcher and is cooked for people's meals.

  Q: How are the second pair of pictures related in a similar way?
    A: Steak is a kind of cow's meat that is prepared by a butcher and is cooked for people's meals.

  Q: What clues helped you decide how the pairs of words were related?
    A: I looked for a connection between a bacon and pig. Bacon is a pig's meat. I then checked to be sure that steak is a cow's meat.

  Q: How do we say this?
    A: Bacon is a pig's meat that people cook and eat, just as steak is a cow's meat that people cook and eat.

### Optional Independent Practice

- If students need additional practice, select the pictures:

  **I-3 Practice:** *potatoes/carrots, beans/peas*

  Q: How are the first pair of pictures related?
    A: A potato and a carrot are the underground root parts of a plant.

  Q: How are the second pair of pictures related in a similar way?
    A: Beans and peas are both seeds of plants, and they grow in pods on the stems of plants.

  Q: What clues helped you decide how the pairs of words were related?
    A: I looked for a connection between a potato and a carrot. A potato and a carrot are the underground root parts of a plant. I checked to be sure that beans and peas are similar parts of plants, the seeds of a plant that grow in pods on the stems of plants.

  Q: How do we say this analogy?
    A: We eat potatoes and carrots, the parts of a plant that grow underground, like we eat beans and peas, the seeds that grow in pods on the stems of plants.

### Thinking About Thinking

  Q: What kind of characteristics did you discuss to describe food?
    A: Whether the food is a plant or animal product. If it is a plant, describe what kind—tree, vine, or small bush—and what part we eat—seed, fruit, leaf, stem, or root. If it is an animal, what kind of animal produces it or is butchered for it, and how it is prepared.

© 2000 CRITICAL THINKING BOOKS & SOFTWARE • WWW.CRITICALTHINKING.COM • 800-458-4849            317

BEGINNING BUILDING THINKING SKILLS LESSON PLANS

DESCRIBING ANALOGIES

**LANGUAGE ARTS EXTENSION**

## LANGUAGE INTEGRATION ACTIVITIES

• Drawing: Ask students to draw two animals in similar situations. Ask them to discuss with a partner each part of the picture that shows an analogy between the animals (what they eat, where they live, with baby animals, etc.)

• Ask students to draw two similar foods (type of food, where we get it, how it is prepared, when we eat it, etc.) Ask students to discuss with a partner each part of the picture that shows an analogy between the foods.

• Story telling: Select a common story or fairy tale about food, such as *Green Eggs and Ham.* Ask students to retell the story as an analogy, such as peas and carrots, instead of eggs and ham. What colors might make them unappealing? How is the analogous story different from the original?

## FOLLOW-UP ACTIVITIES AT HOME

• Ask parents to identify two animals or pets that their children are familiar with and describe something about the two animals that is analogous (what they eat, what food products they supply, where they live, with baby animals, etc.) Parents should then describe the two animals as an analogy and ask the child to describe another analogy about the two animals. (A calf is a baby cow, like a duckling is a baby duck. A calf lives on a farm, like the duckling lives on a pond.)

• Ask parents to identify two foods that their children are familiar with and describe something about the foods that is analogous (where the food comes from, how it is prepared, holidays when the family eats it, etc.). Parents should then describe the two foods as an analogy (We broil a steak, like we boil or fry eggs) and ask the child to describe another analogy about the two foods (We eat steak for dinner, like we eat eggs for breakfast.)

## PICTURE BOOK EXTENSION

• Language experiences with any of the following books extend this lesson and demonstrate how various foods are obtained and prepared across cultures. Additional books on topics in this lesson are listed in the bibliography.

Q: Are there any new ideas about (<u>cabbage, lettuce, beans, peas, cows, or steaks</u>) that we learned from this story?

Q: What ideas or details about (<u>cabbage, lettuce, beans, peas, cows, or steaks</u>) did you get from the pictures?

Q: Is this information true of most (<u>cabbage, lettuce, beans, peas, cows, or steaks</u>)?

• After discussing each story, ask students to add new information about the characteristics of the foods or animals described in the story to the lists, posters, or graphic organizers that you may have used when discussing the pictures.

318    © 2000 CRITICAL THINKING BOOKS & SOFTWARE • WWW.CRITICALTHINKING.COM • 800-458-4849

BEGINNING BUILDING THINKING SKILLS LESSON PLANS                    DESCRIBING ANALOGIES

## SUPPLEMENTAL PICTURE BOOKS

### FOOD

**Beans**

*Growing Colors,* Bruce McMillan
*Jack and the Beanstalk,* Paul Galdone
*Vegetables, Vegetables!,* Fay Robinson

**Cabbage or Lettuce**

*Peter Rabbit,* Beatrix Potter
*Vegetables, Vegetables!,* Fay Robinson

**Peas**

*Peas,* Nicholas Heller
*Vegetables, Vegetables!,* Fay Robinson

**Steak**

*Meat,* Elizabeth Clark

### ANIMALS

**Cow**

*Cows,* Peter Brady
*Farm Animals,* K. Jacobsen
*If It Weren't for Farmers,* Allan Fowler
*Milk,* Donald Carrick
*No Milk,* Jennifer A. Ericsson
*Winter on the Farm,* Laura Ingalls Wilder

**EXERCISE I-4**

# ANALOGIES REGARDING COMMUNITY—EXPLAIN

---

**ANSWERS I-4**

**I-4 Example:** An airplane is driven by a pilot, like a police car is driven by a police officer.

**I-4 Exercise** A grocer sells people clean, safe food at a supermarket. A farmer grows and sells clean, safe food on his or her farm.

**I-4 Practice** A school bus takes people to school to learn what they need, like an ambulance takes people to the hospital to get what they need to feel better.

---

**LESSON PREPARATION**

### OBJECTIVE AND MATERIALS

OBJECTIVE: Students will explain an analogy involving occupations, buildings or vehicles that they see commonly in the community.

MATERIALS: The following pictures are used in this lesson: *airplane (27), ambulance (24), farm (47), farmer (12), grocer (22), hospital (39), pilot (17), police car (25), police officer (18), school (54), school bus (32), supermarket (49).*

### CURRICULUM APPLICATIONS

Social Studies: Define consumer as a user of goods and services; identify how a family depends upon products and services to meet its needs; cite examples of community needs and services; identify jobs within the community and understand how community helpers are an example of interdependence.

© 2000 CRITICAL THINKING BOOKS & SOFTWARE • WWW.CRITICALTHINKING.COM • 800-458-4849          319

BEGINNING BUILDING THINKING SKILLS LESSON PLANS                    DESCRIBING ANALOGIES

## TEACHING SUGGESTIONS
- Model and encourage students to express the following process for explaining an analogy:
  1. I will think how the first pair of pictures are related.
  2. I will look at the three possible answers and decide which one is related to picture three in the same way that the first pair is related.
  3. I will describe that relationship as an analogy.

**MODEL LESSON**

## LESSON

### Introduction

Q: In other lessons you described jobs, buildings, and vehicles that we see in our community.

### Explaining the Objective to Students

Q: In this lesson, we will explain relationships between jobs, buildings, and vehicles.

### Class Activity
- Display the following pictures, grouping them in pairs with some distance between each pair.

**I-4 Example:** *airplane/pilot, police car/police officer*

Q: How are the first pair of pictures related?
 A: An airplane is flown (driven) by a pilot.

Q: How are the second pair of pictures related in a similar way?
 A: A police car is driven by a police officer.

Q: What clues helped you decide how the pairs of words were connected?
 A: I looked for a connection between an airplane and a pilot—a vehicle and who drives it. I then checked to be sure that the police car is driven by a police officer.

Q: How do we say this analogy?
 A: An airplane is driven by a pilot, like a police car is driven by a police officer.

### Guided practice
- Display the following pictures, grouping them in pairs with some distance between each pair.

**I-4 Exercise:** *grocer/supermarket, farmer/farm*

Q: How are the first pair of pictures related?
 A: A grocer works in a supermarket where people buy food. He or she makes sure that the food is clean and safe for people to eat.

Q: How are the second pair of pictures related in a similar way?
 A: A farmer works on a farm where he grows and sells food. He or she makes sure that the food is clean and safe for people to eat.

Q: What clues helped you decide how the pairs of words were related?
 A: I looked for a connection between a grocer and a supermarket— where a grocer sells people clean, safe food. I then checked to be

320          © 2000 CRITICAL THINKING BOOKS & SOFTWARE • WWW.CRITICALTHINKING.COM • 800-458-4849

**BEGINNING BUILDING THINKING SKILLS LESSON PLANS**                    **DESCRIBING ANALOGIES**

sure that a farm is a place where a farmer grows and sells clean, safe food to people.

Q: How do we say this analogy?
  A: A grocer sells people clean, safe food at a supermarket, like a farmer grows and sells clean, safe food on his or her farm.

### Independent Practice

• Display the following pictures grouping them in pairs with some distance between each pair.
  **I-4 Practice:** *school bus, school/ambulance, hospital*

Q: How are the first pair of pictures related?
  A: A school bus carries students to school.

Q: How are the second pair of pictures related in a similar way?
  A: An ambulance carries sick people to the hospital.

Q: What clues helped you decide how the pairs of words were related?
  A: I looked for a connection between a school bus and a school—where a bus takes people to learn what they need there. I then checked to be sure that a hospital is a place where an ambulance takes people get what they need to feel better.

Q: How do we say this analogy?
  A: A school bus takes people to school to learn what they need, like an ambulance takes people to the hospital to get what they need to feel better.

• If students need additional practice, display the following pictures grouping them in pairs with some distance between each pair.

### Thinking About Thinking

Q: What kinds of relationships did you find in the analogies about jobs, buildings, and vehicles?
  A: Vehicles or buildings are used by various workers, which vehicles take people to certain buildings.

### Personal Application

Q: When is it important to understand which buildings or vehicles people use in their work?
  A: To identify jobs and locations correctly; to find something you need or someone whose help you need; to follow directions for errands.

**LANGUAGE ARTS EXTENSION**

### LANGUAGE INTEGRATION ACTIVITIES

• Drawing: Ask students to draw two people at different jobs. Ask them to discuss with a partner each part of the picture that shows an analogy between the jobs (what they do, vehicles they use, where they work, the clothes they wear, the equipment they use, etc.).

• Story telling: Select a common story or fairy tale about jobs or vehicles, such as *Little Toot.* Ask students to retell the story as an analogy, such as

© 2000 CRITICAL THINKING BOOKS & SOFTWARE • WWW.CRITICALTHINKING.COM • 800-458-4849          321

a tractor, instead of a boat. How is the analogous story different from the original? (The little tractor must perform his act of courage and determination on land.)

## FOLLOW-UP ACTIVITIES AT HOME

- Have parents identify two jobs that their children see regularly and ask the child to describe something about the two jobs that is analogous (what they do, vehicles they use, where they work, the clothes they wear, the equipment they use, etc.). Parents should then describe the two jobs as an analogy (A firefighter sometimes works outside when putting out fires, like a farmer sometimes works outside when planting and tending to crops) and ask the child to describe another analogy about the two animals (A firefighter drives a fire truck, like a farmer drives a tractor).

## PICTURE BOOK EXTENSION

- Language experiences with any of the following books extend this lesson and demonstrate how various jobs and vehicles meet individual, family, and community needs. Additional books on topics in this lesson are listed in the bibliography.

  Q: Are there any new ideas about (teachers, schools, farmers, farms, ambulances, hospitals, police cars, and police officers) that we learned from this story?

  Q: What ideas or details about (teachers, schools, farmers, farms, ambulances, hospitals, police cars, and police officers) did you get from the pictures?

  Q: Is this information true of most (teachers, schools, farmers, farms, ambulances, hospitals, police cars, and police officers)?

- After discussing each story, ask students to add new information about the characteristics of the jobs and vehicles described in the story to the lists, posters, or graphic organizers that you may have used when discussing the pictures.

## SUPPLEMENTAL PICTURE BOOKS

### VEHICLES

#### Airplane

*Airplanes,* Dorling Kindersley
*Airport,* Byron Barton
*Bored—Nothing to Do,* Peter Spier

#### Ambulance

*Emergency Vehicles,* Dayna Wolhart
*Emergency,* Snap Shot series

#### Police Car

*Emergency Vehicles,* Dayna Wolhart
*Police Patrol,* Katherine Winkleman

#### School Bus

*The Magic School Bus at the Waterworks,* Joanna Cole
*School Bus,* Donald Crews
*This is the Way We Go to School,* Edith Baer

**BEGINNING BUILDING THINKING SKILLS LESSON PLANS**  **DESCRIBING ANALOGIES**

## OCCUPATIONS
### Farmer
*Family Farm,* Thomas Locker
*Farm Morning,* David McPhail
*Farming Today Yesterday's Way,* Cheryl Walsh Bellville
*If It Weren't for Farmers,* Allan Fowler
*If You Are Not From the Prairie...,* David Bouchard

### Pilot
*I Am A Pilot,* Cynthia Benjamin
*Nobody Owns the Sky,* Reeve Lindbergh

### Police Officer
*Officer Buckle and Gloria,* Peggy Rathman Calde

### Teacher
*Lilly's Purple Purse,* Kevin Hanks
*Miss Malarkey Doesn't Live in Room 101,* Judy Fincher
*My Teacher is My Best Friend,* P. K. Hallinan
*My Great Aunt Arizona,* Gloria Houston

## PLACES
### Farm
*All the Places to Love,* Patricia MacLachlan
*Farm Animals,* E. Posell
*If It Weren't for Farmers,* Allan Fowler.
*If You Are Not From the Prairie,* David Bouchard
*Winter on the Farm,* Laura Ingalls Wilder

### School
*My Teacher's Secret Life,* Stephen Krensky
*School,* Emily Arnold McCully

### Hospital
*Going to the Hospital: Mister Rogers Neighborhood Series,* Fred Rogers

© 2000 CRITICAL THINKING BOOKS & SOFTWARE • WWW.CRITICALTHINKING.COM • 800-458-4849  323

BEGINNING BUILDING THINKING SKILLS LESSON PLANS

TRANSPARENCY MASTERS

# TRANSPARENCY MASTER 1—Attribute Block Pattern

**DIRECTIONS:** If you do not have attribute blocks, you will need three sheets like this one. One sheet should be colored red, one yellow, and one blue. After you color the shapes, cut them apart. Put them in an envelope and write your name on it.

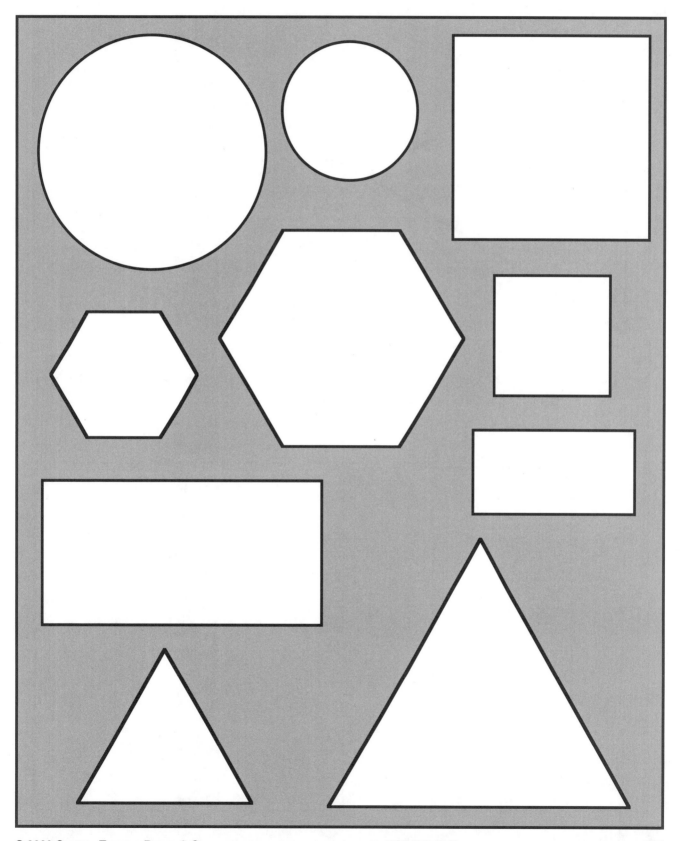

© 2000 CRITICAL THINKING BOOKS & SOFTWARE • WWW.CRITICALTHINKING.COM • 800-458-4849

BEGINNING BUILDING THINKING SKILLS LESSON PLANS                    TRANSPARENCY MASTERS

# TRANSPARENCY MASTER 2—Shape Cards 1

**DIRECTIONS:** Cut out and fold. Use as flash cards.

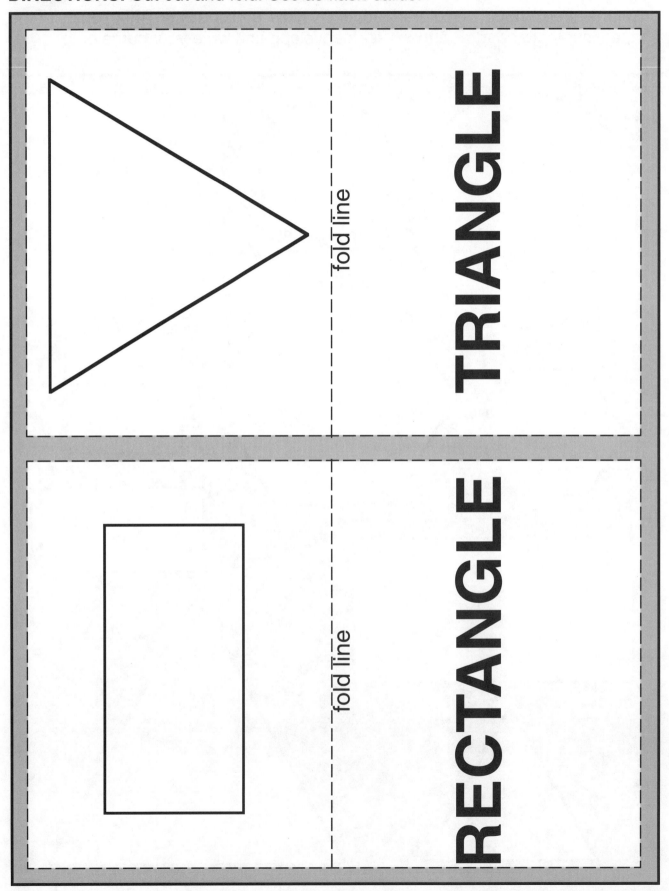

BEGINNING BUILDING THINKING SKILLS LESSON PLANS　　　TRANSPARENCY MASTERS

# TRANSPARENCY MASTER 3—Shape Cards 2

**DIRECTIONS:** Cut out and fold. Use as flash cards.

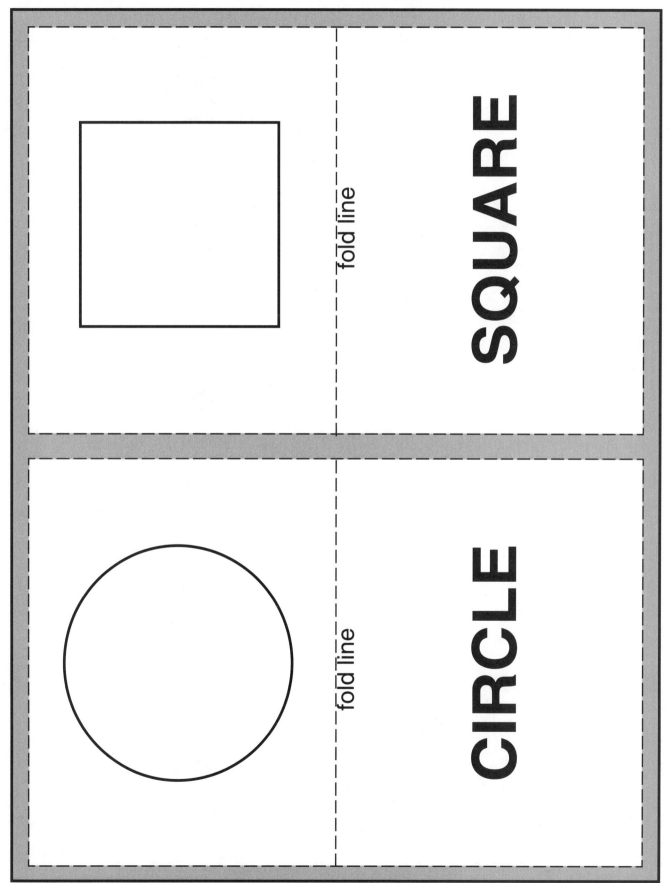

© 2000 CRITICAL THINKING BOOKS & SOFTWARE • WWW.CRITICALTHINKING.COM • 800-458-4849

BEGINNING BUILDING THINKING SKILLS LESSON PLANS        TRANSPARENCY MASTERS

# TRANSPARENCY MASTER 4—Shape Cards 3

**DIRECTIONS:** Cut out and fold. Use as flash cards.

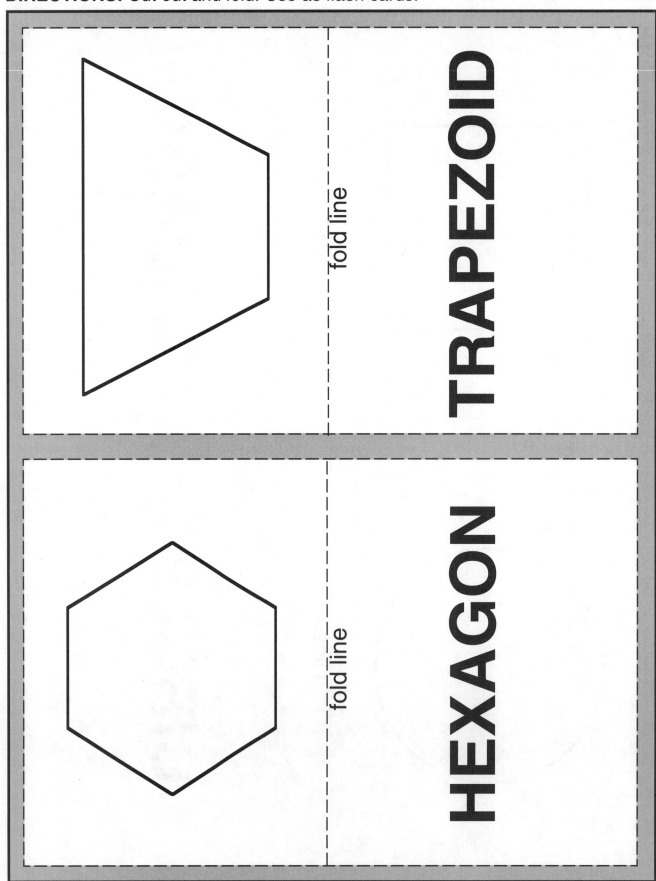

328        © 2000 CRITICAL THINKING BOOKS & SOFTWARE • WWW.CRITICALTHINKING.COM • 800-458-4849

BEGINNING BUILDING THINKING SKILLS LESSON PLANS    TRANSPARENCY MASTERS

# TRANSPARENCY MASTER 5—Matching Shapes

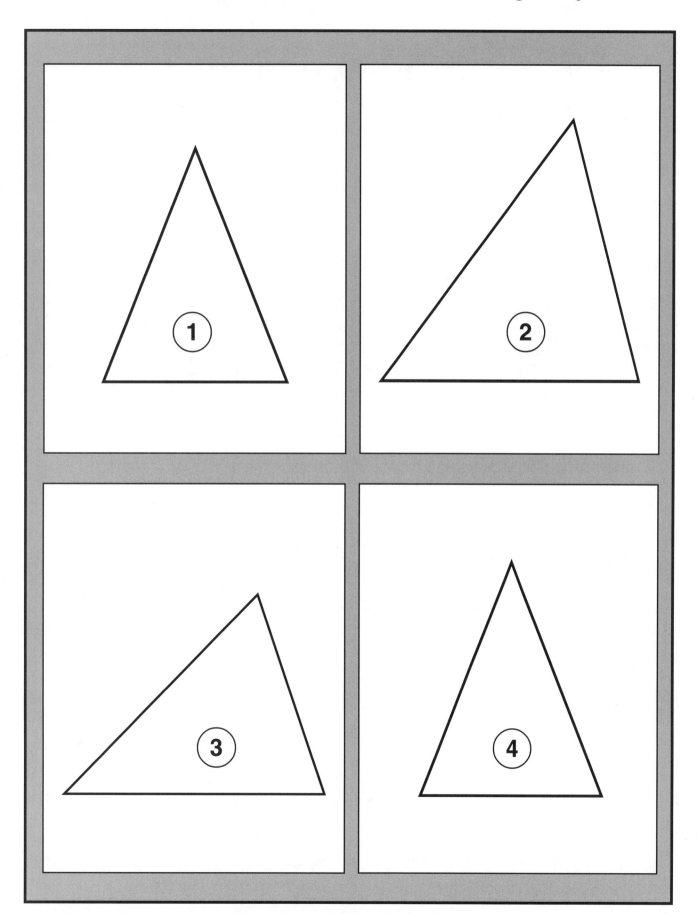

BEGINNING BUILDING THINKING SKILLS LESSON PLANS    TRANSPARENCY MASTERS

© 2000 CRITICAL THINKING BOOKS & SOFTWARE • WWW.CRITICALTHINKING.COM • 800-458-4849    329

BEGINNING BUILDING THINKING SKILLS LESSON PLANS — TRANSPARENCY MASTERS

# TRANSPARENCY MASTER 6—Comparing & Contrasting Shapes

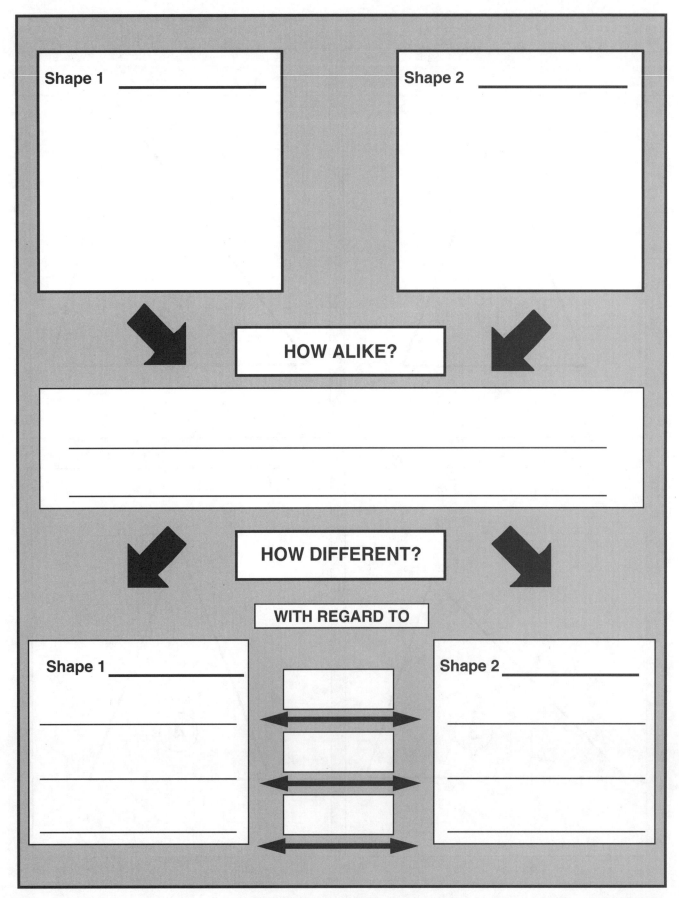

**TRANSPARENCY MASTER 7—Adding or Subtracting Detail**

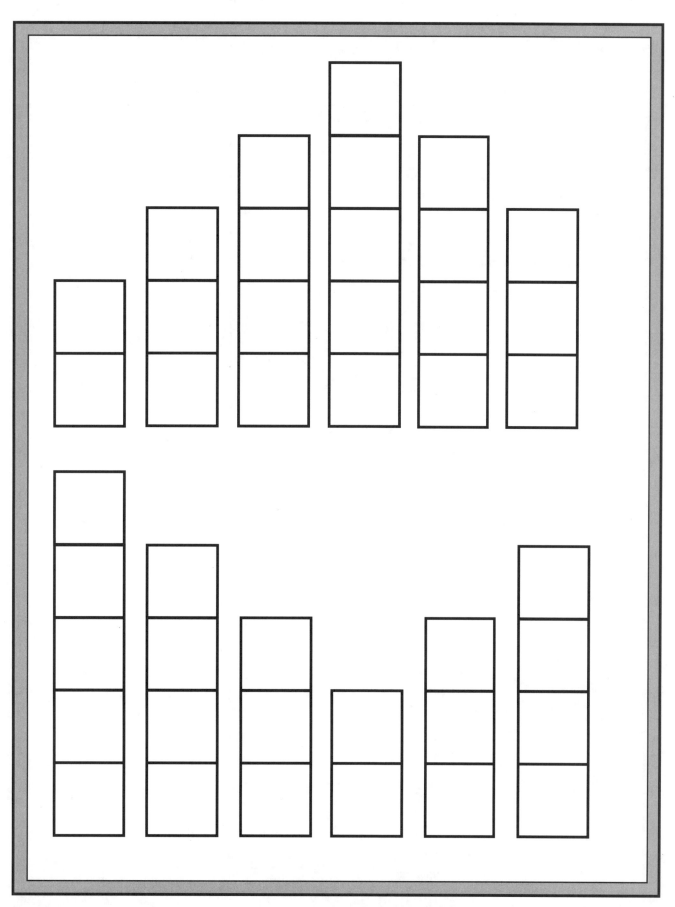

## TRANSPARENCY MASTER 8—Family Tree

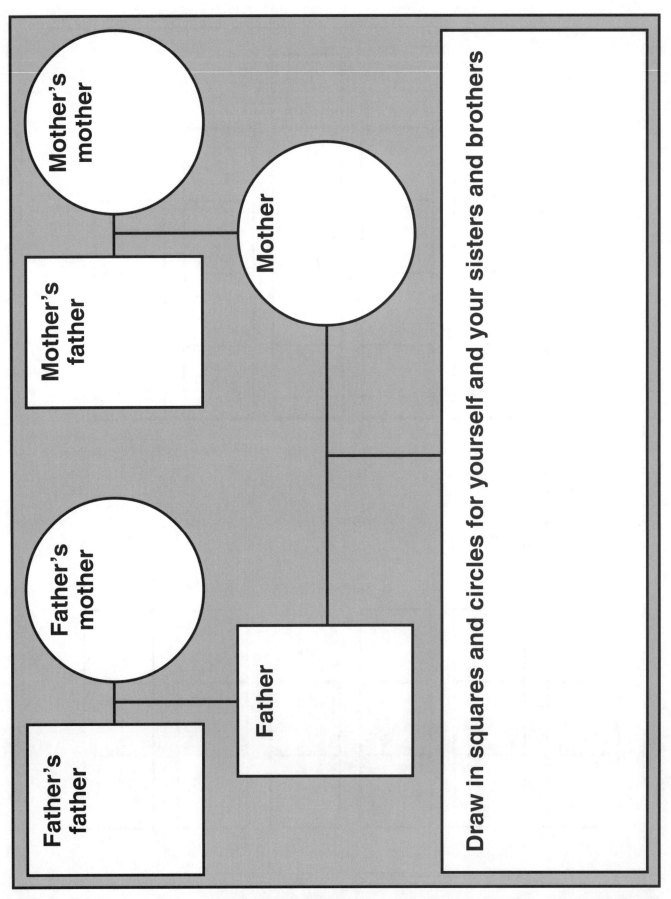

BEGINNING BUILDING THINKING SKILLS LESSON PLANS　　　TRANSPARENCY MASTERS

# TRANSPARENCY MASTER 9—Web Diagram

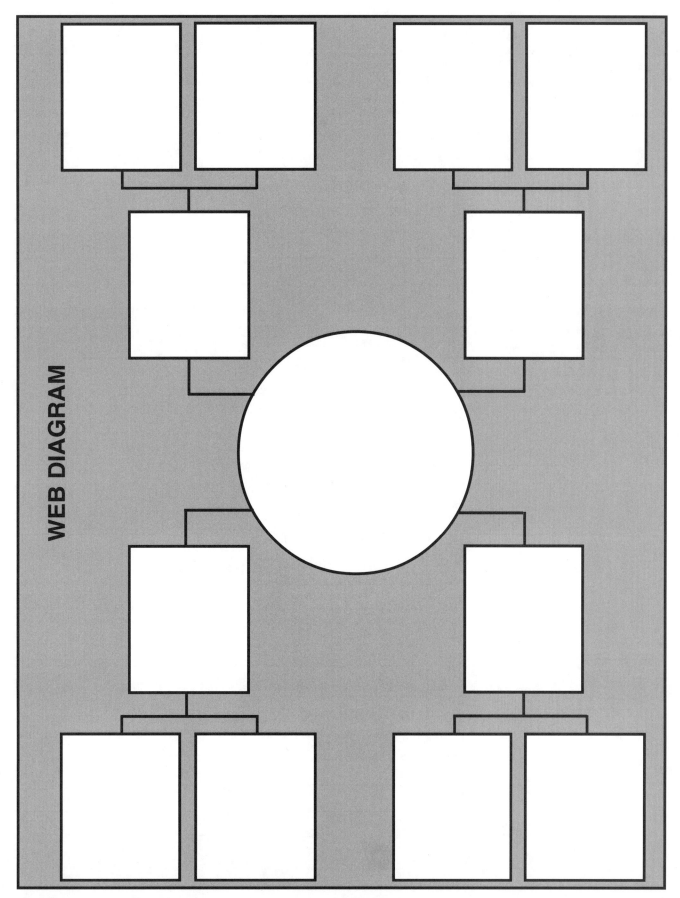

BEGINNING BUILDING THINKING SKILLS LESSON PLANS　　　　TRANSPARENCY MASTERS

# TRANSPARENCY MASTER 10

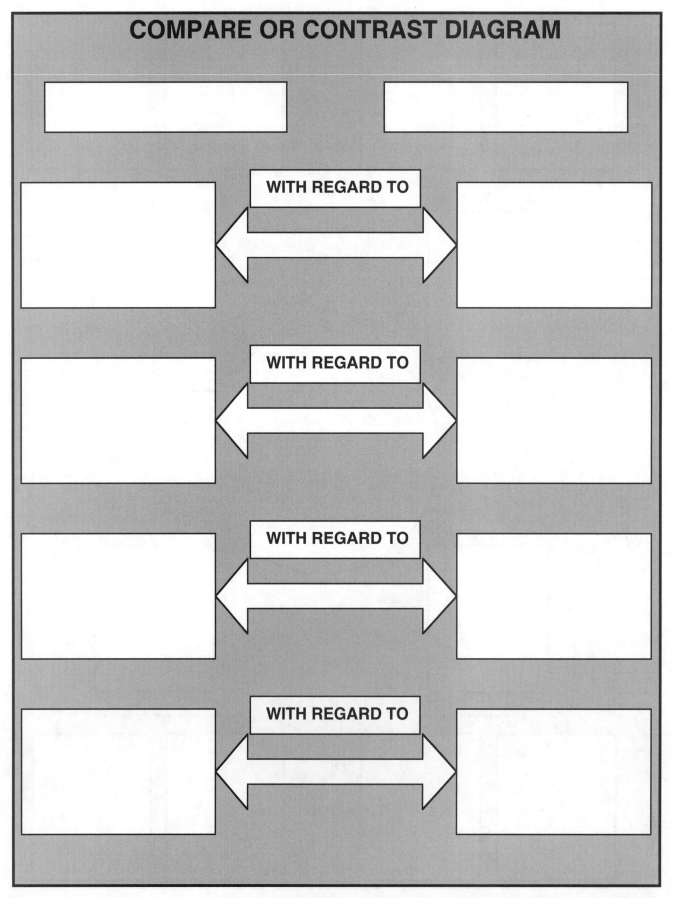

334　　© 2000 CRITICAL THINKING BOOKS & SOFTWARE • WWW.CRITICALTHINKING.COM • 800-458-4849

BEGINNING BUILDING THINKING SKILLS LESSON PLANS — TRANSPARENCY MASTERS

# TRANSPARENCY MASTER 11

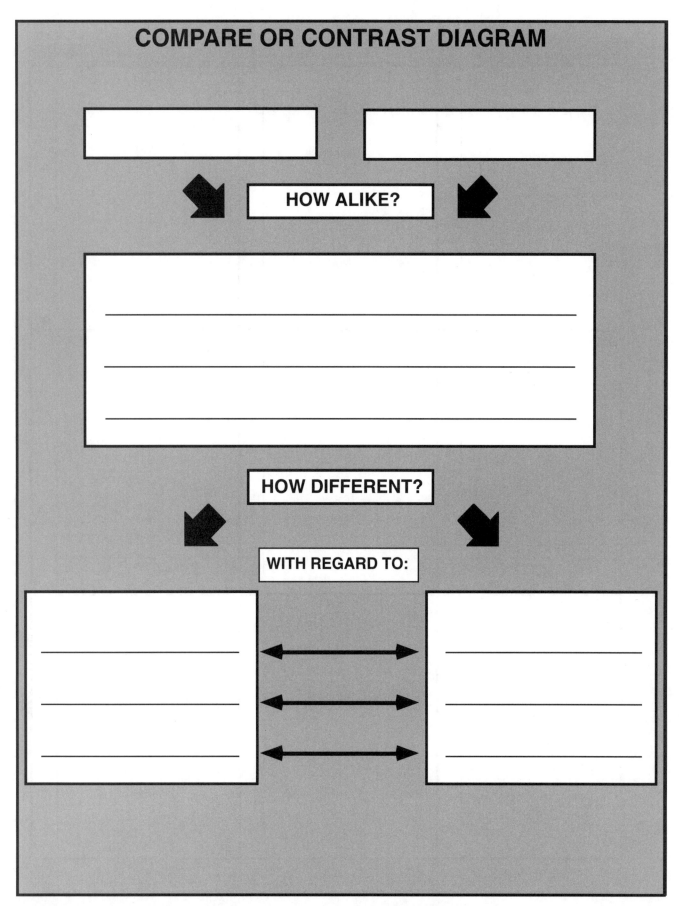

BEGINNING BUILDING THINKING SKILLS LESSON PLANS                    TRANSPARENCY MASTERS

# TRANSPARENCY MASTER 12

LISTENING TIC TAC TOE

336                 © 2000 CRITICAL THINKING BOOKS & SOFTWARE • WWW.CRITICALTHINKING.COM • 800-458-4849

BEGINNING BUILDING THINKING SKILLS LESSON PLANS — TRANSPARENCY MASTERS

# TRANSPARENCY MASTER 13—2 Branching Diagram

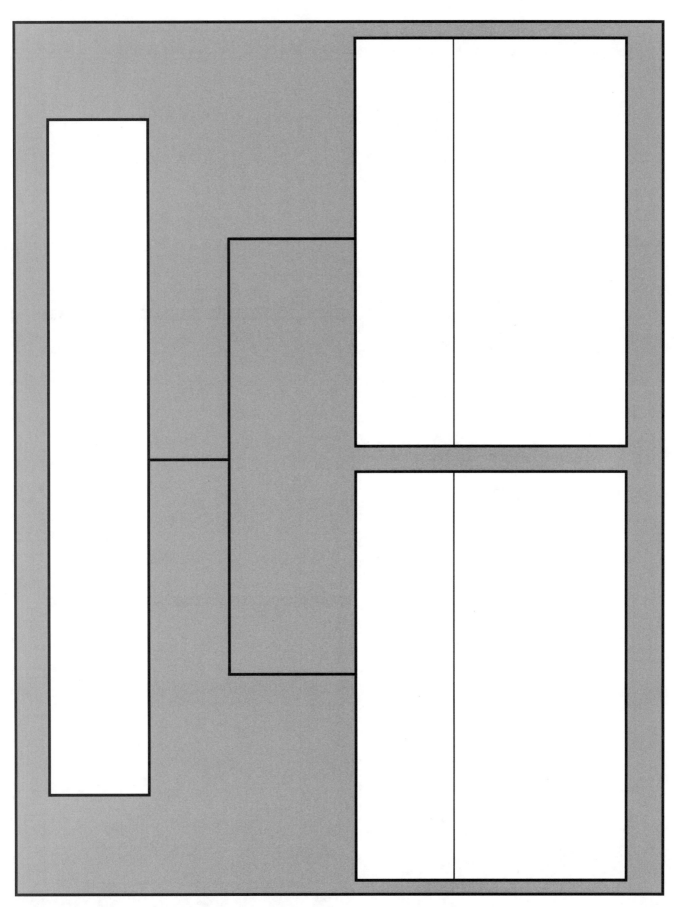

# TRANSPARENCY MASTER 14—3 Branching Diagram

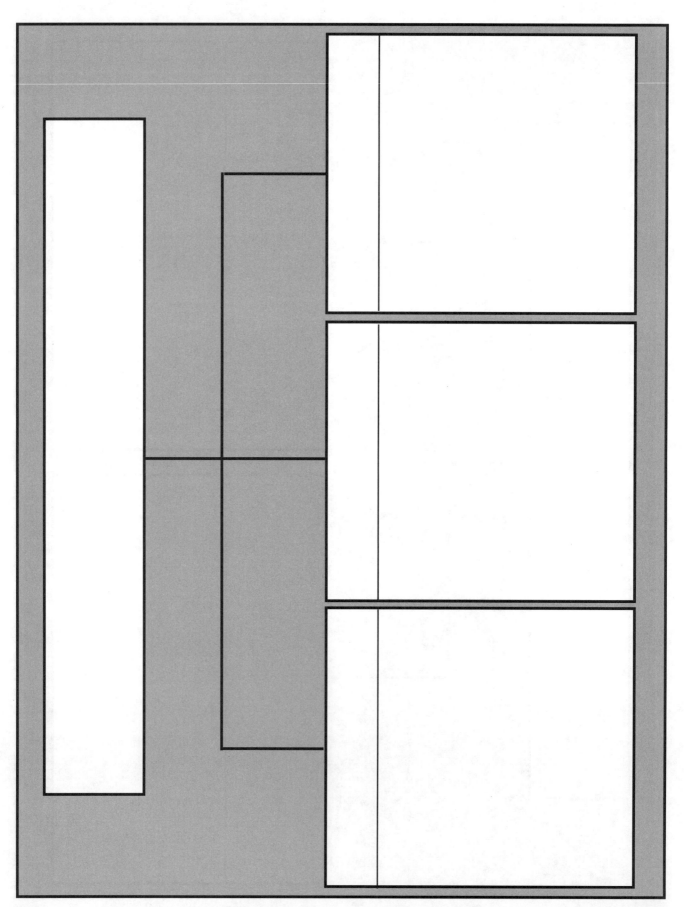

BEGINNING BUILDING THINKING SKILLS LESSON PLANS TRANSPARENCY MASTERS

# TRANSPARENCY MASTER 15—4 Branching Diagram

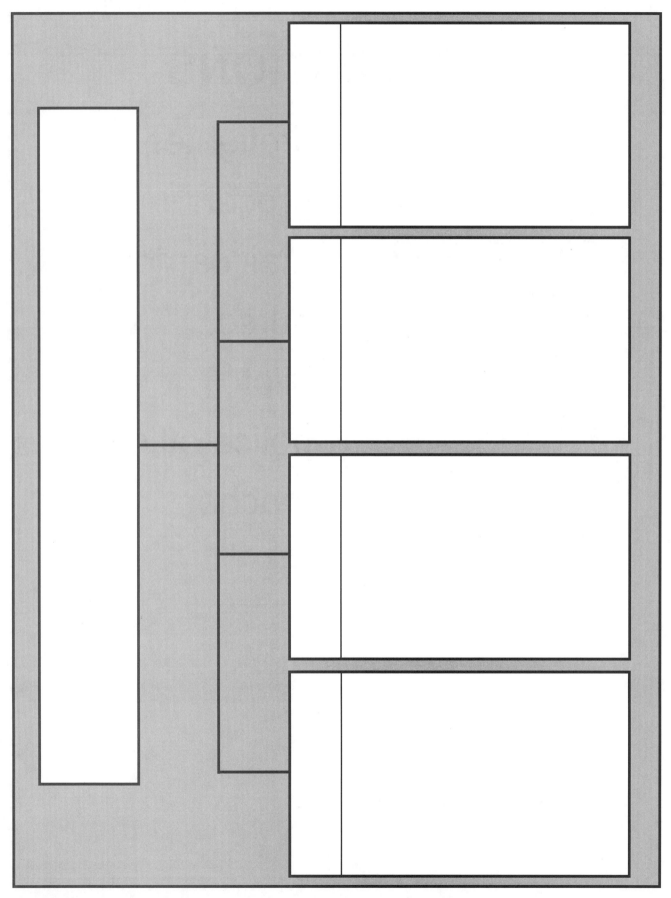

BEGINNING BUILDING THINKING SKILLS LESSON PLANS

## TRANSPARENCY MASTER 15—4 Branching Diagram

© 2000 CRITICAL THINKING BOOKS & SOFTWARE • WWW.CRITICALTHINKING.COM • 800-458-4849 339

BEGINNING BUILDING THINKING SKILLS LESSON PLANS                    TRANSPARENCY MASTERS

# TRANSPARENCY MASTER 16

# OCCUPATIONS

artist

barber

construction
  worker

cook

dentist

doctor

farmer

firefighter

grocer

mail carrier

nurse

pilot

police officer

teacher

340                    © 2000 CRITICAL THINKING BOOKS & SOFTWARE • WWW.CRITICALTHINKING.COM • 800-458-4849

BEGINNING BUILDING THINKING SKILLS LESSON PLANS                    TRANSPARENCY MASTERS

# TRANSPARENCY MASTER 17

# FOOD

| | |
|---|---|
| apple | grapes |
| bacon | ham |
| beans | lettuce |
| bread | milk |
| butter | onion |
| cabbage | orange |
| carrots | peas |
| celery | peach |
| cheese | potato |
| chicken (fried) | rice |
| corn | steak |
| eggs | tomato |

© 2000 CRITICAL THINKING BOOKS & SOFTWARE • WWW.CRITICALTHINKING.COM • 800-458-4849          341

BEGINNING BUILDING THINKING SKILLS LESSON PLANS                    TRANSPARENCY MASTERS

## TRANSPARENCY MASTER 18

# VEHICLES

| | |
|---|---|
| airplane | motorcycle |
| ambulance | police car |
| bicycle | school bus |
| boat | ship |
| bus | tractor |
| car | train |
| fire truck | truck |
| helicopter | |

BEGINNING BUILDING THINKING SKILLS LESSON PLANS                    TRANSPARENCY MASTERS

# TRANSPARENCY MASTER 19

# ANIMALS

| | |
|---|---|
| camel | ostrich |
| chicken | owl |
| cows | pig |
| duck | shark |
| fish | snake |
| frog | spider |
| giraffe | turkey |
| horse | turtle |
| lizard | zebra |

© 2000 CRITICAL THINKING BOOKS & SOFTWARE • WWW.CRITICALTHINKING.COM • 800-458-4849      343

BEGINNING BUILDING THINKING SKILLS LESSON PLANS

TRANSPARENCY MASTERS

## TRANSPARENCY MASTER 20

# BUILDINGS

apartment building

barber shop

barn

farm

fire station

garage

gas station

hospital

house

library

mobile home

playground

police station

post office

restaurant

school

supermarket

344

© 2000 CRITICAL THINKING BOOKS & SOFTWARE • WWW.CRITICALTHINKING.COM • 800-458-4849

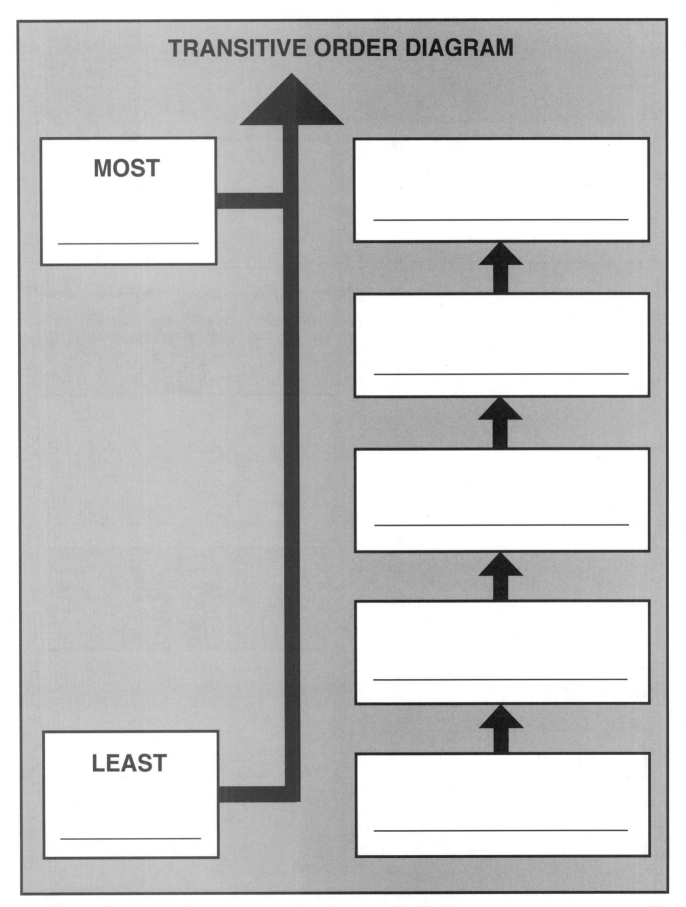

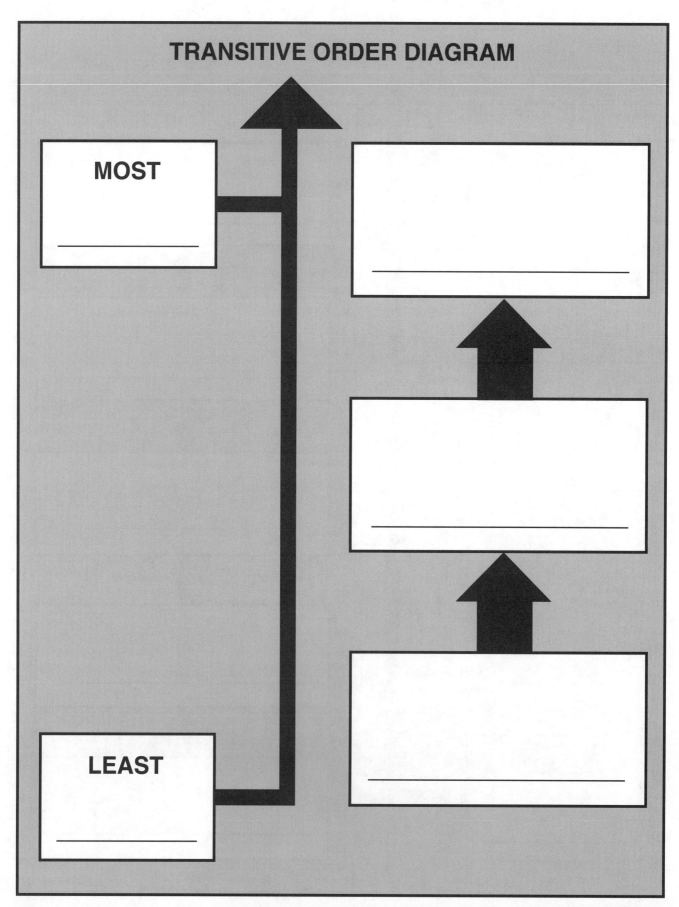

BEGINNING BUILDING THINKING SKILLS LESSON PLANS  TRANSPARENCY MASTERS

# TRANSPARENCY MASTER 23—Class and Members Diagram

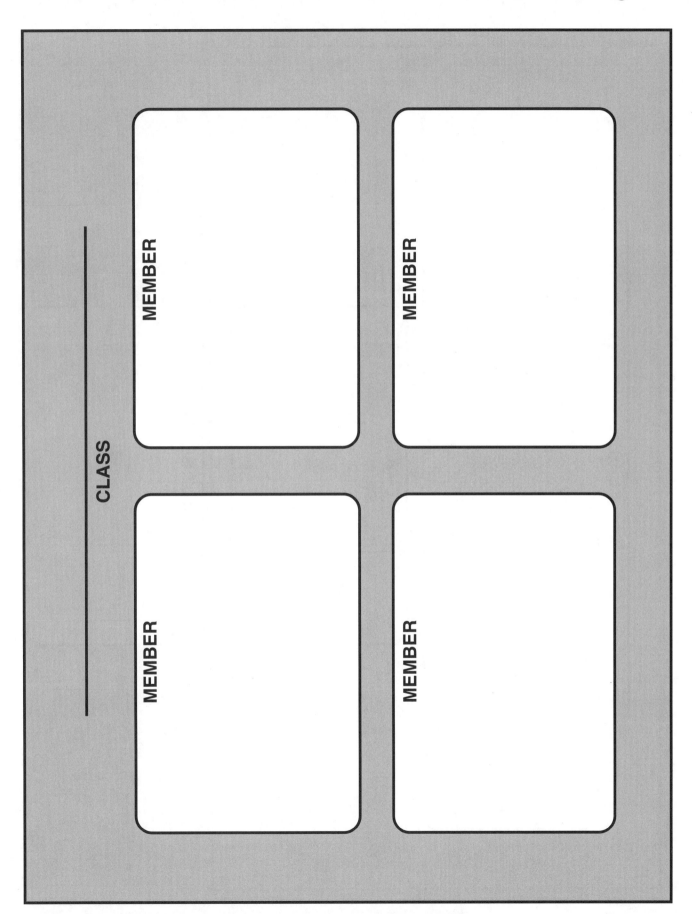

TRANSPARENCY MASTER 23—Class and Members Diagram

© 2000 CRITICAL THINKING BOOKS & SOFTWARE • WWW.CRITICALTHINKING.COM • 800-458-4849   347

BEGINNING BUILDING THINKING SKILLS LESSON PLANS  TRANSPARENCY MASTERS

# TRANSPARENCY MASTER 24—Exception Diagram

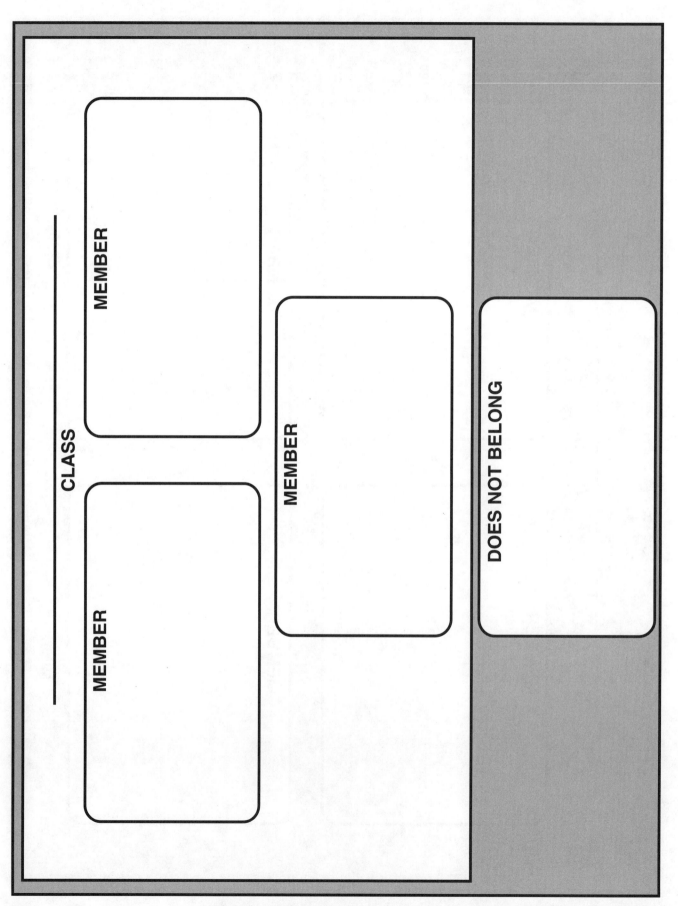

348  © 2000 CRITICAL THINKING BOOKS & SOFTWARE • WWW.CRITICALTHINKING.COM • 800-458-4849

# TRANSPARENCY MASTER 25—Definition Graphic

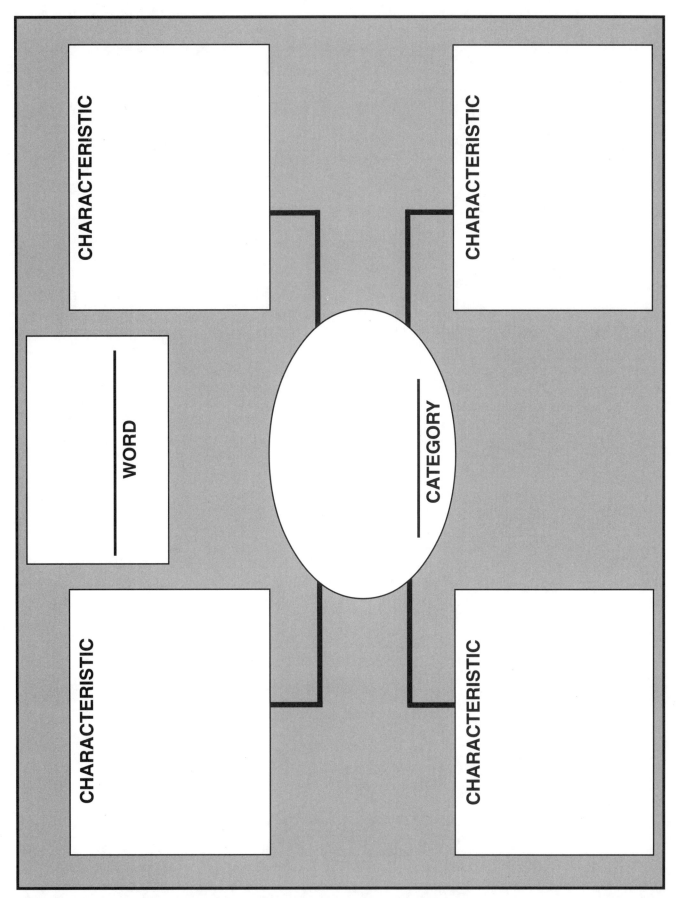

BEGINNING BUILDING THINKING SKILLS LESSON PLANS                    APPENDIX

# BBTS PHOTO CARDS LIST

Cards are printed back to back and numbered. Photo #49 is on the back of photo card #1. There are 96 large cards. Two cards include an inset. There are 98 small cards because the large-card insets are printed as separate cards in the small-card set.

## FAMILY

1. baby
2. toddler girl
3. toddler boy
4. girl
5. boy
6. mother
7. father
8. grandmother
9. grandfather

## OCCUPATIONS

10. construction worker
11. cook
12. farmer
13. mail carrier
14. nurse
15. teacher
16. firefighter
17. pilot
18. police officer
19. doctor
20. dentist
21. artist
22. grocer
23. barber

## VEHICLES

24. ambulance
25. police car
26. pickup truck
27. airplane
28. city bus
29. train
30. bicycle
31. car
32. school bus
33. motorcycle
34. tractor
35. ship
36. motorboat
37. fire truck
38. helicopter

## BUILDINGS

39. hospital
40. library
41. gas station
42. barn
43. barber shop
44. mobile home
45. fire station
46. police station
47. farm
48. restaurant
49. supermarket
50. apartment building
51. post office
52. playground
53. house and garage
54. school

© 2000 CRITICAL THINKING BOOKS & SOFTWARE • WWW.CRITICALTHINKING.COM • 800-458-4849          351

## ANIMALS

55. frog
56. shark
57. fish
58. camel
59. giraffe
60. spider
61. turtle
62. ostrich
63. zebra
64. horse
65. chicken
66. owl
67. turkey
68. lizard
69. snake
70. duck
71. pig
72. cows

## FOOD

73. bread
74. butter
75. cheese
76. ham
77. bacon
78. eggs
79. milk
80. fried chicken
81. steak

## FRUITS AND VEGETABLES

82. carrots
83. onion
84. green beans
85. peas
86. potatoes
87. celery
88. corn
89. rice
90. cabbage
91. lettuce
92. apple branch
93. orange
94. grapes
95. tomatoes
96. peach
A. cooked rice (small cards only)
B. apple (small cards only)

BEGINNING BUILDING THINKING SKILLS LESSON PLANS                                              APPENDIX

# LESSONS USING PHOTO CARDS

- **KEY:** Lesson Reference

  **E** = Describing Things

  **F** = Verbal Similarites and Differences

  **G** = Verbal Sequences

  **H** = Verbal Classification

  **I** = Verbal Analogies

**E-1 Example:** girl (4), grandmother (8), mother (6)

**E-1 Exercise:** baby (1), boy (5), toddler boy (3)

**E-1 Practice:** baby (1), girl (4), toddler girl (2)

**E-2 Example:** baby (1)

**E-2 Exercise:** grandfather (9)

**E-2 Practice:** father (7)

**E-3 Example:** construction worker (10), cook (11), farmer (12)

**E-3 Exercise:** mail carrier (13), nurse (14), teacher (15)

**E-3 Practice:** firefighter (16), pilot (17), police officer (18)

**E-4 Example:** doctor (19)

**E-4 Exercise:** pilot (17)

**E-4 Practice:** mail carrier (13)

**E-5 Example:** bread (73), butter (74), cheese (75)

**E-5 Exercise:** carrot (82), onion (83), orange (93)

**E-5 Practice:** green beans (84), peas (85), potatoes (86)

**E-6 Example:** ham, (76)

**E-6 Exercise:** grapes (94)

**E-6 Practice:** celery (87)

**E-7 Example:** ambulance (24), police car (25), pickup truck (26)

**E-7 Exercise:** airplane (27), city bus (28), train (29)

**E-7 Practice:** bicycle (30), car (31), school bus (32)

**E-8 Example:** train (29)

**E-8 Exercise:** helicopter (38)

**E-8 Practice:** ship (35)

**E-9 Example:** frog (55), snake (69), fish (57)

**E-9 Exercise:** camel (58), horse (64), giraffe (59)

**E-9 Practice:** lizard (68), spider (60), turtle (61)

© 2000 CRITICAL THINKING BOOKS & SOFTWARE • WWW.CRITICALTHINKING.COM • 800-458-4849          353

BEGINNING BUILDING THINKING SKILLS LESSON PLANS                                      APPENDIX

**E-10 Example:** turkey (67)

**E-10 Exercise:** ostrich (62)

**E-10 Practice:** zebra (63)

**E-11 Example:** barn (42), house (53), mobile home (44)

**E-11 Exercise:** fire station (45), gas station (41), police station (46)

**E-11 Practice:** farm (47), restaurant (48), supermarket (49)

**E-12 Example:** apartment building (50)

**E-12 Exercise:** post office (51)

**E-12 Practice:** library (40)

**F-1 Example:** grandmother (8), father (7), mother (6), toddler boy (3)

**F-1 Exercise:** toddler girl (2), baby (1), father (7), grandfather (9)

**F-2 Example:** father (7), grandfather (9)

**F-2 Exercise:** toddler boy (3), toddler girl (2).

**F-3 Example:** dentist (20), doctor (19), nurse (14), police officer (18)

**F-3 Exercise:** farmer (12), grocer (22), nurse (14), pilot (17)

**F-4 Example:** firefighter (16), police officer (18)

**F-4 Exercise:** mail carrier (13), police officer (18)

**F-5 Example:** apple (92), carrot (82), onion (83), orange (93)

**F-5 Exercise:** cheese (75), bacon (77), butter (74), eggs (78)

**F-5 Practice:** green beans (84), corn (88), peas (85), rice (89)

**F-6 Example:** corn (88), rice (89)

**F-6 Exercise:** ham (76), bacon (77)

**F-6 Practice:** peach (96), orange (93)

**F-7 Example:** ambulance (24), car (31), fire truck (37), pickup truck (26),

**F-7 Exercise:** helicopter (38), airplane (27), city bus (28), police car (25)

**F-7 Practice:** ship (35), boat (36), train (29), pickup truck (26)

**F-8 Example:** city bus (28), train (29)

**F-8 Exercise:** bicycle (30), motorcycle (33)

**F-8 Practice:** ship (35), airplane (27)

**F-9 Example:** zebra (63), camel (58), giraffe (59), horse (64)

**F-9 Exercise:** chicken (65), ostrich (62), owl (66), turkey (67)

**F-9 Practice:** lizard (68), frog (55), spider (60), turtle (61)

**F-10 Example:** lizard (68), snake (69)

**F-10 Exercise:** ostrich (62), turkey (67)

354        © 2000 CRITICAL THINKING BOOKS & SOFTWARE • WWW.CRITICALTHINKING.COM • 800-458-4849

**BEGINNING BUILDING THINKING SKILLS LESSON PLANS**                                        **APPENDIX**

**F-10 Practice:** fish (57), frog (55)

**F-11 Example:** house (53), farm (47), playground (52), apartment building (50)

**F-11 Exercise:** police station (46), garage (53), fire station (45), supermarket (49)

**F-11 Practice:** library (40), hospital (39), post office (51), apartment building (50)

**F-12 Example:** restaurant (48) and supermarket (49)

**F-12 Exercise:** barn (42) and garage (53)

**F-12 Practice:** fire station (45) and gas station (41)

**F-13 Example:** doctor (19) and nurse (14)

**F-13 Exercise:** barber (23) and dentist (20)

**F-13 Practice:** grocer (22) and cook (11)

**F-14 Example:** apple (92), tomato (95)

**F-14 Exercise:** cabbage (90), lettuce (91)

**F-14 Practice:** milk (79), butter (74)

**F-15 Example:** city bus (28), school bus (32)

**F-15 Exercise:** airplane (27), train (29).

**F-15 Practice:** tractor (34), pickup truck (26).

**F-16 Example:** chicken (65), duck (70)

**F-16 Exercise:** horse (64), camel (58)

**F-16 Practice:** lizard (68), spider (60)

**F-17 Example:** house (53), mobile home (44).

**F-17 Exercise:** gas station (41), restaurant (48)

**F-17 Practice:** farm (47), playground (52)

**G-1 Example:** baby (1), boy (5), father (7), grandfather (9), toddler boy (3)

**G-1 Exercise:** baby (1), girl (4), grandmother (8), mother (6), toddler girl (2)

**G-2 Example:** cook (11) farmer (12), grocer (22)

**G-2 Exercise:** doctor (19), firefighter (16), pilot (17), teacher (15)

**G-3 Example:** cabbage (90), rice (89), tomato (95)

**G-3 Exercise:** bread (73), potatoes (86), celery (87)

**G-4 Example:** city bus (28), car (31), motorcycle (33), train (29)

**G-4 Exercise:** bicycle (30), boat (36), car (31), tractor (34)

**G-5 Example:** chicken (65), giraffe (59), pig (71)

**G-5 Exercise:** duck (70), ostrich (62), turkey (67)

© 2000 CRITICAL THINKING BOOKS & SOFTWARE • WWW.CRITICALTHINKING.COM • 800-458-4849                        355

**BEGINNING BUILDING THINKING SKILLS LESSON PLANS**                                        **APPENDIX**

**G-6 Example:** apartment building (50), house (53), mobile home (44)

**G-6 Exercise:** house (53), library (40), post office (51), school (54)

**H-1 Example:** baby (1), toddler boy (3), toddler girl (2)

**H-1 Exercise:** girl (4), grandmother (8), mother (6)

**H-2 Example:** artist (21), construction worker (10), farmer (12)

**H-2 Exercise:** dentist (20), doctor (19), nurse (14)

**H-3 Example:** apple (92), orange (93), peach (96)

**H-3 Exercise:** celery (87), lettuce (91), peas (85)

**H-3 Practice:** chicken (65), ham (76), steak (81)

**H-4 Example:** ambulance (24), fire truck (37), police car (25)

**H-4 Exercise:** bicycle (30), boat (36), motorcycle (33)

**H-4 Practice:** airplane (27), city bus (28), train (29)

**H-5 Example:** camel (58), horse (64), giraffe (59)

**H-5 Exercise:** lizard (68), snake (69), turtle (61)

**H-5 Exercise:** pig (71), cow (72), duck (70)

**H-6 Example:** fire station (45), hospital (39), police station (46)

**H-6 Exercise:** barn (42), fire station (45), garage (53)

**H-6 Practice:** library (40), post office (51), school (54)

**H-7 Example:** boy (5), father (7), grandmother (8), mother (6)

**H-7 Exercise:** girl (4), grandmother (8), toddler boy (3), toddler girl (2)

**H-8 Example:** artist (21), barber (23), mail carrier (13), teacher (15)

**H-8 Exercise:** doctor (19), fire fighter (16), pilot (17), police officer (18)

**H-9 Example:** butter (74), cheese (75), milk (79), grapes (94)

**H-9 Exercise:** cabbage (90), celery (87), lettuce (91), potatoes (86)

**H-10 Example:** airplane (27), fire truck (37), school bus (32), train (29)

**H-10 Exercise:** bicycle (30), boat (36), motorcycle (33), tractor (34).

**H-11 Example:** chicken (65), turkey (67), duck (70), pig (71)

**H-11 Exercise:** owl (66), cow (72), horse (64), zebra (63)

**H-12 Example:** apartment building (50), house (53), school (54), mobile home (44)

**H-12 Exercise:** farm (47), library (40), restaurant (48), supermarket (49)

**H-13:** artist (21), dentist (20), farmer (12), grocer (22), mail carrier (13), pilot (17)

**H-14:** bacon (77), green beans (84), carrot (82), celery (87), fried chicken (80), corn (88), grapes (94), orange (93), peach (96), potatoes (86), steak (81), tomato (95)

356                **© 2000 CRITICAL THINKING BOOKS & SOFTWARE • WWW.CRITICALTHINKING.COM • 800-458-4849**

**BEGINNING BUILDING THINKING SKILLS LESSON PLANS**                                    **APPENDIX**

**H-15:** airplane (27), boat (36), city bus (28), car (31), fire truck (37), helicopter (38), school (54), bus (32), ship (35), train (29)

**H-16:** camel (58), pig (71), frog (55), horse (64), ostrich (62), owl (66), snake (69), turkey (67), turtle (61)

**H-17 Exercise:** barber shop (23), fire station (45), house (53), library (40), mobile home (44), police station (46), post office (51), supermarket (49)

**I-1 Example:** chicken (65), corn (88), horse (64), apple (92), bacon (77), onions (83)

**I-1 Exercise:** chicken (65), eggs (78), cow (72), corn (88), bacon (77), milk (79)

**I-1 Practice:** steak (81), cow (72), ham (76), chicken (65), pig (71)

**I-2 Example:** teacher (15), school (54), nurse (14) hospital (39), playground (52), police station (46)

**I-2 Exercise:** barber (23), barber shop (43), cook (11), farm (47), restaurant (48), supermarket (49)

**I-2 Practice:** construction worker (10), pickup truck (26), farmer (12), car (31), motorcycle (33), tractor (34)

**I-3 Example:** rice (89), corn (88), cabbage (90), lettuce (91)

**I-3 Exercise:** bacon (77), pig (71), steak (81), cow (72)

**I-3 Practice:** potatoes (86), carrots (82), green beans (84), peas (85)

**I-4 Example:** airplane (27), pilot (17), police car (25), police officer (18)

**I-4 Exercise:** grocer (22), supermarket (49), farmer (12), farm (47)

**I-4 Practice:** school bus (32), school (54), ambulance (24), hospital (39)

## Note

If you have purchased the small photo cards, you have two extra cards. Card A is cooked rice, to go along with card 89, a rice plant. Card B is a single apple, to go along with card 92, apples on a branch.

© 2000 CRITICAL THINKING BOOKS & SOFTWARE • WWW.CRITICALTHINKING.COM • 800-458-4849          357

# PICTURE BOOKS TO SUPPLEMENT *BEGINNING BUILDING THINKING SKILLS* LESSONS

These picture books for young children were selected because of the richness of their content, the quality of their illustrations, their depiction of concepts across cultures, and their appeal for young children. The list includes fiction and nonfiction books that depict various ethnic groups, books that are humorous, and books that are inspiring. Although other grade-appropriate books may also be used for language arts integration of *Beginning Building Thinking Skills* lessons, these books are commonly available and address curriculum objectives meaningfully.

This bibliography contains some pre-kindergarten books (wordless books, pop-up books, or board books) to provide language stimulation for students whose English usage is underdeveloped. Some picture books commonly used in third or fourth grades are also recommended because they provide content enrichment or because they address rich human themes or ethnic diversity.

Many of the sample lesson plans recommend using picture books after the thinking skill activity. However, for students with limited background or developmental English usage, reading the book aloud and discussing it prior to the thinking activity is recommended. This discussion provides information about the content and enhances students' thinking and their confidence in expressing both their thinking and the concepts depicted in the book.

• **Bold Titles in Italics** designate children's multicultural books that depict the concepts featured in this program in a variety of cultural settings.

**SHAPES AND COLORS**

*Shapes,* Anne Geddes (Cedco Publishing Co., San Rafael, CA, 1997). This picture book shows shapes with ordinary things.

*Spot's Big Book of Colors, Shapes, and Numbers,* Eric Hill (G.P. Putnam's Sons, New York, 1994). This picture book uses simple drawings to illustrate diamond, oval, rectangle, round, square, and triangle.

*Color Farm,* Lois Ehlert (HarperCollins, New York, 1990). The rooster, dog, sheep, cow, pig, and other animals on a farm are drawn using colorful shapes such as square, circle, rectangle, and triangle.

*Color Zoo,* Lois Ehlert (Harper Collins, New York, 1990). Animals found in a zoo are drawn using colorful shapes such as square, circle, rectangle, and triangle.

*Circles, Triangles, and Squares,* Tana Hoban (Macmillan, New York, 1974). Along the city streets, in the kitchen, at the park—circles, triangles, and squares are waiting to be discovered.

• **The Village of Round and Square Houses,** Ann Grifalsoni (Little, Brown, Boston, MA, 1986). This Caldecott Honor Book retelling of a story from Cameroon explains how men and women in this African village create buildings for work and conversation.

*Brown Rabbit's Shape Book,* Alan Baker (Kingfisher Chambers, New York, 1994). Rabbit finds a box of balloons and creates various shapes from them.

*Triangle, Square, Circle,* William Wegman (Hyperion, New York, 1995). Fay, a dog, shows off basic shapes.

## FAMILY MEMBERS

These books describe families with natural or adopted children, families with stepchildren, multigenerational families, alternative family groups, and family members with physical disabilities. Many books illustrate family life across cultures, including a special section on families' experiences coming to America.

- *Families,* Toppers series, Nicola Baxter (Children's Press Groliers, Danbury, CT, 1996). Through interpretation of words and pictures children explore family relationships from the child's viewpoint.
- *People,* Peter Speir (Bantam Doubleday Dell, New York, 1980). This picture book presents numerous descriptions of how people of all ages and cultures fill basic human needs for food, clothing, shelter, love, work, and celebration.
- *Loving,* Ann Morris (Morrow, New York, 1994). All over the world people hold, help, feed, talk, listen, teach, share, and express love for family members and friends.

*My First Family Tree Book,* Catherine Bruzzone (Ideals Children's Books, Nashville, TN, 1992). This record book provides spaces and forms to help primary grade children organize information about their family history.

*Do People Grow on Family Trees?,* Ira Wolfman (Workman, New York, 1991). This book for kids and other beginners in genealogy is intended for older students, but contains ideas for teachers to use in the primary classroom.

*I Got a Family,* Melrose Cooper (Holt, New York, 1993). In rhyming verses, a young girl describes how members of her family make her feel loved.

- *All the Colors of the Race,* Arnold Adoff (Lothrop, Lee & Shepard, New York, 1992). This book explores the inner thoughts and feelings of a child whose unique identity springs from a combination of races and cultures.
- *All the Colors of the Earth,* Sheila Hamanaka (Morrow, New York, 1994). Children come in all the colors of the earth and they are all loved and loveable.

*Happy Adoption Day,* John McCutcheon (Little, Brown, New York, 1996). Parents celebrate the adoption of a child and continue to reassure the child that their love will not go away.

*All the Places to Love,* Patricia MacLachlan (HarperCollins, New York, 1994). Richly detailed pictures depict a young boy's experiences with his family on his grandparents' farm.

- *Masai and I,* Virginia Kroll (Four Winds/Macmillan, New York, 1992). Colorful illustrations depict what a young American girl pictures her life would be like in a Masai family.
- *Going Home,* Eve Bunting (HarperCollins, New York, 1990). Brilliant colors and lyrical prose relate a Mexican farmer worker family's visit with their relatives in Mexico.
- *Tet: The New Year,* Kim-Lan Tran (Modern Curriculum Press, Cleveland, OH, 1992). This book is one of several well-illustrated books created by the Boston, MA Children's Museum to depict celebrations in different cultures.
- *Children of the Wind and Water: Five Stories about Native American Children,* Stephen Krensky (Scholastic, New York, 1994). Stories depict how Muskogee, Dakota, Huron, Tlingit, and Nootka children learn valuable skills.
- *The Hundred Penny Box,* Sharon Bell Mathis (Puffin, New York, 1975). The extended family is pictured in this Newbury Honor Book about a one-hundred-year-old aunt who relates events of her life to the dates on one hundred pennies.
- *Black Is Brown Is Tan,* Arnold Adoff (HarperCollins, New York, 1992). A happy family with a black mother and a white father share experiences.

BEGINNING BUILDING THINKING SKILLS LESSON PLANS                                      BIBLIOGRAPHY

*On The Day You Were Born,* Debra Frasier (Harcourt Brace, New York, 1991). The universe expresses the specialness of each child.

*Arthur's Family Vacation,* Marc Brown (Little, Brown, Boston, MA, 1993). A family must make other plans when it rains during their beach holiday.

*The Canada Geese Quilt,* Natalie Kinsey-Warnock (Dutton, New York, 1992). Worried that family changes will disrupt her familiar life on a Vermont farm in the 1940s, Ariel and her grandmother make a very special quilt

*Home Place,* Crescent Dragonwagon (Aladdin/Macmillan, New York, 1993). As a family hiking in the woods find the ruins of a home, we journey dreamily back to a time when another family lived and loved there.

• ***Too Many Tamales,*** Gary Soto (G.P. Putnam, New York, 1993). Warm oil paintings illustrate a tender, funny story about a Mexican-American family at Christmastime.

*The Car Trip,* Helen Oxenbury (Puffin, New York, 1994). A young boy's car trip with his parents turns out to be less relaxing for his mother and father.

• ***Bigmama's,*** Donald Crews (Greenwillow, New York, 1991). Visiting Bigmama's house in the country, young Donald Crews finds his relatives full of news and the old place and its surroundings just the same as the year before.

*A Sister's Wish,* Kate Jacobs (Hyperion, New York, 1996). A young girl who misses her dad is surrounded by brothers and stepbrothers and longs for a sister.

*Megan's Two Houses,* Erica Jong (Dove Kids, New York, 1984). Humorous drawings and poignant situations relate the lifestyle of the child of divorced parents.

*Robert Lives with His Grandparents,* Martha Whitamore Hickman (Albert Whitman, Morton Grove, IL, 1995). Robert is ashamed to tell his classmates that he lives with his grandparents because his parents have divorced.

*At Daddy's on Saturday,* Linda Walvoord Girard (Albert Whitman, Morton Grove, IL, 1987). Although she feels anger and sadness at her parents' divorce, Katie discovers that she can keep a loving relationship with her father.

*Adoption is For Always,* Linda Walvoord Girard (Albert Whitman, Morton Grove, IL, 1986). This story relates factual information about the adoption process.

*My Daddy,* Susan Paralis (Front Street, Asheville, NC, 1998). Explores the bond between a boy and his father from the boy's point of view.

**Baby**

• *Babies,* Toppers series, Nicola Baxter (Children's Press/Groliers, Danbury, CT, 1996). Through interpretation of words and pictures children explore the needs of babies from the child's viewpoint.

*Happy Birth Day,* Robie Harris (Candlewick, Cambridge, MA, 1996). Muted drawings and prose for young children relate a baby's first day of life.

• ***Welcoming Babies,*** Margy Burns Knight (Tilbury House, Gardiner, ME, 1994). Drawings and text show how a dozen cultures celebrate newborn babies.

*Welcome Little Baby,* Aliki (Greenwillow, New York, 1987). A mother tells her baby what his growing up will be like.

*The Baby's Catalogue,* Janet and Allan Ahlberg (Little, Brown, Boston, MA, 1986). Pictures and labels are categorized according to daily events and common objects of babies and their families.

*Our Teacher Is Having A Baby,* Eve Bunting (Clarion, New York, 1992). A first grade class learns about babies' needs as it prepares for the birth of their teacher's baby.

• ***The World Is Full of Babies,*** Mick Manning (Delacourt/Doubleday Press, New York, 1996). Colorful drawings show how human and animal babies develop before birth and through early childhood.

*I Love You As Much,* Laura Krauss Melmed (Lothrop, Lee and Shepard, New York, 1993). The sentiments of human parents are expressed in animal pictures.

© 2000 CRITICAL THINKING BOOKS & SOFTWARE • WWW.CRITICALTHINKING.COM • 800-458-4849                    361

| | |
|---|---|
| | *The New Baby at Your House,* Joanna Cole (Morrow, New York, 1987). This book helps young children understand what's happening to them and to their family at the birth of a new baby. |
| | *The New Baby: Mister Rogers Neighborhood Series,* Fred Rogers (Putnam, New York, 1989). This book prepares a child to accept a new sibling. |
| | *Eat Up, Gemma,* Sarah Hayes (Morrow, New York, 1994). "Eat up, Gemma!" Mom, Dad, and Grandma always say, but baby Gemma has her own ideas about food. |
| | *Julius, The Baby of the World,* Florence Parry Heide and Judith Heide Gilliland (Morrow, New York, 1995). Lily's parents find her new baby brother extraordinary, but Lilly doesn't agree until a cousin dares to question Julius's charms. |
| | *Arthur's Baby,* Marc Brown (Little, Brown, Boston, MA, 1990). Arthur adjusts to a new baby. |
| | *We Have A Baby,* Cathryn Falwell (Clarion Books, New York, 1993). This book for a new or about-to-be big sister or big brother introduces important things the whole family can do for the baby and shows all the love the baby will give in return. |
| | *Henry's Baby,* Mary Hoffman (Dorling Kindersley, New York, 1993). This story about children whose lives are split between peer group and family describes boys, like Henry, who aren't sure about babies. |
| **Boy** | *Owl Moon,* Jane Yolen (Philomel Division of Putnam and Grosset, New York, 1987). This description of a winter owling hike by a father and son won the Caldecott Medal. |
| | *The Red Barn,* Eve Bunting (Harcourt Brace Jovanovich, New York, 1979). Craig's grandfather teaches him to accept changes in life. |
| | *Mitch and Amy,* Beverly Cleary (Morrow, New York, 1991). The adventures of a nine-year-old twin brother and sister who, despite constant bickering, support each other loyally at home and at school. |
| | *Island Boy,* Barbara Cooney (Viking, New York, 1988). A simple, lovely tale about a boy growing up in a New England island community. |
| | *All the Places to Love,* Patricia MacLachlan (HarperCollins, New York, 1994). Richly detailed pictures depict a young boy's experiences with his family on his grandparents' farm. |
| | • ***Hue Boy,*** Rita Phillips Mitchell (Dial, New York, 1993). In this Caribbean story Hue Boy's discomfort over being small disappears when he "stands tall" for his father's return. |
| | • ***Kofi and His Magic,*** Maya Angelou (Potter/Crown/Random House, New York, 1996). Lilting prose and bright photographs depict the story of a Ghanan boy and his kente cloth. |
| | • ***The Day of Ahmed's Secret,*** Florence Paray Heide and Judith Heide Gilliland, (Morrow, New York, 1995). A boy runs his errands and does his chores celebrating his secret, that he has learned to write his name in Arabic. |
| | • ***Sami and the Time of Troubles,*** Florence Paray Heide and Judith Heide Gilliland, (Clarion, New York, 1992). A boy and his family must live in a basement in war-torn Beirut. |
| | • ***Bar Mitzvah; A Jewish Boy's Coming of Age,*** Erik Kimmel (Viking, New York, 1995). This book describes a Jewish boy's rite of passage. |
| | • ***Baseball Saved Us,*** Ken Mochizuki (Lee and Low, New York, 1995). A Japanese American boy in an internment camp in World War II is helped then and later by playing baseball. |
| | • ***Somewhere in Africa,*** Ingrid Mennen and Niki Daily (Dutton, New York, 1992). A day in the life of a boy in Capetown shows modern, urban South Africa. |

*Climbing Kansas Mountains,* George Shannon (Simon & Schuster, New York, 1996). Sam and his father visit the tall grain elevators that are "Kansas mountains."

- *First Pink Light,* Eloise Greenfield (Writers and Reader Publishing, New York, 1993). A boy struggles to stay awake to greet the return of his father at dawn.

*Like Jake and Me,* Mavis Jukes (Knopf, New York, 1987). An incident with a spider brings a boy and his stepfather closer together.

*Russell and Elisa,* Johanna Hurwitz (Morrow, New York, 1989). Seven-year-old Russell and his three-year-old sister Elisa have adventures with friends and family in their apartment building.

- *Nobiah's Well: A Modern African Folktale,* Donna Guthrie (Ideals Publishing Corp., Nashville, Tennessee, 1993). Sharing precious water with animals, a young boy returns home with only enough for his family, but not for the garden. That evening all the animals he has befriended return and repay Nobiah in full.

- *The Legend of the Indian Paintbrush,* Tomie de Paola (Putnam, New York, 1996). Little Gopher follows his destiny of becoming an artist for his people and brings the colors of the sunset down to earth.

- *Something from Nothing,* Phoebe Gilman (Scholastic, New York, 1993). This retelling of a Russian Jewish story relates how a boy's blanket is transformed as he grows up until nothing but love and memories remain.

## Father

- *Families,* Toppers series, Nicola Baxter (Children's Press/Groliers, Danbury, CT, 1996). Through interpretation of words and pictures children explore family relationships from the child's viewpoint.

*I Love My Father Because,* Laurel Porter-Gaylord (Dutton, New York, 1991). Pictures of animals and their babies illustrate what fathers do.

- *Daddy, Daddy Be There,* Candy Dawson Boyd and Floyd Cooper (Philomel, New York, 1995). A child's pleas express children's needs for a father.

*Owl Moon,* Jane Yolen (Philomel Division of Putnam and Grosset, New York, 1987). This description of a winter owling hike by a father and son won the Caldecott Medal.

*Fishing with Dad,* Michael Rosen (Artisan, New York, 1996). Photographs depict a young boy's experiences fishing with his father.

- *Always My Dad,* Sharon Davis Wyeth (Knopf, New York, 1997). Although a girl does not see her father often, her summer experience at her grandparents' farm reminds her that his absence does not diminish his love.

- *Everett Anderson's Goodby,* Lucille Clifton (Henry Holt, New York, 1983). Everett Anderson has a hard time dealing with the death of his father.

*Horton Hatches the Egg,* Dr. Seuss (Random House, New York, 1968). Commitment makes an elephant the father of a bird.

*My Ol' Man,* Patricia Polacco (Philomel Division of Putnam and Grosset, New York, 1995). A girl recalls her father's stories and the significance of a magic rock.

*Do I Have A Daddy?,* Jeanne Warren Lindsey (Morning Glory Press, Buena Park, CA, 1991). A single mother's answer offers suggestions in explaining a parent's leaving the family.

- *Jafta My Father,* Hugh Lewin (Houghton Mifflin, Boston, MA, 1983). While his father works in the city through the winter, a young South African boy thinks of good times when his father comes home.

*Climbing Kansas Mountains,* George Shannon (Simon & Schuster, New York, 1996). Sam and his father set out on a journey to the tall grain elevators that are "Kansas mountains."

- *First Pink Light,* Eloise Greenfield (Writers and Readers Publishing, New York, 1993). A boy struggles to stay awake for his father's return at dawn's first light.

**BEGINNING BUILDING THINKING SKILLS LESSON PLANS**  **BIBLIOGRAPHY**

*Like Jake and Me,* Mavis Jukes (Knopf, New York, 1984). An incident with a spider brings a boy and his stepfather closer together.

• *Hello Amigos!,* Tricia Brown (Holt, Rinehart & Winston, New York, 1986). Follow the experiences of a Mexican-American boy who lives in the Mission District of San Francisco, on his sixth birthday.

*Daddy's Roommate,* Michael Willhoite (Alyson Publications, Los Angeles, CA, 1990). Some adventures of Daddy and his roommate, Frank.

**Girl**

*I Want to Be,* Thylias Moss (Dial Books, New York, 1994). Beautiful pictures and text relate a girl's aspirations.

*When I Was Young on the Mountain,* Cynthia Rylant (Dutton/Penguin, New York, 1982). Muted illustrations and text relate the details of growing up in rural West Virginia.

*My Mama Had A Dancing Heart,* Libba Moore Gray (Orchard, New York, 1995). A mother and daughter dance through the seasons of the year.

• *Maybe Yes, Maybe No, Maybe Maybe,* Susan Patron (Orchard, New York, 1993). A girl uses her artistic ability to help her older and younger sisters adjust when her family moves to a new apartment.

• *My Painted House, My Friendly Chicken, and Me,* Maya Angelou (Potter/Crown/Random House, New York, 1994). Lilting prose and colorful photographs depict the life of a Ndebele girl in South Africa.

• *The Keeping Quilt,* Patricia Polacco (Simon & Schuster, New York, 1988). A quilt ties together the lives of four generations of Russian immigrants.

*Leah's Pony,* Elizabeth Friedrich (Boyd Mills, Honesdale, PA, 1996). In the Depression of the 1930s a girl sells her beloved horse so that her grandfather may buy back his tractor.

• *The Samurai's Daughter,* Robert San Souci (Dial Books, New York, 1991). This retelling of a legend from the Oki Islands of Japan relates the reunion of a daughter with her exiled father.

*The Rag Coat,* Lauren Mills (Little, Brown, Boston, MA, 1991). Other children laugh at Minna's patchwork coat until she explains the significance of the scraps.

• *Amazing Grace,* Mary Hoffman (Dial Books, New York, 1998). Although classmates say that she cannot play Peter Pan because she is black and a girl, Grace discovers that she can do anything that she sets her mind to do.

• *A Song for Lena,* Hilary Horder Hippely (Simon & Schuster, New York, 1996). As a young girl makes strudel with her grandmother, she learns where songs come from.

• *The Storyteller,* Joan Wehman (Rizolli, New York, 1993). A girl from the Cochiti Pueblo becomes a storyteller by exchanging stories with an elderly woman.

• *Boundless Grace,* Mary Hoffman (Dial Books, New York, 1995). Grace is invited to visit her father and his new family in Africa.

• *Allie's Basketball Dream,* Barbara Barber (Lee and Low, New York, 1993). Determined to play basketball, a young African-American girl is helped by a special friend.

*Insects Are My Life ,* Megan McDonald (Orchard, New York, 1995). No one understands Amanda's devotion to insects.

• *Amelia's Road,* Linda J. Altman (Lee & Low, New York, 1993). This touching tale of the importance of home relates the feelings of Amelia, a child of migrant farm workers, who longs for a home.

• *A Chair for My Mother,* Vera Williams (Morrow, New York, 1984). Daughter, mother, and grandmother share the dream of saving enough coins to buy a new chair to replace one that burned up in the fire that destroyed their apartment.

*The Balancing Girl,* Berniece Rabe (Dutton, New York, 1988). A physically disabled girl proves she is capable of independence.

**BEGINNING BUILDING THINKING SKILLS LESSON PLANS**　　　　　　　　**BIBLIOGRAPHY**

*I Have a Sister, My Sister Is Deaf,* Jeanne Whitehouse Peterson (Harper & Row, New York, 1977). The author shares her enjoyable experiences with her deaf sister.

*Your Best Friend, Kate,* Rick Brown (Bradbury, New York, 1989). Kate's letters to her best friend back home chart her family's extended car trip, and reveal her true affection for her brother with whom she is always fighting.

• ***The Story of Ruby Bridges,*** Robert Coles (Scholastic, New York, 1995). The first black child in an all-white elementary school in the 1960s draws on family values to face a mob.

*Grandaddy's Place,* Helen V. Griffith (Greenwillow, New York, 1987). A young girl learns to appreciate her grandfather and his rural home.

*Mitch and Amy,* Beverly Cleary (Morrow, New York, 1967). Despite constant bickering, a nine-year-old twin brother and sister support each other loyally at home and at school.

**Grandfather**

*Grandfather's Love Song,* Reeve Lindbergh (Viking/Penguin, New York, 1993). Pictures and verse relate a grandfather's love.

*The Red Barn,* Eve Bunting (Harcourt Brace Jovanovich, New York, 1979). Craig's grandfather teaches him to accept changes in life.

*Now One Foot, Now the Other,* Vera Williams (Trumpet Club, New York, 1983). A young boy helps his grandfather recover from a stroke the same way his grandfather taught him to walk.

*Grandaddy's Place,* Helen V. Griffith (Greenwillow, New York, 1987). A young girl learns to appreciate her grandfather and his rural home.

*Goodby, Papa,* Una Leavy (Orchard, New York, 1996). Many adventures that Shane and Peter shared with their grandfather are remembered when he died.

• ***My Grandfather's Journey ,*** Allen Say (Houghton Mifflin, Boston, MA, 1993). Compelling memories of this grandfather's life in America become a poignant account of a Japanese-American family's unique cross-cultural experience.

• ***Grandpa's Face,*** Eloise Greenfield (Putnam and Grosset, New York, 1988). Muted paintings of many generations of a family illustrate the story that appearances do not always show what a person feels.

*Dance at Grandpa's,* Laura Ingalls Wilder, My First Little House Book Series (HarperCollins, New York, 1996). Dreamlike pictures make the experiences of a pioneer family appealing for young children.

• ***Something from Nothing,*** Phoebe Gilman (Scholastic, New York, 1992). This retelling of a Russian Jewish story relates how a boy's blanket is transformed as he grows up until nothing but love and memories remain.

*Happy Birthday, Sam,* Pat Hutchins (Greenwillow, New York, 1978). Grandpa's present allows Sam to reach various items.

*I Dance in My Red Pajamas,* Edith Thacher Hurd (Harper and Row, 1982). A girl and her visiting grandparents form a warm relationship.

• ***Grandfather's Rock: An Italian Folktale,*** Joel Strangis (Houghton Mifflin, Boston, MA, 1993). This Italian folktale, an intergenerational story of love and dependence, relates a plan to keep their beloved grandfather at home when a family can no longer care for Grandfather.

*Stealing Home,* Mary Bartholomew Stolz (HarperCollins, New York, 1992). Thomas and his grandfather find life in their small Florida house changed when Great-aunt Linzy comes to stay.

*The House of Wings,* Betsy Byars (Viking, New York, 1972). Left with his grandfather until his parents are settled in Detroit, Sammy learns to love and respect the old man as they care for an injured crane together.

• ***Grandfather Four Winds and Rising Moon,*** Michael Chanin (Starseed Press,

---

© 2000 CRITICAL THINKING BOOKS & SOFTWARE • WWW.CRITICALTHINKING.COM • 800-458-4849　　　**365**

**BEGINNING BUILDING THINKING SKILLS LESSON PLANS**

**BIBLIOGRAPHY**

Tiburon, CA, 1994). A Native American grandfather teaches his grandson lessons on courage, gratitude, generosity, and faith from an apple tree sacred to their people.

**Grandmother**

*Grandma According to Me*, Karen Magnuson Bell (Dell Yearling, New York, 1992). Pictures and a young girl's conversation lovingly describe her grandmother.

*Something Special for Me*, Vera Williams (Trumpet Club, New York, 1983). A young girl and her mother decide on a birthday present that recalls her grandmother's childhood.

*I Dance in My Red Pajamas*, Edith Thacher Hurd (Harper and Row, New York, 1982). A girl and her visiting grandparents form a warm relationship.

*A Busy Day For A Good Grandmother*, (Margaret K. Mahy/Simon & Schuster, New York, 1993). A very modern grandmother comes to her son's rescue when he cannot stop his teething baby from crying. By trail bike, racing raft, airplane and skateboard, Mrs. Oberon hurries to her son.

• *Abuela,* Arthur Dorros (Dutton, New York, 1991). While riding on a bus with her grandmother, a little girl imagines that they are carried up into the sky and fly over the sights of New York City.

• *A Chair for My Mother,* Vera Williams (Morrow, New York, 1984). Daughter, mother, and grandmother all share the dream of saving enough coins to buy a new chair to replace the one that burned up in the fire.

• *Isla,* Arthur Dorros (Dutton, New York, 1996). A young girl and her grandmother take an imaginary trip to the Caribbean island where the grandmother grew up.

• *Abuela's Weave,* Omar Castaneda (Lee and Low, New York, 1993). A Guatemalan girl and her grandmother grow closer as they weave together.

• *A Song for Lena,* Hilary Horder Hippely (Simon & Schuster, New York, 1996). As a young girl makes strudel with her grandmother, she learns where songs come from.

*Sunshine Home,* Eve Bunting (Clarion, New York, 1994). Family members struggle with their feelings about the grandmother's stay in a nursing home.

• *Babushka Baba Yaga,* Patricia Polacco (Philomel Division of Putnam and Grosset, New York, 1993). Since the villagers are afraid of her, Baba Yaga disguises herself as an old woman to understand the joys of being a grandmother.

• *Mrs. Katz and Tush,* Patricia Polacco (Dell, New York, 1994). A kitten helps an elderly Jewish woman become the "bubee" (grandmother) for an African-American family.

• *The Moon Lady,* Amy Tan (Macmillan, New York, 1992). This story about the importance of caregivers who are not family members relates a grandmother's adventures in China when she was a girl.

• *Chicken Sunday,* Patricia Polacco (Putnam and Grosset, New York, 1992). African-American children earn enough money to buy their grandmother a hat by creating ornamented Russian eggs.

• *Sachiko Means Happiness,* Kimiko Sakai (Children's Book Press, San Francisco, CA, 1995). Sachiko's grandmother's Alzheimer's condition leads her to believe that she herself is the young Sachiko in the family.

• *Things I Like about Grandma,* Francene Haskins (Children's Book Press, San Francisco, CA, 1994). An African-American girl tells of her close relationship with her grandmother.

• *Annie and the Old One,* Miska Miles (Joy Street/Little, Brown, Boston, MA, 1985). This Newbury Honor book relates a Navajo girl's relationship to her grandmother and her heritage.

• *Watch Out for the Chicken Feet in Your Soup,* Tomie de Paola (Prentice-Hall, New

366 © 2000 **CRITICAL THINKING BOOKS & SOFTWARE** WWW.CRITICALTHINKING.COM • 800-458-4849

**BEGINNING BUILDING THINKING SKILLS LESSON PLANS**  **BIBLIOGRAPHY**

York, 1974). Joey is embarrassed by his grandmother's old-fashioned ways until his friend shows great admiration for her.

*Remember Me,* Martha Wild (Albert Whitman, Morton Grove, IL, 1990). Although she may forget some things, Ellie's grandmother remembers the special times they have had.

**Mother**

*My Mama Had A Dancing Heart,* Libba Moore Gray (Orchard, New York, 1995). A mother and daughter dance through the seasons of the year.

*Mom Goes To Work,* Libby Gleeson (Scholastic, New York, 1995). A young child reacts to changes in the family when the mother goes to work.

*Tell Me A Story, Mother,* Angela Johnson (Orchard, New York, 1989). A young girl and her mother remember together her favorite stories of her mother's childhood.

• *Abbeville Anthology of Mother/Daughter Tales,* Josephine Evetts-Sacker (Abbeville Press, New York, 1996). Ten stories from various cultures relate universal themes in mother/daughter relationships.

*I'll Love You Forever,* Robert Munsch (Firefly Books, Ontario, Canada, 1986). Parents' love across generations is poignantly expressed in this short book.

• *Mama, Do You Love Me?,* Barbara J. Joosse (Chronicle Books, San Francisco, CA, 1991). A child living in the Arctic learns that mother's love is unconditional.

*Something Special for Me,* Tomie de Paola (Trumpet Club, New York, 1988). A young girl and her mother decide on a birthday present that recalls her grandmother's childhood.

*I Love You The Purplest,* Barbara J. Joosse (Chronicle Books, San Francisco, CA, 1991). Two boys discover that their mother loves them equally, but in different ways.

*Are You My Mother?,* P. D. Eastman (Random House, New York, 1966). A lost baby bird searches for his mother.

*I Love My Mother Because,* Laurel Porter-Gaylord (Dutton, New York, 1991). Pictures of animal babies illustrate what mothers do.

• *A Chair for My Mother,* Vera Williams (Morrow, New York, 1984). Daughter, mother, and grandmother all share the dream of saving enough coins to buy a new chair to replace one that burned up in the fire.

• *Jonathan and His Mommy,* Irene Smalls-Hector (Little, Brown, Boston, MA, 1992). As a boy and his mother explore their neighborhood, they try various ways of walking—from giant steps and reggae steps to crisscross steps and backward steps.

*Heather Has Two Mommies,* Leslie Newman (Alyson Publications, Los Angeles, CA, 1990). Heather has two mommies: Mama Jane and Mama Kate.

**Toddler**

*When I Was Young: A Four Year Old's Memoir of Her Youth,* Jamie Lee Curtis (HarperCollins, New York, 1993). A four-year-old describes how her life has changed.

• *Glorious Angels,* Walter Dean Myers (HarperCollins, New York, 1995). Photographs and verse about children around the world, especially young children, depict the variety and timelessness of childhood experiences.

*Baby Says,* John Steptoe (Morrow, New York, 1992). A toddler tries every trick in the book to connive his big brother into lifting him out of the playpen, much to brother's distress and baby's delight.

*I Can,* Helen Oxenbury (Random/Firefly Books, Ontario, Canada, 1986). This board book shows what a toddler can do.

• *More, More, More, Said the Baby,* Vera Williams (Greenwillow, New York, 1990). Caldecott Award-winning illustrations convey the special relationships be-

© 2000 CRITICAL THINKING BOOKS & SOFTWARE • WWW.CRITICALTHINKING.COM • 800-458-4849        367

tween toddlers and a father, a mother, and a grandmother, including interracial families.

*Your First Step,* Henri Sorenson (Lothrop, Lee and Shephard, New York, 1991). A child's first steps and young animals' first experiences happen at the same time.

• *Brown Angels,* Walter Dean Myers (HarperCollins, New York, 1993). Verse and photographs of young children show the richness of African-American childhood.

*I'll Love You Forever,* Robert Munsch (Random/Firefly Books, Ontario, Canada, 1986). A toddler's adventures are related in this story.

*I Want To Be,* Tony Ross (Kane/Miller Book Publishers, New York, 1993). Now that she has mastered the use of her potty, the little girl decides it is time to grow up. But she's not sure how to do it or what to be.

**FAMILIES COME TO AMERICA**

• *How My Parents Learned to Eat,* Ina R. Friedman (Houghton Mifflin, Boston, MA, 1984). When an American sailor courts a Japanese girl, each tries, in secret, to learn the other's ways of eating.

• *Angel Child, Dragon Child,* Michele Maria Surat (Scholastic, New York, 1989). After Nguyan Moa hits the red-haired boy with a snowball, her school mates try to devise a plan to bring the rest of her family from Vietnam.

• *How My Family Lives in America,* Susan Kuklin (Macmillan, New York, 1992). A Puerto Rican family, a Senegalese family, and a Chinese family from Taiwan relate and depict their lives in America.

• *How Many Days to America?* Eve Bunting (Clarion Books, New York, 1988). Caribbean families risk danger to cross the Florida straits to America.

• *A Long Way to a New Land,* Joan Sandin (Harper Row, New York, 1981). In the late 1800s Swedes settle in America.

• *An Ellis Island Christmas,* Maxinne Rhea Leighton (Puffin, New York, 1992). Polish immigrants at the turn of the century enter America at Ellis Island.

• *Leaving for America,* Roslyn Bresnick-Perry (Children's Book Press, San Francisco, CA, 1992). Transliterated from Yiddish, this story relates the experience of a young Jewish girl leaving a small Russian village in the 1920s.

• *Tree of Cranes,* Allen Say (Houghton Mifflin, Boston, MA, 1991). A Japanese boy learns about Christmas when his mother decorates a pine tree with paper cranes.

• *Dia's Story Cloth: The Hmong People's Journey of Freedom,* Dia Cha (Lee and Low Books, New York, 1996). The Denver Museum of Natural History exhibits the story cloth made by Hmong people to depict their migration from China to Laos, Thailand, and finally to America.

• *Who Belongs Here? An American Story,* Margy Burns Knight (Tilbury House, Gardiner, ME, 1994). A Cambodian boy raises questions regarding who is an American.

• *Ghost Train,* Paul Yee (Groundwood Books, Ontario, Canada, 1996). A ghostly train ride brings a young girl peace in this story of early Chinese immigration to the United States and the building of Western railroads.

• *Family Pictures (Cuadros de Familias),* Carmen Lomas Garza (Children's Book Press, San Francisco, CA, 1990). In bilingual text and pictures an artist relates growing up in a Hispanic community in Texas.

• *Hello Amigos!,* Tricia Brown (Holt, Rinehart & Winston, New York, 1986). Follow the experiences of a Mexican-American boy who lives in the Mission District of San Francisco, on his sixth birthday.

• *When Jessie Came Across the Sea,* Amy Hest (Candlewick Press, Cambridge, MA, 1997). A thirteen-year-old Jewish orphan immigrates to New York City, where she sews lace to earn money to bring her grandmother to the United States.

**BEGINNING BUILDING THINKING SKILLS LESSON PLANS**                                    **BIBLIOGRAPHY**

**OCCUPATIONS** | These books describe the duties, training, products, and work requirements of various occupations. Many books illustrate occupations across cultures, including pictures and stories of people of various ethnic groups in America. These books emphasize community interdependence to which each occupation plays a significant role, and individual choice in selecting a profession.

- *People,* Peter Speir (Bantam Doubleday Dell, New York, 1980). This picture book presents numerous descriptions of how people of all ages and cultures fill basic human needs for food, clothing, shelter, love, work, and celebration.
- *Richard Scarry's What Do People Do All Day?,* Richard Scarry (Random House, New York, 1968). The many occupations, vehicles, and buildings featured in *Beginning Building Thinking Skills* lessons are depicted in humorous drawings and text.
- *Who Does This Job?,* Pat Upton (Bell Books, Honesdale, PA, 1991). This simple book shows how various jobs (farmers, grocers, teachers, doctors, mail carriers, cooks, police officers, and firefighters) are dependent on each other.

*Taxi: A Book of City Words,* Betsy and Guilio Maestro (Clarion, New York, 1992). The buildings and businesses are described on a wild taxi ride.

- *Hats, Hats, Hats,* Ann Morris, (Mulberry/Morrow, New York, 1989). Different hats show us about the culture, materials, significance, and uses of hats, including identifying hats associated with jobs.
- *Hands,* Jane Yolen (Sundance, Salem, OR, 1993). How we use our hands at home and in our jobs shows their significance across cultures.

**Artist** | *Sketching the Outdoors in Summer,* Jim Arnosky (Lothrop, Lee & Shepard, New York, 1988). This book provides drawings of landscapes, plants, animals, and other aspects of nature, including the artist's comments on how or why he drew them.

- *Getting to Know the World's Artists,* Mike Venezia (Children's Press, Chicago, 1990). This series of nineteen books for primary-grade students includes biographies of DaVinci, Michelangelo, Diego Rivera, Mary Cassatt, Rembrandt, Picasso, etc.

*Miss Rumphius,* Barbara Cooney (Puffin, New York, 1994). Great-aunt Alice Rumphius was once a little girl who loved the sea, loved to visit faraway places, and wished to do something to make the world more beautiful.

*The Painter who Loved Chickens,* Oliver Dunrea (Farrar, Straus & Giroux, New York, 1995). This whimsical story of a painter who painted many chickens and eggs features several species of chickens.

*Painting the Wind,* Michelle Dionetti (Little, Brown, Boston, MA, 1996). Entranced by the paintings of Vincent Van Gogh, for whom her mother worked as a housekeeper, Claudine is saddened when the townspeople turned against him.

*A Blue Butterfly,* Bijou LeTord (Dell, New York, 1995). A story about Claude Monet relates experiences of this artist.

**Barber** | - *Uncle Jed's Barbershop,* Margaret Mitchell (Simon & Schuster, New York, 1993). Despite her emergency illness and the Great Depression, Sarah Jean is able to share her uncle's dream of having his own barbershop. Richly detailed drawings depict the lives of an extended African-American family in the South in the 1930s.

**Construction Worker** | - *Working Hard with the Busy Mixer,* Francine Hughes (Scholastic, New York, 1993). Photographs and simple text show the parts of a cement mixer and the work of construction workers.

© 2000 CRITICAL THINKING BOOKS & SOFTWARE • WWW.CRITICALTHINKING.COM • 800-458-4849          369

BEGINNING BUILDING THINKING SKILLS LESSON PLANS                                                    BIBLIOGRAPHY

- *Building a House,* Byron Barton (Hampton Brown, New York, 1992). A machine digs a hole. A cement mixer pours the foundation. Carpenters, bricklayers, electricians, plumbers, and painters do their part.
- *Dig, Drill, Dump, Fill,* Tana Hoban (Morrow, New York, 1992). Photographs taken at urban building sites show the stages of constructing a building.

*Road Builders,* B.G. Hennessy (Viking, New York, 1994). The jobs and machinery involved in road building are depicted and explained.

*Machines At Work,* Byron Barton (HarperCollins, New York, 1987). Workers use a variety of machines to demolish one building and build another.

**Cook**

- *Getting Ready for a Career in Food Service,* Bill Lund (Children's Press/Groliers, Danbury, CT, 1996). Readers learn the duties of cooks and the knowledge and skills being a cook requires.

**Dentist**

*Going to the Dentist: Mister Rogers Neighborhood Series,* Fred Rogers (Putnam, New York, 1991). This book prepares a child to go to the dentist.

*Doctor DeSoto,* William Steig (Farrar, Straus, & Giroux, New York, 1997). A clever mouse dentist outwits his wicked fox patient.

*My Dentist,* Rockwell Harlow (Morrow, New York, 1987). The young narrator explains her visit to the dentist and the equipment her dentist uses.

**Doctor**

*Going To the Doctor,* T. Barry Brazelton (Addison Wesley, Reading, MA, 1996). Photographs and text by this famous pediatrician explain to children the equipment and procedures of a medical checkup.

*Going to the Doctor: Mister Rogers Neighborhood Series,* Fred Rogers (Putnam, New York, 1991). This book prepares a child to go to the doctor.

*I Am A Doctor,* Cynthia Benjamin (Barron, New York, 1994). This board book offers pictures and information about what doctors do.

**Farmer**

*If It Weren't for Farmers,* Allan Fowler (Children's Press/Groliers, Danbury, CT, 1996). Readers discover intriguing facts about farmers and farm products.

*If You Are Not From the Prairie...,* David Bouchard (Simon & Schuster, New York, 1995). Poetry and highly detailed drawings relate life on a modern farm on the prairie.

*Family Farm,* Thomas Locker (Dial, New York, 1988). A farm family nearly loses their home until they hit on the idea of raising and selling pumpkins and flowers to supplement their corn and milk sales.

*Farm Morning,* David McPhail (Harcourt Brace Jovanovich, New York, 1991). A young girl and her father explore the barnyard.

*Midnight Farm,* Reeve Lindbergh (Puffin/Pied Piper, New York, 1987). Susan Jeffers illustrated this story of nighttime on a farm.

*Market Day,* Eve Bunting (HarperCollins, New York, 1995). Irish children experience the excitement of going to market.

- *Chicken Man,* Michelle Edwards (Morrow, New York, 1994). Rody is in charge of the chicken house on the kibbutz in Israel's Jezreel Valley. When Rody is transferred to different positions, the chickens cleverly arrange for Rody's return.
- *Back Home,* Gloria Jean Pinkney (Dial/Penguin, New York, 1992). Husband Jerry Pinkney illustrated this story of a young African-American girl in the 1950s, riding a train to North Carolina to visit her grandparents' farm.

370          © 2000 CRITICAL THINKING BOOKS & SOFTWARE WWW.CRITICALTHINKING.COM • 800-458-4849

*The Scarebird*, Sid Fleischman (Harcourt Brace, New York, 1988). A lonesome farmer creates a scarecrow for a friend until he makes friends with a homeless boy.

**Firefighter**

• *Fire Fighters,* Ray Broekel (Children's Press/Groliers, Danbury CT, 1981). Simple text, labels, and photographs explain the work of a firefighter.

*"Fire! Fire!" Said Mrs. McGuire*, Bill Martin Jr. and Richard Egielski (Harcourt Brace, New York, 1996). Contemporary pictures and humorous rhymes tell about emergency workers responding to a fire that turns out to be a birthday cake.

*Working Hard with the Busy Fire Truck,* Jordan Horowitz (Scholastic, New York, 1993). Photographs and simple text show the parts of a fire truck and the work of fire fighters.

*The Little Firefighter*, Margaret Wise Brown (HarperCollins, New York, 1993). Bright drawings recreate the 1932 edition of this classic story.

**Grocer**

• *A Busy Day at Mr. Kang's Grocery Store*, Our Neighborhood series, Alice Flanagan (Children's Press/Groliers, Danbury CT, 1996). With photojournalistic style and simple text, this book depicts what a grocer must do to provide food to his customers.

• *The Potato Man,* Megan McDonald (Orchard, New York, 1991). Grandpa tells about the vegetable peddlers of New York in the twenties.

*Eats*, Arnold Adoff (Morrow, New York, 1992). A collection of original poems celebrating the author's love affair with shopping, preparing, and finally devouring favorite culinary delights.

*Market Day*, Eve Bunting (HarperCollins, New York, 1995). Irish children experience the excitement of going to market.

**Mail Carrier**

*The Jolly Postman*, Janet and Allan Ahlberg (Little, Brown, Boston, MA 1986). The postman delivers letters to fairy tale characters.

**Nurse**

*Nurses*, Robert James (Rourke, Vero Beach, FL, 1995). This book explains what nurses do.

**Pilot**

*I Am A Pilot*, Cynthia Benjamin (Barron Educational Series, Hauppauge, New York, 1994). This board book offers pictures and information about what pilots do.

• *Nobody Owns the Sky,* Reeve Lindbergh (Candlewick, Cambridge, MA, 1996). Charles Lindbergh's daughter created this biography of Bessie Coleman, an African-American farm girl who became the first licensed woman pilot.

**Police Officer**

*Officer Buckle and Gloria*, Peggy Rathman Calde (Putnam, New York, 1995). Elementary children ignored Officer Buckle's safety tips until Gloria the police dog accompanied him. Caldecott Award book.

**Teacher**

*My Teacher's Secret Life*, Stephen Krensky (Simon & Schuster, New York, 1996). Fanciful pictures and prose depict young children's humorous misconceptions about teachers.

*Miss Malarkey Doesn't Live in Room 101*, Judy Fincher (Walker, New York, 1995). A fanciful book explores the young children's misconceptions about teachers.

*My Teacher is My Friend*, P. K. Hallinan (Ideals, Nashville, Tennessee, 1989). Fanciful drawings show what a teacher does for children.

*My Great Aunt Arizona*, Gloria Houston (HarperCollins, New York, 1997). An Appalachian girl grows up to be a teacher.

*Lilly's Purple Purse,* Kevin Hanks (Greenwillow, New York, 1996). Lilly's admiration for her male elementary teacher and teaching is shaken in a dispute over her new purple purse.

*Our Teacher Is Having A Baby,* Eve Bunting (Clarion, New York, 1992). A first grade class learns about babies' needs as it prepares for the birth of their teacher's baby.

*The Sub,* P.J. Petersen (Dutton, New York, 1993). Two boys switch seats when they have a substitute teacher.

*Today Was A Terrible Day,* Patricia Reilly Giff (Puffin, New York, 1987). A boy's bad day at school is outweighed by his realization that he can read.

*Ruby the Copycat,* Peggy Rathmann (Scholastic, New York, 1991). Ruby insists on copying Angela, until her teacher helps her discover her own creativity.

*Ramona the Brave,* Beverly Cleary (Morrow, New York, 1975). Ramona has many difficulties until she finally wins a truce with the first-grade teacher.

**FOOD**

These books describe the source and processing of various foods. Many books illustrate food preferences and preparation across cultures. They emphasize primary-grade science and health concepts regarding food selection and basic information on plants and animals that supply food and social studies concepts on community interdependence in acquiring various foods.

*What's on My Plate?,* Ruth Belov Grose (Simon & Schuster, New York, 1991). Good humor, simple text, and vibrant illustrations tell where food comes from.

*A Book of Fruit,* Barbara Hirsh Lember (Ticknor and Fields / Houghton Mifflin, New York, 1994). Photographs show where fourteen fruit are grown.

*Growing Colors,* Bruce McMillan (Lothrop, Lee & Shepard, New York, 1988). Photographs of green peas, yellow corn, red potatoes, purple beans and other fruits and vegetables illustrate the many colors of nature.

*Meat,* Elizabeth Clark (Carolrhoda, Minneapolis, MN, 1996). This book contains basic information about meat.

*Eating the Alphabet,* Lois Ehlert (Voyager / Harcourt Brace, New York, 1987). Pictures of fruit and vegetable include all those featured in *Beginning Building Thinking Skills* lessons.

*We Love Fruit,* Fay Robinson (Children's Press / Groliers, Danbury, CT, 1992). Readers discover intriguing facts about fruit.

*Vegetables, Vegetables!,* Fay Robinson (Children's Press / Groliers, Danbury, CT, 1992). Readers discover intriguing facts about vegetables.

*Vegetables,* Wake (Carolrhoda, Minneapolis, MN, 1996). This book contains basic information about vegetables.

*What Am I? Looking Through Shapes at Apples and Grapes,* N. N. Charles (Blue Sky / Scholastic, New York, 1994). Illustrations with cut out shapes and rhyming riddles introduce a variety of fruit.

*Vegetable Garden,* Douglas Florian (Voyager / HBJ, New York, 1991). A family plants a vegetable garden and helps it grow.

*Growing Vegetable Soup,* Lois Ehlert (Harcourt Brace, New York, 1987). A father and a child grow vegetable soup together.

*More Than Just A Vegetable Garden,* Dwight Kuhn (Silver Burdett / Prentice Hall, Englewood Cliffs, New Jersey, 1990). Text and photos present life among the animals and plants in a vegetable garden.

*Eats,* Arnold Adoff (Morrow, New York, 1992). A collection of original poems celebrating the author's love affair with shopping, preparing, and finally devouring favorite culinary delights.

BEGINNING BUILDING THINKING SKILLS LESSON PLANS                    BIBLIOGRAPHY

**Apples**

*Apples of Your Eye,* Allan Fowler (Children's Press/Groliers, Danbury, CT, 1994). Readers discover intriguing facts about apples.

*Apples,* Easy Readers series, Ann Burckhardt (Children's Press/Groliers, Danbury, CT, 1996). Easy-to-Read science books introduce students to apples.

*Johnny Appleseed,* Steven Kellogg (Morrow, New York, 1988). This book describes Johnny Appleseed's route.

*The Apple Pie Tree,* Zoe Hall, (Blue Sky/Scholastic, New York, 1996). An apple tree grows leaves and flowers, and then produces fruit, while in its branches robins make a nest, lay eggs, and raise a family.

**Bacon**

*Don't Forget the Bacon,* Pat Hutchins (Morrow, New York, 1994). A boy becomes confused about what he should bring home from the grocery store, but remembers "and don't forget the bacon."

**Beans**

*Vegetables, Vegetables!,* Fay Robinson (Children's Press/Groliers, Danbury, CT, 1992). Readers discover intriguing facts about vegetables.

*Growing Colors,* Bruce McMillan (Lothrop, Lee & Shepard/Morrow, New York, 1988). Photographs of green peas, yellow corn, red potatoes, purple beans, and other fruits and vegetables illustrate the many colors of nature.

*Jack and the Beanstalk,* Paul Galdone (Clarion/Houghton Mifflin, New York, 1974). This retelling is based on the 1807 version of the classic story.

**Bread**

• *Bread, Bread, Bread,* Ann Morris (Mulberry/Morrow, New York, 1993). Different cultures vary the ingredients, preparation, significance, and uses of bread.

*The Unbeatable Bread,* Lyn Littlefield Hoops (Dial/Penguin, New York, 1996). Special bread draws people and animals to a feast.

*Seven Loaves of Bread,* Ferida Wolff (Tambourine/Morrow, New York, 1993). When Milly, who does the baking on the farm, gets sick, Rose discovers that there are very good reasons for making extra loaves of bread to share.

• *Too Many Tamales,* Gary Soto (Putnam, New York, 1993). Warm oil paintings illustrate a tender, funny story about a Mexican-American family at Christmastime.

• *Forri the Baker,* Edward Myers (Dial, New York, 1995). Forri, the best village baker in the town of Ettai, makes some pretty oddly-shaped loaves which provoke criticism until he rescues the village from barbarian attack.

• *Tony's Bread,* Tomie De Paola (Putnam and Grosset, New York, 1996). A baker from Milan bakes unusual bread for an Italian nobleman.

**Butter**

*Butter,* Wake (Carolrhoda, Minneapolis, MN, 1990). This book provides information on the processing of butter.

**Cabbage**

*Vegetables, Vegetables!,* Fay Robinson (Children's Press/Groliers, Danbury, CT, 1992). Readers discover intriguing facts about vegetables.

**Carrot**

*Vegetables, Vegetables!,* Fay Robinson (Children's Press/Groliers, Danbury, CT, 1992). Readers discover intriguing facts about vegetables.

• *Tops and Bottoms,* Janet Stevens (Harcourt Brace, New York, 1995). Detailed pictures of growing vegetables illustrate this Caldecott Honor book, which is based on an African trickster tale regarding which part of the vegetable one eats.

*The Carrot Seed,* Ruth Krauss (Scholastic, New York, 1989). Whimsical drawings relate a boy's wait for a carrot seed to grow.

© 2000 CRITICAL THINKING BOOKS & SOFTWARE • WWW.CRITICALTHINKING.COM • 800-458-4849          373

**BEGINNING BUILDING THINKING SKILLS LESSON PLANS** **BIBLIOGRAPHY**

**Celery**

*The Celery Stalks at Midnight,* James Howe (Avon/Macmillan, New York, 1984). Using his observations of white vegetables as evidence, Chester the cat is convinced more than ever that the rabbit Bunnicula is a vampire.

**Cheese**

*The Old Man Who Loved Cheese,* Garrison Keillor (Little, Brown, Boston, MA, 1996). This story about a man's love for stinky cheese names many kinds of cheese.

**Chicken**

*Meat,* Elizabeth Clark (Carolrhoda, Minneapolis, MN, 1996). This book provides information on the processing of various meats.
• *Chicken Sunday,* Patricia Polacco (Putnam and Grosset, New York, 1992). Chicken dinners and eggs take on special significance for an African-American family and their Russian immigrant friend.

**Corn**

*Corn,* Easy Readers series, Ann Burckhardt (Children's Press/Groliers, Danbury, CT, 1996). Easy-to-Read science books introduce students to corn.
• *The Legend of Food Mountain,* Graciela Carrilo (Children's Book Press, San Francisco, CA, 1995). This retelling of a legend describing how corn came to the Aztecs features English and Spanish text and colorful illustrations.
• *Corn Is Maise: The Gift of the Indians,* Aliki (HarperCollins, New York, 1986). Facts about the history and uses of corn are presented in an appealing, easy-to-read book.

**Eggs**

*Green Eggs and Ham,* Dr. Seuss (Random House, New York, 1960). Fantastic drawings and repetitious rhyme make this story about food preferences a classic children's book.
• *Down the Road,* Alice Schertle (Browndeer/Harcourt Brace, San Diego, 1995). Hettie is careful with the eggs on her first trip to the market until she stops to pick apples.
*Egg! A Dozen Eggs, What Will They Be?* A.J. Wood (Little, Brown, Boston, MA, 1993). A fold-out book encourages readers to predict what kind of creature hatches out of twelve different eggs.
*The Easter Egg Farm,* Mary Jane Auch (Holiday, New York, 1992). Pauline the hen lays unusual eggs which her owner thinks are beautiful, and together they work to open an Easter egg farm.
*Too Many Eggs: A Counting Book,* M. Christina Butler (David Godine, Boston, MA, 1985). Readers help count the number of eggs in a birthday cake.
*The Egg Tree,* Katherine Milhous (Aladdin, New York, 1950). This Caldecott Award book explains Easter eggs.
• *The Talking Eggs: A Folktale from the American South,* Robert D. San Souci (Dial, New York, 1989). A Southern folktale in which kind Blance, following the instructions of an old witch, gains riches, while her greedy sister makes fun of the old woman and is duly rewarded.
*Chickens Aren't The Only Ones That Lay Eggs,* Ruth Heller (Putnam, New York, 1981). This colorful, factual book about eggs includes many other animals that lay eggs, including ostriches, turkeys, snakes, spiders, turtles, lizards, frogs, sharks, and fish.
• *Chicken Sunday,* Patricia Polacco (Putnam and Grosset, New York, 1992). Chicken dinners and eggs take on special significance for an African-American family and their Russian immigrant friend.

**Grapes**

*We Love Fruit,* Fay Robinson (Children's Press/Groliers, Danbury, CT, 1992). Readers discover intriguing facts about fruit.

374 © 2000 CRITICAL THINKING BOOKS & SOFTWARE WWW.CRITICALTHINKING.COM • 800-458-4849

**BEGINNING BUILDING THINKING SKILLS LESSON PLANS**                    **BIBLIOGRAPHY**

• *Freedom's Fruit,* William H. Hooks (Alfred A. Knopf, New York, 1996). Conjured grapes are part of a plot to win a slave's freedom.

**Ham**

*Meat,* Elizabeth Clark (Carolrhoda, Minneapolis, MN, 1996). This book provides information on the processing of meat.

*Green Eggs and Ham,* Dr. Seuss (Random House, New York, 1960). Fantastic drawings and repetitious rhyme make this story about food preferences a classic children's book.

**Lettuce**

*Vegetables, Vegetables!,* Fay Robinson (Children's Press/Groliers, Danbury, CT, 1992). Readers discover intriguing facts about vegetables.

*Peter Rabbit,* Beatrix Potter (F. Warne, London, 1987). The original edition of the adventures of Peter Rabbit includes his quest for lettuce.

**Milk**

*No Milk,* Jennifer A Ericsson (Tambourine, New York, 1993). In a repetitive text, a boy tries to milk a cow.

*Milk,* Donald Carrick (Greenwillow, New York, 1985). This book describes the entire process by which milk goes from the cow to our homes.

*Jeremy Kooloo,* Tim Mahurin (Dutton, New York, 1995). In this ABC book Jeremy the cat drinks a whole carton of milk.

*In the Night Kitchen,* Maurice Sendak (Harper & Row, New York, 1970). In a little boy's dream-fantasy he helps three fat bakers get milk for their cake batter.

**Onion**

*Vegetables, Vegetables!,* Fay Robinson (Children's Press/Groliers, Danbury, CT, 1992). Readers discover intriguing facts about vegetables.

• *Tops and Bottoms,* Janet Stevens (Harcourt Brace, New York, 1995). Detailed pictures of growing vegetables illustrate this Caldecott Honor book, which is based on an African trickster tale regarding which part of the vegetable one eats.

**Orange**

*We Love Fruit,* Fay Robinson (Children's Press/Groliers, Danbury, CT, 1992). Readers discover intriguing facts about fruit.

*Each Orange Had Eight Slices,* Paul Giganti (Morrow, New York, 1994). This original counting book uses familiar objects to introduce beginning math concepts and reinforce visual literacy.

*Citrus Fruit,* Wake (Carolrhoda, Minneapolis, MN,1996). This book provides information on oranges

*We Love Fruit,* Fay Robinson (Children's Press/Groliers, Danbury, CT, 1992). Readers discover intriguing facts about fruit.

**Peach**

*James and the Giant Peach,* Roald Dahl (Disney, New York, 1996). This picture book edition relates a young boy's adventures with six insects on a giant peach.

*I Will Tell You A Story of A Peach Stone,* Nathan Zimelman (Lothrop, Lee & Shepard, New York, 1976).

**Peas**

*Vegetables, Vegetables!,* Fay Robinson (Children's Press/Groliers, Danbury, CT, 1992). Readers discover intriguing facts about vegetables.

*The Pea Patch Jig,* Thatcher Hurd (HarperTrophy, New York, 1986). A mouse family's adventures with tomatoes and peas are based on a folk song.

© 2000 CRITICAL THINKING BOOKS & SOFTWARE • WWW.CRITICALTHINKING.COM • 800-458-4849        375

**BEGINNING BUILDING THINKING SKILLS LESSON PLANS**　　　　　　　　　　　　　　**BIBLIOGRAPHY**

**Potato**

*Potatoes*, Easy Readers series, Ann Burckhardt (Children's Press/Groliers, Danbury, CT, 1996). Easy-to-Read science books introduce students to potatoes.

*Vegetables, Vegetables!*, Fay Robinson (Children's Press/Groliers, Danbury, CT, 1992). Readers discover intriguing facts about vegetables.

• *Jamie O'Rourke and the Big Potato: An Irish Folktale,* Tomie DePaola (Putnam, New York, 1992). A leprechaun offers a lazy man a potato seed instead of a pot of gold.

*The Amazing Potato,* Milton Meltzer (HarperCollins, New York, 1992). This book introduces the history, effects and current uses of the potato.

**Rice**

• *Everybody Cooks Rice,* Noral Dooley (Carolrhoda Books, Minneapolis, MN, 1991). Pictures and recipes show how rice is cooked in nine cultures.

• *Rice,* Lynne Merrison (Carolrhoda, Minneapolis, MN, 1990). This book provides information on the processing of rice.

• *The Rajah's Rice: A Mathematical Folktale From India,* David Barry (Putnam, New York, 1994). Doubling grains of rice sixty-four times would make India knee-deep in rice.

*Chicken Soup With Rice,* Maurice Sendak (HarperCollins, New York, 1991). Chicken soup is a unifying theme to present an illustrated tour of the months of the year.

**Steak**

*Meat,* Elizabeth Clark (Carolrhoda, Minneapolis, MN, 1996). This book provides information on the processing of meat.

**Tomato**

*Vegetables, Vegetables!,* Fay Robinson (Children's Press/Groliers, Danbury, CT, 1992). Readers discover intriguing facts about vegetables.

*The Pea Patch Jig,* Thatcher Hurd (HarperTrophy, New York, 1986). A mouse family's adventures with tomatoes and peas are based on a folk song.

*Tomato,* Barrie Watts (Silver Burdett, Englewood Cliffs, NJ, 1990).

**VEHICLES**

These books depict the structure, uses, and operation of various vehicles. They also inform young readers about the occupations and skills involved in operating various vehicles, as well as showing community interdependence regarding transportation.

*Wings, Wheels, and Sails,* Tom Stacy (Random House, New York, 1995). This question-answer book offers interesting, illustrated facts about cars, airplanes, bicycles, helicopters, trains, ships, and boats.

*Steven Biesty's Incredible Cross Sections,* Steven Biesty (Dorling Kindersley, New York, 1995). Highly detailed pictures of cross-sections help children understand how many vehicles work.

• *Richard Scarry's What Do People Do All Day?,* Richard Scarry (Random House, New York, 1968). The many occupations, vehicles, and buildings featured in *Beginning Building Thinking Skills* lessons are depicted in humorous drawings and text.

*On the Go,* Ann Morris (Morrow, New York, 1994). Photographs form a series of multicultural images of people riding, walking, sailing, and being carried.

*What's Inside?,* (Dorling Kindersley, New York, 1992). Detailed pictures show the interiors of several vehicles, including ambulances, fire engines, and trucks.

*Machines As Big as Monsters,* Paul Strickland (Puffin Penguin, New York, 1989). Huge machines (helicopters, tractors, trucks) perform huge tasks.

376　　　© 2000 CRITICAL THINKING BOOKS & SOFTWARE www.criticalthinking.com • 800-458-4849

**BEGINNING BUILDING THINKING SKILLS LESSON PLANS**                                    **BIBLIOGRAPHY**

*Promise I'll Find You,* Heather Patricia Ward (Firefly, Buffalo, New York, 1994). Different transportation is described to assure a loved one of being found.

*Going Places,* Snap Shot series (Oxford University Press, Oxford, England, 1995). This board book offers detailed pictures and information about vehicles.

*I Spy A Freight Train: Transportation in Art,* Lucy Mickle Thwait (Greenwillow, New York, 1996). This book features art masterpieces by famous artists and little text to show the following forms of transportation: airplanes, bicycles, trains, and boats.

*Rush Hour,* Christine Loomis (Houghton Mifflin, Boston, MA, 1996). People rush to work and home again on buses, cars, bicycles, etc.

*Richard Scarry's Cars, Trucks, and Things That Go,* Richard Scarry (Golden Books, Racine, WI, 1974). Various vehicles are colorfully illustrated and described.

**Airplane**

*Airplanes,* Mighty Machines series (Dorling Kindersley, New York, 1995). Detailed pictures show many types of airplanes.

*Airport,* Byron Barton (Trophy / Harper Collins, New York, 1987). Large illustrations follow passengers as they prepare to board an airplane.

*Flight,* Robert Burleigh (Philomel Division of Putnam and Grosset, New York, 1992). This picture book relates Lindbergh's flight across the Atlantic Ocean.

*Flying,* Donald Crews (Mulberry / Morrow, New York, 1986). Simple pictures and words make this story of an airplane flight suitable for beginning readers.

*Going on an Airplane: Mister Rogers Neighborhood Series,* Fred Rogers (G.P. Putnam, New York, 1989). Prepares a child for his first airplane trip.

**Ambulance**

*Emergency Vehicles,* Cruisin' series, Dayna Wolhart (Children's Press / Groliers, Danbury, CT, 1991). Readers learn about the equipment, design, and use of various emergency vehicles.

*Emergency,* Snap Shot series (Oxford University Press, Oxford, England, 1995). This board book offers detailed pictures of emergency vehicles, including an ambulance.

**Bicycle**

*BMX Bicycles,* Rollin' series, Barbara Knox (Children's Press / Groliers, Danbury, CT, 1996). Readers learn about the equipment, design, and use of bicycles.

*Amazing Bikes,* Trevor Lord (Knopf, New York, 1992). This book in the Eyewitness Juniors series shows the diversity and structures of bicycles.

*How Is A Bicycle Made?* Henry Horenstein (Simon & Schuster, New York, 1993). This story shows how frame, wheels, gears, and pedals come together to form a sleek, shiny two-wheeler.

*Hello, Two Wheeler,* Jane Mason (Grosset and Dunlop, New York, 1995). A boy is reluctant to ride his bicycle because his friends no longer ride bicycles with training wheels.

*D. W. Rides Again!* Marc Brown (Little, Brown, Boston, MA, 1996). D. W. has graduated from a tricycle to her first two-wheeler, but first needs to find out where the brakes are!

*My Bike,* Donna Jakob (Hyperion, New York, 1994). A boy recognizes his progress in learning to ride a bicycle.

*The Red Racer,* Audrey Wood (Simon & Schuster, New York, 1996). Nona tries to get rid of her junky old bike so that she can get a Deluxe Red Racer.

**Boat**

*Ships and Boats,* Eye Opener series (Dorling Kindersley, New York, 1995). Detailed pictures show many types of ships and boats.

© 2000 CRITICAL THINKING BOOKS & SOFTWARE • WWW.CRITICALTHINKING.COM • 800-458-4849

**BEGINNING BUILDING THINKING SKILLS LESSON PLANS**                                    **BIBLIOGRAPHY**

*Little Toot,* Hardie Gramatky (Putnam/Grosset, New York, 1939). A little tug boat
saves an ocean liner.

*Boats on the River,* Marjorie Flack (Viking, New York, 1991). This classic Caldecott
Honor book depicts different kinds of boats.

*Sail Away,* Donald Crews (Greenwillow, New York, 1986). Simple pictures and
words make this story of a sailboat in a storm suitable for beginning readers.

*Ships,* Richard Humble (Barnes and Noble, Oxford, England, 1995). Text and
photographs depict a variety of boats and ships.

*Three Days on a River in a Red Canoe,* Vera Williams (Morrow, New York, 1984). A
canoe journeys along a river carrying the family on a camping tour.

*The Wreck of the Zephyr,* Chris Van Allsburg (Houghton Mifflin, New York, 1983). A
boy's ambition to be the greatest sailor in the world brings him to ruin when he
misuses his new ability to sail his boat in the air.

**Bus**

*Is There Room on the Bus?,* Helen Piers and Hannah Giffard (Simon & Schuster, New
York, 1996). In this counting story an alliterative array of animals travel in a
rickety bus.

*Where's That Bus?,* Eileen Brown (Simon & Schuster, New York, 1991). Rabbit and
Mole become too distracted to recognize the frequent passing of the bus.

*The Wheels on the Bus,* Paul Zelinsky (Dutton, New York, 1990). The wheels on the bus
go around, the wipers go swish, the doors open and close, and the people go in
and out in this movable book version of the children's song.

• *Abuela,* Arthur Dorros (Dutton, New York, 1991). While riding on a bus with her
grandmother, a little girl imagines that they are carried up into the sky and fly
over the sights of New York City.

*My Place in Space,* Robin and Sally Hirst (Orchard, New York, 1990). Henry tells the
bus driver exactly where he lives, positioning himself precisely in the universe.

**Car**

*Jack Tractor: Five Stories from Smallbill's Garage,* Karen Ludlow and Willy Imax
(Crown, New York, 1995). Fanciful stories about Benny the Tow Truck describe
his adventures with a tractor, different kinds of cars, and a motorcycle.

*Cars, Cars, Cars,* Grace Maccarone (Scholastic, New York, 1995). This Easy Reader
book shows different kinds of cars.

*Cars,* Eye Opener series (Dorling Kindersley, New York, 1995). Detailed pictures
show many types of cars.

*Taxi: A Book of City Words,* Betsy and Guilio Maestro (Clarion, New York, 1992). The
buildings and businesses are described on a wild taxi ride.

*Chitty Chitty Bang Bang,* Ian Fleming (Knopf, New York, 1989). Two children
persuade their father, an inventor, to purchase and restore an old car which turns
out to have magical powers.

**Fire Truck**

• *Fire Fighters,* R. Broekel (Children's Press/Groliers, Danbury CT, 1981). Simple
text, labels, and photographs explain the work of a firefighter.

*Fire Trucks,* Easy Reader series, Peter Brady (Children's Press/Groliers, Danbury,
CT, 1996). Readers learn about the equipment, design, and use of fire trucks.

*Emergency Vehicles,* Cruisin' series, Dayna Wolhart (Children's Press/Groliers,
Danbury, CT, 1991). Readers learn about the equipment, design, and use of
various emergency vehicles.

*Fire Engines,* Anne Rockwell (Dutton, New York, 1986). This board book offers
simple pictures and information about fire trucks.

*Working Hard with the Busy Fire Truck,* Jordan Horowitz (Scholastic, New York, 1993).

378          © 2000 **CRITICAL THINKING BOOKS & SOFTWARE** WWW.CRITICALTHINKING.COM • 800-458-4849

**BEGINNING BUILDING THINKING SKILLS LESSON PLANS**                                        **BIBLIOGRAPHY**

Photographs and simple text show the parts of a fire truck and the work of firefighters.

*Fire Truck: Nuts and Bolts,* Jerry Boucher (Carolrhoda, Minneapolis, MN, 1993). This book shows the steps in building a fire truck.

*All Aboard Fire Trucks,* Teddy Slater (Grosset & Dunlap, New York, 1991). This book illustrates and describes many kinds of fire trucks.

**Helicopter**

*Emergency Vehicles,* Cruisin' series, Dayna Wolhart (Children's Press/Groliers, Danbury, CT, 1991). Readers learn about the equipment, design, and use of various emergency vehicles.

*Budgie, the Little Helicopter,* HRH Duchess of York (Simon & Schuster, New York, 1989). Budgie and Pippa the airplane help out in a crisis.

**Motorcycle**

*Motorcycles,* Rollin' series, Jackson Jay (Children's Press/Groliers, Danbury, CT, 1996). Readers learn about the equipment, design, and use of motorcycles.

*Dirt Bike Racer,* Matt Christopher (Little, Brown, Boston, MA, 1979). Twelve-year-old Ron Baker restores a minibike.

*Jack Tractor: Five Stories from Smallbill's Garage,* Karen Ludlow and Willy Imax (Crown, New York, 1995). Fanciful stories about Benny the Tow Truck describe his adventures with a tractor, cars, and a motorcycle.

**Police Car**

*Emergency Vehicles,* Cruisin' series, Dayna Wolhart (Children's Press/Groliers, Danbury, CT, 1991). Readers learn about the equipment, design, and use of various emergency vehicles.

*A Day in the Life of a Police Officer,* E. Arnold (Scholastic, New York, 1994). Photographs show the daily activities of police officer Kathy Murphy.

*Police Patrol,* Katherine Winkleman (Walker & Co., New York, 1996). Describes the activities at a police station and the duties of different types of officers.

**School Bus**

*School Bus,* Donald Crews (Morrow, New York, 1993). Climb aboard the bright yellow school bus. It will pick you up, take you to school, and bring you home again.

• ***This is the Way We Go to School,*** Edith Baer (Scholastic, New York, 1990). Describes the many different modes of transportation children all over the world use to get to school.

*The Magic School Bus Series,* Joanna Cole (Scholastic, New York, 1986). This whole series of amusing nonfiction books for children, the school bus is the vehicle that takes them on adventures.

**Ship**

*Ships and Boats,* Eye Opener series (Dorling Kindersley, New York, 1995). Detailed pictures show many types of ships and boats.

*Ships,* Richard Humble (Barnes and Noble, Oxford, England, 1995). Text and photographs depict a variety of boats and ships.

*Harbor,* Donald Crews, (Morrow, New York, 1987). Liners, tankers, tugs, barges, ferries, and fireboats fill a big city harbor with color and excitement.

**Tractor**

*If It Weren't for Farmers,* Allan Fowler (Children's Press/Groliers, Danbury, CT, 1996). Readers discover intriguing facts about farmers and farm products.

© 2000 CRITICAL THINKING BOOKS & SOFTWARE • WWW.CRITICALTHINKING.COM • 800-458-4849

**BEGINNING BUILDING THINKING SKILLS LESSON PLANS**     **BIBLIOGRAPHY**

*Tractors,* Cruisin' series, Gil Chandler (Children's Press/Groliers, Danbury, CT, 1996). Readers learn about the equipment, design, and use of tractors.

*Tractors,* Easy Readers series, Peter Brady (Children's Press/Groliers, Danbury, CT, 1996). Readers learn about the equipment, design, and use of tractors.

*Katy and the Big Snow,* Virginia Lee Burton (Houghton Mifflin, Boston, MA, 1942). Katy the tractor helps people in many difficult situations, including a big snowfall.

*Jack Tractor: Five Stories from Smallbill's Garage,* Karen Ludlow and Willy Imax (Crown, New York, 1995). Fanciful stories about Benny the Tow Truck describe his adventures with a tractor, cars, and a motorcycle.

*Leah's Pony,* Elizabeth Friedrich (Boyd Mills, Honesdale, PA, 1996). In the Depression of the 1930s a girl sells her beloved horse so that her grandfather may buy back his tractor.

**Train**

*Freight Train,* Easy Readers series, Peter Brady (Children's Press/Groliers, Danbury, CT, 1996). Readers learn about the equipment, design, and use of freight trains.

*Freight Train,* Donald Crews (Greenwillow, New York, 1978). This classic Caldecott Honor book features little text and simplified pictures of freight trains.

*Trains,* Eye Opener series (Dorling Kindersley, New York, 1995). Detailed pictures show many types of trains.

*The Little Engine That Could,* Watty Piper (Barbour, New York, 1997). This children's classic demonstrates persistence.

*Train Song,* Diane Siebert (HarperTrophy, New York, 1990). Rhymed text and illustrations describe a variety of trains.

*Steam Locomotive,* Keith Mosely (Compass, Long Beach, CA, 1989). This pop-up book shows the operation of a steam locomotive.

*Steam Train Ride,* Evelyn Clarke Mott (Walker, New York, 1991). Photographs depict a young boy's experience riding a steam locomotive and learning how it works.

*Freight Train,* Donald Crews (Morrow, New York, 1992). When the freight train stands still, we can count the cars, name their colors, and identify their functions. But then the train picks up speed, it becomes a blur of color, speed, and sound.

*Train Leaves the Station,* Eve Merriam (Henry Holt, New York, 1992). Simple pictures of trains illustrate this simple rhyme.

*Country Crossing,* Jim Aylesworth (Simon & Schuster, New York, 1995). Recreates the sights and sounds at a country crossing one summer night, as an old car patiently awaits the passing of a long and noisy freight train.

*The Polar Express,* Chris Van Allsburg (Houghton Mifflin, New York, 1985). This Caldecott winners tells of a magical train trip to the North Pole on Christmas Eve.

*Shortcut,* Donald Crews (Greenwillow, New York, 1992). Children taking a shortcut by walking along railroad tracks find excitement and danger when a train approaches.

• ***Ghost Train,*** Paul Yee (Groundwood Books, Ontario, 1996). A ghostly train ride brings a young girl peace in this story of early Chinese immigration to the United States and the building of Western railroads.

*Journey,* Guy Billout (American Education Publishing, Columbus, Ohio, 1993). Soft, yet vibrant art reveals the experiences of a boy who boards a train for a long journey.

*Sunday Outing,* Gloria Jean Pinkney (Dial/Penguin, New York, 1992). Husband Jerry Pinkney illustrated this story of a young African-American girl in the 1950s, riding a train to North Carolina.

*The Owl Who Became the Moon,* Jonathan London (Dutton, New York, 1993). While riding on a train at night, a young boy listens and watches as he passes many creatures in their wilderness homes.

**380**     © 2000 CRITICAL THINKING BOOKS & SOFTWARE WWW.CRITICALTHINKING.COM • 800-458-4849

| | **BEGINNING BUILDING THINKING SKILLS LESSON PLANS** | **BIBLIOGRAPHY** |

- ***Death of the Iron Horse,*** Paul Goble (Bradbury/Macmillan, New York, 1987). In a act of bravery and defiance against the white men encroaching on their territory in 1867, a group of young Cheyenne braves derail and raid a Union Pacific freight train.

*All Aboard Trains,* Mary Harding (Putnam, New York, 1989). This book illustrates and describes freight trains and passenger trains.

**Truck**

*Pick-Up Trucks,* Rollin' series, James Koons (Children's Press/Groliers, Danbury, CT, 1996). Readers learn about the equipment, design, and use of pickup trucks.

*The Little Black Truck,* Libba Moore Gray (Simon & Schuster, New York, 1994). Dreamlike drawings depict the story of a little truck that is refurbished for a new life.

*Truck,* Donald Crews (Morrow, New York, 1991). A big red truck full of tricycles makes its way from the loading dock to city streets, through a tunnel, and over miles of highway to its destination.

*All Aboard Trucks,* Lynn Conrad (Putnam, New York, 1989). This book illustrates and describes trucks in the neighborhood, trucks around town, and trucks in the country.

*Trucks,* Eye Opener series (Dorling Kindersley, New York, 1995). Detailed pictures show many types of trucks.

*Diggers and Dump Trucks,* Eye Opener series (Dorling Kindersley, New York, 1995). Detailed pictures show many types of trucks and heavy machinery.

*Road Builders,* B.G. Hennessy (Penguin, New York, 1994). This book describes the many trucks needed to build a road.

**ANIMALS**

These books depict the body structure, habitats, food chain relationships, and survival needs of various types of animals.

*What Animal Am I? An Animal Guessing Game,* Iza Trapani (Whispering Coyote Press, Danvers, MA, 1992). This book models animal riddles with pictures.

*The Big Red Barn,* Margaret Wise Brown (HarperCollins, New York, 1989). Rhymed text and illustrations introduce the many different animals that live in the big barn.

*Hoot, Howl, Hiss,* Michelle Koch (Greenwillow, New York, 1991). Depicts the sounds that animals make in the woods, by the pond, in the jungle, at the farm, or in the mountains.

*Egg! A Dozen Eggs, What Will They Be?* A. J. Wood (Little, Brown, Boston, MA, 1993). A fold-out book encourages readers to predict what kind of creature hatches out of twelve different eggs.

*Early Morning in the Barn,* Nancy Tafuri (Greenwillow, New York, 1983). An almost wordless book illustrates the journey of three chicks as they explore the barnyard.

*Farm Morning,* David McPhail (Harcourt Brace Jovanovich, New York, 1985). A young girl and her father explore the barnyard.

*Farm Animals,* New True series, K. Jacobsen (Children's Press/Groliers, Danbury, CT, 1981). This richly illustrated, easy-to-read book provides answers to young students' basic questions about farm animals.

*A First Look at Animals with Horns,* Millicent E. Selsamn and Joyce Hunt (Walker, 1989). This book discusses characteristics of animals with horns.

*The Owl Who Became the Moon,* Jonathan London (Dutton, New York, 1993). While riding on a train at night, a young boy listens and watches as he passes many creatures in their wilderness homes.

*In the Tall, Tall Grass,* Denise Fleming (Holt, New York, 1991). Rhymed text presents

© 2000 CRITICAL THINKING BOOKS & SOFTWARE • WWW.CRITICALTHINKING.COM • 800-458-4849          381

a toddler's view of creatures, such as ants, bees, and moles, found in the grass from lunchtime to nightfall.

*Sketching the Outdoors in Summer*, Jim Arnosky (Lothrop, Lee & Shepard, New York, 1988). This book provides drawings of landscapes, plants, animals, and other aspects of nature, including comments from the artist on how or why he drew them.

*The Trek*, Ann Jonas (Greenwillow, New York, 1985). The city streets become a jungle, then a desert, as a child forges her way to school, observing and avoiding the wild animals posing as trees, chimneys, fences, even fruit.

*Insects and Creepy Creatures* (Dorling Kindersley, New York, 1995). Detailed pictures of many types of insects.

*I Spy A Freight Train: Transportation in Art,* Lucy Mickle Thwait (Greenwillow, New York, 1996). This book features art masterpieces by famous artists and little text to show animals as transportation.

*Chickens Aren't The Only Ones That Lay Eggs,* Ruth Heller (Grosset and Dunlop, New York, 1981). This colorful, factual book about eggs includes many other animals that lay eggs, including ostriches, turkeys, snakes, spiders, turtles, lizards, frogs, sharks, and fish.

*Reptiles,* Robert Matero, Eyes on Nature series (Kidsbooks, Chicago, 1994). Text and photographs of the physical characteristics, habits, and natural environment of various reptiles.

*Birds We Know,* New True series, M. Friskey (Children's Press / Groliers, Danbury, CT, 1981). This richly illustrated, easy-to-read book provides answers to young students' basic questions about familiar birds.

*Life in a Pond,* Rookie Read About Science series, Allan Fowler (Children's Press / Groliers, Danbury, CT, 1996). Young students discover intriguing facts about fish.

*African Animals,* New True series, J. W. Purcell (Children's Press / Groliers, Danbury, CT, 1982). This richly illustrated, easy-to-read book provides answers to young students' basic questions about familiar African animals.

*Night Birds,* New True series, (Children's Press / Groliers, Danbury, CT, 1996). This richly illustrated, easy-to-read book provides answers to young students' basic questions about night birds.

**Camel**

*Desert Mammals,* Elaine Landau (Children's Press / Groliers, Danbury, CT, 1996).

*Pamela Camel,* Bill Peet (Houghton Mifflin, Boston, MA, 1984). A dejected circus camel finds recognition along a railroad track.

**Chicken**

*Chickens*, Easy Readers series, Ann Burckhardt (Children's Press / Groliers, Danbury, CT, 1996). This easy-to-read science book introduces students to well-known farm animals.

*The Chicken or the Egg,* Rookie Read About Science series, (Children's Press / Groliers, Danbury, CT, 1993). Young students discover intriguing facts about chickens.

*If It Weren't For Farmers,* Rookie Read About Science series, (Children's Press / Groliers, Danbury, CT, 1993). Young students discover intriguing facts about farms and farm animals.

*The Rooster's Gift,* Pam Conrad (Harper Collins, New York, 1996). Rooster thinks that his gift makes the sun come up until one morning he oversleeps.

*The Painter Who Loved Chickens,* Oliver Dunrea (Farrar, Straus & Giroux, New York, 1995). This whimsical story of a painter who painted many chickens and eggs features several species of chickens.

*Here a Chick, There a Chick,* Bruce McMillan (Lothrop, Lee & Shepard, New York,

1983). Photographs of baby chicks are used to illustrate such opposite concepts as inside/outside, asleep/awake, and alone/together.

- ***Chicken Sunday,*** Patricia Polacco (Putnam and Grosset, New York, 1992). Chicken dinners and eggs take on special significance for an African- American family and their Russian immigrant friend.

*The Bossy Gallito,* Lucia Gonzalez (Scholastic, New York, 1996). In this retelling of a Cuban folktale, a bossy rooster seeks help to clean his beak.

*The Little Red Hen,* Paul Galdone (Clarion/Houghton Mifflin, New York, 1973). This modern retelling of the classic story is illustrated with humorous pictures.

- ***Hattie and the Fox,*** Mem Fox (Aladdin, New York, 1986). Hattie's discovery of a fox in the bushes creates varying reactions among barnyard animals.

*Good Morning Chick,* Mirra Ginsburg (Morrow, New York, 1992). A little chick pops out of its shell. With Mama by its side it explores the barnyard.

*Chicken Little,* Steven Kellogg (Morrow, New York, 1987). Chicken Little and her feathered friends are all aflutter about a mysterious bump on the head.

- ***Chicken Man,*** Michelle Edwards (Morrow, New York, 1994). Rody is in charge of the chicken house on the kibbutz in Israel's Jezreel Valley. When Rody is transferred to different positions, the chickens cleverly arrange for Rody's return.

*The Easter Egg Farm,* Mary Jane Auch (Holiday, New York, 1992). Pauline the hen lays unusual eggs which her owner thinks are beautiful, and together they work to open an Easter egg farm.

*The Hoben Chicken Emergency,* Daniel Pinkwater (Prentice-Hall, New York, 1977). Arthur goes to pick up the turkey for Thanksgiving dinner but comes back with a 260-pound chicken.

*The Surprise Family,* Lynn Reiser (Greenwillow, New York, 1994). A baby chicken accepts a young boy as her mother and later becomes a surrogate mother for some ducklings that she has hatched.

*Chanticleer and the Fox,* Barbara Cooney (HarperCollins, New York, 1986). An adaptation of the "Nun's Priest's Tale" from the Canterbury Tales.

*Big Fat Hen,* Keith Baker (Harcourt Brace & Co., New York, 1994). Big Fat Hen counts to ten with her friends and all their chicks

**Cow**

*Cows,* Easy Readers series, Peter Brady (Children's Press/Groliers, Danbury, CT, 1996). This easy-to-read book introduces students to well-known farm animals.

*If It Weren't for Farmers,* Allan Fowler (Children's Press/Groliers, Danbury, CT, 1996). Readers discover intriguing facts about farmers and farm products.

*Milk,* Donald Carrick (Greenwillow, New York, 1985). Describes the entire process by which milk goes from the cow to our homes.

*Winter on the Farm,* Laura Ingalls Wilder, My First Little House Book Series (Harper Collins, New York, 1994). A boy is responsible for his two calves during the winter.

*No Milk,* Jennifer A. Ericsson (Tambourine/Morrow, New York, 1993). In a repetitive text, a boy tries to milk a cow.

*The Cow That Went Oink,* Bernard Most (Harcourt Brace, New York, 1990). Whimsical prose and pictures relate the adventures of an unusual cow.

*The Cow That Wouldn't Come Down,* Paul Brett Johnson (Orchard, New York, 1993). In a humorous story, an elderly lady tries to keep her cow from flying.

*Two Cool Cows,* Toby Speed (Putnam, New York, 1995). Lyrical text and whimsical pictures put a new twist on "The cow jumped over the moon!"

- ***The Silver Cow: A Welsh Tale,*** Susan Cooper (Atheneum/Macmillan, New York,

**BEGINNING BUILDING THINKING SKILLS LESSON PLANS**     **BIBLIOGRAPHY**

1983). The father of a young Welsh boy gifted with a magic cow manages to destroy all the good things the cow has brought to their lives.

**Duck**

*Quack and Honk,* Rookie Read About Science series, (Children's Press/Groliers, Danbury, CT, 1993). Young students discover intriguing facts about ducks.

*Make Way for Ducklings,* Robert McClosky (Viking, New York, 1969). The story of a family of mallards trying to find a safe home in busy Boston.

*I Am A Duck, Francois Crozat* (Barron's Educational Series, Hauppauge, New York, 1995). This book from a series of nonfiction board books features colorful pictures and interesting facts about ducks.

*The Surprise Family,* Lynn Reiser (Greenwillow, New York, 1994). A baby chicken accepts a young boy as her mother and later becomes a surrogate mother for some ducklings that she has hatched.

*Secret Place,* Eve Bunting (Clarion, New York, 1996). A young boy finds ducks in a small patch of wilderness in the middle of a big city.

• ***Why Ducks Sleep on One Leg,*** Sherry Garland (Scholastic, New York, 1993). This retelling of a Vietnamese folktale is illustrated by Jean and Mou-sien Tseng.

• ***The Tale of the Mandarin Ducks,*** Katherine Paterson (Scholastic, New York, 1990). This retelling of a Japanese folktale is illustrated in a Japanese style.

• ***The Story About Ping,*** Marjory Flack and Kurt Weiss (Viking, New York, 1933). This children's classic relates the adventures of a duck on the Yangtze River.

*Have You Seen My Duckling?* Nancy Tafuri (Morrow, New York, 1991). Mother Duck asks the bird, the turtle, the beaver, and the fish, "Have you seen my duckling?"

*Farmer Schulz's Ducks,* Colin Thiele (Harper & Row, New York, 1988). In an Australian story, a young girl solves the problem of how to keep the ducks safe when they cross the road.

*The Tale of Jemima Puddleduck,* Beatrix Porter (Ladybird, Auburn, ME, 1993). Jemima Puddleduck's desire to hatch her own eggs leads her away from the farm and into the hands of a treacherous fox.

*Bently & Egg,* William Joyce (HarperCollins, New York, 1992). A shy frog takes on a special role as he looks after a duck's egg.

**Fish**

*My Visit to the Aquarium,* Aliki (HarperCollins, New York, 1993). A boy discovers the characteristics of marine and fresh water creatures.

*Fishes,* Brian Wildsmith (Oxford University Press, Oxford, England, 1995). Children learn the names of groups of fish.

*Swimmy,* Leo Lionni (Pantheon/Random House, New York, 1963). A little black fish in a school of red fish finds a way of protecting them from natural enemies.

*Crinkleroot's 25 Fish Every Child Should Know,* Jim Arnosky (Simon & Schuster, New York, 1993). This resource book helps students understand the variety of fish.

*Come Back, Salmon,* Molly Cone (Sierra Club, Santa Fe, New Mexico, 1992). Students clean up a nearby stream, stock it with salmon, and preserve it as a place where salmon can return to spawn.

*The Great Adventures of Wo Ti,* Nathan Zimelman (Macmillan, New York, 1992). Carp outwit a predator.

*A Fish in His Pocket,* Denys Cazet (Watts/Grolier, New York, 1987). All through school Russell the bear is worried about the little orange fish in his pocket, until he figures out how to return it to its pond.

• ***Nessa's Fish,*** Nancy Luenn (Atheneum/Macmillan, New York, 1990). Nessa's ingenuity and bravery save from animal poachers the fish she and her grandmother caught to feed everyone in their Eskimo camp.

384     © 2000 CRITICAL THINKING BOOKS & SOFTWARE WWW.CRITICALTHINKING.COM • 800-458-4849

**BEGINNING BUILDING THINKING SKILLS LESSON PLANS**                                        **BIBLIOGRAPHY**

*Blue Sea,* Robert Kalan (Greenwillow, New York, 1979). Large illustrations of fish show size and spatial concepts.

**Frog**
*Frog, Where Are You?,* Mercer Mayer (Puffin/Dial, New York, 1969). This book is one of a series of wordless books about having a frog as a pet.
*Amazing Frogs & Toads,* Barry Clarke (Alfred A. Knopf, New York, 1990). This book from the Eyewitness Juniors series, produced by the London Natural History Museum, features large pictures and unusual facts about frogs.
*The Fascinating World of Frogs and Toads,* Barron's Educational Series, Hauppauge, New York, 1993). This nonfiction series on animals features colorful pictures and interesting facts.
*In The Great Meadow, Skid Crease* (Firefly Books, Buffalo, New York, 1994). A frog and a snake try to teach each other how to move and learn about friendship.
*Frog,* Michael Chinery (Troll Associates, New York, 1991). This book from the Life Story series offers detailed photographs of frogs.
*Extremely Weird Frogs,* Sara Lovett, (John Muir, Santa Fe, New Mexico, 1996). Photographs, drawings, and text relate unusual facts about frogs.
*A Boy, A Dog, and A Frog,* Mercer Mayer (Dial, New York, 1985). A boy and a dog try unsuccessfully to catch a frog.
*Fenton's Leap,* Liba Moore Gray (Simon & Schuster, New York, 1994). Fenton, a nearsighted frog, leaps when he gets glasses.
*Hop, Jump,* Ellen Stohl Walsh (Harcourt Brace, New York, 1993). Bored with hopping, Frog discovered dancing.
*Jump, Frog, Jump!* Robert Kalan (Morrow, New York, 1992). This cumulative story repeats, "This is the turtle that slid into the pond and ate the snake that dropped from a branch and swallowed the fish that swam after the frog...".
*Frogs, Toads, Lizards, and Salamanders,* Nancy Parker (Morrow, New York, 1996). Profiles of amphibians and reptiles are complemented by labeled scientific drawings and maps.
*Bently & Egg,* William Joyce (Harper Collins, New York, 1992). A shy frog takes on a special role as he looks after a duck's egg.
*The Frog Goes to Dinner,* Mercer Mayer (Dial, New York, 1974). Boy secretly puts Frog into his pocket and takes him along when the family goes to a fancy restaurant.

**Giraffe**
*Giraffe and a Half,* Shel Silverstein, (HarperCollins, New York, 1964). This humorous book includes a poem on giraffes.
*Giraffe: The Sentinel of the Savannas,* Helen Roney Statler (Lothrop, Lee, and Shepard, New York, 1989). This book describes the physical characteristics, habits, natural environment, and different species of giraffes.
*I Am A Giraffe,* Francois Crozat (Barron's Educational Series, Hauppauge, New York, 1995). This book from a series of nonfiction board books features colorful pictures and interesting facts about giraffes.

**Horse**
*Horses,* New True series, K. Jacobsen (Children's Press/Groliers, Danbury, CT, 1981). This richly illustrated, easy-to-read book provides answers to young students' basic questions about horses.
*Horses, Horses, Horses,* Rookie Read About Science series, Allan Fowler (Children's Press/Groliers, Danbury, CT, 1992). Young students discover intriguing facts about horses.

© 2000 CRITICAL THINKING BOOKS & SOFTWARE • WWW.CRITICALTHINKING.COM • 800-458-4849                385

*Horses and Ponies,* (Usborne/EDC, Tulsa, Oklahoma, 1995). This board book offers realistic pictures and vocabulary to describe horses and ponies.

*The Black Stallion Picture Book,* Walter Farley (Random House, New York, 1979). This simplified version of a children's' classic tells how a black stallion saved a boy's life.

*The Mare on the Hill,* Thomas Locker (Dial/Penguin, New York, 1985). Richly detailed oil paintings depict a mare's surroundings.

• *The Girl Who Loved Wild Horses,* Paul Goble (Aladdin/Simon & Schuster, New York, 1990). This retelling of a Native American legend relates a story about a girl who prefers to spend her time with horses. This book includes two Native American poems about horses.

• *Turquoise Boy: A Navajo Legend,* Terri Cohlene (Watermill Press, Vero Beach, FL, 1990). This retelling of a Navajo legend relates how horses came to the Navajo People.

*Fritz and the Beautiful Horses,* Jan Brett (Houghton Mifflin, Boston, MA, 1949). Fritz, the pony excluded from the beautiful horses, saved the children of the walled city.

• *The Rainbow-Colored Horse,* Antonio Martorell (Warne/Penguie, New York, 1978). This Puerto Rican folktale relates the adventures of a youngest son who captures the colored horse that has been trampling his father's fields.

*Knots on a Counting Rope,* Bill Martin Jr. and John Archambault (Holt, Rinehart & Winston, New York, 1987). A poetic story about a blind boy's horse race as told by his grandfather.

*One Good Horse: A Cowpuncher's Counting Book,* Ann Herbert Scott (Greenwillow, New York, 1990). While a cowboy and his son check cattle, they count things that they see.

*Ride a Cock Horse to Banbury Cross & A Farmer Went Trotting Upon His Gray Mare,* Randolph Caldecott (Orchard, New York, 1988). This book published in the 1800s is based on the nursery rhyme in which people go to Banbury Cross to see a fine lady.

*Black Gold,* Marguerite Henry (Simon & Schuster, New York, 1992). This is the history of a great racing horse named Black Gold, his trainer, and jockey.

## Lizard

*Lizard in the Sun,* Joanne Ryder (Mulberry Books, New York, 1990). Pictures and prose describe a day in the life of a lizard.

*Lizard's Song,* George Shannon (Morrow, New York, 1992). No matter how hard he tries, a bear can't remember the song Lizard teaches him.

*Amazing Lizards,* Trevor Smith (Alfred A. Knopf, New York, 1990). This book from the Eyewitness Juniors series, produced with the London Natural History Museum, features large pictures and unusual facts about lizards.

*Reptiles,* Robert Matero, Eyes on Nature series (Kidsbooks, Chicago, 1994). Text and photographs illustrate the physical characteristics, habits, and natural environment of various species of lizards.

*Frogs, Toads, Lizards, and Salamanders,* Nancy Parker (Morrow, New York, 1996). Profiles of amphibians and reptiles are complemented by labeled scientific drawings and maps.

## Ostrich

*Ostriches,* New True series, E.U. Lepthien (Children's Press/Groliers, Danbury, CT, 1993). This richly illustrated, easy-to-read book provides answers to young students' basic questions about familiar birds.

**BEGINNING BUILDING THINKING SKILLS LESSON PLANS**                    **BIBLIOGRAPHY**

*The Cuckoo Child,* Dick King-Smith (Hyperion/Walt Disney, New York, 1993). With the unknowing help of his pet geese, 8-year-old Jack Dow decides to raise an ostrich on his father's farm.

• *Lion and the Ostrich Chicks, and Other African Folk Tales,* Bryan Ashley (Atheneum/Macmillan, New York, 1986). Includes four traditional tales told by the Hausa, Angolan, Masai, and Bushmen people of Africa.

**Owl**

*Animal Lore and Legend: Owl,* Vee Browne (Scholastic, New York, 1995). These retellings of Seneca, Zuni, and Picuris legends are interspersed with information about and photographs of owls.

• *Owl Lake,* Keizaburo Tejima (Philomel Division of Putnam and Grosset, New York, 1987). This description of a day in the life of a family of owls is illustrated in pictures that resemble Japanese woodcuts.

*Owl Moon,* Jane Yolen (Philomel Division of Putnam and Grosset, New York, 1987). This depiction of a winter owling hike by a father and son won the Caldecott Medal.

*Owl Babies,* Martin Waddell (Candlewick Press, Cambridge, MA, 1992). Three baby owls whose mother goes out for the night try to stay calm until she returns.

*A Toad for Tuesday,* Russell E. Erickson (Lothrop, Lee & Shepard, New York, 1974). On Thursday a toad is captured by an owl who saves him to eat on Tuesday, the owl's birthday, but the intervening five days change his mind.

*What Game Shall We Play?,* Pat Hutchins (Greenwillow, New York, 1990). When the animals ask each other what game they should play, Owl has an answer.

*The Great White Owl of Sissinghurst,* Dawl L. Simmons (Margaret K. McElderry Books/Macmillan, New York, 1993). Three children visiting Sissinghurst Castle are intrigued by the great white owl that sleeps under the roof of the garage.

*The Owl Who Became the Moon,* Jonathan London (Dutton, New York, 1993). While riding on a train at night, a young boy listens and watches as he passes many creatures in their wilderness homes.

*Tiger With Wings: The Great Horned Owl,* Barbara Juster Esbensen (Orchard, New York, 1991). Describes the hunting techniques, physical characteristics, mating ritual, and nesting and child-rearing practices of the great horned owl.

**Pig**

*Pigs,* Easy Readers series, Ann Burckhardt (Children's Press/Groliers, Danbury, CT, 1996). Easy-to-read science books introduce students to well-known farm animals.

*Smart, Clean Pigs,* Rookie Read About Science series, (Children's Press/Groliers, Danbury, CT, 1993). Young students discover intriguing facts about pigs.

*Babe the Gallant Pig,* Dick King-Smith (Random House, New York, 1995). A piglet is adopted by an old sheepdog and learns a special skill.

*Charlotte's Web,* E. B. White (HarperCollins, New York, 1952). Wilbur the pig learns about life and death through his friendship with Charlotte the spider.

*Pigs,* Robert Munsch, (Annicle Press, Buffalo, New York, 1995). This whimsical story relates what happens when pigs take over.

*Oink,* Arthur Geisert (Houghton Mifflin, Boston, MA, 1991). Baby pigs get into trouble.

*Chester the Worldly Pig,* Bill Peet (Houghton Mifflin, Boston, MA, 1980). A disgruntled pig sets his sights on more than being something to eat.

*I Am A Pig,* Francois Crozat (Barron's Educational Series, Hauppauge, New York, 1995). This book from a series of nonfiction board books features colorful pictures and interesting facts about pigs.

© 2000 CRITICAL THINKING BOOKS & SOFTWARE • WWW.CRITICALTHINKING.COM • 800-458-4849

BEGINNING BUILDING THINKING SKILLS LESSON PLANS                                                                BIBLIOGRAPHY

• *Juan Bobo And The Pig – A Puerto Rican Folktale,* Felix Pitre (Lodestar/Dutton, New York, 1993). This folktale, spiced with Spanish words and some modern twists, tells the high-spirited adventures of Puerto Rico's folk hero, Juan Bobo.

*The Three Little Wolves and the Big Bad Pig,* Eugene Trivizas (Macmillan, New York, 1993). In a twist on the folktale, the pig is the villain.

**Shark**

*The Best Way to See a Shark,* Rookie Read About Science series, (Children's Press/ Groliers, Danbury, CT, 1993). Young students discover intriguing facts about sharks.

*Sharks,* Sea Life series, June Behrens, (Children's Press/Groliers, Danbury, CT, 1990). This easy-to-read book answers young students' questions about sharks.

*Sharks,* Jane Resnick, Eyes on Nature series (Kidsbooks, Chicago, 1994). Text and photographs the physical characteristics, habits, and natural environment of various species of sharks.

*Sharks: The Super Fish,* Helen Roney Statler (Lothrop, Lee, and Shepard, New York, 1989). This book describes the physical characteristics, habits, natural environment, and different species of sharks.

*Clark, the Toothless Shark,* Corinne Mellor, Pop Up Book (Artist Writer's Guild, Racine, Wisconsin, 1994). Mermaids make Clark gold teeth.

**Snake**

*It's Best to Leave a Snake Alone,* Rookie Read About Science series, (Children's Press/ Groliers, Danbury, CT, 1992). Young students discover intriguing facts about snakes.

*A Snake in the House,* Faith McNulty, (Scholastic, New York, 1994). An escaped snake finds clever places to hide.

*Amazing Snakes,* Alexandra Parsons (Alfred A Knopf, New York, 1990). This book from the Eyewitness Juniors series, produced with the London Natural History Museum, features large pictures and unusual facts about snakes.

*Explore the World of Snakes,* Chris Mattison (Derrydale Books, New York, 1991). This book from a nonfiction series features colorful pictures and interesting facts.

*The Fascinating World of Snakes,* Barron's Educational Series, Hauppauge, New York, 1993. This book from a nonfiction series on animals features colorful pictures and interesting facts.

*Extremely Weird Snakes,* Sara Lovett, (John Muir, Santa Fe, New Mexico, 1996). Photographs, drawings, and text relate unusual facts about snakes.

*In The Great Meadow, Skid Crease* (Firefly Books, Buffalo, New York, 1994). A frog and a snake try to teach each other how to move and learn instead about friendship.

*Reptiles,* Robert Matero, Eyes on Nature series (Kidsbooks, Chicago, 1994). Text and photographs illustrate the physical characteristics, habits, and natural environment of various species of snakes.

*Hide and Snake,* Keith Baker (Harcourt Brace Jovanovich, New York, 1991). A brightly colored snake challenges readers to a game of hide and seek as he hides among familiar objects.

*The Girl Who Wore Snakes,* Angela Johnson (Orchard Books, New York, 1993). Ali buys several snakes and wears them all home. For children fascinated by snakes, this is an experience to relish. For those afraid, it is reassurance.

*Mouse Count,* Ellen Stoll Walsh (Harcourt Brace Jovanovich, New York, 1991). The illustrations and text proceed from 1 to 10 and then count backward from 10 to 1 as ten mice outsmart a snake.

*The Snake: A Very Long Story,* Bernard Waber (Houghton Mifflin, New York, 1978). A snake goes on a very long trip, only to face a big surprise at the end.

388                    © 2000 CRITICAL THINKING BOOKS & SOFTWARE WWW.CRITICALTHINKING.COM • 800-458-4849

**BEGINNING BUILDING THINKING SKILLS LESSON PLANS**

**BIBLIOGRAPHY**

*Snake In, Snake Out,* Linda Banchek (Crowell, New York, 1978). The antics of a woman's pet snake and parrot illustrate spatial concepts such as in, out, under, and over.

*Snakes,* Sarah Lovett (John Muir, Santa Fe, New Mexico, 1993). Pictures and text describe the physical characteristics and behavior of twenty unusual snakes, including the dwarf puff adder.

**Spider**

*Spiders,* New True series, I. Polendorf (Children's Press/Groliers, Danbury, CT, 1982). This richly illustrated, easy-to-read book provides answers to young students' basic questions about spiders.

*Spiders Are Not Insects,* Rookie Read About Science series, (Children's Press/ Groliers, Danbury, CT, 1996). Young students discover intriguing facts about spiders.

*Amazing Spiders,* Alexandra Parsons (Alfred A. Knopf, New York, 1990). This book from the Eyewitness Juniors series, produced by the London Natural History Museum, features large pictures and unusual facts about spiders.

*The Very Busy Spider,* Eric Carle (Putnam, New York, 1985). Farm animals try to divert a busy spider from spinning her web, but she persists and produces a thing of both beauty and usefulness.

*Miss Spider's Wedding,* David Kirk (Scholastic, New York, 1995). In this rhymed story friends try to convince Miss Spider that Mr. Arachnid would be a better mate.

• *The Adventures of Spider,* Joyce Cooper Arkhurst (Little, Brown, Boston, MA, 1994). Six West African tales explain how spiders got various characteristics.

• *Anansi the Spider,* Gerald McDermott (Henry Holt, New York, 1987). This retelling of an Anansi legend from Ghana is a Caldecott Honor Book.

• *The Spider and the Sky God: An Akan Legend,* Deborah M. Newton Chocolate (Troll Associates, New York, 1993). This retelling of a legend from Ghana explains how Anansi the Spider tricked the Sky God for payment for his stories.

*The Fascinating World of Spiders,* (Barron's Educational Series, Hauppauge, New York, 1993). This book from a nonfiction series on animals features colorful pictures and interesting facts.

*Itsy Bitsy Spider,* Iza Trapani (Whispering Coyote Press, Danvers, MA, 1993). Whimsical drawings illustrate the popular song.

*Like Jake and Me,* Mavis Jukes (Knopf, New York, 1987). An incident with a spider brings a boy and his stepfather closer together.

• *A Story, a Story,* Gail E. Haley (Atheneum/Macmillan, New York, 1970). An African folktale tells about a spider man who bargains with the Sky God to bring stories to earth.

*Charlotte's Web,* E. B. White (Harper Row, New York, 1952). Wilbur the pig learns about life and death through his friendship with Charlotte the spider.

*Insectlopedia,* Douglas Florian (Harcourt, Brace & Jovanovich, New York, 1998). Fanciful pictures illustrate poems about spiders and insects.

**Turkey**

*Turkeys That Fly and Turkeys That Don't,* Rookie Read About Science series (Children's Press/Groliers, Danbury, CT, 1994). Young students discover intriguing facts about turkeys.

**Turtle**

*Turtles Take Their Time,* Rookie Read About Science series (Children's Press/ Groliers, Danbury, CT, 1992). Young students discover intriguing facts about turtles.

© 2000 CRITICAL THINKING BOOKS & SOFTWARE • WWW.CRITICALTHINKING.COM • 800-458-4849

**BEGINNING BUILDING THINKING SKILLS LESSON PLANS**                                          **BIBLIOGRAPHY**

*Into the Sea*, Brenda Z. Guiberson (Henry Holt, New York, 1972). Detailed illustrations depict baby turtles' rush to the sea.

*Box Turtle at Long Pond*, William T. George (Greenwillow, New York, 1989). On a busy day, Box Turtle searches for food, basks in the sun, and escapes a raccoon.

*And Still the Turtle Watched*, Sheila MacGill Callahan (Puffin Penguin, New York, 1991). In this retelling of a legend of the Delaware people, the changes and challenges of modernization are seen through the eyes of a turtle.

*Jump, Frog, Jump!* Robert Kalan (Morrow, New York, 1992). "This is the turtle that slid into the pond and ate the snake that dropped from a branch and swallowed the fish that swam after the frog."

**Zebra**

*Zebras*, New True series, E.U. Lepthien (Children's Press/Groliers, Danbury, CT, 1994). Richly illustrated, easy-to-read books provide answers to young students' basic questions about zebras.

*Greedy Zebra*, Mwenye Hadithi and Adrienne Kennaway (Little, Brown, Boston, MA, 1991). This retelling of a Kenyan story explains how the zebra got its stripes.

• *Zebra,* Caroline Arnold (Morrow, New York, 1992). In Africa herds of *"pundia milia"* roam over the dry, grassy plains. In America a group of zebras lives at a theme park.

**BUILDINGS**

These books were selected because they show how purposes and materials shape buildings across cultures.

• *Round Buildings, Square Buildings, Buildings that Wiggle Like a Fish,* Phillip M. Isaacson (Alfred Knopf, New York, 1988). This book explores architectural styles around the world, depicting churches, bridges, cliff dwellings, tombs, and a variety of public buildings.

• *Richard Scarry's What Do People Do All Day?,* Richard Scarry (Random House, New York, 1968). The many occupations, vehicles, and buildings featured in *Beginning Building Thinking Skills* lessons are depicted in humorous drawings and text.

• *Children Just Like Me,* Barnabas Kindersley (DK Publishing, New York, 1994). Photographs depict the homes, schools, and culture of children worldwide.

*Town and Country,* Alice and Martin Provensen (Browndeer Press/Harcourt, Brace & Jovanovich, New York, 1984). Pictures and text compare and contrast life in a big city and on a farm near a village.

*Dig, Drill, Dump, Fill,* Tana Hoban (Morrow, New York, 1992). Photographs taken at urban building sites provide ringside seats for all the construction action.

• *Taxi: A Book of City Words,* Betsy and Guilio Maestro (Clarion, New York, 1992). The buildings and businesses are described on a wild taxi ride.

*Everything Has a Place*, Patricia Lillie (Greenwillow, New York, 1993). Text and pictures assign a cow to a barn, a dish to a cupboard, a family to a house, and other things to their places

• *Homes*, Toppers series, Nicola Baxter (Children's Press/Groliers, Danbury, CT, 1996). Through interpretation of words and pictures children explore homes from the child's viewpoint.

**Apartment Building**

• *Tar Beach* , Faith Ringgold (Crown Books, New York, 1991). For city children, the "beach" is the roof of their apartment building.

*Russell and Elisa*, Johanna Hurwitz (Morrow, New York, 1989). Seven-year-old Russell and his three-year-old sister Elisa have adventures with friends and family in their apartment building.

BEGINNING BUILDING THINKING SKILLS LESSON PLANS                                                    BIBLIOGRAPHY

*Maybe Yes, Maybe No, Maybe Maybe,* Susan Patron (Orchard, New York, 1993). A girl uses her artistic ability to help her older and younger sisters adjust when her family moves to a new apartment.

• *Apartment Three,* Ezra Jack Keats (Macmillan, New York, 1986). A young boy and a blind man who plays the harmonica interact in a rundown apartment building.

*Nuts to You!,* Lois Ehlert (Harcourt, Brace & Jovanovich, New York, 1998). A rascally squirrel has an outdoor adventure in a city apartment.

*The Gardener,* Sara Stewart (Farrar, Strauss & Giroux, New York, 1995). A girl who loves gardening transforms the roof of her office building.

**Barber Shop**

• *Uncle Jed's Barbershop,* Margaret Mitchell (Simon & Schuster, New York, 1993). Despite her emergency illness and the Great Depression, Sarah Jean's uncle realized his dream of his own barbershop. Richly detailed drawings illustrate the lives of an extended African American family in the South in the 1930s.

**Barn**

*If It Weren't for Farmers,* Allan Fowler (Children's Press/Groliers, Danbury, CT, 1996). Readers discover intriguing facts about farmers and farm products.

*The Red Barn,* Eve Bunting (Harcourt Brace Jovanovich, New York, 1979). Craig's grandfather teaches him to accept changes in life.

*The Big Red Barn,* Margaret Wise Brown (HarperCollins, New York, 1989). Rhymed text and illustrations introduce the different animals that live in the big barn.

*Winter on the Farm,* Laura Ingalls Wilder, My First Little House Book Series (Harper Collins, New York, 1994). A boy is responsible for his two calves during the winter.

*Barn Dance,* Bill Martin, Jr. (Henry Holt, New York, 1986). A group of chicks visit all their barnyard buddies.

**Farm**

*If It Weren't for Farmers,* Allan Fowler (Children's Press/Groliers, Danbury, CT, 1996). Readers discover intriguing facts about farmers and farm products.

*Winter on the Farm,* Laura Ingalls Wilder, My First Little House Book Series (Harper Collins, New York, 1994). A boy tends his two calves during the winter.

*If You Are Not From the Prairie...,* David Bouchard (Simon & Schuster, New York, 1995). Poetry and highly detailed drawings relate life on a modern farm on the prairie.

*Going to Sleep on the Farm,* Wendy Cheyette Lewison, (Dial/Penguin, New York, 1992). Enchanting pictures show how animals on the farm go to sleep.

*All the Places to Love,* Patricia MacLachlan (HarperCollins, New York, 1994). Richly detailed pictures depict a young boy's experiences with his family on his grandparents' farm.

*Haystack,* Bonnie and Arthur Geisert (Houghton Mifflin, Boston, MA, 1995). Detailed drawings show the significance of a haystack on a farm.

• *Back Home,* Gloria Jean Pinkney (Dial/Penguin, New York, 1992). Husband Jerry Pinkney illustrated this story of a young African-American girl in the 1950s, riding a train to North Carolina to visit her grandparents' farm.

*Midnight Farm,* Reeve Lindbergh (Puffin/Pied Piper, New York, 1995). Susan Jeffers illustrated this story of nighttime on a farm.

*Family Farm,* Thomas Locker (Dial, New York, 1988). A farm family nearly loses their home until they hit on the idea of raising and selling pumpkins and flowers to supplement their corn and milk sales.

*Farm Morning,* David McPhail (Harcourt Brace Jovanovich, New York, 1985). A young girl and her father explore the barnyard.

© 2000 CRITICAL THINKING BOOKS & SOFTWARE • WWW.CRITICALTHINKING.COM • 800-458-4849          391

*Farming Today Yesterday's Way*, Cheryl Walsh Bellville, (Carolrhoda, Minneapolis, MN, 1984). Photographs show and the text describes a farm that uses early methods of farming.

*Climbing Kansas Mountains*, George Shannon (Bradbury Press, New York, 1993). Sam and his father set out on a journey to the tall grain elevators that are "Kansas mountains."

*What a Wonderful Day to Be a Cow*, Carolyn Lesser (Knopf, New York, 1995). Farm scenes teach the months of the year.

*Amelia's Road*, Linda J. Altman (Lee & Low Books, 1993). This touching tale of the importance of home relates the story of Amelia, a child of migrant farm workers, longs for a home with a fine yard and shade tree.

*A Prairie Alphabet*, Yvette More (Tundra Books, Plattsburgh, New York, 1992). Highly detailed pictures relate life on a prairie farm to the alphabet.

*A Prairie Year*, Yvette More (Tundra Books, Plattsburgh, New York, 1994). Highly detailed pictures relate life on a prairie farm to the seasons.

**Fire Station**

• *Fire Fighters*, New True series, R. Broekel (Children's Press, Chicago, 1985). Simple text, labels, and photographs explain the work of a fire fighter.

*Fire Truck to the Rescue*, Ann Martin (Scholastic, New York, 1994). Photographs and simple text depict firefighting.

*The Fire Station*, Robert Munsch and Michael Martchenko (Annick Press, New York, 1995). A sister and brother have amusing adventures at a fire station.

*Working Hard with the Busy Fire Truck*, Jordan Horowitz (Scholastic, New York, 1993). Photographs and simple text show the parts of a fire truck and the work of fire fighters.

**Garage**

*Play Garage*, (Dorling Kindersley, New York, 1996). This detailed examination of things that people commonly store in their garages offers suggestions for creative projects.

**Gas Station**

*Jack Tractor: Five Stories from Smallbill's Garage*, Karen Ludlow and Willy Imax (Crown, New York, 1995). Fanciful stories about Benny the Tow Truck describe his adventures with a tractor, different kinds of cars, and a motorcycle.

**Hospital**

*Going to the Hospital: Mister Rogers Neighborhood Series*, Fred Rogers (G.P. Putnam, New York, 1989). Prepares a child for his first visit to the hospital.

*Going Home*, Margaret Wild (Scholastic, New York, 1994). While waiting to leave the hospital, Hugo dreams of adventures with exotic animals in faraway lands.

*Why Am I Going to the Hospital?*, Claire Ciliotta and Carol Livingston (Carol Publishing, New York, 1981). This helpful guide explains what one sees and does at the hospital.

**House**

• *Homes*, Toppers series, Nicola Baxter (Children's Press/Groliers, Danbury, CT, 1996). Through interpretation of words and pictures children explore homes from the child's viewpoint.

• *Houses and Homes*, Anne Morris (Mulberry, New York, 1992). Photographs, labels, and little text describe the homes around the world.

*A House is a House for Me*, Mary Anne Hoberman (Puffin, New York, 1982). Rhyme and drawings depict different characteristics of a home.

**BEGINNING BUILDING THINKING SKILLS LESSON PLANS**                                                    **BIBLIOGRAPHY**

*The Little House*, Virginia Lee Burton (Houghton Mifflin, Boston, MA, 1978). The classic Caldecott Award book relates the history of a little house as a city changes.

• *The Village of Round and Square Houses*, Ann Grifalsoni (Little, Brown, Boston, MA, 1986). This Caldecott Honor Book retelling of a story from Cameroon explains how men and women in this African village create buildings for work and conversation.

*Pictures of Home*, Colin Thompson (Simon & Schuster, New York, 1992). British schoolchildren's writing and Thompson's remarkable drawings make this book a fanciful exploration of what makes a home.

• *Homemade Houses: Traditional Houses from Many Lands*, John Nicholson (Allen and Unwin, St. Leonards, Australia, 1993). This resource book offers pictures and descriptions of two or three houses from various cultures for each of the following types of dwellings: mobile homes, houses of reed, grass, and bamboo, houses of earth and clay, houses of wood, and houses of stone.

• *The House I Live In: At Home in America*, Isadore Seltzer (Scholastic, New York, 1992). This book offers pictures and descriptions of American houses whose design was influenced by various cultures, regions, and periods of American history.

*Building a House*, Byron Barton (Hampton Brown, New York, 1992). A machine digs a hole. A cement mixer pours the foundation. Carpenters, bricklayers, electricians, plumbers, and painters do their part.

*Home Place*, Crescent Dragonwagon (Aladdin Books, New York, 1993). As a family hiking in the woods happen on the ruins of a home that existed long ago, we journey dreamily back to a time when another family lived and loved.

**Library**

*The Library*, Sarah Stewart (Farrar, Strauss, New York, 1995). A girl with too many books starts a library.

*Check It Out: The Book About Libraries*, Gail Gibbons (Harcourt Brace, New York, 1985). This book explains what is found in a library and how different libraries serve their community.

**Mobile Home**

*Someplace Else*, Carol Saul (Simon & Schuster, New York, 1995). An older woman tries out many kinds of houses (apartment buildings, beach cottages, mountain cabins) until she finds the perfect home for her—a mobile home.

**Playground**

*Maisy Goes to the Playground*, Lucy Cousins (Candlewick, Cambridge, MA, 1992). Flaps and tabs show a mouse's activities in the park.

*The Playground*, Kate Duke (Dutton, New York, 1986). Playground equipment is highlighted in this board book.

• *Rebel,* Allan Baille, (Ticknor & Fields / Houghton Mifflin, New York, 1994). An army marches over Burma's dust plains to destroy a playground while children watch.

**Post Office**

*Hi,* Gio Coalson (Philomel, New York, 1994). While waiting in line with her mother at the post office, Margarita greets the patrons who come in carrying different types of mail.

*Will Goes to the Post Office*, Olof and Lena Landstrom (Farrar, Straus & Giroux, New York, 1994). Delightfully ingenuous Will sets off to the post office to pick up what turns out to be an enormous package.

© 2000 CRITICAL THINKING BOOKS & SOFTWARE • WWW.CRITICALTHINKING.COM • 800-458-4849                    393

**BUILDING THINKING SKILLS LESSON PLANS**                    **BIBLIOGRAPHY**

**Restaurant**

*The Frog Goes to Dinner*, Mercer Mayer (Dial, New York, 1974). A boy secretly puts a frog into his pocket and takes him along when the family goes to a fancy restaurant.

• ***The Paper Crane,*** Molly Bang (Mulberry Books, New York, 1987). A mysterious man pays for his restaurant dinner with a paper crane that magically comes alive.

**School**

*Will I Have a Friend?*, Miriam Hoban (Macmillan, 1989). Jim's anxieties on his first day of school are happily forgotten when he makes a new friend.

*School*, Emily Arnold McCully (Harper & Row, 1987). A curious little mouse decides to find out what school is all about.

*My Teacher's Secret Life*, Stephen Krensky (Simon & Schuster, New York, 1996). Fanciful pictures and prose depict young children's humorous misconceptions about teachers.

*Mitch and Amy*, Beverly Cleary (Morrow, New York, 1991). The adventures of a nine-year-old twin brother and sister who despite constant bickering, support each other loyally at home and at school.

• ***Mayfield Crossing,*** Vaunda Micheaux Nelson (Putnam, New York, 1993). In 1960, African-American children experience prejudice for the first time when their school closes and they are sent to a larger school.

*The Sub*, P.J. Petersen (Dutton, New York, 1993). Two boys switch seats when they have a substitute teacher.

*Shark in School*, Patricia Reilly Giff (Delacorte, New York, 1994). When Matthew finds out from J.P., the weird girl next door, that their teacher loves to read, he worries that everyone at his new school will know he's a terrible reader.

• ***The Story of Ruby Bridges,*** Robert Coles (Scholastic, New York, 1995). The first black child to attend an all-white elementary school in the 1960s draws on family values to face a mob.

*Maisy Goes to School*, Lucy Cousins (Candlewick, Cambridge, MA, 1992). Flaps and tabs allow a mouse to do activities such as paint pictures, feed fish, and practice addition and subtraction.

*Annabelle Swift, Kindergartner*, Amy Schwartz (Orchard, New York, 1991). Although some of the things her older sister taught her at home seem a little unusual at school, other lessons help make Annabelle's first day in kindergarten a success.

*The Art Lesson*, Tomie De Paola (Putnam, New York, 1997). Having learned to be creative in drawing pictures at home, young Tommy is dismayed when he goes to school and finds the art lesson there much more regimented.

*I Spy School Days: A Book of Picture Riddles*, Jean Marzollo, (Scholastic, New York, 1995). The "reader" must find the answer to a riddle in photographs of school.

**Supermarket**

*A Busy Day at Mr. Kang's Grocery Store* , Our Neighborhood series, Alice Flanagan (Children's Press/Groliers, Danbury, CT, 1985). With photojournalistic style and simple text, this book depicts what a grocer must do to provide food to his customers.

*Market*, Ted Lewin (Lothrop, Lee and Shepard, New York, 1996). Simple text and brilliant illustrations depict how people in many countries sell and buy goods that we usually buy in supermarkets.

*The Shopping Basket*, John Burningham (Candlewick Press, Cambridge, MA, 1996). A boy tells a fantastic story explaining why he did not get what his mother requested.

*Tommy at the Grocery Store*, Bill Grossman (HarperCollins, New York, 1991). People of different occupations pick up Tommy at the grocery store.

394          © 2000 CRITICAL THINKING BOOKS & SOFTWARE WWW.CRITICALTHINKING.COM • 800-458-4849